Industry 4.0 and Regional Transformations

This edited volume brings together a group of expert contributors to explore the opportunities and the challenges that Industry 4.0 (smart manufacturing) is likely to pose for regions, firms and jobs in Europe. Drawing on theory and empirical cases, it considers emerging issues like servitization, new innovation models for local production systems and the increase in reshoring.

Industry 4.0 and Regional Transformations captures the complexity of this new manufacturing model in an accessible way and considers its implications for the future. It will be essential reading for advanced students and researchers and policy makers in regional studies, industrial policy, economic geography, innovation studies, operations management and engineering.

Lisa De Propris, Birmingham Business School, University of Birmingham, UK.

David Bailey, Birmingham Business School, University of Birmingham, UK, and Senior Fellow, the UK in a Changing Europe programme.

RSA Regional Studies Association

A leading & impactful community

Routledge
Taylor & Francis Group

Regions and Cities

Series Editor in Chief
Joan Fitzgerald, *Northeastern University, USA*

Editors

Roberta Capello, *Politecnico di Milano, Italy*
Rob Kitchin, *Maynooth University, Ireland*
Jörg Knieling, *HafenCity University Hamburg, Germany*
Nichola Lowe, *University of North Carolina at Chapel Hill, USA*

In today's globalised, knowledge-driven and networked world, regions and cities have assumed heightened significance as the interconnected nodes of economic, social and cultural production, and as sites of new modes of economic and territorial governance and policy experimentation. This book series brings together incisive and critically engaged international and interdisciplinary research on this resurgence of regions and cities, and should be of interest to geographers, economists, sociologists, political scientists and cultural scholars, as well as to policy-makers involved in regional and urban development.

For more information on the Regional Studies Association visit www.regionalstudies.org

There is a **30% discount** available to RSA members on books in the ***Regions and Cities*** series, and other subject related Taylor and Francis books and e-books including Routledge titles. To order just e-mail Luke McNicholas (Luke.McNicholas@tandf.co.uk), or phone on +44 (0)20 701 77545 and declare your RSA membership. You can also visit the series page at www.routledge.com/Regions-and-Cities/book-series/RSA and use the discount code: **RSA225**

139. Regional Economic Development and History
Edited by Marijn Molema and Sara Svensson

140. Rural Development in the Digital Age
Exploring Neo-Productivist EU Rural Policy
Edited by Martin Pělucha and Edward Kasabov

141. Smart Cities and Connected Intelligence
Platforms, Ecosystems and Network Effects
Nicos Komninos

142. Industry 4.0 and Regional Transformations
Edited by Lisa De Propris and David Bailey

For more information about this series, please visit:
www.routledge.com/Regions-and-Cities/book-series/RSA

Industry 4.0 and Regional Transformations

Edited by
Lisa De Propris and David Bailey

Routledge
Taylor & Francis Group
LONDON AND NEW YORK

First published 2020
by Routledge
2 Park Square, Milton Park, Abingdon, Oxon OX14 4RN

and by Routledge
605 Third Avenue, New York, NY 10017

First issued in paperback 2021

Routledge is an imprint of the Taylor & Francis Group, an informa business

Publisher's Note
The publisher has gone to great lengths to ensure the quality of this reprint but points out that some imperfections in the original copies may be apparent.

British Library Cataloguing-in-Publication Data
A catalogue record for this book is available from the British Library

Library of Congress Cataloging-in-Publication Data
A catalog record has been requested for this book

ISBN 13: 978-1-03-223662-9 (pbk)
ISBN 13: 978-0-367-17841-3 (hbk)

DOI: 10.4324/9780429057984

Typeset in Bembo
by Newgen Publishing UK

Contents

Figures

Tables

Contributors

David Bailey is Professor of Business Economics at the Birmingham Business School, UK, and a Senior Fellow of the ESRC's UK in a Changing Europe programme, exploring the impacts of Brexit on UK automotive and manufacturing. He has written extensively on industrial and regional policy, especially in relation to manufacturing and the automotive industry. He has been involved in a number of recent projects, including the Horizon 2020 RISE project MAKERS, where he led the Work Package on Industrial Policy. He is Editor-in-Chief of the leading journal *Regional Studies* and is Chair of the RSA Europe Think-Tank and policy forum. He is also a regular media commenter and newspaper columnist.

Marco Bellandi is Professor of Applied Economics at the Department of Economics and Management at Florence University, Italy. He is Dean of the School of Economics and Management at the University of Florence, member of the Advisory Board of the Confucius Institute at the University of Florence, fellow of the *Fondazione per la Ricerca e l'Innovazione* and Member of the Scientific Committee for the Strategic Plan of the Metropolitan City of Florence. He has published extensively on industrial districts and paths of local development in dynamic cities, local systems with embedded large firms, and high-tech clusters. More recently he has studied the challenges of Industry 4.0 and servitization for local systems of production.

Oscar F. Bustinza is Associate Professor of Management at the University of Granada, Spain. His work analyses product-service innovation, demand chain management and drivers of firm's boundaries choice based upon data-driven analysis. His research has been published in a wide range of peer-reviewed journals. He has also been Principal Investigator on a number of Spanish and European projects.

Cristina Chaminade is Full Professor in Innovation Studies at Lund University, Sweden and Adjunct Professor at Aalborg University, Denmark. Her research focuses on global networks and the processes of knowledge creation and adoption that underpin innovations and the transformation towards sustainable forms of living (economic, social and environmental), and how they are affected by and affect institutions. She has worked on innovation in developing countries such as China, India, South Africa, Thailand, and Brazil for over 15 years. She has been an advisor to international organizations such as the European Commission, UNCTAD, the OECD and UN-ECLAC. She has published in journals, books and handbooks in the fields of innovation, development studies and knowledge management.

Agnieszka Chidlow is Head of the Department of Strategy & International Business at the Birmingham Business School, UK and Visiting Professor at the School of International Business, Southwestern University of Finance and Economics in China. She is a co-founder and Vice-President of the Programme of the Academy of International Business Research Methods–Shared Interest Group. Her research looks at the internationalization of firms and methodological issues of international business research, and has been published in leading international journals as well as books. She has editorial experience on leading international journals.

Rosemary Coates is Executive Director of the Reshoring Institute and President of Blue Silk Consulting. She is a seasoned executive with 25 years' experience in supply chain management, operations management, project management and systems consulting. She has consulted with a wide range of global and domestic clients on operations systems and processes. She also has considerable international experience and has worked for extended periods in Asia and Europe. Her experience spans a broad range of industries, including high technology, software, chemicals, healthcare, consumer products, industrial products, food distribution, transportation, publishing, retail, oil and gas.

Giancarlo Corò is Professor of Applied Economics at Ca' Foscari University of Venice, Italy. His research topics cover the development and innovation of production systems, the economic analysis of global value chains, and the study of economic complexity at the international and local levels. He has widely published and has made a significant contribution to scholarly debates on these topics.

Lisa De Propris is Professor of Regional Economic Development in the Birmingham Business School, University of Birmingham, UK. She has expertise in manufacturing, Industry 4.0, technological change, service clusters/districts, creative industries, regional economic development, industrial policy and EU cohesion policy. She has published widely on these themes in academic journals and books, and has presented at international conferences and high-level meetings, including at the European Commission and the OECD, as well as having advised governments and firms. She was the Lead Investigator on the Horizon 2020 RISE project MAKERS and is the Policy Debates Editor for the *Regional Studies* journal.

Mafini Dosso is an economist and policy analyst at the Joint Research Centre of the European Commission in Seville, Spain. Her research interests span industrial research and innovation, industrial development, innovations policies and systems, entrepreneurial ecosystems and firm dynamics. She has contributed to several European and international reports on the innovation investments and technological developments of the world's leading companies. Her current work focuses on qualitative research on global corporate innovation networks and on the policy issues and implications of the Industry 4.0 paradigm in Europe. Since 2017, she has also contributed to policy and research collaborations for evidence-based innovation policy making in Sub-Saharan Africa.

Claudio Fassio is a researcher at the Department of Business Administration of the University of Lund, Sweden, and a research associate at CIRCLE, University of Lund and BRICK, University of Torino, Italy. His research interests cover science, technology and innovation, with a focus on the interplay between innovation and internationalization strategies of firms and the international mobility of skilled individuals. His research has been published in journals such as *Research Policy*, *Industrial and Corporate Change*, *R&D Management* and *Industry & Innovation*. He is the coordinator of the Vinnova-funded three-year Platform Project 'Sweden's position in global value chains'. He has also acted as consultant to a number of governmental agencies in different countries.

Steffen Kinkel is Professor of International Management and Networked Business at Karlsruhe University of Applied Sciences, Germany. His main research interests include socio-economic analysis and technology assessment, innovation management, new business models, scenario building and foresight in different technology areas and industries, as well as for innovation and industrial policy. His second strand of interest covers global value chains with a focus on global production and R&D strategies, economic assessment and strategic management.

Max Nathan is Senior Fellow in Regional Economic Development at the Birmingham Business School and is Deputy Director of the ESRC/UK government-funded What Works Centre for Local Economic Growth. He is an economic geographer with a background in public policy. His research focuses on urban economic development, in particular: the economics of immigration and diversity; innovation systems and tech clusters; and public policy for cities, especially policy design and evaluation. He has over 15 years' public policy experience in think-tanks, consultancy and government, including at the DCLG as an ESRC-DCLG Senior Policy Adviser. He also co-founded the Centre for Cities, where he ran the research programme for the Centre's first three years.

Diletta Pegoraro is a doctoral researcher at the Birmingham Business School, UK. Her research focuses on firms' reshoring strategies with a comparative analysis across the UK, the US and Italy.

Arianna Pittarello is an analyst at the Veneto Chambers of Commerce, Italy. She is a member of the Research Centre in the Veneto Chambers of Commerce (UCV). During the MAKERS project, she was seconded to the University of Birmingham, where she studied job polarizations and skill mismatching in European countries.

Monica Plechero is Research Fellow at the Department of Economics and Management, University of Florence, Italy. Focusing on firms (specifically SMEs), clusters/districts and regional innovation systems, her research covers the globalization of innovation and regional innovation systems in both emerging and developed countries. In her research, she seeks to understand institutional and organizational conditions that can lead to regional and industrial development and different trajectories.

Paulina Ramirez is Lecturer in Innovation and International Business at the Birmingham Business School, UK. Her research covers innovation and technological change, global innovation networks, national and regional innovation systems and innovation in the life sciences and the bio-economy. She has worked on a number of EU-funded projects on topics related to innovation and technological change, and is presently collaborating with EU researchers looking at the fragmentation of the innovation value chain and the globalization of innovation. Within the Horizon 2020 RISE project MAKERS, her work has focused on interactions between national and regional innovation systems and global innovation networks in the transformation of industries.

Erica Santini is a postdoctoral researcher at the University of Trento, Italy. Her main research field covers structural changes and learning processes in local manufacturing systems that foster new paths of development. In the Horizon 2020 RISE project MAKERS, she was a postdoctoral researcher at the Fondazione per la Ricerca e l'Innovazione, where she focused on investigating the impact of technological change on the knowledge transfer processes in traditional manufacturing areas.

Antonella Trevisanato is an analyst at the Veneto Chambers of Commerce, Italy. She is a member of the Research Centre in the Veneto Chambers of Commerce (UCV). During the MAKERS project, she was seconded to the University of Birmingham, where she studied job polarizations and skill mismatching in European countries,

Claudia Vecciolini is Research Associate at the Institute for Industrial Strategy, King's College London. Her research interests focus on knowledge and innovation systems, regional development, manufacturing, Industry 4.0 and international business. She has extensive experience in qualitative research. Her recent work includes research on the digitization of manufacturing supply chains, including the development of related policy.

Ferran Vendrell-Herrero is Senior Lecturer in Business Economics at the Birmingham Business School, UK. His research looks at the innovation, digitization and internationalization dynamics of small and large organisations in the manufacturing and creative industries. His work has been published in a range of journals, including *Regional Studies.* He has played a major role in 'Servitisation', the growing academic community studying the implementation of services in manufacturing companies, by initiating and scientifically directing the International Conference on Business Servitisation.

Mario Volpe is Associate Professor of Political Economy at the Universita' di Venezia Ca' Foscari, Venice, Italy. His research focuses on the internationalization processes of local productive systems and local economic development. He has written both books and scholarly papers on these topics and frequently presents at international conferences and high-level meetings, such as at the OECD.

Preface

MAKERS: the project. The people. The ideas

The MAKERS project was a multi-stakeholder platform funded under the Horizon 2020 MSCA-RISE programme that brought together business, academia and policy makers for three years from 2016 to 2019. Led by the Birmingham Business School (at the University of Birmingham, UK), its academic partners included Universita' di Venezia Ca' Foscari (Italy); Aston University (UK), the University of Granada (Spain); Fakultät für Informatik und Wirtschaftsinformatik Hochschule -Karlsruhe (Germany); Universite' de Neuchatel (Switzerland); the University of Lund (Sweden); and the National University Singapore (Singapore). Policy stakeholders included the Fondazione Recerca e Innovazione – Firenze (Italy); UnioncamereVeneto (Italy); the Centre for European Policy Studies, Brussels (Belgium); and VINNOVA, Sweden's Innovation Agency (Sweden). Finally, business stakeholders included BASIC, Paris (France); Galdon Software (Spain); Steinbeis Transferzentren GmbH (Germany); Rieke Packaging Systems (UK); and the Reshoring Institute, San Diego (US).

MAKERS' research agenda was way ahead of the game when we started. Our focus was on Smart Manufacturing or Manufacturing 4.0 with the objective of understanding how new technologies were going to impact on firms' business models, on the innovation capabilities of EU regions and on the dynamics and geography of global value chains. In particular at the beginning of the project, the main question was to what extent the wave of new technologies inherent in Industry 4.0 was going to cause a shock for sectors, regions, firms and markets, given the extent and the breadth of the disruption and of the change required. Examples of these include: shocks to firms where digital technology will replace more labour; shocks to supply chains where connected digital technology will allow real-time communications between physically distant machines without human intervention; shocks to existing sectors superseded by the rise of new sectors; and shocks to traditional learning and innovation processes as new technologies force discontinuities.

The overarching aim of MAKERS was to identify factors and pathways to enable regional economies to embrace such disruptive industrial transformations in view of sustaining their longer-term socio-economic growth and prosperity.

The unit of analysis of our research has been mainly the regional economy and locally embedded systems of production; this has allowed us to focus on the impact of technological change not just at the firm level, but more crucially at the systemic level, namely at the intersection between buyers–suppliers relationships and between knowledge flows between people and firms. The systemic and relational perspective of MAKERS' analysis meant that we were able to overcome the efficiency-based and firm-based arguments often associated with Industry 4.0, and to offer a broader and more holistic understanding of the impact of new technology on inter-firm relations, on systems and on the producer–consumer nexus. We have called this Industry 4.0+ to stress that new technologies have a wider transformative power on the nature of business and markets, on the dynamics of innovation and learning, and on the implementation of an ecological agenda.

MAKERS observed recent trends with many case studies from across the EU and the US, and a wealth of data. Evidence-based analysis informed policy considerations that are discussed in the final chapters of the volume.

This open access volume aims to be our contribution to a very lively and fast-moving debate, and we thank the partners for their contributions and enthusiasm throughout the project and the writing of this volume.

1 Disruptive Industry 4.0+

Key concepts

Lisa De Propris and David Bailey

1.1 Introduction

Innovation matters and the process of creating new knowledge that can be translated into innovations drives the competitiveness of firms, industries and places. Our analysis starts with a critical overview of the dynamics of technological change and the impact on the economy and society; drawing on the idea of a 'techno-economic paradigm' (Perez, 2010), we try to unravel the breadth and depth of the transformative impact one must expect from the technological change brought about by the Fourth Industrial Revolution (FIR). A host of new technologies is triggering economic and social change: both shift the techno-socio-economic paradigm of the economy and society. Notably, technological change disrupts the organisation of production and the use of production factors (labour and capital) and consumption. We introduce the idea of Industry 4.0+ as the deployment of all the technologies of the FIR that will trigger a transformational shift in the techno-socio-economic paradigm attuned to a green economy and society. This needs to be recognised as a key part of any effort to deliver inclusive socio-economic growth.

1.2 Technological change

A new wave of technological innovations has started to fundamentally alter how we make things, and it signals the start of an era of huge change. To fully understand this, it is worth starting from the idea of Kondratiev's long waves (Kondratieff and Stolper, 1935). The idea of Kondratiev's waves is that after a certain period of time (he found about 50 years), technologies exhaust their potential for new ideas to boost the economy; they slow down until a critical mass of new technologies comes into fruition all at once. This then kicks off a new technological wave that is able to trigger a spate of new applications in new processes and new products (ibid). Kondratiev suggested that radical inventions could revolutionise the techno-economic nature of economies. Indeed, the subsequent spawning of countless minor and incremental innovations could penetrate every aspect of the economy.

Such technological waves linked technological change with cycles in the global economy. Kondratiev saw such major cycles as driven by endogenous forces that therefore unravel organically. The endogeneity of the cycles conceptualised by Kondratiev (1979) drew on the work of Schumpeter (1942), who argued that although technology was exogenous to the economy, it was endogenous to the technology from which it was generated. Indeed, technology was agued to be path-dependent and the translation of inventions into innovations that were economically viable was endogenous to the environment and proceeded along what Perez (2010) called a 'deployment trajectory' where incremental innovations spawn from radical innovations. Kondratiev's waves have been consequently criticised in the methods underpinning the marking of cycles, but have remained widely accepted as a way of capturing the economy as a dynamic process that can be described with major cycles of 'transformation in the productive forces' (ibid, p. 23).

Whether technological change is evolutionary (for instance, Isaacson, 2014) or revolutionary (Kondratiev, 1979), there seems to be break-points that mark the introduction of new technologies whilst old ones are still being phased out. Such technological breaches therefore crack the dominant technological paradigm with a disruptive force that undermines its usefulness and desirability. The systemic transformative change in the economy and society comes from endless incremental innovations and applications derived from such new technologies.

Technological change is somewhat endogenous, in the sense that its roots are in the techno-economic system itself. Truly disruptive changes tend to be technology pushed: this means that long gestation periods might be inevitable before a switch is triggered and ultimately a new techno-economic paradigm takes over. Indeed, the incomplete exploitation of existing – albeit mature – technologies confirms to firms the continued presence of profit-making opportunities in untapped markets and prevents them from taking the risk of investing in new technologies which might still lack 'proof of concept' or clear market-ready applications. The apathy and risk-aversion of demand also delay the translation of inventions into innovations and new products and processes.

The strategic accumulation of inventions culminates in a disruptive technological breakpoint when the economy experiences what we call a 'technological limbo'. This is a status where a mature technology has mostly exhausted its applicability and its leverage on productivity gains, as well as having shown constraints and drawbacks (see combustion engine technology and pollution, for instance), whilst at the same time, a suite of new alternative technologies are emerging without any of them standing out as clear winners. A technological limbo occurs when technologically pushed inventions that were brewing in the background start challenging the existing mature technology, although ignored by the economy which is still occupied with exhausting incremental innovations.

Revising the conceptualisation of Kondratiev's waves with Perez (2010), we pinpoint the existence of the phase that we call a technological limbo to be the trigger point of the new technological revolution which then unfolds with an exploration phase before accelerating to finally reach a maturity phase. The exploration of what new technologies can do occurs with the introduction of radical changes leading to the consolidation of a new paradigm defining a new technological trajectory, which then peaks when the dominant technology shows signs of constraints. The passage between the old and new technology of course encounters great resistance from the incumbent technology adopters, together with the inertia of the production and consumption systems attached and accustomed to the incumbent technology.

This technological limbo is exited when the new technology starts being assimilated by the socio-economic system; namely, when risk-taking entrepreneurs develop and take to market new products that experimental consumers start buying, or when new processes are designed and developed that firms adopt and test before being rolled out as a standard. Connected and unconnected inventions result from the creation of new knowledge or experimental and experiential discoveries.

Tracking the deployment of a technology trajectory with its impact on long-term growth, the exploration and adoption stages are those where we can argue the economy benefits the most. The impact of new technologies on growth depends not only on changes to production, but crucially on changes to the techno-economic paradigm that Perez (2010: 194) defines as 'the way socio-institutional structures are organised'. Only the acceleration of technological adoption together with the adaptation of demand, consumption and use of new products, practices and routines can allow for the full exploitation of the growth potentials associated with a new wave.

The disruption of new technologies in each wave fundamentally changes which resources are used and how they are used, as well as reshaping the organisation of production. New sectors are created while others become obsolete. This dynamism resets the economy and sparks growth again. Economic change is followed by equally profound chances in consumption, use and access to markets, as well as in ways of life. This is why we argue that each wave ushers in disruptive change to the economy and society.

However, the impact of technological change on (sections of) society is costly. For example, we can note the following: changes in the labour market due to new skill requirements in the economy can cause a skills gap and skills obsolescence, leading to unemployment and polarised labour markets; new products can alter daily consumption habits and choices as well as the provision of services; and new forms of business and new markets can sharpen a digital divide, leading to consumption exclusions.

The social cost of the initial shock will flatten out when the socio-economic system starts a process of adaptation to the new technologies that culminates in all aspects of society embracing the myriad of incremental innovations that new technologies are translated into. At this point, the economy and society are locked into what will become the dominant technology (see Figure 1.1).

In summary, when deployed, new technologies will disrupt the economy and society, ushering in a new techno-socio-economic paradigm.

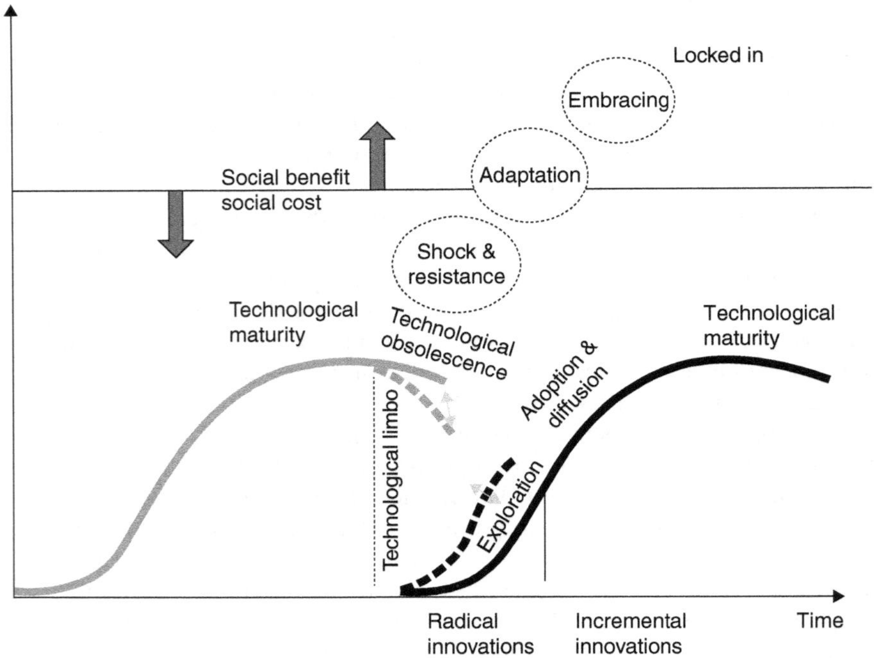

Figure 1.1 Technological change.
Source: Authors' adaptation from Perez (2010).

1.3 Technological revolutions

Tying into the argument that technological change occurs in waves, there have been a number of important contributions that have recently elaborated on the nature and timing of the technological change that is now unfolding. Whilst agreeing on their revolutionary underpinnings and making a case for a series of *technological* revolutions triggering concomitant *industrial* revolutions starting from the first appearance of automation and steam power in the late 1700s, the different contributions fundamentally disagree on how many *revolutions* there have been.

The main reasons for this difference lies on the definition of revolution. In one of the first publications on this topic, Perez (2010) make a robust case for there having been five technological revolutions, on the basis that each marks a shift in the techno-economic paradigm that introduces new key inputs, new sectors, new organisational models and new profit opportunities. Indeed, if '[n]ew technology systems not only modify the business space, but also the institutional context and even the culture in which they occur' (Perez, 2010: 188), then she argues that the first appearance of automation with the spinning machine in the 1700s needs to be separate from the introduction of steam in the 1800s. Merging the latter two into one wave led other contributions to suggest that one can record four main industrial revolutions, starting with Rifkin (2011) and Berger (2014), in parallel to GTAI (2014); Deloitte (2015); Siemens (2015); the EU Parliament (2015); McKinsey (2015); and the EU Commission (2016). Breaking ranks, the OECD (2017a) and Marsh (2013) refer to the next production revolution as the new industrial revolution.

A first wave of technological change in contemporary history starts with innovations related to steam power, cotton, steel and railways, coupled with mechanisation and the surge of the factory system. This marked the 'first' industrial revolution between the last decades of the eighteenth century and the first half of the nineteenth century. Cottage industries were dwarfed or replaced. Industrial districts (Marshall, 1923) were often seedbeds of those developments, even if progressively challenged by the increasing importance of economies of scale in bigger factories, leading to the industrialisation of rural spaces and the emergence of industrial cities and regions.

The Second Industrial Revolution was triggered by the introduction of electricity, heavy and mechanical engineering and synthetic chemistry in the second half of the nineteenth century. This spanned a few decades until the arrival of oil and the automobile. New sectors emerged, not only those related to the automotive systems, and others were given a different identity, as in the case of many consumable goods with the consolidation of the large-scale production model. Standardised demand was satisfied by mass production thanks to internal economies of scale. Even more complex business forms, such as multinational firms, developed.

The Third Industrial Revolution was prompted by innovations in electronics and computers, petrochemicals and aerospace, together with demand becoming more volatile in many sectors in the last decades of the twentieth century. Mass markets broke up and more flexible organisational forms such as firm clusters and industrial districts became pivotal points for development, thanks to their flexibility and innovation. At the same time, new technologies enabled faster communications and transport that pushed and accelerated a process of globalisation in production, commerce and sociocultural integration.

1.4 The Fourth Industrial Revolution

The conceptual framework above helps us to understand the breadth and depth of the transformative impact that must be expected from the current Fourth Industrial Revolution (FIR). A host of new technologies that started being developed in the mid-1980s is driving a wave of change in a new emerging techno-economic paradigm. These new technologies include: biotech, nanotech, neuro-technologies, green and renewables, 16 information and communication technologies (ICT), and mobile tech, 3D, artificial intelligence, robotics, sensoring, space technology and drones.

A cluster of new technologies and sectors rapidly evolved from such a basis and are now driving what is seen as a fourth revolution. The embryos of some of these new technologies can be traced back to the mid-1980s, but to witness their impact on production and sectors, we had to wait until the turn of the century. This current wave is creating a completely new production model inside the factory and between firms. It is already referred to as 'Industry 4.0', 'Manufacturing 4.0' or 'smart manufacturing'.

Four main changes capture the emerging manufacturing model. Firstly, digital technologies are increasingly adopted throughout the production process, and between producers and customers. Inside factories, intelligent machines will enhance both the productivity and the flexibility of productions that will deliver 'mass customised' products. Between firms, digital technology will enable the integration and orchestration of distant machines along the value chain. There is a palpable concern that the combined effect of digitalisation and robotisation will alter the balance between labour and capital inputs, with inevitable consequences for jobs, wealth distribution and societal equity.

Secondly, new pathways to value creation will be activated. In particular, 'servitisation' is the symbiosis between traditional manufacturing sectors with services, whereby the value to the customer is no longer associated (only) with the ownership of the product itself but also with the services that enable the enjoyment of the product's intrinsic functions. Customers are therefore buying services together with the product, or even the service that the product provides, rather than the product itself. Servitised products already exist in some industries such as aerospace; however, the extension of this model to a wide set of goods thanks to the opportunities opened up by digital technologies and the rate of introduction of new offers requires a fundamentally different business model for the firms.

Thirdly, some of the new technologies lend themselves to efficiently scaling down productions, opening up new opportunities for small producers which can tap into market niches for personalised, customised and innovative products. These need to be produced in small batches or even as unique pieces. Such niche markets require customers to co-innovate or even co-produce with the manufacturer or the maker. Digital communications and 3D printing technology, for instance, enable innovators and inventors to again become manufacturers, as was the case during the First Industrial Revolution, and to connect directly with markets. Closer interaction between innovators, manufacturers and customers translates into more distributed manufacturing, whereby customers source or commission the making of products locally.

Finally, almost all new technologies can be deployed to enhance the environmental sustainability of production processes and consumption via energy saving, bio-based products and fuel, remanufacturing and reusing of components.

For our purposes, there is one important point that is worth making. Each wave of technological change is the outcome of scientific exploration inside and across disciplines, leading to breakthroughs in the propositional knowledge we have of our world and in extended parts of prescriptive knowledge.

Its effects ripple across the economy through a myriad of channels and over time: technological change will alter the organisation of sectors and places, institutional frameworks and consumption models, as well as the distribution of wealth, income and jobs across regions and classes. The awareness, access to and adoption of such new technologies on behalf of firms and systems will vary depending on their internal capabilities and processes. Inevitably technological changes will tend to be perceived as exogenous shocks by firms, industrial districts, production and socio-economic systems. The last wave introduces a complete new array of knowledge whose usefulness and applicability are still to be fully revealed.

1.5 The current debate on Industry 4.0

This widely used term has already been defined in a number of different ways by think-tanks, business leaders, international organisations and policy makers. Advanced economies as well as manufacturing-intensive economies such as China have also identified how it would apply in their own context. This section critically overviews the recent and current debate on a new manufacturing model that is at the moment understood to fall under the concept of Industry 4.0.

The term was coined in Germany in 2011, when the Federal Government launched a project in relation to industry-science partnerships called *Industrie 4.0*. It described the impact that the 'Internet of Things' was going to have on the organisation of production thanks to a new interplay between humans and machines and a new wave of digital application to manufacturing production. The German government (GTAI, 2014) made *Industrie 4.0* its high-tech strategy to be delivered through a concerted effort of key national stakeholders such as industry associations and *Fraunhofer* Institutes.

The main motive for this drive to increase production efficiency is due to the nature of sectors and the composition of German industries. Germany has developed a competitive advantage in the engineering, machinery, equipment and auto sectors. These are historically able to capture and maximise labour productivity with process innovations that have included mechanisation and more recently automation. These sectors also present an efficient minimum scale, so firms are medium to large-sized. After a long period of a favourable euro regime, Germany has accumulated a large trade surplus, especially with emerging economies. Nevertheless, this has started to be squeezed by the very same Asian economies (South Korea and China) which have now started to compete in the same markets. *Industrie 4.0* has therefore been a deliberate strategy to enable German manufacturing firms to maintain high productivity levels in their factories in order to continue exporting mechanical engineering products and equipment (e.g. auto and machinery), as well as to build capabilities to export the very same 'efficient factory model' underpinning their competitive advantage. Indeed, Deutsche Bank (2014) suggested that Germany's adoption of *Industrie 4.0* was to become the 'factory outfitter of the world'.

A number of initiatives emerged from this such as the *Industrie 4.0 Platform*, *SmartFactory* and the technology network called *it's OWL*. Such policy endorsement triggered a buzz amongst manufacturing business leaders, who then started to circulate the term to suggest that a new generation of digital technologies was capable of redefining the use and role of a new generation of machinery. The introduction of these machines was argued to transform the factory and inter-factory supply chains in cyber-physical spaces thanks to cloud computing, the Internet of Things and automation. The opportunity presented itself when some German multi-national firms – already adopting advanced technology and literally on the technological frontier – saw this new wave of innovations coming to fruition.

Captured by a business-focused narrative, *Industrie 4.0* started being celebrated for the impact it was expected to have inside the factory, as mentioned above. New technologies such as the Internet of Things, AI, robotics and automation were all argued to bring greater efficiency, productivity, responsiveness, flexibility and ultimately seamless integration of the supply chain into manufacturing production (Deusche Bank, 2014).

Efficiency was mostly understood here as cost-efficiency, energy-efficiency and labour-efficiency, often summed up by the futuristic idea of 'light out factories' with no lights and no heating (*Wall Street Journal*, 2002; Heng, 2014). Factory automation leading to job polarisation and job obsolescence is emerging as a main challenge (Cowen, 2013; Brynjolfsson and McAfee, 2014). Increased productivity would come from automation enabling more flexible processes, shortened lead times, better control of the value chain flow and better quality control. Responsiveness would be greatly enhanced by the data collected thanks to cloud computing. Data can be collected during production on site and along the supply chain, as well as from consumers and users. Data provides information and feedback to be used to enhance processes and responses. Linked to the above, automation and data feed into the ability of firms to maximise their flexibility by producing in smaller batches: this is often referred to as mass customisation. Amongst many of the changes, Siemens (2015) notes the 'integration of value chains with seamless engineering' and a combination of cloud technology and data analytics. Bosch (2017) emphasises that technology is able to globally connect factories across the value chain to design and produce customised products, with flexible processes relying on versatile connected machinery complementing humans, short modification cycles and no rejects or inventory.

In a nutshell, the real game changer is argued to be digital technology that applied across the board is expected to change products and processes as well as to reorganise supply chains (Baur and Wee, 2015; Schmidt et al., 2015; Germany Federal Ministry of Education and Research, 2015). Thus, almost everything becomes 'smart' if digitally connected or enabled. The tight link between digital technology and *Industrie 4.0* has been also unpacked by countless reports by business service consultancies, such as KPMG (2016, 2017), BCG (2018), PwC (2016), McKinsey (2015) and Berger (2014), which have each offered their interpretations, visions of the future and adoption in specific sectors and countries.

In summary, there is a growing debate on what a smart factory and a connected factory will look like once all the relevant technologies have been deployed. These new cyber-physical spaces will transform the flow and use of inputs in the factory, but more fundamentally will transform the whole supply chain across upstream and downstream suppliers. In this regard, the Internet of Things, robotics, sensoring, space technology and mobile technology enabling machine-to-machine communications will allow the coordination of complex production operations via a seamless integration of functions residing not necessary in the same locale.

1.6 A more disruptive Industry 4.0+

However, the impact that the FIR should and could have is much more disruptive than designing a 'lights out factory'. In the MAKERS project, researchers have worked on a broader definition of Industry 4.0+, arguing that the deployment of all the technologies of the FIR will trigger a transformational shift in the techno-socio-economic paradigm attuned to a green economy and society. Only a holistic definition of Industry 4.0+ can deliver opportunities for inclusive socio-economic growth (see Figure 1.2).

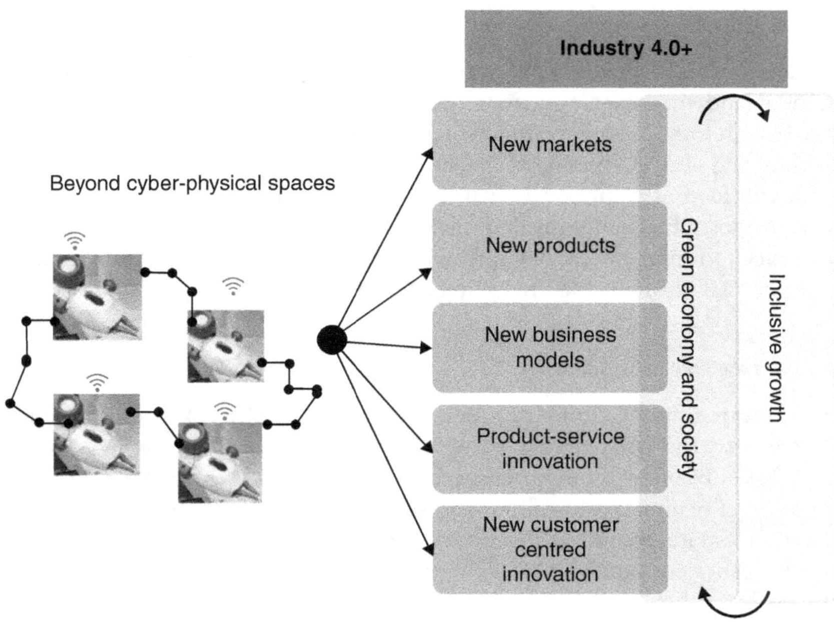

Figure 1.2 Industry 4.0+.

Source: Authors' elaboration.

Here it is argued that the disruptive and transformative changes of Industry 4.0+ can be clustered into five areas.

1.6.1 New markets

Looking at the broad spectrum of the technologies linked to the FIR, new markets will be created by firms, governments and consumers; these new markets will capture new consumption needs as well as pushing new technology-driven offers. Crucially, what will be new about these are the channels connecting production with consumers, users and accessers; indeed, the integration of digital technologies in products will change the channels through which people can buy, use, access or stream goods and services. Such new channels will branch out in a multitude of new modes of consuming, using or accessing depending on the product or service. The functionality and operability of these new markets – channels and modes – will depend on the producers' ability to activate and accustom consumers to them. There are concerns about digital divides resulting in actual digital exclusion as against empowerment.

1.6.2 New products

These new technologies will result in radically new products (goods and services). The way in which the latter are (and will be) 'digitally enabled or connected' will alter the way in which products are actually accessed, used or consumed, what needs they satisfy and what new uses they create. Examples of this are automotive and other forms of transport, mechanical engineering equipment and manufacturing in a broader sense (see below). Fundamental changes in biology, chemistry, medicine and pharmaceuticals will create new diagnostics and new treatments as well as new ways of administering them; such changes will feed into the food chain and bio-based industries. A drastic shift away from a fossil fuel economy and towards a bio-based economy will open up opportunities for completely new products that will have advanced functionalities, but crucially sustainable life cycle expectations.

1.6.3 Product service innovation

Product service innovation (Bustinza et al., 2017; Dimache and Roche, 2013) refers to the current debate on how manufacturing is moving from a product-based business model to a service-based business. This is the so-called servitisation *of* manufacturing (ibid) and suggests a cross-fertilisation of service practices and strategies to manufacturing in order to create a product-service system. It pushes consumers to overcome the need to own products, but rather to hire or lease them; in other words, the relationship between producer and consumer does not end with the sale, but is extended and weaved into a long-term relationship where the product is substituted by a use-oriented service or a result-oriented service (Baines et al., 2017).

1.6.4 New business models

Drawing on the above, to deliver in new markets, new products and a new product-service continuum, firms will be required to explore new business models. Digital technologies will offer a suite of opportunities – some of which are already entering current everyday life – in relation to both business-to-consumer and business-to business markets. Considering the subjects covered in Sections 1.6.1–1.6.3 above, firms will need to experiment in a business environment where increasingly firms face an innovation-production-consumption continuum. Co-innovation with consumers in the design of products can in extreme cases lead to unique, personalised offers that then materialise or become available (production); co-innovation in the delivery can also reflect elements of servitisation whereby the relationship between firm and customer is extended and renewed in the long term.

1.6.5 New customer-centred innovation

Cloud technology, big data and data analytics are a few of the technologies that will allow the design, manufacturing and delivery of personalised products (goods and services) thanks to a two-way flow of information and data between producers and customers. Equally, for instance, 3D printing will allow production at the point of consumption, reducing time lags, disruption, storage, stockpiling and so on. In summary, technology will deliver customer-centred continuous and incremental innovation.

1.7 Disrupting value creation and the organisation of production

The disrupting impact of Industry 4.0+ is likely to have manifold ramifications. On one level, new technologies will change the organisation of production between firms, whether they are co-located in the same region or territory in local systems of production or are linked by globally stretched supply chains. Technological change is expected to disrupt the spatial organisation of production depending on whether firms and systems are able to adapt and shift onto a new trajectory of change. On another level, the adoption and application of new technologies will also disrupt the parameters and the processes of value creation for firms, leading to a radical rethink of value creation along the supply chain in the past described by the 'smile curve' (Mudambi, 2008).

From a business economics perspective, it has been argued that firms can achieve a sustained competitive advantage by creating value from innovation but also by capturing this value (i.e. profiting) in markets and to a greater extent than their rivals (see Bailey et al., 2018, 2019). While originally developed in the context of business strategy, the idea that nations and regions should also be interested in capturing – in a sustainable way – a part of the value they help create and/or co-create with other entities is also gaining recognition in the literature (ibid).

Recent developments in place-based strategy represent moves in the right direction since they recognise both value creation and value capture, but unfortunately largely ignore the distribution of value capture and hence the sustainability of the value-creation process. To fill this gap, Bailey et al. (2019) have advocated place-based strategies that cross-fertilise industrial with business strategy, proposing positioning and value capture through building bottleneck assets with the aim of fostering sustainable value creation and the capturing of co-created value. The scale and speed of the challenge posed by the FIR (De Propris/WEF, 2016) also bring into sharp relief the need for new policy approaches to capture value at the regional and national levels as completely new value chains emerge (see Bailey et al., 2018). Taking the example of the auto industry, Bailey et al. (2018) suggest that the changes involved in Industry 4.0 and the shift to autonomous, connected and electric cars will require firms to position themselves in a completely new personal mobility ecosystem, offering opportunities for supply chain firms to reposition as this new value chain develops. This is beyond traditional 'intersectoral' upgrading as such, but rather is upgrading linked to the creation of a new value chain, which they term 'new value chain upgrading'. Some of the regional industrial policy implications of these issues are explored by Bailey and De Propris in the final chapter of this volume.

Value creation will also come from firms engaging with customers via new business models that will disrupt market relationships by locking consumers or users into a long-term relationship with firms as products are transformed into services. This is discussed by Vendrell-Herrero and Bustinza in Chapter 2. Servitisation is a new strategy that bundles services and products together and allows products to be uniquely personalised and to delegate the running and maintenance of the product to the firms. Indeed, servitisation not only provides a means for product differentiation, but also locks customers into a long-term relationship with the firm during the entire use life cycle. Servitisation is therefore seen as an opportunity to boost value creation and thereby the competitive advantage of European manufacturing firms. To date, however, no cross-country comparison has been attempted to establish the extent to which European firms have adopted servitisation strategies. Drawing on the ORBIS database (BvD), a map of servitisation activities across the EU-28 is presented. The method has recently been described in the literature and consists of observing the percentage of manufacturing firms that have a secondary North American Industry Classification System (NAICS) classification in knowledge-based services. The main findings report a weak but positive bivariate correlation between servitisation and both manufacturing value added as percentages of GDP (World Bank) and value in the Digital Economy and Society Index (Eurostat). Additionally, manufacturing and the development of digital capabilities are found to be substitutes and not to co-locate, implying that access to digital competences matters, but that firms need to strategically decide to pursue it.

Value creation also hinges on the innovativeness and ingenuity of people. However, the nature and the pervasiveness of this wave of new technologies will alter the balance between labour and capital, as well as change the skills, abilities and competences required in the workplace. This is explored by Pittarello, Trevisanato and De Propris in Chapter 3, using job vacancies data for the UK, Germany and Italy. Overall, the pace and breadth of the adjustments that firms are required to make will shape their ability to leverage new technologies (Pittarello, Trevisanato and De Propris, 2019).

1.8 Systemic disruptions and trajectories of change

The overwhelming narrative on automation, robotics, digitalisation and related technologies, in particular their application to the organisation of production within the firm and especially in *factories*, underplays the fact that firms do not operate in isolation regardless of their size, but rather are nodes in spatial and sectoral systems. Firms are key actors in deciding on innovation, capital and intangible investment, labour and skills, the location of production, the organisation of production and so on. However, they take decisions and function subject to the environment that surrounds them. Small and medium-sized firms in particular are embedded in local production systems that are enmeshed in regional economies that can be either specialised or diversified, with some presenting a significant service sector (Corò et al., 2017; Chaminade et al., 2017; Bellandi et al., 2017), especially in terms of services (OECD, 2010).

However, we would argue that technological change cannot deliver inclusive social and economic growth, as advocated in the Industry 4.0+ model, unless we understand its disrupting impact at the systemic level. In particular, we focus on two intersecting systems: the local system of production with micro-, small and medium-sized firms, and the global system of production coordinated by multi-national firms. We look at these in turn.

The extensive debate on drivers of regional economies and in particular on the local systems of production that can shape the growth or demise of regions left a grounded understanding of why and how regional industries emerge, grow and at times decline (Bellandi, De Propris and Santini, 2019a; Isaksen and Trippl, 2014; Capello and Nijkamp, 2010). However, such debate has evolved in a context where firms were operating within a stable and known technological paradigm. The innovation capacity of firms was tightly linked to the systemic knowledge and know-how they could assess and leverage through dense socio-economic exchanges connecting the local productive fabric. Learning and innovation processes differ across such systems depending on the nature of the innovation infrastructure therein. The innovation literature distinguished between science and technology-based (STI) and learning-by-doing, by-using and by-interacting (DUI) innovation modes (Lundvall, 2016); the former characterises innovation processes, for instance, in university-centred clusters in the US (Becattini et al., 2009), such as in ICT, and in regional innovation systems, such as the Cambridge biotech cluster (Cooke, 2002). The STI innovation mode has been used to explain processes of incremental innovation in sectors which are more high tech and where innovation has tended to be science-pushed and underpinned by codified knowledge. On the other hand, local production systems in relatively mid- or low-tech industries have been argued to innovate via a DUI learning mode, whereby learning and innovation is argued to occur via the sharing, exchange and transmission of often tacit knowledge eased by co-location as well as strong socio-cultural ties (Dei Ottati, 2009). The vast literature on Marshallian industrial districts has expanded on the latter and has introduced the concept of decentralised innovation creativity to capture the fact that innovation relies on 'the decentralization of the sources of new knowledge' (Bellandi, 1996: 354).

The current technological shift poses some clear challenges to local systems of production of small and medium-sized firms, especially those relying on a DUI learning mode. The key questions here are: how will the system access new technologies? How will technological change the systemic knowledge base? Which actors will drive or hinder the necessary transformative process of adaptation? This volume includes five contributions that unpack such issues with novel conceptual propositions and enlightening case study analysis.

In the first, Bellandi, Chaminade and Plechero (in Chapter 4) introduce a novel conceptual framework for understanding how different knowledge bases (analytic, synthetic and symbolic) can be accessed and combined at different territorial scales, looking at which mechanisms can be used to favour positive transformation paths in local productive systems. They apply such framework to the role of combinatorial knowledge for sustainable transformation under the impact of global challenges, such as those posed by Industry 4.0+. Case studies in Italy and Sweden illustrate the multi-scalarity of knowledge bases combined in different paths of industrial transformation addressing the challenge of technological change.

Next, in Chapter 5, Bellandi, Santini, Vecciolini and De Propris challenge dominant approaches to Industry 4.0 that effectively favour large firms in the application of new digital technologies, leaving local productive systems (LPSs) of small firms with the gloomy prospect of either declining or becoming dependent on large technological companies. Instead, in a broader approach, such as the one developed by the MAKERS project, Industry 4.0+ contemplates the possibility for such LPSs to integrate new technologies into existing socio-economic systems, allowing them to thrive; this would be the case for so-called 'Mark 3 industrial districts'. Here, appropriate solutions combine new digital-based technologies in processes of production and products, and possibly other innovations, with a renewed integration with artisan and creative capabilities. Such solutions require not just adaptations internal to single firms, but more crucially a collective rerouting that involves the recombination of productive knowledge at the system level.

Following on from this, Ramirez in Chapter 6 analyses initial efforts to motivate a regional transition towards a sustainable and innovative forest-based bio-economy in the Värmland Region of Sweden. The chapter discusses the notion of a bio-economy socio-technical system based on the development of renewable biological resources and its implications for local manufacturing systems. The account highlights the importance of place-specific dynamics of transition processes, such as the existence of a local natural resource with the potential to become a new source of raw materials, new regional visions and policies, and the role of local formal and informal institutions in the process of transition towards new regional environmentally sustainable socio-technical systems. The main focus of the chapter is on the role of agency and new policy initiatives strongly influenced by the need to address major societal challenges in processes of regional diversification. The multi-scalar nature of the change is also analysed.

The next regional study comes from Coro and Volpe (in Chapter 7), who provide an analysis of firms' adoption of the latest digital technologies in the Veneto region, one of the main manufacturing areas in Italy. The chapter focuses on factors that enable firms to adopt technologies related to Industry 4.0, with special attention being paid three main aspects: human capital, international openness and financial structure. The empirical analysis is based on a sample of firms that operate in the manufacturing, construction and business services. They unearth a heterogeneous use of Industry 4.0 technologies across different industries, allowing for the identification of distinct technology frontiers between sectors. The findings also reveal a positive relationship between the adoption of digital technologies and openness to international markets, as well as with highly skilled and highly educated human capital. Indeed, digital users show greater productivity than other firms. However, financial performance is less clear. In fact, firms that adopt new digital technologies have a more balanced financial structure, but they do not show higher profitability ratios than non-users. This result depends on a longer-run return on investment and on a different labour and capital ratio inside the firm.

Finally in this section, Fassio and Nathan in Chapter 8 look at the evolution of Industry 4.0 producers in Sweden during the 2000s and early 2010s. Like many industries before it, manufacturing is being reshaped by new technology. Much existing analysis on the FIR or 'Industry 4.0' has focused on users and, more broadly, on awareness and levels of readiness in existing businesses. Using MONA microdata, the analysis reveals smart manufacturing clusters in Stockholm and other Swedish cities with distinctive ecosystem features.

1.9 A new local-global continuum

The hyper-globalisation (Friedman, 2005) that was witnessed in the 1990s and early 2000s appears to be over; we are seeing signs of an emerging debate that is acknowledging fundamental change in the attitudes towards and the strategies related to globalisation. From a blind and unchallenging infatuation with globalisation in all its forms, including the globalisation of markets and production, culture and tastes, a deep untrustworthiness towards it emerged following the 2008 financial crisis. Indeed, society first started questioning, doubting and rejecting the claims that globalisation was not only inevitable but also had to be encouraged in order to allow markets to work efficiently, benefiting consumers and creating wealth (McGrew, 1998). The globalisation of production in particular led to the offshoring of labour-intensive manufacturing functions from advanced economies to low-income economies driven by the creation of multi-national enterprises' global value chains. The disappearance of entire industries in some regions of Europe and the US created large masses of unemployed or under-employed communities (Bell and Blanchflower, 2018) whose livelihood and sense of identity remained depressed for decades due to a lack of job alternatives. These communities expanded as a consequence of the 2008 financial crisis, shedding light to the real 'losers' in advanced economies of 'globalisation 3.0' as discussed by Baldwin (2019).

The recent debate on de-globalisation is discussed in Pegoraro, De Propris and Chidlow in Chapter 9, where they also present compelling evidence that the economic activities of firms show signs of *de-globalising*. A new appreciation of the value of manufacturing activities in light of the current geopolitical turmoil in terms of jobs and inclusive growth, as well as the emergence of new technologies with all their implications (*The Economist*, 2009), are creating a new continuum linking local places with global spaces. Understanding emerging de-globalisation forces matters since changes in technological paradigms and in the nature of markets can significantly impact on firms' location decisions in relation to manufacturing activities (Mudambi et al., 2018; Li and Bathelt, 2018; Chidlow et al., 2015; Chidolow et al., 2009). More specifically, such location decisions can relate to the adaptation of a reshoring strategy, which involves bringing back the manufacturing activity (or part of it) from a foreign market to a home market.

This latter development is explored by Kinkel, Pegoraro and Coates in Chapter 10, who compare reshoring trends across the EU and the US by focusing on three selected European regions, namely Veneto in Italy, Baden-Württemberg in Germany and the West Midlands in the UK. They explore whether a reshoring strategy is a viable solution for sustainable competitiveness or not, and evidence on reshoring in the US, with three criteria highlighted to be considered in adopting a reshoring strategy. The direct link between reshoring and technological change is unpacked further by Kinkel in Chapter 11 as he investigates the relationship between investments in new digital production technologies, which are currently discussed under headings such as 'Industry 4.0 (I4.0)' or 'Industrial Internet of Things (IIoT)', and reshoring or backshoring decisions of manufacturing companies. It is assumed that the use of Industry 4.0 technologies may affect global value chains in two ways: firstly, the increased productivity provided by Industry 4.0 production technologies may neutralise the cost-factor advantages of offshoring locations and make labour arbitrage less appealing; and, secondly, increased flexibility provided by Industry 4.0 technologies may provide an incentive for firms to locate production close to their European customers and regain some of the responsiveness lost in fine-sliced global supply chains.

The empirical test is based on a large dataset of almost 1,300 German manufacturing companies from the European manufacturing survey (EMS). This dataset has the advantage of including variables on both reshoring and investments in modern production technologies, and a number of additional control variables.

In Chapter 12, Mafini offers an interesting insider's perspective on the EU policy agenda for Industry 4.0 and discusses the underlying rationales of policies. For these purposes, the chapter builds upon recent major communications and documents of the European Commission, as well as key initiatives and platforms launched to support the transition of European industries and territories towards the fourth industrial era. In doing so, it puts forward an integrated background and a multi-dimensional policy approach of EU frameworks, including, for instance, 'Industrial Renaissance, Industrial Modernisation and Key Enabling Technologies' (KETs) and the 'Digitizing European Industry initiative' – dedicated to stimulating, accelerating and monitoring Industry 4.0. Finally, the uptake of Industry 4.0 in the research and innovation strategies smart specialisation strategy is examined, relying initially on information from the European Commission's Eye@RIS3 platform.

Following this perspective on EU policies, in the final chapter of the volume, Bailey and De Propris reflect on the extent to which technological change – including AI – inherent in the FIR will require further adjustments to EU regional and cohesion policies in order to allow the latter to have a 'transformative' power. In so doing, Chapter 13 considers the evolution of EU policies in terms of vision, objectives and instruments since the 1990s. Priorities have changed over time, but, the authors argue, have always been underpinned by a concern for inter-regional socio-economic cohesion. The disruptions brought about by FIR technologies have the potential to introduce new layers of socio-economic divides. The chapter discusses whether and how new technologies will widen economic divergence between low- and high-performing regions and states or, alternatively, whether and how they might allow some regions to 'leap-frog' with a consequent faster catching up. The chapter concludes with a 'call to arms' for a transformative regional industrial policy given the scale of change coming.

References

Amison, P. and Bailey, D. (2014). Phoenix industries and open innovation? The Midlands advanced automotive manufacturing and engineering industry. *Cambridge Journal of Regions, Economy and Society*, 7(3): 397–411.

Asheim B., Boschma R. and Cooke, P. (2011). Constructing regional advantage: platform policies based on related variety and differentiated knowledge bases. *Regional Studies*, 45(7): 893–904.

Bailey, D. (2016) Follow that (driverless) cab! *Birmingham Post.* Available at: www.birminghampost.co.uk/business/business-opinion/follow-that-driverless-cab-11817752.

Bailey, D. (2017) Electric vehicle market sparks into life as ICE age comes to end? *Birmingham Post*. Available at: www.birminghampost.co.uk/business/business-opinion/electric-vehicle-market-sparks-life-13354818.

Bailey, D. and De Propris, L. (2014) Manufacturing reshoring and its limits: the UK automotive case. *Cambridge Journal of Regions, Economy and Society*, 7(3): 379–398.

Bailey, D., Pejic, D. and Pegoraro, D. (2018) Case studies of EU value chain upgrading. MAKERS Paper, D5.2. MAKERS/European Commission. Available at: www.makers-rise.org/wp-content/uploads/2018/02/D5.2-Paper-on-a-case-study-of-value-chain-upgrading-protected.pdf.

Bailey, D., Pitelis, C. and Tomlinson, P. (2018) A place-based developmental regional industrial strategy and/for sustainable capture of co-created value. *Cambridge Journal of Economics*, 42(6): 1521–1542.

Bailey, D., Pitelis, C. and Tomlinson, P. (2019) Strategic management and regional industrial strategy: cross-fertilisation to mutual advantage. *Regional Studies*.

Baines, T., A Z Bigdeli, O F Bustinza, V Guang Shi, J Baldwin, and K Ridgway (2017) Servitization: revisiting the state-of-the-art and research priorities. *International Journal of Operations & Production Management*, 37(2): 256–278.

Baldwin, R. (2019) *The Globotics Upheaval: Globalisation, Robotics and the Future of Work*. New York, Oxford University Press.

Barca, F. (2011) Alternative approaches to development policy: intersections and divergences. In OECD, *OECD Regional Outlook 2011*. OECD Publishing, pp. 215–225.

Barca, F., McCann, P. and Rodríguez, P. (2012) The case for regional development intervention: place-based versus place-neutral approaches. *Journal of Regional Science*, 52(1): 134–152.

Baur, C. and Wee, D. (2015) Manufacturing's next act. McKinsey and Company, Available at: www.mckinsey.com/business-functions/operations/our-insights/manufacturings-next-act.

BCG (2018) Embracing Industry 4.0 – and rediscovering growth. Available at: www.bcg.com/capabilities/operations/embracing-industry-4.0-rediscovering-growth.aspx.

Bell, D.N. and Blanchflower, D.G. (2018). Underemployment in the US and Europe (No. w24927). National Bureau of Economic Research.

Becattini, G., Bellandi, M. and De Propris, L. (eds.) (2009). *A Handbook of Industrial Districts*. Cheltenham: Edward Elgar.

Bellandi, M. (1996) Innovation and change in the Marshallian industrial District. *European Planning Studies*, 4(3): 357–368. DOI: https://doi.org/10.1080/09654319608720351.

Bellandi, M. and De Propris, L. (2017). New forms of industrial districts. *Economia e Politica Industriale*, 44(4): 411–427.

Bellandi, M., De Propris, L. and Santini, E. (2019a) Endogenous rerouting and longevity in systemic organisations of production. In F. Hervas and J.-L. Belussi (eds), *Agglomeration and Firm Performance*. Springer, pp. 207–222.

Bellandi, M., De Propris, L. and Santini, E. (2019b). An evolutionary analysis of industrial districts: the changing multiplicity of production know-how nuclei. *Cambridge Journal of Economics*, 43(1): 187–204.

Bellandi, M. and Santini, E. (2018) Territorial servitization and new local productive configurations: the case of the textile industrial district of Prato. *Regional Studies*, 53: 356–365.

Bellandi, M. et al. (2017) Deliverable D3.1. Available at: www.makers-rise.org/wp-content/uploads/2018/03/D3.1-Paper-on-the-impact-of-new-technology-on-the-organisation-of-production-in-high-tech-districts-or-clusters.-Protected.pdf.

Bellandi, M., Santini, E., De Propris, L. and Vecciolini, C. (2018) *A Place-Based View on Industry 4.0 in Systems of SMEs*. Mimeo.

Berger (2014) Industry 4.0: the new Industrial Revolution – how Europe will succeed. Roland Berger Strategic Consultants.

Berkeley, N., Bailey, D., Jones, A. and Jarvis, D. (2017) Assessing the transition towards battery electric vehicles: a multi-level perspective on drivers of, and barriers to, take up. *Transportation Research Part A: Policy and Practice*, 106: 320–332.

BNEF (Bloomberg New Energy Finance) (2016) Electric vehicles to be 35% of global new car sales by 2040. Available at: https://about.bnef.com/blog/electric-vehicles-to-be-35-of-global-new-car-sales-by-2040.

BNEF (Bloomberg New Energy Finance) (2017) Electric cars to reach price parity by 2025. Available at: https://about.bnef.com/blog/electric-cars-reach-price-parity-2025.

Bosch (2017) Intelligent systems for the flexible factory 4.0. Available at: www.bosch.com/explore-and-experience/industry-4-0-flexible-production-line.

Brynjolfsson, E. and McAfee, A. (2014) The second machine age: work, progress, and prosperity in a time of brilliant technologies. W.W. Norton.

Bustinza O.F., Vendrell-Herrero, F., Santini, E., Bellandi, M. and De Propris, L. (2017) Servitization on manufacturing. MAKERS Report. Available at: www.makers-rise.org/wp-content/uploads/2018/02/Deliverable-1.2-protected.pdf.

Capello, R. and Nijkamp, P. (eds.). (2010). *Handbook of Regional Growth and Development Theories*. Edward Elgar.

Chaminade, C., Bellandi, M., Plechero, M. and Santini, E. (2017) A paper on the role of RIS and NIS on manufacturing upgrading, including a case study analysis on the role of knowledge transfer to upgrade the textile industry in Europe. MAKERS Report. Available at: www.makers-rise.org/wp-content/uploads/2018/03/D2.2-A-paper-on-the-role-of-RIS-and-NIS-on-manufacturing-upgrading.pdf.

Chidlow, A., Holmström-Lind, C., Holm, U. and Tallman, S. (2015) Do I stay or do I go? Sub-national drivers for post-entry subsidiary development. *International Business Review*, 24(2): 266–274.

Chidlow, A., Salciuviene, L., and Young, S. (2009) Regional determinants of inward FDI distribution in Poland. *International Business Review*, 18(2): 119–133.

Cooke, P. (2002) Regional innovation systems: general findings and some new evidence from biotechnology clusters. *Journal of Technology Transfer*, 27(1): 133–145.

Corò, G., Volpe, M., Pejcic, D. and De Propris, L. (2017) Paper on technological upgrading in manufacturing in the light of the new manufacturing model, MAKERS Paper, D1.1. MAKERS/European Commission. Available at: www.makers-rise.org/wp-content/uploads/2017/10/D1.1-Manufacturing-4.0-protected.pdf.

Cowen, T. (2013) *Average Is Over*. Dutton.

De Propris, L., Ramirez, P., Robinson, P., Bailey, D. and Pegoraro, D. (2017) EU positioning in key manufacturing GVCs. MAKERS Paper, D5.1. MAKERS/European Commission. Available at: www.makers-rise.org/wp-content/uploads/2017/10/D5.1-Glocal-value-chains-protected.pdf.

De Propris, L./WEF (World Economic Forum) (2016) How the Fourth Industrial Revolution is powering the rise of smart manufacturing. Available at: www.weforum.org/agenda/2016/06/how-the-fourth-industrial-revolution-is-powering-the-rise-of-smart-manufacturing.

Dei Ottati, G. (2009) Semi-automatic and deliberate actions in the evolution of industrial districts, in G. Becattini, M. Bellandi and L. De Propris (eds), *A Handbook of Industrial Districts*. Edward Elgar, pp. 204–215.

Deloitte (2015) Industry 4.0: challenges and solutions for the digital transformation and use of exponential technologies. Available at: www2.deloitte.com/content/dam/Deloitte/ch/Documents/manufacturing/ch-en-manufacturing-industry-4-0-24102014.pdf.

Deutsche Bank (2014) Industry 4.0: upgrading of Germany's industrial capabilities on the horizon. Available at: www.dbresearch.com/PROD/RPS_EN-PROD/PROD0000000000451959/Industry_4_0%3A_Upgrading_of_Germany%E2%80%99s_industrial_ca.pdf.

Dimache, A. and Roche, T. (2013). A decision methodology to support servitisation of manufacturing. *International Journal of Operations and Production Management*, 33(11–12), 1435–1457.

The Economist (2009) International: turning their backs on the world. 19 February.

EU Parliament (2015) Industry 4.0: digitalisation for productivity and growth. Briefing.

European Commission (2014) *Communication: Towards an Industrial Renaissance. COM/2014/014 Final.* Brussels: European Commission.

European Commission (2016) Industry 4.0. Brussels: European Commission.

Friedman, T.L. (2005). *The World is Flat: A Brief History of the Globalised World in the 21st Century*. Allen Lane/Penguin.

Germany Federal Ministry of Education and Research (2015) Platform Industrie 4.0. Available at: www.plattform-i40.de/PI40/Navigation/EN/Home/home.

Gowling, W.L.G. (2016) Are you data driven? UK Autodrive White Paper. Available at: https://landing.gowlingwlg.com/driverless/?utm_source=driverless-vehicles-regulating-moral-programming-in-order-to-move-forward&utm_medium=gowlingwlg-website&utm_campaign=autodrive#download.

GTAI (2014) *Industrie 4.0: Smart Manufacturing for the Future*. German Trade and Invest.

Heng, S. (2014) Industry 4.0: upgrading of Germany's industrial capabilities on the horizon. Available at: https://ssrn.com/abstract=2656608.

Hildreth, P. and Bailey, D. (2013) The economics behind the move to 'localism' in England. *Cambridge Journal of Regions, Economy and Society*, 6(2): 233–249.

Isaacson, W. (2014) *The Innovators: How a Group of Hackers, Geniuses, and Geeks Created the Digital Revolution*. Simon & Schuster.

Isaksen, A. and Trippl, M. (2014) Regional industrial path development in different regional innovation systems: a conceptual analysis (No. 2014/17). Lund University, CIRCLE-Center for Innovation, Research and Competences in the Learning Economy.

Kinkel, S., Dewanti, R.T., Zimmermann, P. and Coates, R. (2017) *Measuring Teshoring Trends in the EU and the US*. MAKERS Report. Available at: www.makers-rise.org/wp-content/uploads/2018/02/D4.1-Measuring-reshoring-trends-in-the-EU-protected.pdf.

Kondratieff, N.D. (1979). The long waves in economic life. *Review* (Fernand Braudel Center), II(4): 519–562.

Kondratieff, N.D. and Stolper, W.F. (1935) The long waves in economic life. *Review of Economics and Statistics*, 17(6): 105–115.

KPMG (2016) The factory of the future. Industry 4.0 –The challenges of tomorrow. Available at: https://assets.kpmg/content/dam/kpmg/es/pdf/2017/06/the-factory-of-the-future.pdf.

KPMG (2017) Beyond the hype: separating ambition from reality in Industry 4.0. Available at: https://home.kpmg/xx/en/home/insights/2017/05/beyond-the-hype-separating-ambition-from-reality.html.

KPMG/SMMT (2015) Connected and autonomous vehicles – the UK economic opportunity. Available at: https://home.kpmg.com/content/dam/kpmg/pdf/2015/04/connected-and-autonomous-vehicles.pdf.

KPMG/SMMT (2016) *The Digitalisation of the UK Automotive Industry*. Available at: www.smmt.co.uk/wp-content/uploads/sites/2/smmt_the-digitalisation-of-the-uk-auto-industry_kpmg-apr-2017.pdf.

Li, P. and Bathelt, H. (2018) Location strategy in cluster networks. *Journal of International Business Studies*, 49(8): 967–989.

Lundvall, B.Å. (2016) Innovation as an interactive process: from user–producer interaction to the national systems of innovation. In B.Å. Lundvall (ed.), *The Learning Economy and the Economics of Hope*. Anthem Press, pp. 61–84.

Marsh, P. (2013) *The New Industrial Revolution: Consumers, Globalization and the End of Mass Production*. Yale University Press.

Marsh, P. (2015) *New Manufacturing: Opportunities and Policies: How Ideas in Production Industry Can Re-energise the World Economy*. Report for the OECD Centre on Entrepreneurship, SMEs and Local Development.

Marshall, A. (1923) *Industry and Trade*, 4th edn. Macmillan.

McCann, P. and Ortega-Argilés, R. (2015) Smart specialization, regional growth and applications to European Union cohesion policy. *Regional Studies*, 49(8): 1291–1302.

McGrew, A.G. (1998) The globalisation debate: putting the advanced capitalist state in its place. *Global Society*, 12(3): 299–321.

McKinsey (2015) Manufacturing's next act. Available at: www.mckinsey.com/business-functions/operations/our-insights/manufacturings-next-act.

McKinsey (2016) Disruptive trends that will transform the auto industry. Available at: www.mckinsey.com/industries/high-tech/our-insights/disruptive-trends-that-will-transform-the-auto-industry?cid=other-eml-ttn-mip-mck-oth-1612.

McKinsey Global Institute (2012) *Manufacturing of the Future: The Next Era of Global Growth and Innovation*. McKinsey.

Mudambi, R. (2008) Location, control and innovation in knowledge intensive industries. *Journal of Economic Geography*, 8(5): 699–725.

Mudambi, R., Li, L., Ma, X., Makino, S., Qian, G. and Boschma, R. (2018) Zoom in, zoom out: geographic scale and multinational activity. *Journal of International Business*, 49(8), 929–941.

Muller, P., Devnani, S., Julius, J., Gagliardi, D. and Marzocchi, C. (2016). *Annual Report on European SMEs 2015/2016 – SME Recovery Continues*. Contract number: EASME/COSME/2015/012. European Union.

OECD (2010) *SMEs, Entrepreneurship and Innovation*. OECD Publishing.

OECD (2015) *ICTs and Jobs: Complements or Substitutes? The Effects of ICT Investment on Labour Market Demand by Skills and by Industry in Selected Countries*. OECD Digital Economy Working Papers, No. 259. OECD Publishing.

OECD (2016) *Science, Technology and Innovation Outlook 2016: Megatrends Affecting Science, Technology and Innovation*. OECD Publishing.

OECD (2017a) *Small, Medium, Strong: Trends in SME Performance and Business Conditions*. OECD Publishing.

OECD (2017b) *The Next Production Revolution: Implications for Governments and Business*. OECD Publishing.

Pegoraro, D., De Propris, L. and Bailey, D. (2017) *Paper on Reshoring Trends and Drivers of Shorter Value Chains*. MAKERS Report. Available at: www.makers-rise.org/wp-content/uploads/2017/10/D4.2-Reshoring-protected.pdf.

Pejcic, D., Bailey, D. and Pegoraro, D. (2018) *Paper on a Case Study of Value Chain Upgrading*. MAKERS Report. Available at: www.makers-rise.org/wp-content/uploads/2018/02/D5.2-Paper-on-a-case-study-of-value-chain-upgrading-protected.pdf.

Perez, C. (2010) Technological revolutions and techno-economic paradigms. *Cambridge Journal of Economics*, 34(1): 185–202.

Pittarello, A., Trevisanato, A. and De Propris, L. (2019) *Report on the Employment Transformation in EU Manufacturing Sectors*. MAKERS Report to the EU Commission. Available at: www.makers-rise.org/wp-content/uploads/2019/05/Skills-report_final.pdf.

PwC (2016) *Industry 4.0: Building the Digital Enterprise*. Available at: www.pwc.com/gx/en/industries/industries-4.0/landing-page/industry-4.0-building-your-digital-enterprise-april-2016.pdf.

Ramirez, P. and Ciappei, S. (2018) *Paper on the Impact of GINs on Manufacturing Upgrading*. MAKERS Report. Available at: www.makers-rise.org/wp-content/uploads/2018/03/D2.1-Paper-on-the-impact-of-GINs-on-manufacturing-upgrading.pdf.

Rifkin, J. (2011) *The Third Industrial Revolution*. Palgrave Macmillan.

Rifkin, J. (2013) *The Third Industrial Revolution: How Lateral Power is Transforming Energy, the Economy, and the World*. Palgrave Macmillan.

Rifkin, J. (2014) *The Zero Marginal Cost Society: The Internet of Things, the Collaborative Commons, and the Eclipse of Capitalism*. Palgrave Macmillan.

Rodrik, D. (2004) *Industrial Policy for the 21st Century*. Cambridge, MA: John F. Kennedy School of Government.

Rodrik, D. (2008) *One Economics, Many Recipes: Globalization, Institutions, and Economic Growth*. Princeton University Press.

Santini, E. and Bellandi, M. (2017) *Paper on the Impact of New Technology on the Organisation of Production in High-tech Districts or Clusters*. MAKERS Report. Available at: www.makers-rise.org/wp-content/uploads/2018/03/D3.1-Paper-on-the-impact-of-new-technology-on-the-organisation-of-production-in-high-tech-districts-or-clusters.-Protected.pdf.

Schmidt, R., Möhring, M., Härting, R., Reichstein, C., Neumaier, P. and Jozinović, P. (2015) Industry 4.0: potentials for creating smart products: empirical research results. Conference Proceedings. International Conference on Business Information Systems.

Schumpeter, J.A. (1942) *Capitalism, Socialism and Democracy*. New York: Harper.

Schwab, K. (2016) *The Fourth Industrial Revolution*. Geneva: World Economic Forum.

Simoudis, E. (2015) The innovation-driven disruption of the automotive value chain (part 1). Synapse Partners. Available at: http://synapsepartners.co/2015/04/06/the-innovation-driven-disruption-of-the-automotive-value-chain-part-1.

Simoudis, E. (2017) A new value chain for next-generation personal mobility. *Re-imagining Corporate Innovation with a Silicon Valley Perspective Blog*. Available at: https://corporate-innovation.co/2017/04/25/a-new-value-chain-for-next-generation-mobility.

Volpe, M. and Coro', G. (2018) *Paper on Cluster Upgrading with Case Studies*. MAKERS Report. Available at: www.makers-rise.org/wp-content/uploads/2018/03/D3.2-Paper-on-cluster-upgrading-with-case-studies.-Protected.pdf.

Walker, J. and Johnson, C. (2016) *Peak Car Ownership: The Market Opportunity of Electric Automated Mobility Services*. Rocky Mountain Institute. Available at: www.rmi.org/wp-content/uploads/2017/03/Mobility_PeakCarOwnership_Report2017.pdf.

Wall Street Journal (2002) Workers aren't included in lights-out factories. Available at: www.wsj.com/articles/SB1037666065632825628.

World Bank (2017) *Trouble in the Making? The Future of Manufacturing-Led Development*. World Bank.

2 Servitization in Europe

Ferran Vendrell-Herrero and Oscar F. Bustinza

2.1 Introduction: motivation, definitions and research objectives

As a result of a reduction in transport costs, a rise in offshoring of European and US production to developing economies in the 1990s changed the way the global economy was conceptualized during the twentieth century (Krugman and Venables, 1995). Countries like China, India, Turkey and Mexico benefited from production offshoring and other foreign direct investments from Western economies, significantly improving their manufacturing industry. Over the years, these countries have become increasingly competitive and could threaten the manufacturing leadership of Europe and the US as the latter functioned during the twentieth century (Baldwin, 2016).

Advanced economies are characterized by high wages, high skills and high disposable income. Business models that focus on the exploitation of economies of scale thus became obsolete for European manufacturers at the turn of the twenty-first century. With the rapid rise of Asia's global production, firms in advanced economies must increase customization while maintaining high levels of scalability and efficiency in order to develop and maintain a competitive advantage. New competitive conditions require a better understanding of what drivers and bottlenecks can enable manufacturing sectors to transition to more innovation-intensive and difficult-to-imitate business models. One way of sustaining the competitive advantage of these sectors in the medium and longer term is through bundling products and services and/or through digital upgrading of product features (Porter and Heppelman, 2014). This chapter endeavours to better understand and to quantify the use of these business models in Europe.

Product and service firms have conventionally been thought of as largely independent entities. Evidence suggests, however, that potential synergies between products and services could ultimately enhance consumer satisfaction. The business strategy of bundling products and services in manufacturing sectors is known as the *servitization* of manufacturing (Bustinza, Vendrell-Herrero and Baines, 2017). In servitization, production firms attempt to enhance product features and capabilities, as well as consumer satisfaction, and to increase product differentiation by including services that support product capabilities during the product's entire life cycle in their business portfolio. By incorporating services as an integral part of the product to be sold, firms gain more customizable offerings. The services provided are not homogeneous; they differ substantially in their levels of risk and competition, and their potential to create competitive advantages. Some manufacturers create wealth by offering a wide range of 'break-fix' services (e.g., maintenance), while others develop more sophisticated outcome-based contracts (Visnjic, Neely and Jovanovic, 2018). Successful examples of the latter include Rolls-Royce's TotalCare solution and Xerox's delivering 'pay-per-click' scanning, copying and printing of documents.

In Europe, the rise of servitization is evidence of a business environment that has significantly dented the weight of manufacturing's contribution to GDP. The European manufacturing industry has been in relative decline for the last 30 years and has recently reached an all-time minimum of 15% of total GDP, a share that the European Commission has been committed to raise to 20% as part of its 2020 Agenda (Veugelers, 2013). European initiatives have also been devoted to promoting servitization across manufacturing firms (Hojnik, 2016). Despite this growing interest, no research as yet grounds how to map the heterogeneities in servitization activity across Europe (Lafuente, Vaillant and Vendrell-Herrero, 2018).

One stream of research does, however, focus on the territorial aspect of servitization (Vendrell-Herrero and Wilson, 2017). This research underscores the importance of the Knowledge-Intensive Business Services (KIBS) sector (Horvath and Rabetino, 2018; Seclen-Luna and Barrutia-Güenaga, 2018) and provides some isolated pictures of servitization activity in Europe (Crozet and Millet, 2017; Gomes et al., 2018; Sforzi and Boix, 2018). This research stream focuses on secondary datasets and thus considers a large and broad set of representative firms. A summary of these methods is given in Table 2.1.

Crozet and Millet (2017) use data from the French fiscal authority to differentiate between sales from products and sales from services. These authors visualize that 70% of French manufacturers are servitized, but their method suffers from two limitations. Firstly, the sample can be neither extrapolated (data from different fiscal authorities might not be comparable) nor scalable (data are confidential; no repositories exist to merge data from various countries). Secondly, the data could over-represent servitization, as they account for all types of services (basic as well as advanced) and do not consider the option of bundling products and services.

The figures obtained by Gomes et al. (2018) and Sforzi and Boix (2018) are considerably more pessimistic, although their methods are scalable to all EU-28 countries and consider only knowledge-based (advanced) services. Both articles use ORBIS, a Bureau van Dijk (BvD) service that provides firms' balance sheet statements and covers a wide spectrum of countries. The method used by Sforzi and Boix (2018) focuses on searching keywords in the description of the business. By examining firms located in specifically industrial districts

Table 2.1 Measuring servitization using secondary sources

Method	*Source*	*Articles*	*Range*	*Advantages/limitations*
Identifies product firms with positive service sales	Compustat	Suarez, Cusumano and Kahl (2013)	42% (US)	Does not include firms selling bundles of products and services. Inflated by multi-sector firms. The method is rich for firm-level analysis but not scalable or extrapolable to other territories Intensive and extensive margins of servitization.
	Fiscal Authorities and Central Banks	Crozet and Millet (2017)	70% (France)	
		Ariu (2016)	8% (Belgium)	
Identifies product firms with service business in their description*	BvD (any)	Neely (2008)	10–60%#	Depends largely on the firm's description. Only extensive margin of servitization
		Sforzi and Boix (2018)	3.4% (Italy) and 5.7% (Spain)	
Identifies product firms with a secondary service sector**	BvD (ORBIS)	Gomes et al. (2018)	3.9% (Spain) and 9.8% (Germany)	Secondary sectors are not compulsory to declare, so it is difficult to build a firm-level control sample. Only extensive margin of servitization. The information is highly reliable when it comes to representing territories.
		Opazo et al. (2018)	n.a.##	
		Sforzi and Boix (2018)	3.6% (Spain)	

Notes:

* Usual keywords for knowledge-based services: research, development, scientific, advertising, design, software, programming, consultancy, streaming, engineering, leasing, usage, creative, intermediation and brokerage.

** Commonly used secondary NAICS codes for knowledge-based services: 518 'Data Processing, Hosting, and Related Services'; 519 'Other Information Services'; 54 'Professional, Scientific, and Technical Services'; 56 'Administrative and Support and Waste Management and Remediation Services'; and 811 'Repair and Maintenance'.

\# The study has a large number of countries.

\#\# The study does not have a control sample of non-servitized firms.

for 2011, the authors conclude that 5.7% of Spanish manufacturing firms and 3.4% of Italian manufacturing firms are servitized. Gomes et al. (2018) delve more deeply into ORBIS, exploiting the full capacity of the sample by identifying the firms' secondary sector. This method enables identification of firms with manufacturing as the primary industry and knowledge-based services as a secondary industry. In comparing Germany and Spain, Gomes et al.'s (2018) study obtains figures in the same range as Sforzi and Boix (2018). For 2014, they find that 3.89% and 9.79% of product firms are servitized in Spain and Germany, respectively. Conceptually and methodologically, this method seems superior to the others. Our chapter thus aims to estimate current servitization activity for all EU-28 countries with the methodology proposed by Gomes et al. (2018), thereby making an important academic contribution to the literature.

Beyond mapping servitization in Europe, another objective of this study is to depict what inputs drive servitization activities in a given country. We focus on the role of two inputs: manufacturing and digital territorial capabilities. By collecting reliable information on these constructs from the World Bank (manufacturing) and Eurostat (digital exposure), we test three important postulates, two of them bivariate relationships and the third testing multivariate and joint effects.

The first question we attempt to answer is how the manufacturing fabric in a country relates to the percentage of product firms implementing service business models in the same territory. For the case of Spanish autonomous communities, Lafuente, Vaillant and Vendrell-Herrero (2017) identify a virtuous circle of KIBS activity and employment growth in manufacturing sectors. Similarly, for a sample of 121 European regions, Horváth and Rabetino (2018) find that a solid industrial fabric correlates highly with the development of entrepreneurial projects based on the implementation of knowledge-based services. This research stream seems to indicate a positive link between manufacturing and servitization activities at the country level, but this relationship has not yet been explicitly tested. We help to fill this knowledge gap by representing graphically the correlation between these variables and considering the level of economic development as a moderator of this relationship.

Our second goal is to determine whether a direct relationship exists between digitization and servitization activities. Since digital upgrading and smart products are key elements for servitization, these variables are clearly linked at the firm level (Coreynen, Matthyssens and van Bockhaven, 2017; Vendrell-Herrero et al., 2017a). No empirical studies have demonstrated this relationship with a spatial analysis, although the theory of digital dark matter has been proposed (Greenstein and Nagle, 2014; Vendrell-Herrero et al., 2017b). This theory suggests that digitization activity correlates positively with servitization activity at the country level, since more digital infrastructure increases the capacity of businesses and customers in the region to develop more complex business models. We test this suggestion by picturing the digitization–servitization link and considering economic development as a moderating variable. Our final exercise evaluates graphically and through simple regression analysis whether the industrial fabric and digital infrastructure should be seen as substitutes for each other or as complementary.

The following sections provide more details on the data and measurement of the different concepts used, including their geographical mapping. The relationships explained above are then tested. Subsequently, the results and provides various policy recommendations are discussed.

2.2 Mapping servitization across the EU-28: sources, data and variables

To analyse the European geography of servitization activity, as well as this activity's correlation with other country-level variables, we construct a unique database. The data are drawn from multiple sources, including ORBIS (BvD), the World Bank and Eurostat. The sample focuses on the 28-country European Union (including the UK) and collects information for the most recent year available for each variable considered.[1]

As discussed in the previous section and in Table 2.1, there are various ways to compute a country-level measure of servitization activity through secondary databases. We understand the best approach to be that followed by Gomes et al. (2018) and Opazo, Vendrell-Herrero and Bustinza (2018). This approach consists of identifying the percentage of manufacturing firms with a secondary sector in the knowledge-based service sector.[2]

We cleaned the data to ensure comparability between the different countries. After downloading the data from ORBIS for 2017, we identified outliers that required correction. The outliers were three countries with very low values and three countries with extremely high values. The countries at the bottom of the group were Estonia, Malta and Italy, with a percentage of servitized manufacturers of 1% or lower. The countries at the top were Hungary, Slovakia and the Czech Republic, with over 35% servitization,[3] exactly double that of the next-lowest country, Belgium (18%). The figures for all six of these countries were adjusted following the quartile imputation technique (Muñoz and Rueda, 2009). We imputed the average of the bottom quartile (1.97%) to the three countries at the bottom and the average of the top quartile (10.34%) to the three countries at the top.

Figure 2.1 maps the servitization activity in Europe. To simplify the visual analysis, the variable is divided into quartiles. Countries with the highest servitization activity include some of the usual suspects and reflect the apparent concentration of servitization in central Europe. These countries include the Benelux countries, Germany, Hungary Slovakia and the Czech Republic. The top three countries are Belgium (18.5%), Germany (12%) and the Netherlands (11%). The second quartile includes countries with 4.7–9% servitized manufacturers – very rich countries such as Austria (6.5%) and Sweden (5.5%), and relatively poor ones such as Greece (5.5%) and Bulgaria (4.8%). The third

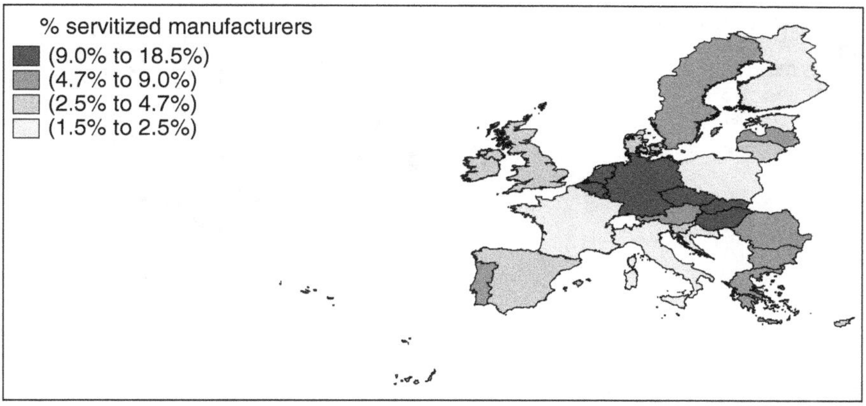

Figure 2.1 Mapping servitization intensity, EU-28.

quartile includes Spain (4.2%), Ireland (3%), the UK (3.1%) and Denmark (3.7%), and the bottom quartile countries like France (2%) and Finland (1.6%).

This study approximates the manufacturing activity of a country as the manufacturing value added as a percentage of GDP. The literature widely accepts this measure as a way to understand the manufacturing strength of an economy (Aquilante, Bustinza and Vendrell-Herrero, 2016; Haraguchi, Cheng and Smeets, 2017). The data were obtained from the World Bank's open data (https://data.worldbank.org/indicator/NV.IND.MANF.ZS) and are from 2016, which is the most recent year available.

Figure 2.2 maps the manufacturing activity in Europe, dividing the data in this figure into quartiles. The manufacturing industry in the countries in the top quartile generates 20–35% of the GDP. Among these countries we find Ireland (35%), the Czech Republic (27%), Hungary (24%) and Germany (23%). The second quartile represents countries with manufacturing value added representing 15–20% of GDP. This category includes countries such as Italy (16%), Finland (17%), Austria (18%) and Poland (20%). Countries with manufacturing value added of 12–15% of GDP compose the third quartile, exemplified by the Netherlands (12%), Spain (14%), Sweden (15%) and Denmark (15%). The bottom quartile contains countries with manufacturing value added of 5–12% of GDP. Surprisingly, countries with a long tradition in manufacturing, such as France (11%) and the UK (10%), are now at the bottom of the classification.

This study computes an economy's level of digitization using the Digital Economy and Society Index (DESI) provided by Eurostat (https://ec.europa.eu/digital-single-market/en/desi). DESI is a composite index that takes values between 0 and 1. It contains information from relevant indicators of country-level digital performance and infrastructure, providing information

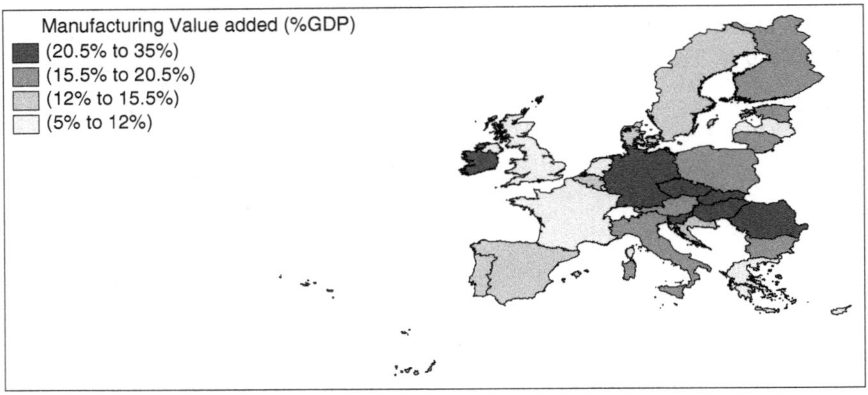

Figure 2.2 Mapping manufacturing intensity, EU-28.

on connectivity, digital skills, the use of internet by citizens and businesses, availability of digitalized public services and development of the ICT sector. This index has been used in previous research that attempts to map the digital capabilities of European countries (Moroz, 2017). Here, we use the DESI for 2017, in which the maximum was 0.67 (Denmark) and the minimum 0.31 (Romania).

Figure 2.3 maps the DESI for the EU-28. The colours of the countries indicate the quartile to which other variables of interest belong. The DESI ranges from 0.56 to 0.67 for the leading group, which includes mostly Scandinavian countries (Sweden, Finland and Denmark lead, with very similar values), the Benelux countries (the Netherlands with 0.64, followed by Belgium with 0.58 and Luxembourg with 0.57) and the UK (0.58). The second quartile (0.51–0.56) is exemplified by German-speaking countries (Germany and Austria both have an index of 0.54) and Ireland (0.55). The third quartile countries, with a DESI of 0.41–0.51, are the Latin countries (Spain and Portugal with an index of 0.51, followed by France with 0.48). With the exception of Italy (0.38), the bottom quartile (0.31–0.41) is composed of EU emerging economies, including Romania (0.31), Bulgaria (0.35) and Poland (0.40).

2.3 Measuring servitization across the EU-28

Our first objective is to disentangle whether manufacturing and servitization are positively correlated, as implied by Lafuente, Vaillant and Vendrell-Herrero (2017), and Horváth and Rabetino (2018). Figure 2.4 shows the possible correlations between these variables for the full sample and three subsamples based on level of income.[4] Our results show a weak (not statistically

Figure 2.3 Mapping digitization intensity, EU-28.

significant) but positive correlation between servitization and manufacturing (0.091). Interestingly, this correlation is considerably stronger for low- and medium-income groups (0.414 and 0.649, respectively), and even statistically significant at 5% for medium-income groups. However, it is negative for the high-income group (-0.363). Our results thus show that income level moderates the relationship between manufacturing and servitization. Manufacturing drives servitization for relatively poor countries, but has the opposite effect once countries reach a certain income threshold. One explanation for this result is that the richest countries are less dependent on the manufacturing-installed base to deploy service business models. As these countries have more resources, they can obtain manufacturing knowledge from other business ecosystems.

Another consideration is whether digitalization drives servitization (Coreynen, Matthyssens and van Bockhaven, 2017; Greenstein and Nagle, 2014; Vendrell-Herrero et al., 2017b). We analyse this issue in Figure 2.5. The correlation of digitization and servitization is also weak, but slightly higher than that of manufacturing and servitization (0.115 vs. 0.091). In the case of digitization, however, the moderating effect of income groups is practically non-existent. Medium-income groups show essentially no correlation (0.002), and this correlation becomes moderately negative for low- and high-income groups (-0.121 and -0.372, respectively). None of these correlations is statistically significant.

Our bivariate analysis seems to reflect that servitization is not strongly linked to manufacturing and digitization. However, bivariate analysis is limited and introducing more correlates sometimes uncovers new relationships. To better evaluate the relationship between these variables, we undertake multivariate analysis.

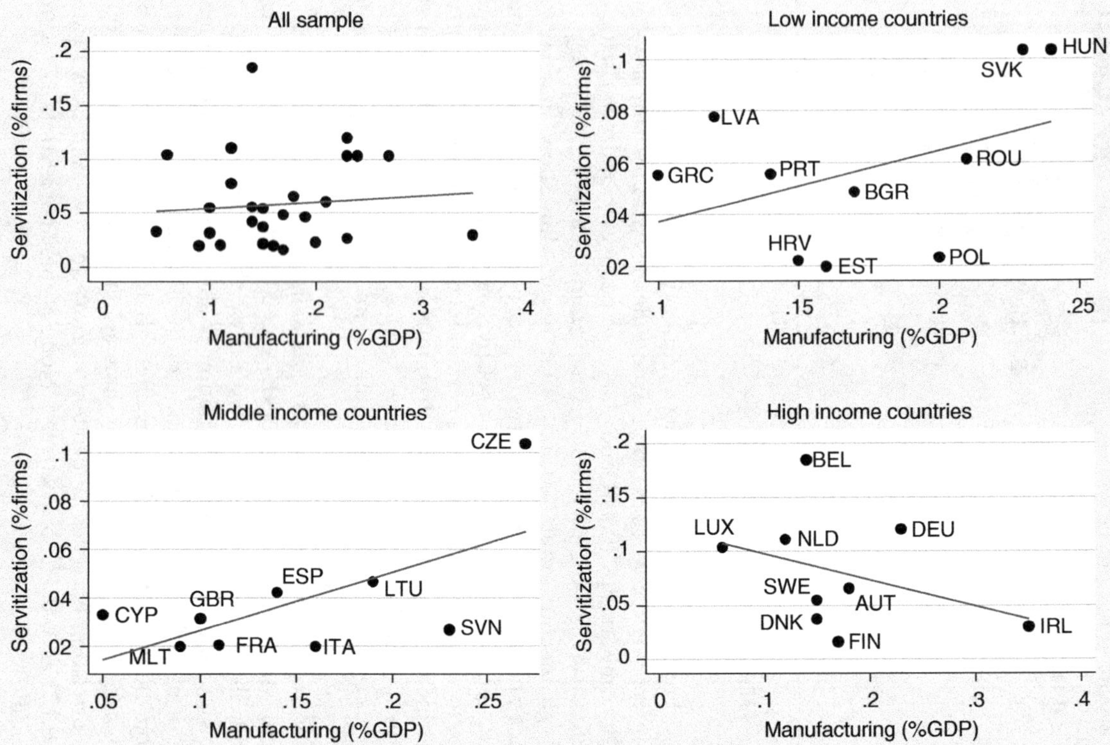

Note: Pairwise bivariate correlations are 0.091, 0.414, 0.649 & –0.363 respectively.

Figure 2.4 Manufacturing and servitization, by income groups.

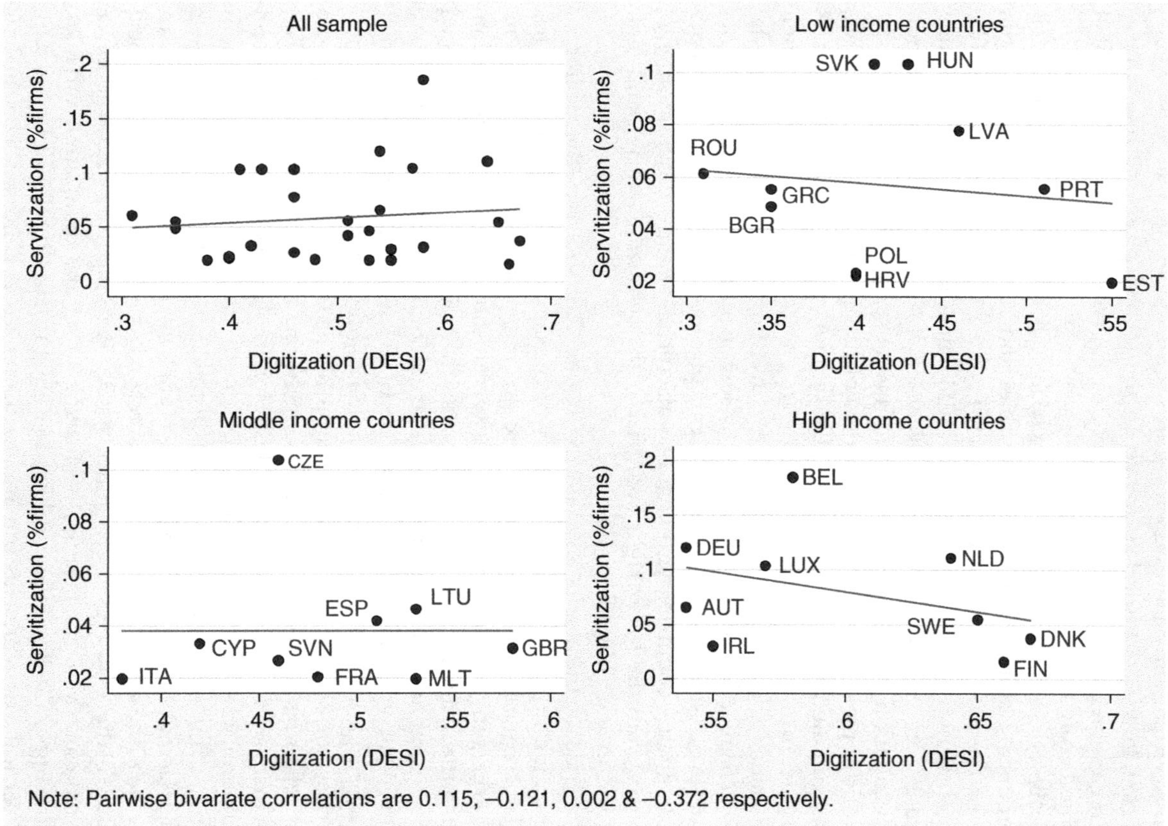

Figure 2.5 Digitization and servitization, by income groups.

The multivariate analysis proposed in this chapter has two phases. First, we attempt to explain graphically how manufacturing, digitization and servitization are interrelated. This analysis already shows some tendencies that require confirmation through statistical inference. In the second phase, we thus undertake regression analysis to confirm/reinforce the results obtained in the initial graphical analysis.

Graphical representation of three variables is complex. One method is to produce a scatter plot of two variables and represent the third by the size (or form or colour) of the marker. Figure 2.6 does precisely this. The horizontal and vertical axes show the DESI values and manufacturing value added as percentages of GDP, respectively. Panel A contains the information on distribution of the 28 EU countries in the scatter plot. One characteristic of this plot is that dotted lines represent the median values of manufacturing and digitization variables, roughly defining four quadrants. Countries positioned in the upper-right quadrant are characterized by relatively high manufacturing and high digitization (e.g., Ireland), whereas countries in the lower-left quadrant are characterized by low manufacturing and low digitization (e.g., Greece). The other quadrants present mixed options; the upper left identifying countries with high manufacturing and low digitization (e.g., Hungary), and the lower right countries with low manufacturing and high digitization (e.g., Belgium).

The size of the circles in Panel B (Figure 2.6) indicates the degree of servitization in the country. It is thus worth examining which quadrant has the largest markers. Theoretically, there are three answers to this question. First, synergetic effects could occur between manufacturing and digitization, making the quadrant with the largest circles the upper right. Secondly, manufacturing and digitization could be seen as substitutes for each other, making the quadrant with the largest circles one of the mixed solutions (upper left or lower right). Thirdly, manufacturing and digitization could exert a negative effect on servitization, making the quadrant with the largest circles the lower left. A visual analysis of Panel B suggests that the quadrants with the largest circles are the mixed solutions. This result implies that manufacturing and digitization are substitutes for each other and that policy makers should focus on stimulating only one of those inputs if the aim is to boost service business models across the industrial fabric. A complementary graphical analysis to show how the three variables are inter-related would use three-dimensional graphs. To this end, Figure 2.7 presents a 3D bar graph in which the lower axes represent a binary measure of manufacturing and digitization variables, and the upper (high) and lower (low) axes the median (Panel A in Figure 2.6). The vertical axis represents the average degree of servitization. This analysis shows even more clearly that mixed (low-high or high-low) combinations boost servitization activity.

As a final exercise, we conduct a regression analysis to validate the results obtained in the graphical analysis (Figures 2.6 and 2.7) through statistical inference. Table 2.2 reports the results of the regression analysis. The dependent

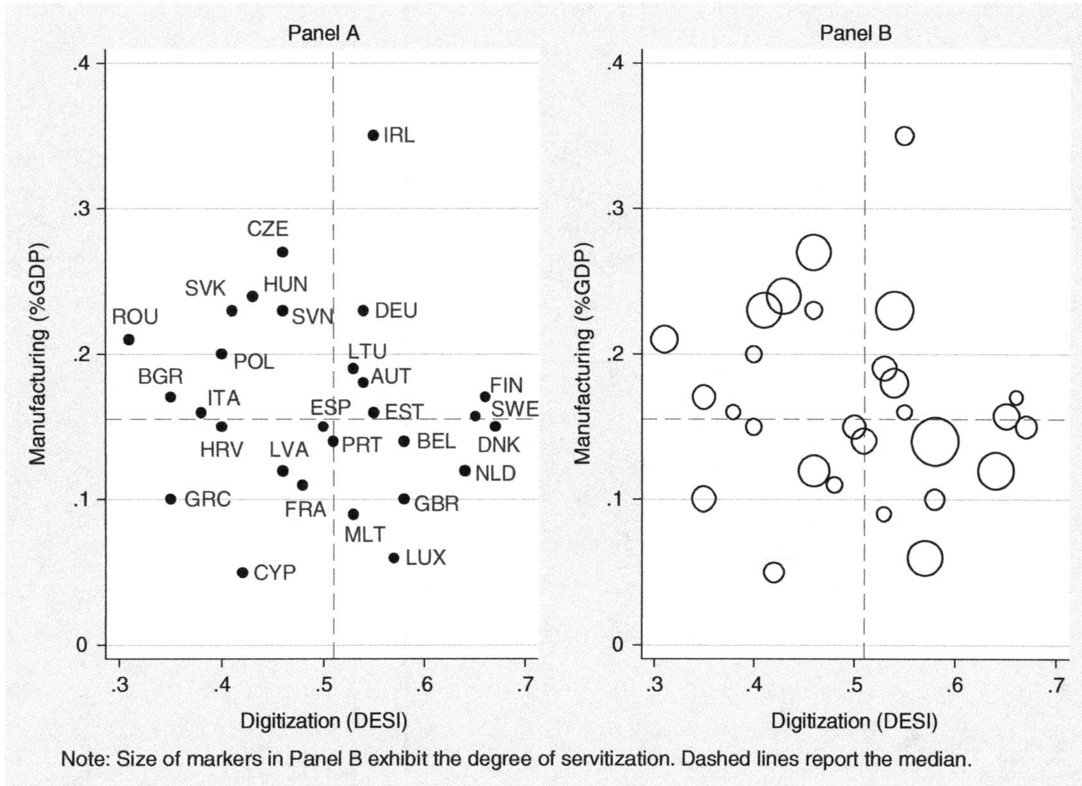

Figure 2.6 Digitization and manufacturing distribution.

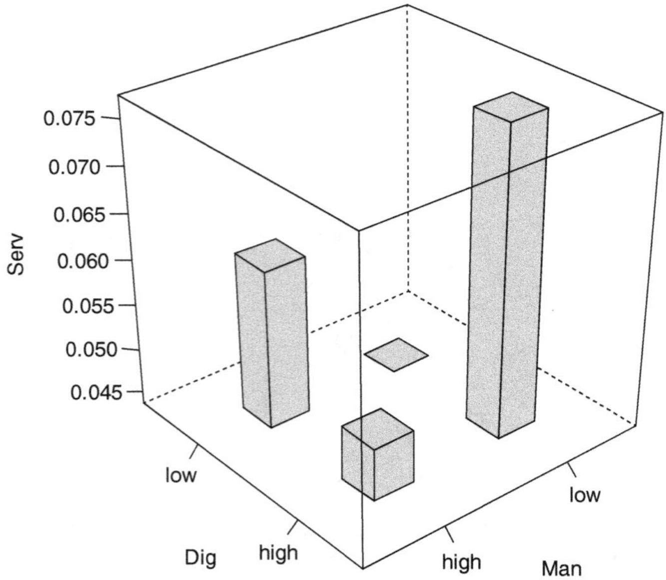

Figure 2.7 The relationship between digitization, manufacturing and servitization.

Table 2.2 Regression analysis

	(1)	*(2)*
[1] DESI	0.479**	0.451*
	(0.220)	(0.228)
[2] Manufacturing (% GDP)	1.395**	1.423**
	(0.618)	(0.603)
[1] * [2]	-2.669**	-2.804**
	(1.247)	(1.179)
Constant	-0.193*	-0.177
	(0.108)	(0.111)
Income group FE	NO	YES
N	28	28
R^2	0.114	0.159

Notes:
Robust standard errors in parentheses.
Dependent variable: % of manufacturing firms that are servitized.
* $p < 0.10$, ** $p < 0.05$, *** $p < 0.01$.

variable is servitization, and the independent variables are manufacturing value added as a percentage of GDP, the digitization index (DESI) and the interaction between these two variables. To control for income heterogeneity, we include income group fixed effects in column 2. The model's fit is good, as the R^2 ranges from 11% to 16%.

In both columns, the parameters of manufacturing and digitization are positive and statistically significant (at 5% in most cases). However, the combined effect captured by the interaction term is negative, indicating that increasing both variables (manufacturing and digitization) at the same time has damaging outcomes in terms of the servitization level.

So, the results of the regression analysis confirm that digitization and manufacturing in isolation are positive enablers for servitization, but our results suggest that combining both in the same territory can produce negative consequences in terms of servitization activity. Our graphical and regression analysis suggest that countries with a focus in developing a territorial servitization strategy should specialize in developing manufacturing strength or digital capabilities, but not both at the same time.

2.4 Discussion and conclusions

The implementation of services in the manufacturing industry (servitization) is an increasingly relevant topic. A consolidated academic community currently focuses on how these business models are deployed (Bustinza, Vendrell-Herrero and Baines, 2017) and what drivers and bottlenecks enable and hinder successful implementation of product-service innovation (Bustinza et al., 2018).

The literature also pays increasing attention to the territorial aspects of servitization (Lafuente, Vaillant and Vendrell-Herrero, 2017, 2018). More studies seek to determine how many manufacturers in a territory are servitized. This question is hard to answer because no formal registers are available to catalogue firms deploying these business models and secondary sources are not designed to collect direct information on servitization. Some research examines the data repositories of central banks or fiscal authorities to quantify indirectly the degree of servitization in specific countries (Ariu, 2016; Crozet and Millet, 2017), but this method is usually non-scalable, as it is nearly impossible to access this type of data for more than one country. Other studies use ORBIS (or other BvD data sources) to measure servitization activity (Gomes et al., 2018; Neely, 2008; Opazo, Vendrell-Herrero and Bustinza, 2018; Sforzi and Boix, 2018). Ours is the first research study to provide a cross-country comparison of servitization activity in the EU-28 – a major contribution to the literature.

The cross-country exercise is instructive. We learn that servitization activity seems to be concentrated in Central Europe, particularly in the Benelux countries, Germany, Hungary, Slovakia and the Czech Republic. According to these results, servitization is led by neither the 'old European historical glories' (France, the UK, Spain and Italy) nor the Scandinavian countries. Our study is consistent with current research highlighting the economic emergence of the Visegrád Group (Piotrowicz, 2015; Prokop, Stejskal and Kuvíková, 2017) and the political and economic European leadership of Germany and the Benelux countries (Nurgent, 2017).

A second aim of this study is to identify what causes a country's level of servitization. As we operate with a small sample, our analysis contains three main regressors: income level; the degree of manufacturing; and digitization exposure. As these variables were extracted from very reliable sources, including Eurostat and the World Bank, our findings are relevant for industrial policy.

We find that the countries with the highest servitization specialize in either the industrial fabric or digitization infrastructure and that these inputs of servitization seem to be substitutes for each other. The only country that excels in servitization activity and has high degrees of both manufacturing and digitization exposure is Germany. The other leaders in servitization, such as Belgium and Hungary, specialize in either digitization or manufacturing, respectively.

Our results must be taken with caution. The measure of servitization used has several advantages, but also drawbacks. For instance, legislation governing firms of a certain size whose operations and sales are divided among different sectors is not homogeneous throughout Europe, and our method may produce some outliers. We have made an effort to avoid this problem by cleaning the database of this noise through the quartile imputation method, but the data collected are still subject to bias and criticism. With more homogeneity in future legislation, the method used here will become significantly more reliable. Another limitation of this research is its cross-sectional design. This design is intentional, since the primary aim of this chapter is to produce a preliminary mapping of servitization activity in Europe.

Our goal is to pave the way for future studies of territorial servitization that uncover the geographical composition of servitization inside and outside European boundaries. To this end, we designed a benchmark methodological context as the basis for future longitudinal work, seeking to estimate not only the degree of servitization activity at the country level, but also its rate of growth.

Acknowledgements

We acknowledge support from the European Commission under the Horizon 2020- Marie Skłodowska-Curie Actions project 'MAKERS: Smart Manufacturing for EU Growth and Prosperity', grant agreement number 691192, and the Spanish Government under Grant ECO2014-58472-R.

Notes

1 The most recent year is 2017 for servitization and digitization and 2016 for manufacturing value added.
2 Following standard practice (see the bottom of Table 2.1), we used the following secondary NAICS codes to identify knowledge based services: 518 'Data Processing, Hosting, and Related Services'; 519 'Other Information Services'; 54 'Professional, Scientific, and Technical Services'; 56 'Administrative and Support and Waste Management and Remediation Services'; and 811 'Repair and Maintenance'.
3 The best explanation of these values is that declaring secondary industry codes is legally binding in these countries.
4 The income level is obtained by sorting the countries by GDP per capita and clustering them into three groups (high, medium and low) based on their ranking.

References

Aquilante, T., Bustinza Sánchez, O.F. and Vendrell-Herrero, F. (2016). Services in European manufacturing: servinomics explained. *Bruegel Blog*. Available at: http://bruegel.org/2016/03/services-in-european-manufacturing-servinomics-explained.

Ariu, A. (2016). Services versus goods trade: a firm-level comparison. *Review of World Economics*, 152(1), 19–41.

Baldwin, R. (2016). *The Great Convergence*. Cambridge, MA: Harvard University Press.

Bustinza, O.F., Vendrell-Herrero, F., Parry, G. and Myrthianos, V. (2013). Music business models and piracy. *Industrial Management & Data Systems*, 113(1), 4–22

Bustinza, O.F., Vendrell-Herrero, F. and Baines, T. (2017). Service implementation in manufacturing: an organisational transformation perspective. *International Journal of Production Economics*, 192, 1–8.

Bustinza, O.F., Vendrell-Herrero, F., Gomes, E., Lafuente, E. et al. (2018). Product-service innovation and performance: unveiling the complexities. *International Journal of Business Environment*, 10(2), 95–111.

Coreynen, W., Matthyssens, P. and van Bockhaven, W. (2017). Boosting servitization through digitization: pathways and dynamic resource configurations for manufacturers. *Industrial Marketing Management*, 60, 42–53.

Crozet, M. and Milet, E. (2017). Should everybody be in services? The effect of servitization on manufacturing firm performance. *Journal of Economics & Management Strategy*, 26(4), 820–841.

Gomes, E., Bustinza, O., Tarba, S., Khan, Z. and Ahammad, M. (2018). Antecedents and implications of territorial servitization. *Regional Studies*. DOI: https://doi.org/10.1080/00343404.2018.1468076.

Greenstein, S. and Nagle, F. (2014). Digital dark matter and the economic contribution of Apache. *Research Policy*, 43(4), 623–631.

Haraguchi, N., Cheng, C.F.C. and Smeets, E. (2017). The importance of manufacturing in economic development: has this changed? *World Development*, 93, 293–315.

Hojnik, J. (2016). The servitization of industry: EU law implications and challenges. *Common Market Law Review*, 53(6), 1575–1623.

Horváth, K. and Rabetino, R. (2018). Knowledge-intensive territorial servitization: regional driving forces and the role of the entrepreneurial ecosystem. *Regional Studies*, DOI: https://doi.org/10.1080/00343404.2018.1469741.

Krugman, P. and Venables, A. J. (1995). Globalization and the inequality of nations. *Quarterly Journal of Economics*, 110(4), 857–880.

Lafuente, E., Vaillant, Y. and Vendrell-Herrero, F. (2017). Territorial servitization: exploring the virtuous circle connecting knowledge-intensive services and sustainable new manufacturing businesses. *International Journal of Production Economics*, 192, 19–28.

Lafuente, E., Vaillant, Y., and Vendrell-Herrero, F. (2018). Territorial servitization and the manufacturing renaissance in knowledge-based economies. *Regional Studies*, 3(3), 313–319.

Moroz, M. (2017). The level of development of the digital economy in Poland and selected European countries: a comparative analysis. *Foundations of Management*, 9(1), 175–190.

Muñoz, J.F. and Rueda, M. (2009). New imputation methods for missing data using quantiles. *Journal of Computational and Applied Mathematics*, 232(2), 305–317.

Myrthianos, V., Vendrell-Herrero, F., Bustinza, O.F. and Parry, G. (2014). Evaluating firm profitability during the servitization process of the music industry. *Strategic Change*, 23(5–6), 317–328.

Neely, A. (2008). Exploring the financial consequences of the servitization of manufacturing. *Operations Management Research*, 1(2), 103–118.

Nugent, N. (2017). *The Government and Politics of the European Union*. New York: Palgrave Macmillan.

Opazo, M., Vendrell-Herrero, F. and Bustinza, O.F. (2018) Uncovering productivity gains of digital and green servitization: implications from the automotive industry. *Sustainability*, 10(5), 1524.

Piotrowicz, W. (2015). Information technology and systems in the Visegrád group of countries (Czech Republic, Hungary, Poland, and Slovakia): a literature review. *Journal of Global Information Technology Management*, 18(2), 77–93.

Porter, M. E. and Heppelmann, J. E. (2014). How smart, connected products are transforming competition. *Harvard Business Review*, 92(11), 64–88.

Prokop, V., Stejskal, J. and Kuvíková, H. (2017). The different drivers of innovation activities in European countries: a comparative study of Czech, Slovak, and Hungarian manufacturing firms 1. *Ekonomicky Casopis*, 65(1), 31–45.

Seclen-Luna, J.P. and Barrutia-Güenaga, J. (2018). KIBS and innovation in machine tool manufacturers: evidence from the Basque country. *International Journal of Business Environment*, 10(2), 112–131.

Sforzi, F. and Boix, R. (2018). Territorial servitization in Marshallian industrial districts: the industrial district as a place-based form of servitization. *Regional Studies*, DOI: https://doi.org/10.1080/00343404.2018.1524134.

Suarez, F.F., Cusumano, M.A. and Kahl, S.J. (2013). Services and the business models of product firms: an empirical analysis of the software industry. *Management Science*, 59(2), 420–435.

Vendrell-Herrero, F., Bustinza, O.F., Parry, G. and Georgantzis, N. (2017a). Servitization, digitization and supply chain interdependency. *Industrial Marketing Management*, 60, 69–81.

Vendrell-Herrero, F., Myrthianos, V., Parry, G. and Bustinza, O. (2017b). Digital dark matter within product service systems. *Competitiveness Review*, 27(1), 62–79.

Vendrell-Herrero, F., and Wilson, J.R. (2017). Servitization for territorial competitiveness: taxonomy and research agenda. *Competitiveness Review*, 27(1), 2–11.

Veugeleres, R. (2013). Manufacturing Europe's future. *Bruegel Blog*. Available at: http://bruegel.org/2013/10/manufacturing-europes-future.

Visnjic, I., Neely, A. and Jovanovic, M. (2018). The path to outcome delivery: interplay of service market strategy and open business models. *Technovation*, 72, 46–59.

3 Jobs 4.0

Arianna Pittarello, Antonella Trevisanato and Lisa De Propris

3.1 Introduction

Technology has always driven firms' requirements for skills and knowledge, as well as having changed the nature and content of occupations. This chapter presents cross-country evidence of firms' demand for labour to shed some light on firms' skills requirements, using firms' declared vacancies data from the UK, Italy and Germany. Given the current technological transformation, we want to ascertain what occupations firms are actually seeking to address their medium-term skills needs.

Several studies have shown that the adoption of new technologies (such as computers in the 1980s) was complementary to hiring employees for non-routine jobs, but was a substitute for workers who performed routine jobs, indicating that the demand for different types of jobs is heterogeneous (Autor et al., 2003). In fact, some evidence has documented the correlation between the adoption of computer-based technologies and the increased use of college-educated labour at the industry level. This is referred to as skill-biased technological change, suggesting that technological adoption has destroyed routine jobs (manual and cognitive), whilst increasing less-skilled jobs and high-skilled jobs (Acemoglu, 2002, Autor et al., 2003, Katz and Autor, 1999, Kemeny and Rigby, 2012). So technological change – and in part manufacturing offshoring – resulted in a so-called job polarisation (Autor and Dorn, 2013); that is, the simultaneous increase of employment in the highest- and lowest-skill occupations, as middle-skill occupations disappeared. Job polarisaton of course is linked to a widening wage polarisation and the much-discussed plague of broadening income inequality in advanced economies (OECD, 2019).

The emergence of a wave of new technologies is often referred to as the Fourth Industrial Revolution (FIR) and a fast-growing debate is unpacking its implications for firms, consumers, workers and society more widely. In the chapter, we focus on the impact that in particular automation and digitalisation are expected to have on the labour market and the demand for skills. As suggested above, previous technological shocks were shown to cause significant job losses, especially in the short term, but over the longer term, as the economy adapted to the changes and started to grow again, jobs were eventually created.

So this time round, technological change is also expected to cause labour market adjustments and to trigger medium- and long-term growth and development (see Chapter 1), which in turn will create a new and growing demand for labour, notwithstanding the fact that this demand will be for new jobs or jobs with new and different types of skills and competences (McKinsey Global Institute, 2017).

The purpose of this chapter is to explore firms' demand for skills with vacancies data in the context of a disruptive technological change that has been unfolding for the last couple of years thanks to firms' adoption of FIR technologies. We want to gauge whether firms are anticipating and preparing for the skills requirements of the future by looking at their current demand for labour (i.e. vacancies).

The chapter will proceed as follows. Section 3.2 will briefly present the recent literature on the impact of technological change on the labour market. Section 3.3 will discuss the current debate on the future of work given the spead of FIR technologies. Section 3.4 will present the data and methodology. Section 3.5 will discuss the findings, and a short conclusion will recap the chapter.

3.2 Technological change and job polarisation

3.2.1 Background

Drawing on a large literature on both job polarisation and skill mismatch, we here note a few points to frame the empirical analysis that follows. Technological change and the efficiency-seeking internationalisation strategies of multi-national firms since the 1980s have led to major shifts in labour markets, resulting in job and wage polarisation with evidence primarily from the US (Autor and Dorn, 2013; Autor and Handel, 2013; Boehm, 2014). This has led to overarching concerns with growing intra-country income inequality. Between 1983 and 2007, the growth of low paid jobs was mostly in services and, in particular, personal care jobs (Dwyer, 2013). Other contributions find that job polarisation worsened following the 2008 financial crisis as the subsequent recession was followed by jobless recoveries in the short term (Goos et al., 2014).

Technological change is also argued to trigger imbalances in the labour market between demand and supply in the form of a skill mismatch: this concept captures the degree of heterogeneity in the labour market across a number of dimensions such as skills, industrial sector and location. Significant differences in the skills workers have and those required by firms tend to lengthen the time that it takes to match individuals with jobs. This frictional unemployment is of course a cost to the economy and can cause wide-ranging social difficulties. A skill mismatch can be a short-lived and transitory imbalance in the labour market. More fundamentally, if not addressed, it can lead to structural skill shortages, i.e. linked to megatrends such as digitalisation (Brunello et al., 2019).

In times of rapid technological change, firms face skill challenges not only when hiring but also with their existing labour force. We refer to *'on-the-job' skill mismatch* when workers are either over- or under-skilled for their jobs (vertical on-the-job mismatch) or have different skills/qualifications from those required for the jobs (horizontal on-the-job mismatch) (McGuinness, Pouliaka and Redmond, 2018). This mismatch leads to either redundancy or to the mismatched employees earning less than would otherwise be the case (Bárcena-Martín, Budría and Moro-Egido, 2012). This form of mismatch is dependent on rigidities in the labour market. For example, in a hire-and-fire context, an 'on-the-job' skill mismatch might be limited, but firms pass on to individuals the cost and risk of training and retraining. Conversely, where firms face constraints in terms of firing employees, they might more proactively seek to address the skill mismatch of their labour force with on-the-job training and retraining, and implement a sort of life-long training to ensure that their labour force has the appropriate skills and competences.

Public policy interventions to manage or reduce such skill mismatches are crucial for the long-term growth of an economy and the shared prosperity of its people. This will be discussed at the end of the chapter.

3.3 The skills of the future

Projections, estimations and scenario painting have started to describe what changes in the workplace and labour market the rise of FIR technologies are likely to trigger. To appreciate the scale and pervasiveness of the technological change we are facing, predictions suggest that about two-thirds of children in primary school today are likely to be in occupations that do not yet exist (World Economic Forum, 2018). In the labour market, according to the McKinsey Global Institute (2017), automation and digitalisation will displace up to 30% of the workforce by 2030, especially in advanced economies (namely up to 800 million people) and up to 375 million will switch occupational category by learning new skills. Jobs will be lost primarily in 'physical work in predictable environments and data collection and processing', whilst there will a demand for new skills and especially advanced cognitive capabilities such as logical reasoning and creativity (ibid). With automation and digitalisation also expected to hit high-skill jobs performing routine cognitive tasks, we are again looking at a skill-biased technological change that is likely to result in job polarisation with low-skill and high-skill jobs expected to increase (OECD, 2018). Indeed, technological change is thought to potentially involve jobless growth, making unemployment and under-employment a major business risk globally (De Propris/World Economic Forum, 2016). It has been estimated that 'as many as 45 percent of the activities individuals are paid to perform' are open to automation according to Chui et al. (2015). This conclusion is supported by other studies (Frey and Osborne, 2013; PwC, 2017), though not all envisage such profound effects (e.g. Arntz et al., 2016). It should be noted that automation will affect not just routine and codifiable activities, but also those requiring tacit knowledge and experience (and hence activities where developed countries have a comparative advantage; Rifkin 2014). According to the OECD (2015), around '60% of occupations could have 30% or more of their constituent activities automated'. Such changes would dramatically transform the vast majority of occupations, possibly leading either to jobless growth and/or further job polarisation in the labour markets of developed economies (OECD, 2015).

Changes in the skill content of jobs will become clear relatively quickly, bringing about abrupt job losses in the most affected occupations and affecting some sectors more than others, while job creation will be delayed as individuals grapple with an emerging demand for new skills and seek to acquire them via education and training. This mistiming will create unemployment, which can be frictional or structural depending on the ability and commitment of the education sector, policy makers and businesses to train, retrain or uptrain individuals.

In this disrupted context, education and training are crucial. PwC (2018) explores different labour market scenarios and finds that people feel they are increasingly responsible for their skill development and that access to jobs will depend on people's ability 'to brand and sell their own skills' (PwC, 2014: 19). In other words, in order to respond to changes in the workplace, people are expected to acquire and develop their own skills, adapt to flexible work patterns and environments, and autonomously identify job and career opportunities. Inevitably, this will translate in a *skill divide* that is probably determined from the very early education and training opportunities that individuals might have.

Looking at firms' demand for labour can therefore provide a valuable insight into what occupations they are seeking in the short term and to gauge whether they are already anticipating skills needs that they are missing in their current workforce. We do this with firms' job vacancy data for Italy, Germany and the UK.

3.4 Job vacancy data

3.4.1 German job vacancy data

Vacancy data for Germany was extracted from the Job Vacancy Survey carried out by the Institute for Employment Research (IAB) since 1989 (for more details, see www.iab.de/en/iab-aktuell.aspx). It is the only survey in Germany that measures the development of the unmet labour demand in a representative and statistically robust way. The survey data is subject to strict data protection and confidentiality regulations. This is guaranteed by the Institute for Employment Research as well as the Institute Economic Research & Consulting, which are currently conducting the survey on behalf of the IAB. The population of the main survey in the fourth quarter of every year consists of all firms in Germany with at least one employee subject to social security contributions.

A new stratified random sample is drawn every year from this population. It is stratified by region, seven firm-size classes as well as 23 industries based on the 2008 German classification of industries (NACE rev. 2). This creates a three-dimensional sampling matrix. The dataset covers the entire unfilled labour demand in Germany (structure of vacancies, future labour demand) and identifies the entire number of vacancies in the German labour market (last new hiring and the last case of a failed recruitment effort). Moreover, the survey offers information on lapsed vacancies and on employers' perceptions of recent labour market policy developments, and the special questionnaire examines employers' attitudes and firms' use of current labour market instruments. From this source, we have created a database with information about the number of vacancies in Germany grouped by occupations, regions, firm size and sector classification.

3.4.2 Italy: Excelsior dataset

Job vacancy data in Italy was collected via the Excelsior Information System; since 1997, this has been one of the main Italian sources of information on labour market forecasts. This survey is promoted and produced by Unioncamere (Italian Association of the Chambers of Commerce) with the participation of the Ministry of Labour and the EU (for more details, see https://excelsior.unioncamere.net/eng). It provides detailed and reliable data about the demand for labour by Italian firms both in the short term and in the long term, by region and sector. It also provides information about the specific characteristics of the occupational profiles required by firms, such as age, educational level, type of contract, work experience, difficulty in recruiting specific profiles and need for further training. Moreover, it is aimed at informing policy makers in relation to policies concerning the labour market and the education and training system, ultimately in order to favour the matching between labour supply and demand. The Excelsior survey is included in the official statistics produced on an annual basis within the Italian National Statistical System (SISTAN). The Excelsior Information System is based on data collected through an annual sampled survey conducted on more than 100,000 Italian enterprises (corresponding to about 8% of the total number of Italian companies) operating in the agriculture, manufacturing and service sectors. Firms must be registered with the Business Register and have at least one employee.[1]

3.4.3 The UK: employer skills survey data

The UK Employer Skill Survey is a survey covering approximately 90,000 employers and contains data on vacancies, skills shortages, employee skill gaps and training (for more details, see www.skillssurvey.co.uk/index.htm). It distinguishes between different types of vacancies – e.g. hard-to-fill and skill-shortage vacancies. The data is disaggregated by regions (NUTS 1), vacancy types by occupation (relying on nine Standard Occupational Classification

Major Groups), by broad skill level and by sector disaggregation (13 sectors). Data is also available at the level of Local Enterprise Partnerships and Local Education Authorities. The available vacancy data include:

- number of total vacancies;
- number of hard-to-fill vacancies;
- number of a skills shortage vacancies (prompted or unprompted);
- number of vacancies as a percentage of all employment;
- number of under-utilised staff (i.e. those whose skill levels are above those required in the job they do).

3.5 Methodology

Data is classified using the Eurostat/Isco08 skills classification. We distinguish high-, medium- and low-skill occupations. High-skill occupations include managers, professionals, technicians and associate professionals. Medium-skill occupations include craft and related trades workers, clerical support workers, and skilled agricultural, forestry and fishery workers. Finally, low-skill occupations include elementary occupations, plant and machine operators and assemblers, and service and sales workers. Vacancy data was available only for the following periods: 2011–14 for Germany, 2011–15 for Italy and only the discrete years 2011, 2013 and 2015 for the UK. The unique database we have constructed with firms' job vacancies captures employers' needs and planning in terms of current and near-future skill requirements. In other words, they are telling us what skill they seek on the labour market demand side. Therefore, we can use the job vacancies database as a prediction of firms' skill composition demand at different levels by country.

3.6 Job vacancies trends

We analyse the distribution of vacancies at the national level and the regional level for Germany, Italy and the UK, also considering firms' size and sector. Below we present our findings by country.

3.6.1 Germany

The German data shows that the number of medium-skill vacancies is higher than those of low- and high-skill vacancies, and this is consistent over the period 2011–14. However, the growth rate of vacancies for high- and low-skill jobs is greater than for medium-skill jobs, so over the period firms are seeking to recruit more at the top and bottom ends of the labour market. This suggests a trend towards a possible job polarisation. The positive growth rates of vacancies suggest that in Germany, the labour market is lively and firms are seeking to hire; we cannot say whether they are replacing staff or expanding, but only that they are seeking occupations with specific skills. Consistently, the recovery period in Germany has been characterised by two-thirds of the vacancies being in medium-skill occupations.

Tables 3.1 and 3.2 show the shares of vacancies by skill categories and by firms' size and by region at a more fine-grained level of analysis. In terms of vacancy shares by firm size, small firms (10–49 employees) are seeking medium- and low-skill workers, while medium-sized firms have over the period increasingly focused their recruitment on low- and high-skill jobs. Overall, by 2014, small and medium-sized firms showed the strongest demand for high-skill jobs. The most important results are that the vacancy growth rates are quite high for low- and high-skill occupations for micro-firms (0–9 employees) and medium-sized firms (50–249 employees). The demand for medium- and low-skill workers is negative for large firms (>250 employees) over the period.

3.6.2 Germany's manufacturing sector

What is happening in the German manufacturing sector? In general, growth rates are decreasing and more significantly so for low-skill jobs, even if they are less in demand (see Tables 3.3 and 3.4). Vacancies for medium-skill workers are stable over the period, but these occupations are the most sought-after. Finally, vacancies for high-skill workers suffered mostly in 2013, with a drop of 5,000 in 2012–13, but bounced back in 2013–14.

3.6.3 Germany's business service sector

In the business services sector, only demand for high-skill jobs increased consistently over the entire period and picked up in 2014, whereas the growth rates of vacancies for medium- and low-skill jobs fluctuated with alternating positive and negative growth rates. Overall, the job market seems to be more volatile for low- and medium-skill jobs than for high-skill jobs. This suggests that firms are constantly and increasingly seeking to fill high skill-positions. We cannot tell from the data whether this is related to upskilling or churning strategies (see Tables 3.5 and 3.6).

3.6.4 Italy

In Italy the number of vacancies for medium-skill jobs is significantly higher than in the others two categories, as we saw in the case of Germany. In general, the number of vacancies has fallen over the entire period for all three categories of skills in 2012–13, followed by a slight increase in 2014–15. Stagnation in the job market mirrored a long recession that Italy experienced following the 2008 financial crisis and the austerity policies forced on the country in the following decade. Stagnation meant that those in jobs hung on to their positions, so there was no need to replace them; in addition, firms were not looking to expand and therefore were not hiring. In Italy there is no sign of job polarisation and

Table 3.1 Germany: vacancy shares by firms' size and skills classification, 2011–14

	2011			*2012*			*2013*			*2014*		
	High-skill	*Medium-skill*	*Low-skill*	*High-skill*	*Medium-skill*	*Low-skill*	*High-skill*	*Medium-skill*	*Low-skill*	*High-skill*	*Medium-skill*	*Low-skill*
1–9 employee	14.4	26.9	16.0	20.2	25.9	27.8	30.5	26.8	16.1	19.6	28.1	27.4
10–49 employee	33.0	34.7	34.4	29.4	42.3	40.5	25.7	34.9	42.6	28.3	37.0	31.7
50–249 employee	25.3	24.8	33.0	19.3	20.6	15.3	21.5	26.4	24.1	27.0	25.1	29.3
>250 employee	27.3	13.6	16.6	31.2	11.2	16.3	22.3	11.8	17.2	25.1	9.8	11.6

Source: Authors' elaboration based on IAB Job Vacancy Survey Data.

Table 3.2 Germany: vacancy variation rates by firms' size and skills classification, 2011–14

	2011–2012			*2012–2013*			*2013–2014*			*2011–2014*		
	High-skill	*Medium-skill*	*Low-skill*	*High-skill*	*Medium-skill*	*Low-skill*	*High-skill*	*Medium-skill*	*Low-skill*	*High-skill*	*Medium-skill*	*Low-skill*
1–9 employee	59.0	-13.4	56.7	69.1	1.6	-19.1	-33.0	20.9	61.6	80.3	6.5	104.8
10–49 employee	1.0	9.5	6.1	-2.1	-18.9	47.1	15.2	22.1	-29.1	13.8	8.5	10.6
50–249 employee	-13.7	-25.5	-58.2	24.9	25.8	119.6	31.2	9.5	15.6	41.5	2.7	6.2
> 250 employee	29.2	-25.6	-11.4	-19.8	3.2	46.7	17.3	-4.5	-35.5	21.5	-26.7	-16.2
Total	13.4	-10.1	-9.9	11.9	-1.9	39.7	4.4	15.3	-4.8	32.5	1.7	19.8

Source: Authors' elaboration based on IAB Job Vacancy Survey Data.

Table 3.3 Germany: absolute values of vacancies by skills classification in the manufacturing sector, 2011–14

	2011	*2012*	*2013*	*2014*
High-skill	20,591	19,938	14,549	19,982
Medium-skill	46,653	49,136	45,794	45,884
Low-skill	7,124	8,261	7,252	5,871
Total	74,368	77,335	67,595	71,737

Source: Authors' elaboration based on IAB Job Vacancy Survey Data.

Table 3.4 Germany: vacancy variation rates by skills classification in the manufacturing sector, 2011–14

	2011–2012	*2012–2013*	*2013–2014*	*2011–2014*
High-skill	-3.2	-27.0	37.3	-3.0
Medium-skill	5.3	-6.8	0.2	-1.6
Low-skill	16.0	-12.2	-19.0	-17.6
Total	4.0	-12.6	6.1	-3.5

Source: Authors' elaboration based on IAB Job Vacancy Survey Data.

Table 3.5 Germany: absolute values of vacancies by skills classification in the business service sector, 2011–14

	2011	*2012*	*2013*	*2014*
High-skill	87,836	99,205	100,977	115,848
Medium-skill	316,952	259,945	257,079	299,894
Low-skill	92,076	73,204	92,102	86,440
Total	496,864	432,354	450,158	502,182

Source: Authors' elaboration based on IAB Job Vacancy Survey Data.

Table 3.6 Germany: vacancy variation rates by skills classification in the business service sector, 2011–14

	2011–2012	*2012–2013*	*2013–2014*	*2011–2014*
High-skill	12.9	1.8	14.7	31.9
Medium-skill	-18.0	-1.1	16.7	-5.4
Low-skill	-20.5	25.8	-6.1	-6.1
Total	-13.0	4.1	11.6	1.1

Source: Authors' elaboration based on IAB Job Vacancy Survey Data.

as the demand for labour improved from 2014, all skill profiles were sought, but medium-skill jobs still accounted for two-thirds of all vacancies.

In Italy micro-enterprises (1–9 employees) show the greatest demand for medium- and low-skill labour, whereas large firms seem to seek to hire high-skill labour. Medium-sized firms are less active in the labour market across all levels of skills (see Table 3.7). In general, all the enterprises suffered during the recession years, as negative variation rates between 2011 and 2013 show in Table 3.8; firms started hiring again in 2014 when the first positive signs of growth started to appear. All firms sustained the labour market until 2015; however, whilst large firms sought high- and mid-skill labour, micro-firms and small firms were seeking low- and medium-skill profiles. This can be particularly worrying as the adoption of new FIR technologies requires firms to upskill their labour force and some of this upskilling involves high-skill occupations. Italy's industrial structure is chartered by small firms and their ability to retain and retrain their human capital will be a precondition for their survival.

3.6.5 Italy's manufacturing sector

An overview of vacancies in the manufacturing sector reflects a weak demand for labour across all skill levels and a slight recovery in 2015 (see Table 3.9), and growth rates turning positive only in 2014–15, especially for low-skill and high-skill profiles (see Table 3.10). Again, the data suggests a lack of job polarisation in Italy, but growth trends suggest an increasing acceleration of vacancies for low-skill and high-skill profiles.

3.6.6 Italy's business service sector

In the business services sector, the data shows similar patterns, with vacancies picking up after 2014 across all levels of skills. Half of the vacancies are in medium-skill occupations, although low-skill and high-skill profiles are growing faster than medium-skill profiles.

3.6.7 The UK

In the UK, the number of vacancies seems to be greater for high- and low-skill jobs, which is different from what we found in Germany and Italy. In general, the number of vacancies grew steadily between 2011 and 2015, suggesting that firms were seeking to hire, although as we can see in Table 3.13, mostly in low-skill and medium-skill occupations. We find that in the UK, the most active firms were the micro-enterprises (0–24 employees – note that the UK firm size classification is different from that in Germany and Italy) in 2011, with the greatest vacancy shares, around 60% for medium- and low-skill jobs; however, by 2015, medium (100–249 employee) and large (>250 employees) firms large accounted for about 50% of high-skill vacancies, and small firms (25–99 employees) accounted for 40% of low-skill vacancies (see Table 3.13).

Table 3.7 Italy: vacancy shares by firms' size and skills classification, 2011–15

	High-skill	*Medium-skill*	*Low-skill*	*High-skill*	*Medium-skill*	*Low-skill*	*High-skill*	*Medium-skill*	*Low-skill*	*High-skill*	*Medium-skill*	*Low-skill*	*High-skill*	*Medium-skill*	*Low-skill*
1–9 employees	30.4	46.7	32.2	27.9	44.7	33.9	27.9	44.2	29.2	25.7	42.1	30.2	23.8	41.6	32.5
10–49 employees	21.8	21.5	26.4	17.5	19.2	23.6	20.4	22.0	24.8	18.9	23.5	24.2	18.0	22.5	24.2
50–249 employees	18.4	10.8	18.5	19.8	10.5	17.4	19.0	10.6	18.1	19.3	10.8	18.5	20.2	9.9	16.6
250 and more employees	29.4	21.0	22.9	34.8	25.5	25.1	32.6	23.2	27.9	36.1	23.5	27.1	38.0	25.9	26.7

Source: Authors' elaboration based on Excelsior Data.

Table 3.8 Italy: vacancy variation rates by firms' size and skills classification, 2011–15

	High-skill	*Medium skill*	*Low-skill*	*High-skill*	*Medium skill*	*Low-skill*	*High-skill*	*Medium skill*	*Low-skill*	*High-skill*	*Medium skill*	*Low-skill*	*High-skill*	*Medium skill*	*Low-skill*
1–9 employees	-39.3	-26.3	-21.1	-1.2	-10.8	-30.1	-5.0	4.6	14.3	13.0	13.8	30.9	-35.6	-21.7	-17.6
10–49 employees	-46.6	-30.9	-33.0	14.7	3.4	-15.0	-4.3	17.2	8.3	16.3	10.2	21.4	-31.8	-7.7	-25.2
50–249 employees	-28.7	-24.9	-29.9	-5.4	-9.1	-15.6	4.9	12.2	13.1	27.7	5.5	9.0	-9.6	-19.2	-27.0
250 and more employees	-21.6	-6.4	-17.8	-7.5	-18.1	-9.9	14.1	11.6	7.4	28.4	26.5	19.5	6.3	8.2	-4.9
Total	-33.7	-22.9	-25.1	-1.4	-9.8	-19.0	3.2	9.8	10.7	22.0	15.0	21.5	-17.7	-12.1	-18.4

Source: Authors' elaboration based on Excelsior Data.

Table 3.9 Italy: absolute value of vacancies by skills classification in the manufacturing sector, 2011–15

	2011	*2012*	*2013*	*2014*	*2015*
High-skill	32,815	24,643	23,370	22,613	31,568
Medium-skill	70,454	53,312	46,568	50,227	58,348
Low-skill	66,475	45,073	35,581	42,155	72,642
Total	169,744	123,028	105,519	114,995	162,558

Source: Authors' elaboration based on Excelsior Data

Table 3.10 Italy: vacancy variation rates by skills classification in the manufacturing sector, 2011–15

	2012/2011	*2013/2012*	*2014/2013*	*2015/2014*	*2015/2011*
High-skill	-24.9	-5.2	-3.2	39.6	-3.8
Medium-skill	-24.3	-12.7	7.9	16.2	-17.2
Low-skill	-32.2	-21.1	18.5	72.3	9.3
Total	-27.5	-14.2	9.0	41.4	-4.2

Source: Authors' elaboration based on Excelsior Data.

Table 3.11 Italy: absolute value of vacancies by skills classification in the business service sector, 2011–15

	2011	*2012*	*2013*	*2014*	*2015*
High-skill	108,138	72,402	70,638	72,428	93,213
Medium-skill	258,331	194,054	167,559	182,045	215,309
Low-skill	169,300	111,645	91,216	102,358	132,223
Total	535,769	378,101	329,413	356,831	440,745

Source: Authors' elaboration based on Excelsior Data.

Table 3.12 Italy: vacancy variation rates by skills classification in the business service sector, 2011–15

	2011–2012	*2012–2013*	*2013–2014*	*2014–2015*	*2011–2015*
High-skill	-33.0	-2.4	2.5	28.7	-13.8
Medium-skill	-24.9	-13.7	8.6	18.3	-16.7
Low-skill	-34.1	-18.3	12.2	29.2	-21.9
Total	-29.4	-12.9	8.3	23.5	-17.7

Source: Authors' elaboration based on Excelsior Data.

Table 3.13 The UK: vacancy shares by firms' size and skills classification, 2011, 2013 and 2015

	2011			*2013*			*2015*		
	High-skill	*Medium-skill*	*Low-skill*	*High-skill*	*Medium-skill*	*Low-skill*	*High-skill*	*Medium-skill*	*Low-skill*
1–24 employees	44.3	61.5	60.0	38.5	52.4	46.6	17.5	29.1	22.5
25–99 employees	22.2	18.1	20.1	24.6	19.0	27.7	28.9	34.3	39.7
100–249 employees	13.5	9.8	9.8	15.6	10.9	14.5	26.8	17.7	27.8
250 and more employees	20.0	10.7	10.2	21.3	17.7	11.1	26.9	18.9	10.0

Source: Authors' elaboration based on Employer Skills Survey Data.

Table 3.14 The UK: vacancy variation rates by firm sizes' and skills classification, 2011, 2013 and 2015

	2013/2011			*2015/2013*			*2015/2011*		
	High-skill	*Medium-skill*	*Low-skill*	*High-skill*	*Mid Skill*	*Low-skill*	*High-skill*	*Medium-skill*	*Low-skill*
1–24 employees	-10.4	-13.4	1.7	-41.0	-17.0	-25.6	-47.1	-28.1	-24.3
25–99 employees	14.1	6.5	80.7	53.4	170.4	120.5	75.0	188.1	298.4
100–249 employees	18.7	13.2	93.8	124.3	143.5	195.0	166.3	175.7	471.8
250 and more employees	10.1	68.3	43.1	64.0	59.9	38.8	80.5	169.2	98.7
Total	3.1	1.5	30.8	30.3	49.7	54.1	34.3	52.0	101.6

Source: Authors' elaboration based on Employer Skills Survey Data.

The variation rates are always positive and high over the period: this suggests that the situation of the job market is quite different in the UK from the other two countries (Table 3.14). Overall, there is a high job mobility market, and the high number of vacancies suggests that workers are moving from one job to another one quite easily.

Growing vacancy rates might be explained in many ways: it might be that firms are replacing mobile talent, expanding the existing labour force or seeking complementary skills. The data cannot tell us anything about this; however, we

Table 3.15 The UK: absolute value of vacancies by skills classification in the manufacturing sector, 2011, 2013 and 2015

	2011	*2013*	*2015*
High-skill	12,203	11,916	13,260
Medium-skill	12,981	10,775	15,328
Low-skill	12,727	11,684	19,209
Total	37,848	34,375	47,797

Source: Authors' elaboration based on Employer Skills Survey Data.

Table 3.16 The UK: vacancy variation rates by skills classification in the manufacturing sector, 2011, 2013 and 2015

	2013/2011	*2015/2013*	*2015/2011*
High-skill	-2.4	11.3	8.7
Medium-skill	-16.6	42.3	18.7
Low-skill	-8.2	64.4	50.9
Total	-9.2	39.0	26.3

Source: Authors' elaboration based on Employer Skills Survey Data.

find large vacancy growth rates for small, medium and large-sized firms from 2011 to 2015 for medium and low skills, whereas large firms are mainly looking for high-skill workers. Meanwhile, micro-firms show signs of withdrawing from the labour market.

3.6.8 The UK's manufacturing sector

In the case of the manufacturing sector, there is no clear evidence of job polarisation in the jobs firms try to fill: in 2011, vacancies were evenly distributed across the different skill categories, while in 2015, the highest demand was for low-skill workers, followed by the medium-skill workers.

In particular, in the manufacturing sector vacancies contracted between 2011 and 2013 (post-crisis), but picked up again in 2013, signalling a dynamism in the sector which was mostly export-driven. Worryingly, however, the vacancies that grew the most were for low- and medium-skill workers.

3.6.9 The UK's business services sector

In the business services sector there appears to be some evidence of job polarisation in 2011 and 2013, while in 2015 vacancies for low-skill and medium-skill workers grew the fastest. In this sector, the data shows an increase of 200,000 vacancies between 2013 and 2015 (see Table 3.17).

Table 3.17 The UK: absolute value of vacancies by skills classification in the business service sector, 2011, 2013 and 2015

	2011	*2013*	*2015*
High-skill	143,099	140,818	182,390
Medium-skill	72,986	71,925	114,218
Low-skill	148,587	150,804	239,918
Total	364,672	363,547	536,526

Source: Authors' elaboration based on Employer Skills Survey Data.

Table 3.18 The UK: vacancy variation rates by skills classification in the business service sector, 2011, 2013 and 2015

	2013/2011	*2015/2013*	*2015/2011*
High-skill	-1.6	29.5	27.5
Medium-skill	-1.5	58.8	56.5
Low-skill	1.5	59.1	61.5
Total	-0.3	47.6	47.1

Source: Authors' elaboration based on Employer Skills Survey Data.

The service sector has very big variation rates in terms of vacancies for all three kinds of workers between 2015 and 2013 and between 2015 and 2011. However, between 2011 and 2013 (post-crisis), the situation appeared quite stationary.

3.7 Conclusions

The novel contribution of this chapter is to explore job vacancies in Germany, Italy and the UK. We used regional, sectoral and firm size data to reveal firms' demand for skills. Our analysis suggests that German and British firms were very active in looking for labour, notably in terms of high-skill labour in Germany and low-skill labour in the UK. Meanwhile, in Italy there was evidence of a stagnant job market where the demand for medium-skill workers was the largest. Finally, it is perhaps surprising that the sectoral analysis suggests that the service sector seems more receptive to Industry 4.0 skills than the manufacturing sector. Job vacancies data provides valuable information on firms' skill needs; however, unfortunately it does not enrich the analysis with details about the why and how of labour market changes. Nevertheless, we feel that a number of policy recommendations can be drawn from our research:

1 There is a need to raise awareness at the firm level of the types of skills needed to adopt new technologies. The extent to which firms still demand low-skill jobs raises some concerns with respect to their possible lack of readiness to fully exploit the benefits of all the FIR technologies. This

means that key stakeholders have a role to play in informing, alerting and advising firms on what skills they need, given the sectors they operate in and the activities they are undertaking. Such skills may be in the local labour market or may need to be acquired via the existing workforce.

2 The education system needs to start updating its programmes to include competences related to FIR technologies in order to avoid structural skill mismatches in the labour market.
3 The fast pace of technological change means that firms will experience rapid skill obsolescence. A solution would be for firms to prioritise constant on-the-job reskilling and upskilling of their internal labour force by accessing general or tailored courses offered by specialist providers, especially for smaller firms who might not have the in-house facilities and scale to invest in competence building.
4 Industry associations and public sector stakeholders can work with the knowledge-intensive business sector by supporting the latter to emerge and develop symbiotically with the industrial specialisation of the regional economy in order to offer tailored, customised and bespoke training programmes.
5 Skills formation is often considered a good example of market failure necessitating government intervention in order to compensate for the private sector's under-investment due to free-riding concerns. However, skills formation will increasingly become a multi-dimensional requirement for firms, government and society. The lack of skills will impact on people's employability and therefore on their job prospects and income. At the same time, governments will need up-to-date skills and competences across their range of departments in order to understand the policy and regulatory implications of technological change. Furthermore, firms can only become or remain competitive if their physical investments in digitally enabled technologies are dovetailed with investment in competence building. This means that skills formation cannot be left solely to schools and universities; firms need to be compelled to proactively invest and plan for the skills they need and will need. Policy needs in turn to incentivise firms to retain and retrain its labour force by introducing, for instance, 'skills vouchers' (similar to innovation vouchers) or programmes such as industrial doctorate programmes or apprenticeships.

Note

1 Public administration, public enterprises in the health sector, public primary and secondary schools, public universities and other no-profit organisations are excluded.

References

Acemoglu, D. (2002) Technical change, inequality, and the labor market. *Journal of Economic Literature* 40: 7–72.

Arntz, M., Gregory, T. and Zierahn, U. (2016) The risk of automation for jobs in OECD countries: a comparative analysis. OECD Social, Employment and Migration Working Papers, No. 189. Paris: OECD Publishing.

Autor, D. (2015) Why are there still so many jobs? The history and future of workplace automation. *Journal of Economic Perspectives* 29: 3–30.

Autor, D. and Handel, M. (2013) Putting tasks to the test: human capital, job tasks, and wages. *Journal of Economics* 3: S56–S96.

Autor, D., Levy, F. and Murnane, R. (2003) The skill content of recent technological change: an empirical exploration. *Quarterly Journal of Economics* 118: 1279–1333.

Bisello, M. (2013) Job polarization in Britain from a task-based perspective. Evidence from the UK Skills Surveys. Discussion paper.

Böhm, M. (2014) The wage effects of job polarization: evidence from the allocation of talents. Econstor Conference paper.

Brunello, G., Wruuck, P. and Maurin, L. (2019) Skill shortages and skill mismatch in Europe: a review of the literature. EIB Working Papers, No. 2019/05

CEDEFOP (2015) Skill obsolescence (%) across countries in 2014. Available at: http://skillspanorama.cedefop.europa.eu/en/indicators/skills-obsolescence.

Chui, M., Manyika, J. and Miremadi, M. (2015) Four fundamentals of workplace automation, *McKinsey Quarterly*, November.

De Propris, L./World Economic Forum (2016) How the Fourth Industrial Revolution is powering the rise of smart manufacturing. Available at: www.weforum.org/agenda/2016/06/how-the-fourth-industrial-revolution-is-powering-the-rise-of-smart-manufacturing.

Bárcena-Martín, E., Budría, S. and Moro-Egido, A. (2012) Skill mismatches and wages among European university graduates. *Applied Economics Letters* 19(15): 1471–75, DOI: https://doi.org/10.1080/13504851.2011.633886.

Dwyer, R.E. (2013). The care economy? Gender, economic restructuring, and job polarization in the US labor market. *American Sociological Review* 78(3): 390–416.

European Vacancy Monitor. European Commission. Available at: https://excelsior.unioncamere.net/eng.

Fernández-Macías, E. (2012) Job polarization in Europe? Changes in the employment structure and job quality, 1995–2007. *Work and Occupations* 39(2): 157–182.

Frey, C.B. and Osborne, M.A. (2013) The future of employment: how susceptible are jobs to computerisation? Oxford Martin School Working Paper, Oxford University.

Goos, M., Salomons, A. and Vandeweyer, M. (2014) *Job Polarization during the Great Recession and Beyond.* Ku Leuven Euroforum.

Hamersma, M., Edzes, A. and van Dijk, J. (2015) Underqualification as an opportunity for low-educated workers. *Government and Policy* 33: 83–103.

Heyman, F. (2018) Job polarization, job tasks and the role of firms. *Economics Letters* 145: 246–251.

Katz, L.F. and Autor, D.H. (1999) Changes in the wage structure and earnings inequality. In O. Ashenfelter and D.E. Card (eds), *Handbook of Labor Economics.* Amsterdam: Elsevier Science.

Kemeny, T. and Rigby, D. 2012. Trading away what kind of jobs? Globalization, trade and tasks in the US economy. *Review of World Economics* 148: 1–16.

McCann, P. and Ortega-Argilès, R. (2015) Smart specialization, regional growth and applications to European Union cohesion policy. *Regional Studies* 49: 1291–1302.

McGuinness, S., Pouliaka, K. and Redmond, P. (2018) Skills mismatch: concepts, measurement and policy approaches. *Journal of Economic Surveys* 32(4): 985–1015.

McKinsey Global Institute (2017) Jobs lost, jobs gained: what the future of work will mean for jobs, skills, and wages. Available at: www.mckinsey.com/featured-insights/future-of-work/jobs-lost-jobs-gained-what-the-future-of-work-will-mean-for-jobs-skills-and-wages.

Moreno-Galbis, E. and Sopraseuth, T. (2014) Job polarization in aging economies. *Labour Economics* 27: 44–55.

Morgado, A., Sequeira, T., Santos, M., Ferriera-Lopes, A. and Reis, A.B. (2014) Measuring labour mismatch in Europe. *Social Research* 1–19.

Niedermayer, K. and Tilly, J. (2016) Short-Time Work in Germany during the Great Recession: A Quantitative Investigation. IAB Conference Proceedings.

OECD (2015) ICTs and jobs: complements or substitutes? The effects of ICT investment on labour market demand by skills and by industry in selected countries, OECD Digital Economy Working Papers, No. 259. Paris: OECD Publishing.

OECD (2018) *Job Creation and Local Economic Development 2018: Preparing for the Future of Work*. Paris: OECD Publishing.

OECD (2019) Inequality. Available at: www.oecd.org/social/inequality.htm.

PwC (2014) The future of work: a journey to 2022. Available at: https://pwc.blogs.com/files/future-of-work-report-1.pdf.

PwC (2017) Will robots steal our jobs? The potential impactof automation on the UK and other major economies. Available at: www.pwc.co.uk/economic-services/ukeo/pwcukeo-section-4-automation-march-2017-v2.pdf.

PwC (2018) Workforce of the future: the competing forces shaping 2030. Available at: www.pwc.com/gx/en/services/people-organisation/workforce-of-the-future/workforce-of-the-future-the-competing-forces-shaping-2030-pwc.pdf.

Rifkin, J. (2014) *The Zero Marginal Cost Society: The Internet of Things, the Collaborative Commons, and the Eclipse of Capitalism*. New York: Palgrave Macmillan.

Skills Panorama (2016) Focus on skills challenges in Europe. Available at: https://skillspanorama.cedefop.europa.eu/sites/default/files/2016_Skills_Challenges_AH.pdf.

UK Commission for Employment and Skills (2018) Employer Skills Survey 2015 of 91,000 employers. Available at: www.gov.uk/government/publications/ukces-employer-skills-survey-2015-uk-report.

World Economic Forum (2018) The future of jobs report. Available at: http://www3.weforum.org/docs/WEF_Future_of_Jobs_2018.pdf.

4 Transformative paths, multi-scalarity of knowledge bases and Industry 4.0

Marco Bellandi, Cristina Chaminade and Monica Plechero

4.1 Introduction

This chapter discusses the role of combinatorial knowledge and its multi-scalarity in shaping the transformation paths of local productive systems (LPSs) that are affected by the gales of contemporary technological change. Specifically, we look at how access to – and the combination of – different knowledge bases at different territorial scales (local/regional, national, international/global) can support different paths of industrial upgrading for LPSs in the face of the challenges posed by Industry 4.0 (I4.0). We adopt the I4.0+ (plus) perspective defined in Chapter 1, which aims to address sustainable development.

Local and regional transformation paths increasingly rely on complex knowledge dynamics (Grillitsch et al., 2018), which require different types of knowledge to inter-relate in order to support some degree of innovativeness in local systems (Asheim et al., 2017; Grillitsch et al., 2017). Such knowledge dynamics refer not only to knowledge that has different degrees of transferability across spaces (tacit vs. codified knowledge), but more crucially involve different knowledge bases: analytic (science-based), synthetic (engineering-based) and symbolic (cultural-based) (Asheim and Coenen, 2005; Asheim and Gertler, 2005).

Traditionally the literature on knowledge bases has argued that synthetic and symbolic knowledge – both with a high tacit content – tends to be accessed only when actors are in close proximity and with limited international interactions (Martin and Moodysson, 2011, 2013). In contrast, analytic knowledge – which has a higher codified content – tends to be accessible at a wider geographical scale. However, recent evidence suggests that synthetic and symbolic knowledge can also be sourced at an international level, which extends the possibility for accessing and combining all knowledge bases at different geographical scales (Martin et al., 2018).

In this chapter, we build on this suggestion and propose a novel conceptual framework that attempts to match different transformative paths with different forms of combinatorial knowledge creation. We assume that matching might involve different knowledge bases that are sourced at all geographical scales, from regional to global. Furthermore, we will discuss how effective sourcing depends on the use of specific mechanisms and on the presence of place-specific conditions (Section 4.2).

This extended framework will be applied to better understand how access to knowledge and any of its combinations can shape alternative models of value creation in LPSs that are embarking on transformative or renewed paths of development in order to take advantage of the opportunities opened up by I4.0. In particular, digital technologies characterize the core of the I4.0 model, and may unlock and enable new value-creation solutions within LPSs that will impact not only on the economic growth of places, but also on their societal development (OCSE, 2016; World Bank, 2017). On the one hand, I4.0 is pushed by the increasing importance of analytical/scientific knowledge supported by digital coding. On the other hand, the outcomes of innovation processes underpinned by I4.0 include an ever-deeper combination of product, service and societal contents. This implies the necessity of accessing both synthetic/engineering and symbolic/cultural knowledge on complex multi-scalar settings (Section 4.3).

In the final section in the chapter, we will discuss these issues in relation to a number of cases studied within the MAKERS project.

4.2 Access and combination of different knowledge bases in the transformative paths of LPSs

4.2.1 Knowledge bases and local path transformation

As already noted, there is a stream in the innovation literature that argues that local/regional path transformation is favoured when different types of knowledge can be accessed, combined and effectively integrated.[1] Combining different types of knowledge is indeed a distinct feature of current innovation processes transforming the nature of a large number of industries (Strambach and Klement, 2012; Grillitsch and Trippl, 2014, Corradini and De Propris, 2015). This is even more so in the context of both disruptive technological challenges brought by Industry 4.0 and when there is a need to pursue sustainable societal as well as environmental goals (Strambach, 2017).[2]

Attending to the degree of codification and the processes of knowledge creation, Asheim and Coenen (2005) and Asheim and Gertler (2005) distinguish between three types of knowledge bases:

- *Analytic knowledge (science-based)* is often created with the application of experiment-based methods. The value is extracted from the application of scientific principles and theoretical modes of learning. Much of its content can be transferred in a codified form (lectures, reports, publications and patents). Often firms rely on collaboration with research organizations for its creation and on research and development (R&D) laboratories for its absorption.

- *Synthetic knowledge (engineering-based)* relies on inductive processes of problem solving. In production contexts, it is associated with the engineering of new results emerging from doing, using and interacting (DUI) forms of learning (Jensen et al., 2007). The value can be extracted by means of socialization and synthesis of the existing knowledge (Herstad et al., 2014).
- *Symbolic knowledge (cultural-based)* concerns cultural contents and aesthetic as well as immaterial values. Its creation relies on a variety of heritage and life notions and images elaborated by means of trained artistic and cultural intuition. The value can be extracted from creativity and contextualized sense making. Whilst it is highly place-specific, as the interpretation of images, design and symbols varies significantly from one location to another, it can also be embedded in artefacts and media communications by means of design and various types of applied and performing arts.

Due to its mostly codified nature, analytical knowledge could be accessed across large geographical distances and, consequently, industries dominated by analytical knowledge bases tend to display a high propensity towards establishing international networks. Synthetic knowledge, meanwhile, combines elements that are tacit and codified in nature, and, as a consequence, such knowledge can be acquired more through local networks and only to a lesser extent through international networks. Finally, symbolic knowledge-creation processes tend to rely significantly on local knowledge networks (Bathelt et al., 2004; Martin, 2011).

When we consider processes of local or regional transformation, should LPSs' access to and ability to combine different knowledge bases be limited, a high risk of path exhaustion if not decline would materialize. On the contrary, when different types of knowledge can be accessed and effectively combined by local actors, this may lead to some forms of path upgrading. Meanwhile, new path creation would require a high degree of combinatorial knowledge, which often implies an extensive use of differentiated knowledge bases as well as complex multi-scalar interactions.[3]

While some of the initial literature on knowledge bases tends to suggest that synthetic and symbolic knowledge will be sourced in local and regional networks while analytical knowledge can be sourced at the international level (Martin and Moodysson 2011, 2013), Martin et al. (2018) suggest that different knowledge bases supporting the processes of transformation of LPSs can be acquired at different scales depending on the needs and capabilities of specific firms. However, they fall short of explaining how this occurs and which mechanisms are more likely to be activated to access the different types of knowledge and at which different geographical scale. This chapter fills this conceptual vacuum.

4.2.2 Multi-scalar mechanisms for knowledge access and combination in local productive systems and knowledge-led transformative paths

A key issue that emerges from the literature that links knowledge bases to transformative paths is that effective combinatorial knowledge processes require local and global spaces to be bridged or connected. Such connections need to be better understood. At the local level, firms and supporting organizations may use a variety of mechanisms to access different knowledge bases (Trippl et al., 2009), such as market mechanisms, networks (e.g. alliances), hierarchies (e.g. via the operations of multi-national corporations) and spill-overs (e.g. mobility). In particular, knowledge is typically exchanged in *markets* when it is embodied in goods or services whose value is potentially easy to measure. Such embodied knowledge is likely to correspond to analytic or codified synthetic types of knowledge. Typical examples would be the use of patents for a new drug development or the acquisition of machinery for a specific engineering process.

Fragments of all types of knowledge may be accessed via *unintended spill-overs* associated with human capital mobility, the monitoring of competitors, or informal single or repeated face-to-face contacts. Spill-overs tend to occur in close geographical proximity, although larger geographical distances are not excluded, for example, through international mobility (Rosenkopf and Almeida, 2003; Song et al., 2003) or temporary geographical proximity (Torre, 2008).

Networks, on the other hand, are based on trust and reciprocity (Powell, 1990). The reciprocal character of network relationships implies that actors have similar or complementary absorptive capacity as well as frequent face-to-face interactions and/or the sharing of habits and collective rules. Networks are a good mechanism for the transmission of know-how and know-who, and, in that respect, they are likely to be used for the collaborative transfer and the absorption of tacit contents prevailing in synthetic and symbolic knowledge. Networks for knowledge creation and innovation can take different forms: R&D contracts, alliances, research consortia, epistemic communities or communities of practice.

Finally, *hierarchies*, which can be inter-firm and intra-firm, are mainly based on power enforcement together with the sharing of private rules, common routines or a history of previous interactions. Those characteristics also reduce institutional distance across space (Martin and Salomon, 2003). By opening subsidiaries in different locations, multi-national corporations (MNCs) can access and absorb tacit and codified synthetic knowledge belonging to different scientific and technological fields that has been accumulated in different countries or regions around the world (Kafouros et al., 2012).

The propensity of firms to use different mechanisms to access distant knowledge will ultimately depend on the availability and transferability of knowledge as well as the capabilities of firms. By availability, we refer to the degree of concentration of that knowledge in specific regions around the world. The sources of highly novel analytic knowledge, highly specialized synthetic knowledge or key symbolic knowledge are sparse and often highly concentrated in specific locations (knowledge hubs). This means that firms located in knowledge hubs have an advantage in terms of access to such knowledge without the need to engage in extra-regional links. However, having access to knowledge is not enough. The ability of the organization to tap into pools of knowledge is strongly related to its absorptive capacity. Transferability is the possibility to transmit and receive knowledge without noise, bias or leaks, and depends on the degree of codification. Hence, availability, absorptive capacity and transferability determine what mechanism firms avail themselves of to access knowledge at different geographical scales.

The question is therefore as follows: at what different geographical scales do the above-mentioned mechanisms help firms and related organizations access different knowledge bases and trigger combinatorial knowledge creation processes enabling local transformations?

We focus our analysis on LPSs (Becattini and Rullani, 1996): these are (relatively) small regions (urban or rural areas, industrial districts, etc.) featuring one or a few productive specializations, which are more or less complementary. The specializations are related to the activity of a cluster of firms and supporting business and public organizations operating in the place. Productive decisions and activities have key roots in local business and socio-cultural and institutional networks.

Table 4.1 provides a schematic summary of the main mechanisms supporting the access of LPSs to different types of knowledge bases that can be leveraged at different geographical scales. The *appropriateness of the mechanisms* and their role for path transformation in LPSs depend on the wealth of knowledge sources in LPSs and the type of proximity that can be used when accessing different knowledge bases.[4]

In *transformative processes*, market mechanisms are used by companies to access internationally available analytic knowledge, for example, through patents (Herstad et al., 2014). However, firms whose innovative processes are driven by the creation and/or the development of new analytic knowledge either cluster in highly innovative hubs around the world or tend to link to key players themselves located in international knowledge hubs. Networking in this case is a preferable mechanism for distant interactions. Firms located in LPSs with strong research infrastructure are also more likely to have high technological capabilities enabling them to actively participate in research networks on a global scale.

Networks and spill-overs facilitating or implying face-to-face interaction are likely to be used intensively for accessing synthetic knowledge at different geographical scales. Networks in general are likely to work better at local or national levels where institutional distance is limited (Martin and Moodysson, 2013; Mattes, 2012). When accessibility to synthetic knowledge is low or networks and spill-overs at the local level fail to provide new inputs for generating value, firms may decide to use the hierarchical channel by opening, for example, a subsidiary abroad (offshoring of R&D) to acquire synthetic knowledge from a distant location (Liu et al., 2013). The MNC might bring in knowledge accumulated from networks with other places that can be reapplied and reused differently in the host location.

On the other hand, symbolic knowledge is highly context-specific and tacit, moving with individuals or being embedded in specific communities (e.g. communities of practice or epistemic communities). Access to symbolic

Table 4.1 Some key mechanisms for firms in LPSs to access different knowledge bases in a multi-scalar setting

Knowledge base / Mechanism	*Markets (within LPS)*	*Markets (beyond LPS)*	*Spill-overs (within LPS)*	*Spill-overs (Beyond LPS)*	*Networks (within LPS)*	*Networks (beyond LPS)*	*Hierarchies (within LPS)*	*Hierarchies (beyond LPS)*
Analytical	Trade (e.g. patents)	Trade (e.g. patents)			R&D collaboration (e.g. research consortium)	Domestic/international R&D collaboration, but some cognitive/organizational proximity necessary) **(this can be key for knowledge creation**)		
Synthetic	Trade (market technologies/goods for codified aspects of engineering process)	Trade (market technologies/goods for codified aspects of engineering process)	Local mobility of human resources and face-to-face interactions	International mobility, temporary geographical proximity	Networks (often informal)	Domestic networks (also informal, but institutional proximity is necessary)	R&D offshoring from MNCs in loco **(this can be key for knowledge renewal)**	International R&D offshoring (e.g. in specialized hubs) **(this can be key for knowledge renewal)**
Symbolic			Local mobility of human resources	National/international recruitment of skilled labour	Networking within local community (e.g. community of practice)	International communities (e.g. in epistemic communities, some social proximity is necessary) **(this can be key for new sense making)**		

Source: Authors' elaboration.

knowledge is therefore expected to be based on networks and spill-overs. Social proximity, temporary proximity or international mobility can compensate for a lack of geographical proximity (Gertler, 2008; Martin and Moodysson, 2011). This is particularly crucial when there is a need for companies in an LPS either to link to places where new creative processes are taking place or to inject a new sense of interpretation and new intangible values in established cultural contexts.

The framework suggested here helps us to draw connections across the fragmented empirical evidence on the geography of different knowledge bases. In particular, by linking knowledge characteristics, types of proximity and mechanisms of transmission, it is possible to reach a better understanding of how different knowledge types at different geographical scales can *generate value* for LPSs embarking on sustainable and transformative paths.

4.3 Geographical scales of competing models in Industry 4.0 technological transformation

Drawing on the conceptual framework presented in Chapter 1 in this volume, it is possible and desirable to include considerations of social and environmental sustainability within and around the pure technical core of the current digital and science-driven industrial transformation that goes by the name of *Industry 4.0*. Such inclusion leads to an expanded perspective, so-called *Industry 4.0 plus (I4.0+)*, that implies the generation of alternatives to mainstream models of value creation and distribution, which otherwise would seem to respond deterministically to 'natural' efficiency-driven arguments. Such Industry 4.0 efficiency-driven arguments would include the centrality of smart and webbed factories and platforms, the ruling of large and multi-national firms, combining mass-customization of products and a very high intensity of capital in core processes, together with market domination, skill polarization, and the digitally driven deterioration of the citizen's control over choices on local public and common goods.

In contrast, I4.0+ is based on the idea that the new technologies should and could be addressed to help bringing sustainable growth, a wide mobilization of human capabilities, and prosperity within territories and their populations of firms, workers and families, as well as between territories. Specifically, the I4.0+ perspective aims at better understanding alternatives in local and regional industrial development that face the current challenges of social, economic and environmental sustainability in models of value creation and distribution.

4.3.1 Alternative I4.0+ models of value creation and distribution

The alternatives to conventional 'efficiency'-based models concern various aspects. We refer to Bellandi et al. (2018) for a broader discussion, but here we evoke briefly the core contents of the composite solutions supporting I4.0+ models as alternatives to the technocratic and centralistic mainstream:

- *Inter-dependencies around smart networked micro-manufacturing* (SNMM): small factories are able to incorporate new digital-based technologies in production processes led by craft skills and care. Small firms managing such factories access international networks of designers, customers and suppliers. Localized pools of SNMM drive a transformation of LPSs specialized in manufacturing into product-service systems incorporating territorial servitization (Bellandi and Santini, 2019).
- *Digital participation and distributed service provision*: an open and enlarging set of digital-based services would allow a territorial servitization of LPSs, with the latter being strong and non-dependent on large oligopolistic providers. Services here include trade, finance, advertising, labour selection and training, enterprise resource planning and relationship management, collaborative knowledge and innovation networks (De Maggio et al., 2009). They may develop on local platforms where small firms and citizens are granted digital sovereignty, information freedom and open access (Morozov and Bria, 2018). Local counterbalancing power should be inserted within and supported by national and supranational anti-trust actions.
- *Makers and smart skills*: operative well-trained skills are still crucial in key phases of value chains if production digital-based technologies are developed not in substitution, but in support of professional/creative processes (Barzotto and De Propris, 2019). This would allow LPSs to meet customer-specific demand in complex ways and expand SNMM. Examples are the matching of materials of variable quality with multi-purpose tools (I4.0 as well), related quality control, prototypes of new digital-based production processes, etc. (Bettiol and Micelli, 2014).
- *Quadruple-helix governance of projects of sustainable socio-economic development*: integrated productive development and innovation projects involve and connect constellations of actors. They include engaged developmental universities, local/regional networks of SMEs non-captured by oligarchies, anchored MNCs forced to relinquish predatory strategies, and civic society, with its more or less local social networks and supporting social innovation towards a common good for a sustainable life (Aoyama and Parthasarathy, 2016).

The contents of alternative manufacturing models under *I4.0+* suggest innovation processes that could promote transformative paths for LPSs characterized by a networked plurality of firms and organizations and by manufacturing specializations grown out of the previous wave of technological change (Perez, 2009). It is apparent that a wide and coordinated introduction of such contents would imply the access, absorption and creative combination of different types of knowledge. This would be the basis for paths of accentuated upgrading in these systems.

4.3.2 Knowledge bases and multi-scalar mechanisms in I4.0+

We now apply the framework presented in Section 4.2 to the models discussed just above under the *I4.0+* perspective in order to derive general suggestions on the relations between transfer mechanisms and the multi-scalar setting for knowledge access and combination that drive transformations in LPSs. The core of such a model, we would suggest, lies in SNMM solutions.[5] Within and around such core, there is a need for the development of digital participation and distributed service provision; the diffusion of neo-maker competences, combining artisan attitudes and digital skills; and the quadruple-helix governance of projects of sustainable socio-economic development.

Our concern now is to understand what the geographical scale of processes of knowledge access and combination for innovation might be both for the mainstream technocratic and centralistic models leading to cyber-physical production organizations and for the *alternative distributed model* (inspired to *I4.0+*). In particular, we want to investigate under what conditions LPSs characterized by a networked cluster of independent specialized business organizations can pursue processes of innovation incorporating the alternative model, and using this support paths of sustained upgrading and regional transformation (path renewal or even path creation).

Starting from the productive core, the basic feature that the *alternative distributed model* shares with the centralistic efficiency-driven model is the importance of codified knowledge in terms of digital coding and software development underlining the I4.0 technologies or their applications. R&D on new types of coding and new applications to multiple fields of scientific and technological problems obviously relates to efforts to create analytical knowledge. Such efforts are concentrated, though non-exclusively, in few 'hot' high-tech hubs around the word. The results of their efforts may be in principle transmitted in codified form at a distance. However, the successful transfer and acquisition of such results require absorptive capacity; in other words, they necessitate pre-existing digital competences internal to users-firms, either to generate new combinations between incoming knowledge and the knowledge bases already present in the firm or just to adopt new technologies developed elsewhere.

Given the breadth and the speed of the development of new digital technologies, the support of specialized intermediary agents in LPSs is also needed. They are knowledge-intensive business or service (KIBS/KIS) providers that combine parts of the analytical knowledge with the synthetic knowledge related to the features and idiosyncrasies of specific technological, production or organizational fields of firms in the LPS. In certain cases, KIBS/KIS providers also combine significant components of symbolic knowledge, as with design-driven innovation (Cooke and Eriksson, 2011). Such combinatorial services may be more or less standardized or customized to the needs of particular users.

Large firms can easily access I4.0 technologies. With their large demand, they rely on the services of national and international KIBS/KIS providers by means of relational contracts and formal networks. Temporary geographical proximity with such international KIBS/KIS providers by means of resident teams is to be expected during the developmental phases or to resolve unexpected shocks in usage, whereas ordinary maintenance and upgrading can be supported at a distance.

Trying to navigate the technological requirements of I4.0 technologies raises very different questions for non-centralized LPSs aiming at *alternative distributed production models*. Here we see two main challenges. Firstly, the single business organizations (even local entities of MNCs) included in these LPSs ordinarily cannot represent a large demand of service within the portfolio of national or international providers of KIBS/KIS. Secondly, it seems plausible that LPSs addressing alternative models to I4.0 should find their competitive advantage in market fields featured by a continuous stream of differentiation, incremental innovations and decentralized creativity, combining the personalization of products and artisan ingenuity. Here, synthetic and symbolic knowledge have key functions in terms of value creation, together with an increasing degree of codification and automation in various phases of the value chain. A real servitization of the variable and differentiated digital components needed by firms belonging to the core productive specializations of the LPS would need geographical proximity and versatility, and the help of various types of mechanisms, also including spill-overs and informal networks. This is a territorial servitization (Lafuente et al., 2017), whereby local KIBS/KIS work in stable contact with the LPS users (Bellandi and Santini, 2019). On the other hand, if the LPS is not able to express an effective territorial servitization, digital services may be acquired by LPS users in standardized forms by means of market relations. This would be a situation where the alternative distributed model to I4.0 has reduced the chances of success. Large national and international providers of KIBS/KIS may also be involved in LPSs. If there is the possibility to develop digital platforms servicing a critical mass of local users with some specific smart and connectivity-enabling components, then large providers may find it profitable to invest in local entities (R&D outsourcing).

Around the productive core, the 'alternative way' also needs to expand from business organizations and networks to wider society. Neo-makers, local digital sovereignty and quadruple helix methods of governance express a function played by the contexts of out-of-the factory life that is deeper and larger than just consumption and labour supply. It concerns knowledge access, value creation and value distribution. Giacomo Becattini saw this relation between *in-factory* and *out-of-the-factory life* at work in the development of industrial districts. He pointed to the neo-artisan tendencies opening windows of opportunities in many non-centralized LPSs in advanced economies in the second half of the 20th century. 'The ever-changing multiplicity of needs demands an exit of capitalist production from the "factory", and its return to a plenty of "laboratories" within the society, searching for artisanship, customized service, ties with historical-cultural and environmental sources of peculiar experiences' (Becattini and Bellandi, 2006: 86). And in the words of Sebastiano Brusco: 'Both the "in-factory" and "out-factory" spheres contribute directly to shape not only the quality of civil life but also productivity levels and market competitiveness' (Brusco, 1996: 155–156).

This perspective on the societal side extolled the importance of geographical and social proximity. The local contents of synthetic and symbolic knowledge, which are at the core of DUI modes of learning and innovation (Jensen et al., 2007), were also drawing from the experiences of ordinary life. It was acknowledged, nonetheless, that trans-local networks, local agents of versatile integration and local centres of services were also needed in order to link the LPS with the development of scientific and technological frontiers (Becattini and Rullani, 1996).

The effective involvement of the societal side is also key in the definition of distributed non-centralistic approaches to the contemporary digital transformation under the *I4.0+* perspective. The opportunity to combine, at various degrees of breadth and depth, the different knowledge bases is open to more than a few bridging, integrating, gatekeeping business actors. In principle, it may involve a multitude of business, socio-cultural and institutional agents.

What differentiates the capacity of LPSs to innovate and take upgrading paths of transformation is both the effective diffusion of combinatorial competencies and the collective capability to share a vision on path transformation. The vision may be led by the idea of a key role played by the development of new analytic or synthetic knowledge. However, the vision in itself has necessarily high local and non-local symbolic contents, since it requires a creative exploration of the opportunities offered by I4.0, in which new values and new senses for interpreting society are collectively constructed (Rullani and Rullani, 2018).

Furthermore, such a vision should be supported by collective (public and private) investments in specific open and multi-disciplinary platforms for the development of combinatorial capabilities and digitally based innovations. The development of such platforms necessarily rests on analytic/scientific knowledge. Weak combinatorial capabilities would probably force the LPS down towards lower paths of transformation, which might plug the LPS within centralistic routes of I4.0 or more generally force it to become subservient to global logics by feeding its economic resources to global chains of production and consumption (Storper, 2009: 155–156).

4.4 Examples from the MAKERS project

In this section, we present some applications of the framework developed in the previous sections to the interpretation of the geographical scales of knowledge links relevant to path transformation in LPSs under I4.0+ perspectives. Facts and reflections are collected from eight cases discussed within the reports of the MAKERS project (see Chapter 1 of this volume).[6]

We would partition the eight cases into three sub-sets. The first one includes the transformations of the 'paper province' in the Swedish Värmland Region and the Viareggio yachting industry in the Tuscany region (Italy). The second sub-set consists of three textile-based LPSs in Prato (Tuscany), Borås (in western Sweden) and St Gallen, Appenzell and Glarus (in eastern Switzerland). The third sub-set corresponds to the mechatronic LPS in Veneto (Italy), the automation LPS in Värtmanland (Sweden) and the life sciences LPS in Tuscany.

Only the Tuscany life sciences LPS has a strong basis in a metropolitan area (Florence), whereas the eastern Switzerland LPS is confined within a set of relatively small cities and it includes traditionally a related variety of sectors around the decreasing textile specialization. All the other LPSs are in reality industrial districts supported by different types of regional innovation systems.

In what follows, we focus in particular on the cases of the first sub-set highlighted, that is, the traditional medium-tech industries (the pulp and paper industry in Värmland and the yachting industry in Viareggio), and their geographical scales, knowledge bases and path transformation under *I4.0+* perspectives. Cases falling under the other two sub-sets will be discussed more briefly so as to provide some complementary observations at the end of the section.

The pulp and paper industry in Värmland and the yachting industry in Viareggio have developed in the past few decades as the main manufacturing specialization of the respective LPSs, with competitive advantages grounded in the relation between a strong basis of synthetic knowledge and specific locational factors. Both cases are interesting because such locational factors have been turned in the last few decades into a strong source of symbolic knowledge, still combining with local synthetic knowledge, but also attracting the activity of providers of analytic knowledge. Both cases can be taken as examples of alternative I4.0+ models that challenge the narrower definition of I4.0 and allow us to look at the geographical scale and knowledge bases of paths to upgraded transformation.

4.4.1 Combinatorial knowledge bases and multi-scalar mechanisms in the transformation of pulp and paper in Värmland (Sweden)

In this case, the locational factor is represented by the proximity to a large land of forests, an abundance of woods that may be easily treated for pulp extraction, and a tradition of preservation of the natural patrimony. The pulp and paper industry has developed for almost a century, with a strong presence of manufacturing plants and R&D laboratories as part of some large national and international companies, together with a population of specialized SMEs, also including those related to forest works.

Chapter 6 in this volume by Ramirez illustrates the emergence of a transformation path, from the traditional pulp and paper specialization to a more differentiated and analytic knowledge-intensive path, which is called the 'forest-based bio-economy', within a plan promoted by a local cluster organization in the last decade. The enduring basis is a multiplicity of nuclei of manufacturing synthetic knowledge, in dialogue with the synthetic knowledge of forest-related activities. Crucial manufacturing synthetic knowledge is hosted within the larger plants and accessed thanks to networks and spill-overs at the local level or through technologies partly acquired on external markets. The access to analytical knowledge has also been important both for the absorption and the development of some more capital-intensive technologies in pulp processes, and for an environmentally sustainable approach to the large-scale exploitation of wood resources.

The cluster initiative in recent years has tried to promote the shift to an economy specialized in the production of renewable biological resources, also with the support of digital technologies. In this cluster initiative, a critical role seems to be played by the strategic orientation of national and regional innovation systems, investments by MNCs embedded in the local economy and the role played by technological intermediaries. New analytic knowledge is developed thanks to the presence of R&D laboratories of large MNCs firms, and networks with local and national universities are also supportive in this respect.

The cluster management agency, the national innovation agency and the international technological intermediaries have been able to elaborate an integrated vision and strategy that has also pulled a wave of investments from distant headquarters of MNCs. This includes reference to the highly symbolic contents of the 'bio-economy' (a combination of the local forest tradition, the green strategy of the national innovation system and EU programmes). Moreover, it provides an answer to relevant manufacturing problems (e.g. the disposal of industrial waste), with the interaction between traditional synthetic know-how (accessed by local spill-overs, informal networks and hierarchies) and analytic knowledge (accessed by local formal network and the R&D laboratories of large vertically integrated firms that can digitally control all the phases of the production processes). Around the productive core, the cluster initiative includes projects aimed at diffusing digital competences and increasing the capacity of small local ICT services to access the new demand of the forest-based bio-economy (see Ramirez, Chapter 6 in this volume).

All in all, this case shows a virtuous combination of all three knowledge bases, accessed with appropriately different mechanisms at different spatial scales. The LPS seems ready for accomplishing a path transformation that could be seen, if realized, as a case of successful path creation (see Table 4.2).

4.4.2 Combinatorial knowledge bases and multi-scalar mechanisms in the transformation of the luxury yachting industry of Viareggio

In this second case, the locational factor is represented by the fact that the luxury yachting industry of Viareggio is located adjacent to an important Tuscan seaside tourist attraction, around Viareggio and Forte dei Marmi, which is associated with an image of high-quality recreational products and services.

As detailed in Chapter 5 in this volume by Bellandi, De Propris, Santini and Vecciolini, the long-term synthetic knowledge base of the yachting system is artisan know-how in small shipbuilding. The industry has evolved in the last few decades thanks to the international inflow of analytic knowledge that has allowed the introduction of new advanced materials, constructive solutions and

Table 4.2 MAKERS cases: combination of knowledge bases in a multi-scalar setting in the pulp and paper industry in Värmland

	Path creation towards I4.0+: use of combined analytical, synthetic and symbolic knowledge at different geographical levels transforming a paper and pulp specialized LPS into a forest based bio-economy LPS							
	Markets (within LPS)	*Markets (beyond LPS)*	*Spill-overs (within LPS)*	*Spill-overs (beyond LPS)*	*Networks (within LPS)*	*Networks (beyond LPS)*	*Hierarchies (within LPS)*	*Hierarchies (beyond LPS)*
Analytical		Digital technologies in the pulp processes and aimed at sustainable environment			R&D collaboration with large firms; networks with local universities	Networks with national universities		
Synthetic		Market technologies related to synthetic processes	Spill-over from domestic/ international MNCs within pulp industry located in LPS		Interactions at local level between traditional and forest-related activities (mediated by cluster organization)	Bridging role in international networks played by local MNCs and technological intermediaries	R&D offshoring from MNC located in LPS	
Symbolic					Bio-economy concept: shared values at local level (emerging from a cluster initiative)	Bio-economy concept: shared values with national and international stakeholders		

Source: Authors' elaboration on MAKERS cases, www.makers-rise.org.

gadgets in the building of top-end boats for recreational uses. Nowadays, the LPS is specialized in the production of luxury yachts, with highly sophisticated and price-inelastic demand from wealthy people.

Each luxury yacht is almost a unique piece, with unique design, artisanship and sophisticated technology, including solutions absorbing many types of smart and connectivity digital components. Analytical knowledge is accessed in various ways, but a key role is played by the R&D offices of the local shipyards (which correspond to the sectoral headquarters of large national and international companies), by formal networks with research organizations supported by a regional intermediary organization, and by market relations and informal networks with providers of technology at local, national and international levels. However, R&D is mainly aimed at the creation of new symbolic knowledge for improving design rather than at the development of new analytic knowledge. Furthermore, the construction of each yacht is highly demanding in terms of practical learning and creativity that involves a large number of specialized SMEs and artisans. This local core of synthetic knowledge is based on reciprocal spill-overs, formal networks with the shipyards and informal networks with the providers of technology. Small-scale and personalized information and communications technology (ICT) services for the yacht industry are granted by an ICT cluster based in the nearby city of Pisa. Various types of initiatives (local fairs, professional schools, etc.) can involve the local citizens in shaping the destiny of the local industry, even if the growth of neo-maker competences seems quite weak and given that related quadruple-helix projects are not surfacing at the moment. Indeed, the main knowledge input into the LPS comes from the *out-factory* relationships associated with requests and demands raised by wealthy buyers from around the world, as well as by the skippers employed by the ship owners.

While the case of this LPS appears quite unique, the luxury yacht industry may be seen as an exemplification of the extreme personalization and co-production that might characterize top-end and niche industries within the I4.0+ model. The uniqueness of each product, the continuous introduction of new solutions and the adoption of the latest technologies make it difficult to classify what path the LPS is following or can follow. Perhaps it points to a class of paths of 'continuous' renewal, where the creativity that drives personalization may become, in subsequent steps, a source of inspiration for part of the local community to reuse the acquired technologies and develop other related business or civic services. This case is led by the development of symbolic and synthetic knowledge and the absorption of analytic knowledge (see Table 4.3). In particular, symbolic knowledge has strong local roots, but it demands multi-scalar flows and mechanisms of creation and image building, combined with the absorption of new analytic and synthetic knowledge. Perhaps the local structure would not support local path creation, but the multi-scalar actors involved in the delivery of highly sophisticated unique products which are present at a local level could favour new value chains and path creation in other places (see Chapter 5 in this volume).

Table 4.3 MAKERS cases: combination of knowledge bases in a multi-scalar setting in the luxury yachting industry

	Continuous path renewal driven by extreme personalization: development of new symbolic and synthetic knowledge with absorption of analytic knowledge							
	Markets (within LPS)	*Markets (beyond LPS)*	*Spill-overs (within LPS)*	*Spill-overs (beyond LPS)*	*Networks (within LPS)*	*Networks (beyond LPS)*	*Hierarchies (within LPS)*	*Hierarchies (beyond LPS)*
Analytical		Digital technologies advance material, new constructive solutions			Networks with research organizations; networks with providers of technologies (weak R&D)	National and international networks with providers of technologies (weak R&D)		
Synthetic			Local companies reciprocal spill-over		Formal networks within the shipyards; informal networks with providers of technologies			
Symbolic					R&D collaborations for new symbolic/design knowledge	R&D collaborations for new symbolic/design knowledge		

Source: Authors' elaboration on MAKERS cases, www.makers-rise.org.

4.4.3 Other cases from the MAKERS project

Other cases from the MAKERS project help to provide supportive insights and qualifications. The textile cases[7] illustrate *transformation paths based on strong synthetic knowledge* as they face the pressure of contemporary challenges. In all three cases, symbolic knowledge has acquired a key role, although playing partially different functions. In the Prato textile district, the image of creativity and quality of 'Made in Italy' is applied to the synthetic knowledge-based capability to rapidly produce an open and variable range of fabrics in very small batches (with a high degree of personalization and with some help given by digital technologies). Here, symbolic knowledge combines directly into strategies of high personalization of products, and the variety of mechanisms for accessing and absorbing new analytic knowledge is still quite low. In the Borås textile district, a strong governance and innovation system at the regional and national levels has promoted a vision that facilitated the absorption of new global analytic knowledge for the development and production of high-tech textile products. Symbolic knowledge seems to play a role in supporting strategic convergence around a collective strategy of analytic knowledge intensification, helped by multi-scalar mechanisms and integration. In the eastern Switzerland district of embroidery and textile machines, a local system supporting innovation and some civic initiatives, coupled with the presence of local diversified research and manufacturing capabilities, also networked at the national and international scales, help combine the synthetic knowledge basis with the creation of new symbolic and analytic knowledge. In this case, symbolic knowledge apparently plays both roles (i.e. personalization and vision).

Such cases appear to confirm some aspects detected in the first sub-set of cases above. Firstly, the high personalization of products demands the guidance of symbolic knowledge coupled with synthetic knowledge. Secondly, a greater opportunity for radical innovation and path creation seems to demand the guidance of analytic knowledge (accessed on a multi-scalar level) coupled with a subservient but necessary role of symbolic knowledge. In all cases, local access to synthetic knowledge cannot be dispensed in LPSs that seem to evoke alternative *I4.0+* models. However, in the stronger cases, the reproduction and creation of synthetic knowledge is also an open field of local converge of multi-scalar strategies.

Finally, the third sub-set includes cases characterized by the greatest *use of analytic knowledge*.[8] Even for these, while any path of upgraded transformation depends crucially on access to and the adoption of analytic knowledge, the extent and depth of the transformation cannot be related only to the degree of local capabilities related to analytic knowledge. In fact, paths consistent with the alternative I4.0+ model, like in Värtmanland, also critically require access to symbolic knowledge for the creative and absorptive functions and at different geographical scales, beyond the presence of strong local pools of synthetic knowledge.

4.5 Conclusions and further research

The previous discussion linking knowledge bases, multi-scalarity and the transformation of LPSs brings some interesting insights for policies (particularly at the regional level) sustaining LPSs. *Firstly*, regional policies do not necessarily have to ensure that all three knowledge bases (synthetic, analytic and symbolic) are co-located in the same LPS. Contrary to what has often been argued in the literature, firms and other innovative organizations could access different knowledge even from distant locations. Regional policies aiming at strengthening LPSs therefore need to go hand in hand with more general policies supporting the use of mechanisms to access knowledge at other geographical scales. Which mechanisms are more adequate depends strongly on the type of knowledge base, the capabilities of the firms located in the region, and conditions allowing access to knowledge. It also depends on which type of model of path transformation is pursued. In particular, and in relation to the challenges of I4.0, it depends on the prevalent vision (e.g. centralistic and technocratic or non-centralistic and distributed) informing public policies and private strategies. *Secondly*, our framework could help extend policies in terms of considering why two firms in the same industry and with similar levels of innovativeness – one located in a knowledge hub and the other one located in a peripheral region – may have very different configurations.

This chapter has some limitations. Firstly, applying a multi-scalar framework to knowledge bases, which brings in knowledge characteristics and meso- and micro- conditions, requires data that are beyond what is currently available. In the short term, dedicated firm-based surveys or case studies in different LPSs around the world could provide a starting point to conduct empirical analysis based on the proposed framework. Secondly, based on the premise that combinatorial knowledge-creating processes involves the sourcing of knowledge at different geographical scales, our focus has been on theorizing when and how these multi-scalar knowledge-sourcing processes will take place. Admittedly, while the sourcing of knowledge is paramount for innovation, it is only one part of combinatorial knowledge-base processes. Knowledge acquired externally needs to be further processed internally, inside both individual firms and related organizations – and among them – within LPSs. In other words, while this chapter provides some insights as to how different knowledge bases are *sourced* using different mechanisms at different scales, it does not discuss how the firm *combines* them into new knowledge. Other chapters of this book consider this more directly, in so doing looking in depth into some of the MAKERS project cases referred to above.

Acknowledgements

We gratefully acknowledge the support by the EU Horizon 2020 project MAKERS, which is a Research and Innovation Staff Exchange under the

Marie Sklodowska-Curie Actions, grant agreement number 691192. All errors remain the authors' responsibility.

Notes

1 See in particular the special issue on knowledge bases in (2017) 93(5) *Economic Geography*.
2 In this latter case, the generation of value often derives from the convergence of unrelated knowledge bases taken from different sectorial contexts and recombined in traditional sectorial specialization (Grillitsch et al., 2017).
3 Various contributions develop concepts and cases around such relations. See Asheim et al. (2011, 2017); Chaminade et al. (2017, 2018); Grillitsch et al. (2017, 2018); Isaksen and Trippl (2016); Manniche et al. (2017); Trippl et al. (2017).
4 Another condition not discussed in this chapter is *appropriability*, which concerns how agents interpret and use the acquired knowledge for extracting value.
5 This also concerns analogous productive solutions outside manufacturing, with precision agriculture, sustainable tourism, creative industries, personalized welfare, etc. (Crespi et al., 2014).
6 A cautionary note is needed: underpinning research on the cases to which we refer was not developed directly for applying and testing of the interpretative framework illustrated here. Therefore, some implications concerning individual cases are speculative. Nonetheless, we are confident about the robustness of the overall comparative panel.
7 See Bellandi et al., Chapter 5 in this volume on Prato; the MAKERS report by Santini and Bellandi (2017), including the case of eastern Switzerland; and Chaminade et al. (2018) on Borås.
8 See Corò and Volpe (Chapter 7 in this volume) on the Veneto mechatronic LPS and the automation LPS in Värtmanland. For the life sciences LPS in Tuscany, See Chapter 6 in this volume.

References

Aoyama, Y. and Parthasarathy, B. 2016. *The Rise of the Hybrid Domain. Collaborative Governance for Social Innovation*. Cheltenham: Edward Elgar.

Asheim, B.T. and Coenen, L. 2005. Knowledge bases and regional innovation systems. Comparing Nordic clusters. *Research Policy*, 34(8), 1173–1190.

Asheim, B.T. and Gertler, M.S. 2005. The geography of innovation: regional innovation systems. In Fagerberg, J., Mowery, D. and Nelson, R. (eds), *The Oxford Handbook of Innovation*. Oxford: Oxford University Press.

Asheim, B.T., Boschma, R. and Cooke, P. 2011. Constructing regional advantage: Platform policies based on related variety and differentiated knowledge bases. *Regional Studies*, 45(7), 893–904.

Asheim, B., Grillitsch, M. and Trippl, M. 2017. Introduction: combinatorial knowledge bases, regional innovation, and development dynamics. *Economic Geography*, 93(5), 429–435.

Barzotto, M. and De Propris, L. 2019. Skill up: smart work, occupational mix and regional productivity. *Journal of Economic Geography*, 19(5), 1049–1075.

Bathelt, H., Malmberg, A. and Maskell, P. 2004. Clusters and knowledge: local buzz, global pipelines and the process of knowledge creation. *Progress in Human Geography*, 28(1), 31–56.

Becattini, G. and Bellandi, M. 2006. Distretti industriali: un paradigma socio-economico' in Fortis, M. and Quadrio Curzio, A. (eds), *Industria e distretti. Un paradigma di perdurante competitività italiana*. Bologna: Il Mulino.

Becattini, G. and Rullani, E. 1996. Local systems and global connections: the role of knowledge. In Cossentino, F., Pyke, F. and Sengenberger, W. (eds), *Local and Regional Response to Global Pressure: The Case of Italy and its Industrial Districts*. Geneva: International Institute for Labour Studies.

Bellandi, M., De Propris, L. and Santini, E. 2018. *Industry 4.0+ Challenges to Local Productive Systems and Place-based Integrated Industrial Policies*. Mimeo.

Bellandi, M. and Santini, E. 2019. Territorial servitization and new local productive configurations: the case of the textile industrial district of Prato. *Regional Studies*, 53(3), 356–365. https://doi.org/10.1080/00343404.2018.1474193.

Bettiol, M., and Micelli, S. 2014. The hidden side of design: the relevance of artisanship. *Design/Issues*, 30(1), 7–18.

Boschma, R. 2005. Proximity and innovation: a critical assessment. *Regional Studies*, 39(1), 61–74.

Brusco, S. 1996. Global systems and local systems. In Cossentino, F., Pyke, F. and Sengenberger, W. (eds), *Local and Regional Response to Global Pressure: The Case of Italy and its Industrial Districts*. Geneva: International Institute for Labour Studies.

Chaminade C., Bellandi M., Plechero, M. and Santini, E., 2017. Paper on the role of RIS/NIS and knowledge transfer on manufacturing upgrading. MAKERS Deliverable 2.2. Available at: www.makers-rise.org/publications.

Chaminade C., Bellandi M., Plechero, M. and Santini, E. 2018. Path renewal and creation in specialized regional innovation systems. A comparative analysis of two textile districts in Italy and Sweden. Paper presented at the Rethinking Clusters: Critical Issues and New Trajectories of Cluster Research workshop, University of Florence, Italy, 3–4 May.

Cooke, P. and Eriksson, A. 2011. Design-driven regional innovation. In Cooke, P., Asheim, B., Boschma, R., Martin, R., Schwartz, D. and Tödtling, F. (eds), *Handbook of Regional Innovation and Growth*. Cheltenham: Edward Elgar.

Corradini, C. and De Propris, L. 2015. Technological diversification and new innovators in European regions: evidence from patent data. *Environment and Planning A: Economy and Space*, 47(10), 2170–2186.

Crespi, G., Fernandez-Arias, E. and Stein, E.H. (eds). 2014. *Rethinking Productive Development: Sound Policies and Institutions for Economic Transformation*. New York: Palgrave Macmillan.

De Maggio, M., Gloor, P.A. and Passiante, G. 2009. Collaborative innovation networks, virtual communities and geographical clustering. *International Journal of Innovation and Regional Development*, 1(4), 387–404.

Gertler, M. 2008. Buzz without being there? Communities of practice in context. In Amin, A. and Roberts, J. (eds), *Community, Economic Creativity, and Organization*, Oxford: Oxford University Press.

Giuliani, E. 2007. The selective nature of knowledge networks in clusters: evidence from the wine industry. *Journal of Economic Geography*, 7(2), 139–168.

Grillitsch, M., Asheim, B.T. and Trippl, M. 2018. Unrelated knowledge combinations: the unexplored potential for regional industrial path development. *Cambridge Journal of Regions, Economy and Society*, 11(2), 257–274. https://doi.org/10.1093/cjres/rsy012.

Grillitsch, M., Martin, R. and Srholec, M. 2017. Knowledge base combinations and innovation performance in Swedish regions. *Economic Geography*, 93(5), 458–479.

Grillitsch, M. and Trippl, M. 2014. Combining knowledge from different sources, channels and geographical scales. *European Planning Studies*, 22(11), 2305–2325.

Herstad, S.J., Aslesen, H.W. and Ebersberger, B. 2014. On industrial knowledge bases, commercial opportunities and global innovation network linkages. *Research Policy*, 43(3), 495–504.

Isaksen, A. and Trippl, M. 2016. Exogenously led and policy-supported new path development in peripheral regions: analytical and synthetic routes. *Economic Geography*, 93(5), 436–457.

Jensen, M.B., Johnson, B., Lorenz, E. and Lundvall, B. 2007. Forms of knowledge and modes of innovation. *Research Policy*, 36(5), 680–693.

Kafouros, M.I., Buckley, P.J. and Clegg, J. 2012. The effects of global knowledge reservoirs on the productivity of multinational enterprises: the role of international depth and breadth. *Research Policy*, 41(5), 848–861.

Lafuente, E., Vaillant, Y. and Vendrell-Herrero, 2017. Territorial servitization: exploring the virtuous circle connecting knowledge-intensive services and new manufacturing businesses. *International Journal of Production Economics*, 192, 19–28.

Liu, J., Chaminade, C. and Asheim, B. 2013. The geography and structure of global innovation networks: a knowledge base perspective. *European Planning Studies*, 21(9), 1456–1473.

Manniche, J., Moodysson, J. and Testa, S. 2017. Combinatorial knowledge bases: an integrative and dynamic approach to innovation studies. *Economic Geography*, 93(5), 480–499.

Martin, R. 2011. The local geographies of the financial crisis: from the housing bubble to economic recession and beyond. *Journal of Economic Geography*, 11(4), 587–618.

Martin, R., Aslesen, H.W., Grillitsch, M. and Herstad, S.J. 2018. Regional innovation systems and global flows of knowledge. In Isaksen, A., Martin, R. and Trippl, M. (eds), *New Avenues for Regional Innovation Systems: Theoretical Advances, Empirical Cases and Policy Lessons*. Cham: Springer.

Martin, R. and Moodysson, J. 2011. Innovation in symbolic industries: the geography and organization of knowledge sourcing. *European Planning Studies*, 19(7), 1183–1203.

Martin, R. and Moodysson, J. 2013. Comparing knowledge bases: on the geography and organization of knowledge sourcing in the regional innovation system of Scania, Sweden. *European Urban and Regional Studies*, 20(2), 170–187.

Martin, X. and Salomon, R. 2003. Knowledge transfer capacity and its implications for the theory of the multinational corporation. *Journal of International Business Studies*, 34(4), 356–373.

Mattes, J. 2012. Dimensions of proximity and knowledge bases: innovation between spatial and non-spatial factors. *Regional Studies*, 46(8), 1085–1099.

Morozov, E., and Bria, F. 2018. *Rethinking the Smart City: Democratizing Urban Technology*. New York: Rosa Luxemburg Stiftung.

OECD. 2016. *Science, Technology and Innovation Outlook 2016: Megatrends Affecting Science, Technology and Innovation*. Paris: OECD Publishing.

Perez, C. 2009. Technological revolutions and techno-economic paradigms. *Cambridge Journal of Economics*, 34(1), 185–202.

Powell, W. 1990. Neither market nor hierarchy. *Research in Organizational Behaviour*, 12, 295–336.

Rosenkopf, L. and Almeida, P. 2003. Overcoming local search through alliances and mobility. *Management Science*, 49(6), 751–766.

Rullani, F. and Rullani, E. 2018. *Dentro La rivoluzione digitale. Per una nuova cultura dell'impresa e del management*. Turin: Giappichelli Editore.

Santini, E. and Bellandi, M. 2017. Paper on the impact of new technology on the 9 organisation of production in high-tech districts or clusters. MAKERS Report. 10. Available at: www.makers-rise.org/wp-content/uploads/2018/03/D3.1-11-Paper-on-the-impact-of-new-technology-on-the-organisation-of-production-in-high-tech-districts-or-clusters.-Protected.pdf.

Song, J., Almeida, P. and Wu, G. 2003. Learning-by-hiring: when is mobility more likely to facilitate interfirm knowledge transfer? *Management Science*, 49(4), 351–365.

Storper, 2009. The economics of context, location and trade: another great transformation? In Becattini, G., Bellandi, M. and De Propris, L. (eds), *A Handbook of Industrial Districts*. Cheltenham: Edward Elgar.

Strambach, S. 2017. Combining knowledge bases in transnational sustainability innovation: microdynamics and institutional change. *Economic Geography*, 93(5), 500–526.

Strambach, S. and Klement, B. 2012. Cumulative and combinatorial micro-dynamics of knowledge: the role of space and place in knowledge integration. *European Planning Studies*, 20(11),1843–1866.

Torre, A. 2008. On the role played by temporary geographical proximity in knowledge transmission. *Regional Studies*, 42(6), 869–889.

Trippl, M., Grillitsch, M. and Isaksen, A. 2017. Exogenous sources of regional industrial change: attraction and absorption of non-local knowledge for new path development. *Progress in Human Geography*, 42(5), 687–705.

Trippl, M., Tödtling, F. and Lengauer, L. 2009. Knowledge sourcing beyond buzz and pipelines: evidence from the Vienna software sector. *Economic Geography*, 85(4), 443–462.

World Bank. 2017. *Trouble in the Making? The Future of Manufacturing-Led Development*. Washington, DC: World Bank.

5 Industry 4.0

Transforming local productive systems in the Tuscany region

Marco Bellandi, Erica Santini, Claudia Vecciolini and Lisa De Propris

5.1 Introduction

The current wave of technological change is affecting local productive systems of specialised SMEs, such as industrial districts (IDs), which still characterise important parts of the European manufacturing sector. Dominant and quite restricted approaches to Industry 4.0 paint a bleak scenario for such IDs, suggesting that they might be doomed to decline or to becoming dependent on large technological companies. Instead, the more holistic approach that has emerged in the MAKERS project of *Industry 4.0+* (and that is presented in Chapter 1 of this volume) illustrates the opportunities that the new technologies can offer to small-scale firms and systems that rely on them, such as IDs, to embark on transformative paths that recombine embedded specialisation with new technologies.

Indeed, a number of solutions are feasible that see new digital technologies being applied to, combined with, meshed in or integrated with capabilities that are intangible, experience-based and creative in order to generate process and product innovations. In IDs and similar productive systems, such combinations and applications do not just require adaptations internal to single firms in relation to their business models and competence pools; rather, they can trigger a *collective rerouting* that occurs at the system level. This implies the recombination of the productive knowledge within an evolving multiplicity of know-how nuclei with any new incoming knowledge, as well as the transformation of the technological foundations, sectoral specialisations, business networks, supply relations, and embedded social relations and institutional support of the local system.

This chapter will be structured as follows. The starting point of our analysis in Section 5.2 is to present the relevant aspects of Industry 4.0+ in relation to local productive systems. Section 5.3 will discuss the processes of knowledge recombination that can occur in IDs, followed by some case studies taken from the Tuscany region in Italy. Some final remarks will conclude the chapter.

5.2 Industry 4.0+ and local productive systems of SMEs

This section illustrates how Industry 4.0+ can support transformative pathways leading to the upgrading and rerouting of local productive systems of SMEs following the diffusion of the digital technologies linked to the Fourth Industrial Revolution (henceforth FIR technologies) (Schwab, 2016). We will present a framework on the dynamics and dimensions of the collective rerouting that IDs need to engage with in order to benefit from the current technological change. For this, a crucial juncture is a clear understanding of what recombinant knowledge implies in such systems, as it will be more extensively discussed in the next section.

It is now well understood that we are experiencing a wave of new technologies that will completely redraw the techno-economic paradigm underpinning our economy and society; these include biotech, nanotech, neurotech, green and renewables, ICT and mobile tech, 3D, AI, robotics, sensoring and space tech. The impact of these new technologies has been captured so far by the extensive debate on Industry 4.0 that kicked off in Germany in the mid-2010s and that has primarily looked at the application of some of these technologies inside factories to increase efficiency, productivity and flexibility. There is, however, an emergent literature on the opportunities they can offer to redefine business models, value-creation processes and industry supply chains (Porter and Heppelmann, 2014; Hermann et al., 2016).

However, the disruptive change that FIR technologies can trigger is wider and greater than the one underpinning the creation of 'smart factories' only. They can lead to a socio-economic transformation driven by the increasing technological capacity of societies and individuals (Hilbert and López, 2011). The pervasive penetration of digital technologies is changing resource reliance and the organisation of production within and between firms, together with creating new sectors whilst making other become obsolete. The current disruptive technologies are completely altering the nature of and the interface between manufacturing and service sectors, as well as the relationship between buyers and suppliers, and between firms and customers.

Some advanced and emerging economies have already started drawing strategies to support firms, regions and sectors to develop and/or adopt such new technologies to sustain their competitive advantage for longer-term jobs and prosperity (see Chapter 13 in this volume for more details on EU policy responses). Indeed, such transformations and adjustments necessitate a clear and supportive policy vision and tools accompanying the experimental and entrepreneurial spirit of firms.

In this scenario, local manufacturing systems of small and medium-sized enterprises (SMEs) also have to adjust their traditional industrial organisation as well as their knowledge configurations to meet such challenges. Historically, some such systems, like many classical IDs, were able to adapt their internal systemic structure thanks to the propelling role played by their underpinning *cognitive structure* and knowledge bases. The cognitive structure of IDs has tended to rest on: (1) mechanisms of learning and creativity within and among the know-how nuclei of the core manufacturing specialisation; (2) latent local resources of trust and adaptability related to a strong sense of local belonging; (3) small firms thriving as life projects for the local community of entrepreneurs, artisans and skilled workers; and (4) policies supporting the provision of public goods specific to local needs (Becattini, 2004). Because of the above, IDs have evolved by branching out into new but still locally embedded knowledge bases supporting the rerouting of their development (Bellandi et al., 2018).

However, the current disruptive technological transformations require a new and delicate balance between *'smart and digital' competencies,* triggered by the FIR, and *manual and artisan skills*, which remain crucial in customisation and innovation processes. Such integration is not a trivial process. Moreover, the reconfiguration of social regulations and human capital that allows for faster access to data and information, as well as the hybridisation of the systemic embedded know-how, are both reliant on the capabilities of systems' *institutional structure* to accommodate such challenges; the latter include formal and informal norms, as well as policy makers and private stakeholders at the local and national levels.

As contemporary global competition is reshaped at a fast pace by technological change, the diffusion of new technologies may act as a springboard for local manufacturing systems of SMEs to help restore the determinants of their local competitiveness. In the 1980s and 1990s, in the wake of post-Fordism, the mutual adjustment of the cognitive and institutional meso-structures of local SMEs systems, such as many classical IDs, was instrumental in the exploration and exploitation of new knowledge bases related to the diffusion of consolidated technologies (Becattini, 2004). However, the traditional internal mechanisms that generated systems' external economies (ibid.) and supported their incremental adaptation and adaptability are no longer sufficient. Instead, we need to better understand what new mechanisms ought to be in place to accommodate the shocks caused by the incoming radical technological changes. The economic and social sustainability of such systems is not necessarily guaranteed since the auto-reproductive capabilities they rely on are likely to be modified. In fact, the nature and dynamics of districts' external economies will adapt as local systems of SMEs experience new solutions to be competitive and successful in the global markets.

New forms of local external economies are emerging, resulting from the integration of material inputs and digital knowledge along the value chain. How new technological knowledge is combined and recombined with the existing sets of knowledge embedded into local manufacturing systems could determine the creation of a new industrial landscape. Indeed, the ability of local production systems to cope with the technological challenge they face cannot be defined only by firm-level solutions, but rather by solutions that are designed and embraced at the system level within IDs. IDs function systemically on a number of levels: the specialised labour pools they are rooted in, the market and non-market mechanisms of business networking, and the reproduction of the social foundations of entrepreneurship and artisanship. These have to adapt to leverage the benefit of FIR technologies.

There are examples of IDs that have been successful and resilient in evolving markets and technologies thanks to their internal features (Belussi and De

Propris, 2013). They are associated to the so-called 'IDs Mark 3' (Bellandi and De Propris, 2017).[1] These are IDs that have evolved to take on variations in response to changes in technology and markets, including: a) product-service specialisations crossing the borders of different statistical economic sectors; b) heterogeneous populations of networked, specialised and innovative SMEs together with flagship trans-local companies and anchored multi-national enterprises (MNEs); c) insertion in policies of regional and national platforms for continuous learning, research and innovation collaborations, international trans-local services; and d) local social embeddedness of the economic activities rooted in a continuous interpretation of cultural heritage and authenticity within the global flows of persons, information and capital (Bellandi and De Propris, 2017).

In many cases, such variations are only partially developed, while the traditional mechanisms, which cumulate self-reinforcing mechanisms of learning and place-specific organisational models, have become largely unsuitable for the renewal of the sets of embedded knowledge and innovation processes, leading systems to become locked into sub-optimal paths (Arthur, 1994; Antonelli, 1999). Even worse, some are unable to adjust their set of knowledge bases and trigger new learning processes in the presence of disruptive challenges (Martin et al., 2016).

5.3 Processes of knowledge recombination

We have recalled above that in classical (Mark 2) IDs, new knowledge generation begins from the exploitation and exploration of knowledge inputs sourced both internally (i.e. the set of specialised knowledge bases) and externally (i.e. foreign markets, business and institutional partnerships). Here interactions within and across the systems' different knowledge bases enable the transformation and integration of internal and external knowledge inputs through processes of learning by doing-using-interacting, the so-called DUI-mode (Jensen et al., 2007), which are embedded into the idiosyncratic structures of each local system (cognitive and institutional systems).

In IDs relying only on DUI modes, the forces dampening adaptability can be particularly strong when the local system and its main manufacturing sector of specialisation, together with complementary industries and subsidiaries services, have reached the phase of maturity (Menzel and Fornahl, 2009; Hervas-Oliver and Albors-Garrigos, 2014). In fact, at maturity, self-reinforcing mechanisms of learning and innovation tend to take the form of incremental change and repetition that confirm known patterns of success. Furthermore, the institutional structure may become unable to remove barriers and inertia related to rent-seeking and coordination problems (Bailey et al., 2010). In these circumstances, the knowledge set embedded in the system becomes progressively obsolete, unable to hybridise with new incoming knowledge and to renew its configuration. Therefore, recalling the 'rigid specialisation trap' concept introduced by Grabher (1993), it may be argued that beyond some threshold and time, local specialisation weakens local learning and innovation, reducing the capacity to reshape the cognitive and institutional structures in the face of non-gradual changes and putting at risk a long-lasting resilient growth (see Staber, 2001; Boschma, 2005; Frenken et al., 2015).

The challenge for DUI mode systems is how to spot, assess and react to maturity entropic effects and to disruptive external challenges. We would argue that two structural conditions affect knowledge generation in local productive systems of SMEs: the composition of specialised knowledge bases; and crucially the breadth of local business networks (Bellandi et al., 2018). The composition of the specialised knowledge bases maps the sectors embedded in the area and, more specifically, the economic activities belonging to every single local *filière*. On the other hand, the breadth of local business networks captures the distance in the interactions between knowledge bases belonging to the same or different *filières*. These interactions can be established either between closely related knowledge bases when they belong to the same *filière* or between distant knowledge bases when they refer to different *filières*. 'Strong ties' can be argued to feature the sharing of closely related knowledge bases, while 'weak ties' allow contacts between distant knowledge bases (Granovetter, 1985). Business networks with enough breadth to encompass both strong and weak ties promote new knowledge generation thanks to the combination of similar and more distant knowledge bases.

Depending on the wealth and composition of specialised knowledge bases and on the breadth of its local business networks, a local productive system can embark on different types of learning processes. In classical IDs, DUI modes of learning rest preferentially on the combination of similar knowledge bases within the *filière* of the main industry or around it. However, Mark 3 IDs should instead include clusters of different *filières* and open business networks. This is highly relevant in the context of technological change, especially since enabling technologies develop across sectors and *filières*, completely redefining them or creating new sectors and *filières*. Indeed, it has been argued that new production technologies increase cross-sectoral interactions (OECD, 2017), bridge distant knowledge bases, and generate in turn much more radical and disruptive innovations (Corradini and De Propris, 2016).

Given the above considerations, we define four possible types of learning processes taking place in DUI mode-based systems as described in Table 5.1.

QUADRANT 4 **Learning by accumulation**	**QUADRANT 3** **Learning by recombination**
QUADRANT 1 **Learning by substitution**	**QUADRANT 2** **Learning by conversion**

Figure 5.1 Learning processes in local productive systems
Source: Authors' elaboration.

We argue that local productive systems characterised by a small set of specialised knowledge bases and by interactions mostly concentrated within the same *filière* are likely to embark on processes of *learning by substitution* (QUADRANT 1). This is because the joint effect of the limited amount of knowledge bases and of interactions constrained within a *filière* addresses DUI learning processes towards substitution at the margin of obsolete sets of knowledge with newer similar knowledge. They correspond to simple sectorial agglomerations of small firms. *Learning by conversion* (QUADRANT 2) occurs in local productive systems endowed with a few knowledge bases dispersed across multiple *filières*. Examples can be found in IDs still presenting Mark 2 features, for instance, in rural local systems combining agriculture and food processing industries, tourism and craft products. In this case, the DUI mode of learning within closely related knowledge bases is weak. However, interactions with other *filières* may enable the exploration of loosely related knowledge bases, leading to the generation of new knowledge by converting external inputs absorbed through weak ties (an example could be the adoption of off-the-shelf digital solutions, be they hardware or software). *Learning by recombination* (QUADRANT 3) occurs in local productive systems that are endowed with a multitude of knowledge bases and where firms engage in cross-*filière* interactions thanks to extensive and diverse business networks. In Mark 3 IDs, learning by recombination supports the exploitation and exploration of internal and external knowledge sources, leading to novel combinations generated through strong and weak ties. Finally, when the system's endowment of knowledge bases is rich, but the interactions take place mostly within the same *filière*, knowledge generation is limited and occurs through processes of *learning by accumulation* (QUADRANT 4). This type is consistent with classical (Mark 2) IDs that tend to be characterised by highly specialised and developed industrial structures, in which the main value chain has spawned into a multiplicity of secondary economic activities underpinned by related knowledge bases. Strong ties across such closely related knowledge bases support learning processes based on the DUI mode, leading at best to the incremental adaptations of the existing composition of knowledge bases.

5.4 Cases

The conceptual framework presented so far has been applied to analyse three contemporary cases of localised industry in Tuscany (Italy), specifically the textile production system in the Prato district, the yachting production system in Viareggio and the houseware production system on the outskirts of the city of Pistoia. The empirical evidence analysed in these case studies results from qualitative data and information collected via semi-structured questionnaires to firms, as well as to local institutional stakeholders between 2017 and 2018, until theoretical saturation is reached (O'Reilly and Parker, 2013).[2]

5.4.1 The Larciano system of plastic products, household and sanitary goods and toilet accessories

The hostile geography of the Larciano area in the hilly Tuscan countryside makes it difficult to accommodate large-scale production. Nevertheless, this territory hosts a significant agglomeration of SMEs specialised in low-value plastic products, such as brooms, buckets and toilet accessories, and, according to the ISTAT 2011 Census data, this industry employs around 29% of the local workforce.

Historically, this system was specialised in the production of brooms, taking advantage of the easy availability of the necessary natural resources in the area, in particular wood and straw. In the mid-twentieth century, a process of local division of labour led some local small firms to specialise in the production of components of the final products (e.g. the handle and bassine broom). However, this process of local division of labour did not go very far, involving only a small number of firms and leaving only a small set of specialised knowledge bases detectable in the system. The local division of labour remained incomplete and did not lead to the emergence of complementary know-how nuclei, such as those related to mechanical tools.

At the end of the 1990s, firms started exploring plastic materials to replace wood and broomcorn. The entrepreneurial leadership of some more structured firms and the involvement of informal networks of firms producing plastic vases for a nearby flowers industry were enough to adjust firms' production processes and the system's organisational model. The transformation required investments in new machineries and greater vertical integration of the production process to take advantage of economies of scale. Thanks to these adjustments, the local production system has grown since then and has been able to survive the long recession that Italy experienced following the 2008 economic crisis.

However, it now faces another wave of technological shocks that will again test the knowledge structure of the system, posing threats but maybe offering some opportunities as well. Industry 4.0+ has the potential to introduce new materials as fossil fuel-based plastic is somewhat decommissioned, digitalisation might force further investments to upgrade the automation of the production process or, again, digitalisation might overturn the whole industry by introducing new cleaning devices.

Some of these challenges are already discussed by local businesses, as the following quote testifies:

> Firm A asked me to start a micro-scale production of buckets with specific characteristics. So, I started to explore various solutions opened up recently with the newest technologies. We do not have a R&D department, so we started some collaborations with local universities and local consultants, investing a large amount of money into the project. We discovered that the 3D printing is neither cheap nor easy to apply in every kind of production. Large investments are needed to adapt the 3D printer to the

> specific production process we need to make buckets. We also need to train workers. We cannot continue to invest. As first-mover, the returns on such an investment are clearly in the long term and we cannot afford the risk. We are not a large firm, and therefore we decided to wait. (Firm in the plastic production system of Larciano)

As already mentioned, FIR technologies are redefining the sources of scale economies and, at the same time, are allowing efficiency to occur at low scale. This should offer an opportunity to production systems like Larciano that can detect the advantages of new technologies in terms of market experimentation and attempt to embrace change through *some* weak ties beyond the *filière*. However, in the case of Larciano, firm-level capabilities force firms to be imitators rather than innovators. At the same time, the thinness of local knowledge bases reduces the interactions across *filières* and the possibilities for recombinant solutions under collective and systemic learning processes. In this case, the rerouting of the local productive system would need a place-based policy supporting investments that trigger a more robust transition from *learning by substitution* to *learning by conversion* processes.

5.4.2 The Prato textile district

The textile industry has a long history in the city of Prato, dating back to the Middle Ages and extending to a set of other contiguous towns. Before the Second World War, until the post-war recovery period, the district was characterised by two parallel circuits of firms: a core of vertically integrated firms producing few types of carded woollen fabrics, at a large scale, for national and international markets; and a secondary circuit made of small craft producers. In the 1950s, the introduction of other fibres besides wool and of new finishing processes allowed the district to widen its range of products and the development of a system of phase specialised SMEs within the textile *filière* (Dei Ottati, 2003). This system also expanded into a range of complementary *filières*, such as textile machinery or tools and dyes for the textile industry. By the 1990s, the Prato district had peaked and since then it has experienced a slow but steady reduction in terms of firms, employees and production capacity. The rate of shrinkage accelerated after 2002 and 2012 (Dei Ottati, 2018).

The cumulative spawning of knowledge and the continuous integration of new competencies in the local textile *filière* has followed a DUI mode based on the multiplicity of local knowledge bases within and around the main textile *filière*, benefiting from an active and committed institutional support. However, the limited interactions between the textile and other *filières* did not allow the activation of mechanisms of learning by recombination and limited the chances of rerouting the local system to new pathways.

Today, a new knowledge base is surfacing around digital technology services. Santini and Bellandi (2018) found that some manufacturing firms have started combining their specialised manufacturing competences with knowledge related to digital services by means of both internal experimentation and external relations (e.g. with universities and private research institutes). However, a large number of the traditional leading firms seem unable to extend their business networks in order to take advantage of these new competences and to explore radically new processes and markets. This means that the system seems quite unable to explore new pathways and reroute its specialisation. Such rerouting would require changes in skills, capital, organisation and of course technologies, but there is not a shared collective vision on strategies of investments. It is probable that any attempt at rerouting will be a stop-start process. The required transformative changes are stalled not only by a lack of breadth in business networks, but also by a lack of institutional coordination, if not by positive resistance to change. It also has to be considered that the possibility for and strength of collective and public actions in the Prato ID have weakened due to the emergence of an adjacent cluster of Chinese textile producers over the last decade. Various problems of social co-existence and economic legality have surfaced; positive linkages between the two systems have not developed yet (Dei Ottati, 2018).

We would argue therefore that two trajectories appear possible for the Prato ID. The first trajectory sees the system remaining locked in the traditional DUI mode of innovation, with reliance on *learning processes by accumulation* within the local *filière* supported by the integration of digital applications in the knowledge bases related to textiles. Along the second trajectory, the resistance to change in many segments of the local *filière* could lock the district into a hardly sustainable condition of *learning by substitution*. This would prevent any transformative change of the local networks, leading to a reduction in the multiplicity of knowledge bases and the continuous shrinkage of the local textile *filière*, until its natural demise.

The Prato textiles district therefore faces the challenges of Industry 4.0+ standing at an historical juncture. Although the first trajectory is desirable and possible, the second one is more likely, although painfully unattractive, due to the observed internal resistance to change, an inability to leverage emerging knowledge bases for renewal, and a fractured socio-cultural fabric.

5.4.3 The Viareggio system of yachting production

The maritime tradition of Viareggio dates back to the fifteenth century, when its coast became a strategic seaport to control the commercial flows in the Tyrrhenian Sea. Supported by the long-standing tradition as fishers and seamen, shipping production in Viareggio took off in the nineteenth century with the production of small ships and, later in the century, of cargo ships and of 30- to 40-metre schooners, mostly used for fishing and commercial purposes. Around the mid-twentieth century, the main shipyards started to produce recreational boats, in the wake of Viareggio's increasing recognition as a popular seaside resort and tourism system. In the 1960s, the introduction of fibreglass in shipbuilding marked a turning point in the traditional meaning associated with the production and utilisation of boats. On the supply side, fibreglass profoundly affected the structure of the shipbuilding supply chain, making a number of traditional activities vanish, especially those that specialised in woodworking, and giving value to the niches of high-quality production that resisted the change. Furthermore, driven by an increasing demand for leisure boats, over the course of the following decades, Viareggio expanded the local shipbuilding supply chain and became a world leader in the production of luxury yachts. Since the 2008 international economic crisis, the Viareggio yachting system has specialised in the production of luxury mega-yachts over 50 metres (accounting for 25% of global production, according to IRPET data), while reducing the production of mid-size yachts. In 2011, the yachting industry absorbed around 25% of the manufacturing employment in the Viareggio area (identified through ISTAT Local Labour Market Areas: ISTAT 2011 Census data).

Today, the Viareggio yachting system organises and coordinates (particularly through the shipyards) a web of suppliers for the fitting of mega-yachts. Shipyards are responsible for design and planning, services, control and assistance, while production is sub-contracted to a rich network of suppliers, including furniture makers, upholsterers, marble producers, suppliers of technological appliances, window fitters, etc. Manufacturing activities are supported by a constellation of services, comprising business services (e.g. training, marketing, legal and certification), maritime and port services. Considering that the building of a yacht requires about 600 suppliers and pulls together up to 70 different competences, we can think of the yachting system as a platform bringing together multiple *filières*. In addition to the first-tier shipbuilding *filière* specialised only in yachting production (e.g. the construction of external structures), we observe a plurality of other *filières*, concurring to the production of each single component for the internal fitting of the yacht-final product, such as those of production of lighting systems, mechanical and engineering firms. Each *filière* can be considered as a sector per se, being endowed with a multiplicity of specialised knowledge bases all aimed at producing individually recognisable products (e.g. appliances, furnishings, upholstery and lighting systems). The multiplicity of knowledge bases and of cross-*filière* interactions favours *learning processes by recombination*, resulting from knowledge sharing through both strong and weak ties. In this regard, the characteristic of the yachting cluster as a platform of *filières* makes it a suitable network structure and composition for the diffusion of FIR technologies and the adoption of an Industry 4.0+ rationale (with a new business model and new products). The multi-sectoral firms also producing components for the yachting system in fact make considerable use of FIR technologies and are applying them to different supply chains, including yachting itself.

5.5 Conclusions

The shift to new paths characterised by the extension of DUI modes of learning to cross-sectoral relations requires large technological and competence investments, and implies radical organisational changes. They are nevertheless at the core of the systemic rerouting to new paths of development and models of local productive systems of SMEs, such as the Mark 3 IDs. In this regard, SMEs face huge constraints, as they require a financial system and local incentive strategies able to sustain such experimental activities. Nonetheless, this systemic reaction would enable the strengthening of diffused creativity and entrepreneurship in the area, repairing the cooperative nexus necessary for a renewed local division of labour. The hybridisation of systemic embedded know-how would allow the system of SMEs to experience new solutions and rethink their product, their processes and their identity in the global markets, driving through new development paths along an Industry 4.0+ direction.

Fruitful rerouting dynamics should be supported by wide-ranging and robust collective and public actions by institutional bodies, addressing productive development at local/regional, national and international (e.g. EU) scales. For example, radical changes to the education and training system would be desirable, as a greater need for multi-disciplinary approaches to learning is becoming necessary in order to face local and global challenges. A new vision for forming human capital as well as increasing public and private investment would reduce competence constraints and skills shortages, as well as reducing the resistance to technological change at the local level. Awareness of the technological opportunities would curb rent-seeking activities and support sharing of successful experiences in terms of exploration, access, adoption and variation of new technologies and markets, with related variations in business models and networks. Eventually, the sharing of successful cases and good practices will help activate imitation processes and reduce the sense of mistrust that many local manufacturing systems of SMEs have experienced over the last decade, as technological change has occurred alongside upheaval in the social, economic and environmental spheres.

Notes

1 The 'classical IDs' that followed successful paths of local development in the second half of the last century can be seen as Mark 2, while the historical IDs of the first Industrial Revolution would be Mark 1 (Bellandi and De Propris, 2017).

2 See Santini et al. (2018) for more details.

References

Antonelli, C. (1999). *The Microdynamics of Technological Change*. London: Routledge.

Arthur, W.B. (1994). *Increasing Returns and Path Dependence in the Economy*. Ann Arbor: University of Michigan Press.

Bailey, D. and De Propris, L. (2014). Manufacturing reshoring and its limits: the UK automotive case. *Cambridge Journal of Regions, Economy and Society*, 7(3), 379–395.

Bailey, D., Bellandi, M., Caloffi, A. and De Propris, L. (2010) Place-renewing leadership: trajectories of change for mature manufacturing regions in Europe. *Policy Studies*, 31(4), 457–474.

Becattini, G. (2004), *Industrial Districts: A New Approach to Industrial Change*. Cheltenham: Edward Elgar.

Bellandi, M. and De Propris, L. (2017). New forms of industrial districts. *Economia e Politica Industriale. Journal of Industrial and Business Economics*, 44(4), 411–427.

Bellandi, M., De Propris, L. and Santini, E. (2018). An evolutionary analysis of industrial districts: the changing multiplicity of production know-how nuclei. *Cambridge Journal of Economics*, 43(1), 187–204.

Bellandi, M., Santini, E. and Vecciolini, C. (2018). Learning, unlearning and forgetting processes in industrial districts. *Cambridge Journal of Economics*, 42, 1671–1685.

Belussi, F. and De Propris, L. (2013). 20 They are industrial districts, but not as we know them! In Giarratani, F., Hewings, G.J.D, and McCann, P. (eds), *Handbook of Industry Studies and Economic Geography*. Cheltenham: Edward Elgar, pp. 479–492.

Boschma, R. (2005). Proximity and innovation: a critical assessment. *Regional Studies*, 39(1), 61–74.

Corradini, C. and De Propris, L. (2016). Beyond local search: bridging platforms and inter-sectoral technological integration. *Research Policy*, 46(1), 196–206.

Dei Ottati, G. (2003). Exit, voice and the evolution of industrial districts: the case of the post-World War II economic development of Prato. *Cambridge Journal of Economics*, 27(4), 501–522.

Dei Ottati, G. (2018). Marshallian industrial districts in Italy: the end of a model or adaptation to the global economy? *Cambridge Journal of Economics*, 42(2), 259–284.

Frenken, K., Cefis, E. and Stam, E. (2015). Industrial dynamics and clusters: a survey. *Regional Studies*, 49(1), 10–27.

Giuliani, E. (2005). Cluster absorptive capacity: why do some clusters forge ahead and others lag behind? *European Urban and Regional Studies*, 12(3), 269–288.

Grabher, G. (1993). The weakness of strong ties: the lock-in of regional development in the Ruhr area. In Grabher, G. (ed.), *The Embedded Firm: On the Socioeconomics of Industrial Networks*. London: Routledge, pp. 255–277.

Granovetter, M. (1985). Economic action and social structure: the problem of embeddedness. *American Journal of Sociology*, 91(3), 481–510.

Hermann, M., Pentek, T. and Otto, B. (2016). Design principles for Industrie 4.0 scenarios. In *Conference Proceedings of the* 49th Hawaii International Conference on System Sciences (HICSS), pp. 3928–3937.

Hervas-Oliver, J.L. and Albors-Garrigos, J. (2014). Are technology gatekeepers renewing clusters? Understanding gatekeepers and their dynamics across cluster life cycles. *Entrepreneurship & Regional Development*, 26(5–6), 431–452.

Hilbert, M. and López, P. (2011). The world's technological capacity to store, communicate, and compute information. *Science*, 332(6025), 60–65.

Jensen, M.B., Johnson, B., Lorenz, E. and Lundvall, B.Å. (2007). Forms of knowledge and modes of innovation. *Research Policy*, 36, 680–693.

Martin, R., Sunley, P., Gardiner, B. and Tyler, P. (2016). How regions react to recessions: resilience and the role of economic structure. *Regional Studies*, 50(4), 561–585.

Menzel, M.P. and Fornahl, D. (2009). Cluster life cycles: dimensions and rationales of cluster evolution. *Industrial and Corporate Change*, 19(1), 205–238.

O'Reilly, M. and Parker, N. (2013). 'Unsatisfactory saturation': a critical exploration of the notion of saturated sample sizes in qualitative research. *Qualitative Research*, 13(2), 190–197.

OECD (2017). *The Next Production Revolution: Implications for Governments and Business*. Paris: OECD Publishing.

Porter, M.E. and Heppelmann, J.E. (2014). How smart, connected products are transforming competition. *Harvard Business Review*, 92(11), 64–88.

Santini, E. and Bellandi, M. (eds) (2018). Paper on the impact of new technology on the organisation of production in high-tech districts or clusters. Official Report to the EU Commission, MAKERS Project. Available at: http://www.makers-rise.org/wp-content/uploads/2018/03/D3.1-Paper-on-the-impact-of-new-technology-on-the-organisation-of-production-in-high-tech-districts-or-clusters.-Protected.pdf.

Staber, U. (2001). Spatial proximity and firm survival in a declining industrial district: the case of knitwear firms in Baden-Wurttemberg. *Regional Studies*, 35(4), 329–341.

Schwab, K. (2016). *The Fourth Industrial Revolution*. Geneva: World Economic Forum.

6 Sustainable manufacturing

Creating a regional forest-based bio-economy

Paulina Ramirez

6.1 Introduction

How regions develop environmentally sustainable new growth paths represents an increasingly urgent challenge for both policy makers and academics interested in sustainable regional renewal. The concern for sustainability comes in the context of increasing perceptions of the scale of contemporary environmental degradation and is leading to growing pressures for changes to existing socio-technical systems as a way of addressing this pressing societal challenge (Geels 2011; Coenen et al. 2015). However, the emergence and diffusion of new socio-technological systems is a complex and long-term process involving significant changes to existing scientific knowledge and technologies, user practices and markets, as well as societal institutions (Geels 2004, 2011). These systemic transitions usually require a re-alignment of multiple technical and social elements in new configurations that are often contested as they can undermine powerful vested interests (Geels 2011; Boshma et al. 2017). Moreover, it is argued that transitions towards sustainable socio-technical systems require purposive action (Smith et al. 2005 in Geels 2011) in the sense that they are the result of policies that consciously address the need for environmental sustainability. Given these conditions, the dynamics of systemic transitions towards green regional economies will differ significantly from the evolutionary processes of regional renewal within existing socio-technical systems discussed in much of the evolutionary economic geography literature (Boschma 2017), which focus on the nature and diversity of local technologies and capabilities, knowledge spill-overs and entrepreneurial responses to new technological and market opportunities.

This chapter describes and analyses initial efforts to establish a new regional growth path based on the transition of Sweden's Värmland Region from a socio-technical system based on the traditional manufacture of pulp and paper towards a forest-based bio-economy. Given the complexity and multitude of factors that influence the regional transition of socio-technical systems, the study of the dynamics of change in one region can help us gain an understanding of the factors and relationships that promote or hinder systemic change. The account highlights the importance of place-specific dynamics of transition processes such as the existence of a natural resource with the potential to become a new source of a renewable biological raw material (in this case the forest); new regional visions and policies; the role of the locality for market formation; and the role of local formal and informal institutions in the emergence and transition towards new regional socio-technical systems. The main focus of the chapter is on the role of agency and new policy initiatives strongly influenced by the need to address major societal challenges such as climate change on processes of regional diversification. The analysis adopts a multi-scalar perspective because many of the key players in Värmland's regional economy are subsidiaries of multi-national corporations (MNCs) or part of their global value chains (GVCs) and global innovation networks (GINs) and because transitions of socio-technological systemic tend to be global in nature, though with important national and regional manifestations.

The chapter is structured as follows: Section 6.2 brings together insights from the literatures on evolutionary economic geography and transitions to discuss changes in socio-economic systems with a focus on environmental sustainability. In Section 6.3 the methodology of the study is presented. Section 6.4 describes and analyses processes of transition towards a sustainable forest-based bio-economy. Section 6.5 discusses the role of agency and the multi-scalar nature of regional transitions to new socio-technical systems. Section 6.6 concludes the discussion.

6.2 Regional transitions towards sustainable socio-technical systems

Evolutionary interpretations of regional development and diversification have emphasised the importance of local knowledge given the path-dependent nature of learning and technological change (Immarino 2005; Castaldi et al. 2015) and much attention has focused on the nature and degree of technological diversity of local knowledge and capabilities which are seen to condition the type of new activities that will be able to develop (Frenken et al. 2007; Nefket et al. 2011; Boschma et al. 2017). In these accounts, novelty is analysed in relation to the existing knowledge base and capabilities of a region, and the main mechanism for local diversification are knowledge spill-overs between industrial sectors (Asheim et al. 2011), whilst the main drivers of innovation and regional renewal are profit-driven firms incentivised by new technological and market opportunities. As argued by Boschma et al. (2017), the focus of recent studies on regional renewal has been on the enabling conditions embodied in regional capabilities, with less attention having been paid to factors that constrain the development of new growth paths and the role of agency in overcoming such obstacles.

Whilst these accounts of the dynamics of regional diversification based on new combinations of previously unconnected technologies (which diffuse through regional economies on the basis of spill-overs – see Castaldi et al. 2015; Boschma et al. 2017) can explain radical and incremental innovation within existing socio-technical systems (Geels 2004), they do not capture the complexities, obstacles and tensions associated with systemic changes of globally dominant techno-economic and social systems. Socio-technical-systems transitions involve not only new technologies but also changes in markets and user practices, as well as institutions (e.g. environmental standards and practices) which are often contested.

It is argued that, in general, private firms have limited incentives to drive sustainability transitions because the goal is related to a collective good (sustainability) associated with numerous instances of market failure (Geels 2011). Moreover, the industries where sustainability transitions are most needed (e.g. transport and energy) tend to be dominated by large MNCs that possess complementary assets (Teece 1986, Rothaermel 2001) (such as specialised manufacturing capabilities and large-scale test trials) that give incumbents a strong position in relation to the entrepreneurial firms that tend to be the first to develop environmental innovations. Therefore, the involvement of incumbent firms that are still embedded in current socio-technical systems in processes of systems transition to a green economy usually requires significant strategic reorientation on their part (Geels 2011). From a regional development perspective, successful transitions towards sustainable local economies therefore require what Coe and Yeung (2015) refer to as a *strategic coupling* between local strategies of regional diversification and the strategic needs of MNCs and their GVCs. This process of strategic coupling has three important characteristics: (i) it is strategic in that it needs intentional and active intervention on the part of both regional authorities and the MNCs active in the region to occur; (ii) it is time-space contingent and is therefore a temporary coalition between local and non-local actors; and (iii) actors from different spatial scales interact (Coe and Yeung 2015). The ability to align regional diversification strategies with those of MNCs is not automatic or always successful (Coe et al. 2004; Dunning and Lundan 2008; Coe and Yeung 2015).

The above discussion suggest that in order to understand processes of regional transitions in line with new, environmentally sustainable, socio-technical systems, the role of agency (including, for example, the collective action by firms and the actions of policy makers) and policy needs to be incorporated into the analysis (Neffke et al. 2016; Boschma 2017; Boschma et al. 2017). The literature suggests that in the case of regional diversification based on the transformation of socio-technical transformation, new entrants such as spin-offs and to a lesser extent diversifying firms will be the key agents of change and the formation of new industries (Neffke et al. 2016; Boschma et al. 2017). However, it is accepted that regional governments can also play an important role as agents of regional transitions by lobbying for the creation of new supporting institutions at the national and global levels. Moreover, when new socio-technical systems are close to the existing knowledge base of a locality, a region can provide a supporting institutional structure for change.

Given that the development of socio-technical transitions are global in nature and scale, especially transitions related to climate change, a multi-scalar perspective that takes into account how global and national processes impact on regional diversification is necessary.

6.3 Methodology

The case study is written following the tradition of 'appreciative theorizing' (Nelson and Winter 1982; Nelson 1994), a theory-building approach widely used in innovation studies and evolutionary theories of innovation and organisational change that concentrates the analysis on the role of actors, relationships and processes that lead to qualitative transformation. Data for the study was collected from 15 semi-structured interviews with representatives from six firms located in the cluster organisation Paper Province (PP) (three MNCs and three SMEs) and nine representatives from the national and regional policy-making system. Interviews took place in 2016, three years after PP won the Vinnväxt competition, and therefore focus on the initial stages of the process of regional diversification and transition.

6.4 Värmland Region's transition towards a sustainable forest-based bio-economy

A structural transition towards a regional bio-economy involves underlying changes in a local economy so that renewable biological resources such as crops, forests, fish, animals and micro-organisms replace fossil fuels and become a major source of raw material for production. In the case of forestry, the biological resource is lignin, a wood component produced as by-product (or waste material) of pulp production, which can potentially be refined into new environmentally friendly fuels, chemicals and lightweight materials (e.g. bio-based household products, composite materials, pharmaceuticals, paper and textiles) (Formas 2012). Lignin has been described as a new 'green gold' because of its potential to replace fossil fuel as a source of energy as well as raw materials. However, many of the technologies related to the bio-economy are still very new to the industrial sector and society. In that sense, the bio-economy represents a new socio-technical system requiring the development of new forms of production and new firms, new markets and changes in user practices as well as new institutions.

The Värmland Region of Sweden has a long history of industrial development based on the forest industry, above all pulp and paper, and deep knowledge of the process technologies underlying these two sectors. At the time that the study took place, there were some 200 companies dedicated to the pulp and paper industry in the region that covered the whole paper and pulp value chain, including companies that manage the forest, paper and pulp mills, all major national and international machine and equipment suppliers, technology and engineering management consultancy firms and other specialised service firms. The majority of the large mills and supplier firms located in the region are the local affiliates of leading global MNCs in the pulp, paper and forest-based industries, and a number of them are also key players in the development of the new technologies used in the industry worldwide. Most of the MNCs located in the region have a long history in the area (in some cases 50–100 years) and are therefore a critical part of the knowledge and competence base of the region. At the same time, these local MNC affiliates are also embedded in the global knowledge systems of their parent firms, which in most cases are headquartered outside the region and often outside Sweden. As well as the large MNCs, the region also hosts many dynamic small and medium-sized enterprises (SMEs). Some of these are stand-alone firms which export and deliver services to international markets, while others mainly supply services and components to the local affiliates of MNCs and are therefore part of the global innovation and production networks of these global firms. The region hosts the University of Karlstad. Whilst the University has played a role in local industrial development, in general academic researchers working in the technological and business fields relevant to local industrial development are few and isolated. Links between the university and local firms do exist, but they tend to be ad hoc and mainly focused on a few PhD placements.

The region also hosts a cluster organisation – PP – established in the late 1990s when concerns about the impact of the decline of the paper and pulp industries in the region motivated the municipality of Karlstad along with other public and private regional actors to establish a cluster organisation. PP was later reorganised into a business association (though it is still mainly a publicly funded organisation) and today has more than 100 member companies. The Management Board of PP includes representatives from the large MNCs as well as SMEs, the regional government of Värmland, the municipal government of Karlstad (which is meant to represent the wider community of the region), the University of Karlstad, as well as a RISE centre (RISE is a network of Research and Technology Organisations, wholly or partly owned by the Swedish state, which perform industrial research and innovation). The regional strategy of PP has been strongly influenced by the leading MNC affiliates operating in the region which are active participants of the Management Board of PP as well as by the Värmland regional government. It is important to note that PP with the support of the Värmland regional government has been the main driving force for the strategic regional transition towards a forest-based bio-economy.

6.4.1 The creation of new regional growth paths

The initial process of transition towards a regional bio-economy can be traced back to the mid- to late 2000s, when the Värmland regional government began to push industry cluster organisations such as PP to adopt a more strategic role in regional industrial development. A number of important initiatives associated with issues of sustainability and innovation were taken by PP in the early 2000s. Examples include the establishment in 2004 of the Packaging Greenhouse, an independent test laboratory for paper and engineering products and services, which played an important part in many regional development projects, as well as the Energy Square (launched in 2007), which aimed to develop new products and services that reduce energy consumption within the global pulp and paper industry.

However, broader attempts towards local industrial diversification were not successful during this period because the representatives of the leading paper and pulp firms in the region could not agree on a common strategy. One of the main obstacles to change at this stage was the fact that the main business of the traditional pulp and paper mills located in the region was packaging (an area of the paper and pulp industry that was not in decline) and they did not see the need for change. Other companies in the region such as machine suppliers and technology consultancy firms (many of them affiliates of large international engineering consultancy firms) were much more open to novel growth paths which opened up new business opportunities; however, their dependence on the large paper and pulp MNCs limited their capacity for change. What existed in the region at this stage was therefore a strongly embedded socio-technical system with no clear motivation for change from a business point of view. In this period, the lack of strategic coupling (or alignment) between MNCs and regional policy makers who perceived the need to create new local growth paths was a significant obstacle to structural change.

The arguments in favour of industrial diversification began to gain increasing support in the paper and pulp industry, both inside and outside the region, from 2012 to 2013 as it became increasingly clear that the traditional business models adopted by the major firms in the industry might not be commercially sustainable over the longer term. This change in the perception of business conditions was the result of both a fall in the global consumption of paper as well as an increasing awareness of the industry's negative environmental impact at a time when sustainable environmental development was becoming a policy priority both within Sweden and at the EU level (e.g. the Lund Declaration of 2009 and the European Climate Change Programme 2000–2004). Interviews with firms and policy makers in the region indicate that this change in business conditions was critical for the creation of a more receptive environment amongst all regional stakeholders for arguments in favour of structural and transformative change. Therefore, what we see is the beginning of a questioning by global industry leaders as well as regional bodies of the sustainability of the dominant socio-technical system in the paper and pulp industry.

Yet, within the region, the challenges associated with the development of a common strategy for industrial renewal and socio-technical transitions were significant. One of the main difficulties confronting PP and its Management Board was that given the importance of MNC affiliates in the local economy (both through their direct investment as well as their influence over suppliers through their control of regional value chains), it was critical to include these firms in any strategy of regional transformation. However, strategic decisions that define the activities of MNC affiliates are usually taken at headquarter level and are driven by considerations which are far removed from the needs of regional development. Therefore, though local management might support regional strategic initiatives which are positive for the locality as well and their affiliates, these proposals for change might not necessarily be supported by headquarters which have different priorities and perceptions of the needs of the whole MNC. Moreover, though local suppliers and service providers might welcome the idea of change, such support may weaken if local collaborative buyer–supplier relationships are disrupted.

What we saw in the Värmland Region at that time is that although important elements of the infrastructure, capabilities and networks that would have enabled the transition towards an environmentally sustainable socio-technical system did exist in the area, the lack of a common regional strategy that could have unified and mobilised local firms or given directionality to the investment of local firms was not present. In the case of this particular region, the deadlock was broken when the leadership of PP in collaboration with the Värmland regional government were able to formulate and articulate a strategy of regional transition towards sustainable development that won the support of global senior managers of MNCs and their regional affiliates as well as other regional firms and stakeholders. Critical to this process was the notion of a *forest-based bio-economy*, a strategy for growth and structural diversification that the mills located in the area could support and sell to headquarters.

6.4.2 A vision and strategy for transition towards a sustainable bio-economy

Critical to Värmland region's success in mobilising regional actors around a common strategy of regional as well as socio-technical transformation was the ability of the leadership of PP to formulate and articulate a regional strategy for growth based on the notion of a *forest-based bio-economy* involving the creation of new regional value chains based on the forestry sector and the use of lignin, a waste material already created by existing paper and pulp mills. As a member of the Management Board of PP noted:

> [T]hree and a half years ago [i.e. 2013], nobody here talked of a bio-economy. Nobody talked about cooperating and different value-chains from the forest, no one … so I think, when I look back, it was about selling a good story about the future. (Interview with a member of the Management Board of PP)

A critical element that galvanised the region into the formulation of a new strategy of regional transition that incorporated the need for sustainability and that later resulted in the notion of a *forest-based bio-economy* was the decision by PP to participate in Vinnova's (Sweden's national agency for innovation systems) Vinnväxt competition. Vinnväxt (Regional Growth through Dynamic Innovation Systems) is a national territorial-based programme which aims to promote sustainable regional growth by developing innovative local environments in specific fields. As part of its mission, Vinnväxt programmes aim to incentivise transformational change towards innovation-driven sustainable growth through the long-term funding of regional initiatives (usually a region receives funding for ten years). The competition for Vinnväxt funding requires regions to formulate a long-term strategy for regional renewal based on innovation and new collaborations (Vinnova 2016) and it explicitly asks regions to work towards ensuring that a proportion of the local economy is based on renewable technologies and practices (interview with Management Board Member of the Paper Province Vinnväxt Initiative):

> The clue was that they asked 'Where will you be in 15 years' time?' and they said 'There has to be a good proportion of renewable'. That was really the important thing. This led us to ask what is renewable? (Interview with a member of the Management Board of PP)

The process of application for Vinnova's Vinnväxt competition opened up an intensive period of collective search and learning amongst firms and regional institutional stakeholders represented on the Management Board of PP to identify a long-term regional sustainable growth strategy. Interestingly, as they prepared their application for the Vinnväxt competition, the Board of PP, including the representatives of the mills and their suppliers, were not clear what could be renewable in the local economy, and numerous workshops, discussions and regional SWOT (strengths, weaknesses, opportunities and threats) analysis were organised around this issue. In the early stages, firms could identify their strengths and the threats they faced, but little clarity existed with respect to future possibilities. Terms such as 'sustainability' and 'bio-economy' were used, but little clarity existed about what they meant.

In their process of search to clarify their strategy, PP came across the notion of a 'forest-based bio-economy', a concept which opened up a scenario of regional renewal that did not challenge the core business or power of existing paper and pulp MNCs. In a forest-based bio-economy, the production of paper and pulp would remain an important part of the regional economy, but the waste produced by traditional paper and pulp manufacturers – above all lignin and heat – would become the raw material for the emergence of new regional value chains. In this scenario, the existing paper and pulp mills could become important players in the creation of new local value chains because of their deep knowledge and capabilities of the process technologies that underpin the innovation in forest-based production. The new strategic idea was therefore to become a large-scale 'regional demonstrator of a forest-based bio-economy' where forest-based industries value chains can be verified, tested and supported. Interviews with local firms and representatives from PP also highlighted that the idea that local firms could contribute to the solution to climate change was an important element of the regional debate, which resulted in the notion of a regional transition towards a forest-based bio-economy gaining widespread support (interviews with representatives of firms and institutions members of the Management Board of PP).

6.4.3 New technological initiatives in the area

In 2013, PP was announced as the winner of Vinnväxt, opening a period of record investment (SEK 130 million over ten years)[1] in the forest industry of Värmland. Winning the competition has incentivised new investments in innovation and industrial renewal, as well as new types of collaborations and networks. At the time of interview, there were 10–15 major innovation projects supported by PP to develop technological and business processes associated with the forest-based bio-economy (this does not include the new investments by the paper mills and machinery and equipment suppliers, which are held under conditions of tight secrecy).

Examples of projects supported by PP include the following.

The LignoCity test-bed

Test-beds are physical or virtual environments in which companies, academia and other organisations can collaborate in the development, testing and introduction of new products, services, processes or organisational solutions. In the case of the LignoCity test-bed, the aim is to develop sustainable processes and products based on the use of lignin as a raw material (at the moment, the lignin value chains are still undeveloped), an area where the region has a strong competitive advantage as lignin is a by-product of pulp mills. The LignoCity test-bed is based on a unique Swedish technology that separates lignin from pulp mills, but can also be used to develop alternative technologies. The project involved opening RISE's demonstration plant to companies interested in evaluating and validating new refining concepts using lignin so that they can develop and scale up the technology to new climate-friendly fuels, chemicals and materials. The project is run by RISE and aims to shorten the time from idea to commercialisation. It is also expected to contribute to the establishment of new companies in Värmland. At the time that this study took place, approximately 20 companies were involved in the project. The project is also part of the region's Smart Specialisation Strategy (http://www.innventia.com/en/About-us/News1/LignoCity–a-new-centre-for-new-green-technologies).

Becoming a regional large-scale demonstrator

Interviews also show that there is a strong belief in PP that the creation of new value chains based on a forest-based bio-economy is not enough and that the success of this regional transformation requires that the region, including the regional government and municipalities, become large-scale 'demonstrators' and users of the bio-economy. The role of public actors in creating demand for bio-economy products, thereby contributing to the creation of a regional market, is seen as a critical element of the regional transition towards a bio-economy. A number of examples were given where public actors could become important users, for example, local hospitals using sheets made from cellulose and a regional and municipal transport system powered by biofuels. This follows already existing examples of municipally owned energy companies that use the waste product from local paper mills (e.g. hot water) as a source of energy.

Regional cooperation for industrial symbiosis within PP

In 2017, PP started a project on industrial symbiosis together with Linköping University, RISE and ten other regional partners. Industrial symbiosis means that residue from one industry becomes the raw material of another. Examples include waste energy from paper mills that can be used by other industries or municipal facilities, but also shared services and logistics solutions. In the project, PP and its partners have to map the different industrial residual streams in the region in order to find circular solutions with multiple beneficiaries.

6.5 The role of agency and the multi-scalar nature of the process of regional transitions to new socio-technical system

As discussed above, a critical factor in Värmland Region's ability to start a process of transition towards a regional forest-based bio-economy was the role of PP. Our interviews indicate that PP was able to develop and articulate a vision of the *forest-based bio-economy* capable of aligning the interests of different regional stakeholders, including the local affiliates of the large MNCs. Moreover, it consistently argued for this idea in the context of significant doubts and initial opposition from a number of powerful MNC affiliates operating in the region. Interviews with local R&D managers indicate that at the time that regional discussions were taking place, the concept of a regional strategy of development based on a bio-economy was very novel. As the R&D manager of one of the large paper mills interviewed explained:

> We were very early to actually put the bio-economy on the agenda – in the Board [Management Board of PP] and in the meetings, to really have that as a strategy. I think we were four or five years earlier than everybody

> else. We were very early adopters of this as a strategy, this is the thing … This would not have happened without Paper Province. (R&D manager, paper mill)

PP also played an important enabling role in the creation of new regional, national and international business and innovation networks that are developing the new forest-based technologies. Moreover, PP and its Management Board has also been a crucial forum for collective learning at the regional level. In collaboration with the Värmland regional government as part of the EU Smart Specialisation Strategy, PP has undertaken a detailed analysis of existing locally based industrial activities and capabilities, knowledge and technology institutions, and infrastructure and the changes required to bring about the transition towards a bio-economy. However, the formulation of the strategy of transitions towards a bio-economy was very strongly influenced by the notion that new strategies for regional development also needed to address societal challenges, in this case climate change (interviews with PP and the Värmland regional government). In this process PP also evolved from being predominantly an industry association representing the interests of firms in the region and creating opportunities for networking to an organisation able to give strategic leadership for a transition of socio-technical system in the region. Our interviews suggest that in this example of regional diversification which involved a process of transition to a new socio-technical system, normal business interactions and market mechanisms would not have resulted in a unified strategic vision. The role of policy-making institutions with a deep understanding of the strategic needs as well as the assets and competencies of the regions was central to the development and implementation of the strategy of regional transitions.

The multi-scalar nature of the transition has also been critical in this process of transition. Though very much focused on the development needs of the region and based on a deep understanding of local assets (the forest), knowledge and capabilities, as well as networks, the process of regional transition has been incentivised, informed and financed by a number of national and international factors. These influences were perceived at different levels, including: the initial incentive to develop a strategy for regional development; the formulation of a regional strategy that also needed to address societal goals; and the need to establish a strategic coupling between the needs of the region and those of the MNC affiliates operating in the area.

6.5.1 The role of regional government and EU policy on clusters and smart specialisation

The Värmland regional government is a member of the Management Board of PP and played a central role in the formulation and development of PP's strategy for regional transition towards a forest-based bio-economy. The contribution of the Värmland regional government has been influenced by its close collaboration with the EU on the formulation of regional strategies for cluster development and smart specialisation. In early to mid-2000s, the regional government set out to challenge the clusters in the region to take on a more strategic role by asking them what kind of local renewal they foresaw for their cluster. In the case of PP, this led to the formulation of the Vinnväxt proposal, which formulated the notion of the forest-based bio-economy.

6.5.2 Vinnova and Swedish national innovation strategy that addresses societal challenges

As discussed above, a critical point in the development of the region was the application for long-term funding from Vinnova's Vinnväxt programme. Vinnväxt's mission is to promote sustainable regional growth and to catalyse a broader transformational change in society towards innovation-driven sustainable growth. The competition demands the formulation of a strategy for regional renewal based on innovation and new collaborations as part of the proposal (Vinnova 2014) as well as a long-term strategic change that addresses issues related to the societal challenges such as climate change and environmental sustainability (interviews with representatives of the Paper Province Vinnväxt Initiative). In its formulation of the forest-based bio-economy, PP was largely influenced by the EU's strategy for a bio-economy and smart specialisation. The notion of addressing climate change has now been integrated into the region's Smart Specialisation Strategy for the region (interviews with representatives of the Paper Province Vinnvaxt Initiative).

6.5.3 The necessity for strategic coupling between the needs of the regions and the MNC affiliates operating in the region

As discussed above, the region hosts a number of MNC affiliates which are deeply embedded in the local economy and are critical to the competences of the region. These firms are also tightly integrated into the knowledge and innovation networks of their parent companies. This double-embeddedness enables these firms to play a significant role in the upgrading of the innovative and manufacturing capabilities of the locality as they can become conduits for the entry of state-of-the-art knowledge into the region. Local affiliates of MNCs can play a significant role in regional renewal when the strategic shifts in the region match the strategic needs of the MNC as a whole. The key point is that the strategic decisions of MNCs are not taken locally, nor are they driven by the needs for regional development; rather, they are driven by the need to meet the interests of global shareholders. When there is strategic convergence between regional development and the needs of MNCs, these firms can bring the significant resources in terms of finance, knowledge and capabilities needed to bring about regional strategic shifts. However, when no strategic match is possible, local MNC affiliates can paralyse regional renewal (as seen in

PP before 2012) or even undermine it by destroying local competences if they withdraw from the area.

The case of PP shows that aligning the interests and strategies of the various MNCs operating in the area and achieving a strategic match between them and the needs for regional renewal can be extremely complex and is often contingent on major drivers for societal change outside the control of the region (in this case major changes in societal values with respect to environmental sustainability and/or radical changes in technology which threaten the existing business models of MNCs).

6.6 Conclusion

This chapter has discussed the initial experiences of regional transition from the traditional manufacture of paper and pulp towards a sustainable forest-based bio-economy. This transformational change represents both a change in the socio-spatial composition of a regional economy as well as a change of socio-technical systems. These major transformations, though still in their initial stages, have been made possible because of the region's deep knowledge of forest-based process technologies and the ability of PP as a cluster organisation to formulate a vision and strategy of regional transformation that unified the main local stakeholders. Directly addressing climate change as a major societal challenge is a central element of the regional diversification strategy, galvanising regional, national and EU support for the new growth path.

The study highlights the role of regional policy-making bodies with a deep understanding of the strategic needs as well as the assets and competencies of their regions as critical agents of regional renewal. This is associated with their ability to formulate new strategies of regional transformative change and mobilise regional stakeholders in processes of learning, searching and implementation. In our study, the ability of regional bodies to play this role was strongly influenced by their interactions with national and EU bodies, which informed, supported and funded their efforts to promote regional transitions.

In the case of a region where MNC affiliates play such a strong role in the local economy, transformational change of socio-technical system required the strategic coupling between the new regional growth paths and the long-term objectives of the global MNCs in the area. In this particular case, a strategic coupling was possible because the sustainability of the existing socio-technical system was beginning to be questioned not only at a regional level but also at a global level, and because the new strategies for regional transformation did not challenge the core business or power of existing MNCs. On the contrary, the notion of the forest-based bio-economy can open up a wide range of new business opportunities for existing firms. However, the experience of the region also shows that when no strategic coupling is achieved, MNCs can block efforts towards both regional diversification when these involve changes in socio-technical systems.

Note

1 The total project budget for PP is SEK 130 million over ten years. Half of the funding comes from Vinnova and half from regional co-funders, such as Värmland Region, Karlstad University, the Värmland municipalities, the County Administrative Board, the County Council, the Forest Board and the PP member companies. See https://www.kau.se/en/research/collaboration-researchers/research-collaboration/vinnvaxt-paper-province-20.

References

Asheim, B.T., Boschma, R. and Cooke, P. 2011. Constructing regional advantage: platform policies based on related variety and differentiated knowledge bases. *Regional Studies*, 45(7): 893–904.

Boschma, R. 2017. Relatedness as driver of regional diversification: a research agenda. *Regional Studies*, 51(3): 351–364.

Boschma, R., Coenen, L., Frenken, K. and Truffer, B. 2017. Towards a theory of regional diversification: combining insights from evolutionary economic geography and transition studies. *Regional Studies*, 51(1): 31–45.

Castaldi, C., Frenken, K and Los, B. 2015. Related variety, unrelated variety and technological breakthrough: an analysis of US state-level patenting. *Regional Studies*, 49: 767–781.

Coe, N., Hess, M., Yeung, H.W.-C., Dicken, P. and Henderson J. 2004. Globalizing regional development: a global production networks perspective, *Transactions of the Institute of British Geographers*, ns 29(4): 468–484.

Coe, N. and Yeung, H.W.-C. 2015. *Global Production Networks: Theorizing Economic Development in an Interconnected World*. Oxford University Press.

Coenen, L., Hansen, T. and Rekers, J.V. 2015. Innovative policy for grand challenges: an economic geography perspective. *Geography Compass*, 9(9): 483–496.

Dunning, J. and Lundan, S. 2008. *Multinational Enterprises and the Global Economy*, 2nd edn. Edward Elgar.

Formas. 2012. Swedish Research and Innovation Strategy for a Bio-based Economy. Swedish Research Council for Environment, Agricultural Sciences and Spatial Planning. Available at: https://www.formas.se/download/18.462d60ec167c69393b91e60f/1549956092919/Strategy_Biobased_Ekonomy_hela.pdf.

Frenken, K., van Oort, F.G. and Verburg, T. 2007. Related variety, unrelated variety and regional economic growth. *Regional Studies*, 41: 685–697.

Geels, F.W. 2004. From sectoral systems of innovation to socio-technical systems: insights about dynamics and change from sociology and institutional theory. *Research Policy*, 33: 897–920.

Geels, F.W. 2011. The multi-level perspective on sustainability transitions: responses to seven criticisms. *Environmental Innovation and Societal Transitions*, 1: 24–40.

Immarino, S. 2005. An evolutionary integrated view of regional systems of innovation: concepts, measures and historical perspectives. *Regional Planning Studies*, 13(4): 497–519.

Neffke, F., Matté, H., Boschma, R. and Henning, M., 2016, Agents of structural change: the role of firms and entrepreneurs in regional diversification. Papers in Evolutionary Economic Geography, Utrecht University.

Nefket, F., Henning, M. and Boschma, R. 2011. How do regions diversify over time? Industry relatedness and the development of new growth paths in regions. *Economic Geography*, 87: 237–265.

Nelson, R.R. 1994. The co-evolution of technology, industrial structure, and supporting institutions. *Industrial and Corporate Change*, 3(1): 47–63.

Nelson, R.R. and Winter, S. 1982. *An Evolutionary Theory of Economic Change*. Harvard University Press.

Rothaermel, F.T. 2001. Incumbent's advantage through exploiting complementary assets via interfirm cooperation. *Strategic Management Journal*, 22: 687–699.

Smith, A., Stirling, A. and Berkhout, F. (2005) The governance of sustainable socio-technical transitions. *Research Policy*, 34(10): 1491–1510.

Teece, D.J. 1986. Profiting from technological innovation: implications for integration, collaboration, licensing and public policy. *Research Policy*, 15(6): 285–305.

Vinnova (2016) *Viinvaxt. A Programme Renewing and Moving Sweden Ahead.* Vinnova.

7 Driving factors in the adoption of Industry 4.0 technologies

An investigation of SMEs

Giancarlo Corò and Mario Volpe

7.1 Introduction

The growing diffusion of a new generation of digital technologies is leading to innovations in communication, production and work to such an extent that several scholars agree that it amounts to new industrial revolution (Bianchi and Labory 2018; Brynjolfsson and McAfee 2014; McQuivey 2013; Schwab 2016). This digital revolution, or Industry 4.0 (I4.0), is expected to increase flexibility, reduce lead times, allow mass customization, enable new services based on big data and create appealing work structures (Heng 2014). Productivity gains might be substantial, opening up opportunities in every industry. At the same time, such changes present a number of challenges, the most significant being increasing job substitution and social inequality (Cowen 2013; Frey and Osbourne 2017).

Given the framework presented in Chapter 1, the aim of this chapter is to provide some empirical evidence of the enabling factors that can assist firms' adoption of specific technologies related to I4.0. Drawing on Frey and Osbourne's (2017) argument on the impact of computerization on jobs, our core objective is to explore the relationship between the adoption of I4.0 technologies and either job creation or destruction. Moreover, we are interested in analysing the synergies between the use of digital technologies and firms' internationalization and financial structure.

There are three main contributions that this chapter makes to the current debate. The first is to provide empirical evidence on the degree of adoption of specific I4.0 technologies by different types of firms, using primary data collected via a survey. Despite the amount of attention that I4.0 has received in the media and in the policy debate, little robust evidence is available on the diffusion of such technologies. The second contribution of is to profile what types of firms are more likely to adopt specific technologies; we find that such firms are more likely to employ high-skill workers, have better links with international markets and have good financial leverage. In other words, there are some enabling factors that facilitate firms' adoption of I4.0 technologies. Moreover, it has emerged that firms tend to adopt combinations of such technologies rather than a single one, which is consistent with the theoretical framework of I4.0 (Platform I4.0 2015). Finally, our evidence shows that firms adopting advanced digital technologies also tend to increase their employment in the short term.

Drawing on Arthur (2009), technology is defined here as an assemblage of practices and components, collections or toolboxes to reach human goals. From this perspective, we consider I4.0 as a cluster of technologies characterized by high levels of connectivity that allow data and information integration in the production and consumption activities. More specifically, we consider I4.0 as including the following seven technologies: robotics, the industrial Internet of Things (IoT), smart products, additive manufacturing (3D printing), big data, augmented reality and the virtualization of IT systems (cloud computing). For the purposes of this work, the expressions 'digital technologies' and 'I4.0 technologies' are interchangeable, since they both refer to the above-listed technologies in line with, among others, the EU definition as spelt out in the I4.0 and digital agendas (EU Parliament 2015a, 2015b) following the German policy that introduced the term *Industrie 4.0* for the first time (Kagermann et al. 2013).

The chapter will proceed as follows. Section 7.2 will discuss the economic literature on the potential of digital innovation and technologies for businesses. Section 7.3 will discuss the uptake of the I4.0 model in Italy. Section 7.4 will present the data collection and outline the methodology employed in the analysis. Sections 7.5 and 7.6 will describe the main findings of the survey and will discuss the relationship between adoption of digital technologies and three different enabling factors: internationalization, financial structure and human capital. Section 7.7 will summarize with a few concluding remarks.

7.2 Digital innovation and technological upgrading

The world of digital technologies is commonly linked to what is now called 'Industry 4.0' (Baur and Wee 2015). This, in turn, is usually associated with the emergence of cyber-physical systems – i.e. highly automated and hyper-connected production processes – that are expected to redraw the organization of production inside the factory (Broy 2013), as well as involving the reorganization of supply chains (Platform I4.0 2015) and a reconceptualization of both products and processes (Schmidt et al. 2015). Therefore, the new industrial paradigm is expected to manifest itself in a multi-faceted way with transformations that are widespread and disruptive.

This idea of I4.0 is linked to similar paradigms that have been often referred to as 'Advanced Manufacturing', 'Integrated Industry', 'Smart Industry' or 'Smart Manufacturing' (Hermann et al. 2015). These latter concepts are similar, but tend to emphasize distinct aspects; therefore, there is no consensus on *one* definition of I4.0 (Hermann et al. 2015; Liao et al. 2017). The difficulty in defining the phenomenon is partly due to the different perceptions that companies and stakeholders hold regarding digitization and I4.0. Sommer (2015) has shown that the importance of change is widely recognized, even though very few companies are ready to invest, or are already investing, in that direction.

In the current debate, I4.0 is often assumed to be linked to the Fourth Industrial Revolution (Schwab 2016), following the previous three that are widely accepted in the literature and are associated, respectively, with steam power, electricity and computerization (Rullani 1989). Other authors, by contrast, consider today's digital innovation still as the tail end of the Third Industrial Revolution that started in the 1970s with the introduction of computers in business processes (Gordon 2016). According to Thames and Schaefer (2016), the main goals of I4.0 are to achieve a higher level of productivity and efficiency, as well as a higher level of automation. These will allow mass customization of products, fast adaptation of production chains, innovative value chain organizations, and new types of services and business models (Shafiq et al. 2015, 2016). The economic potential of this transformation could be huge (Rüßmann et al. 2015), but its evaluation is very difficult because of the vast number of technologies involved and of the different maturity levels for each of the technologies (Schröder 2016; Hermann 2015; Hofmann and Rüsch 2017). For a more detailed literature review and discussion of I4.0, see Liao et al. (2017), Lu (2017) and Kang et al. (2016).

Although the aim of this chapter is not to elaborate on whether I4.0 is associated either with a revolutionary industrial paradigm shift (Schwab 2016) or with an evolutionary process of digitalization that started in the 1970s (Gordon 2016), it is worth highlighting a couple of points that will help frame the following empirical analysis. Firstly, there are some elements of originality in the current phase of digitalization that distinguish 'Industry 4.0' from the computerization of the 1970s and 1980s, such as the combination of different technologies into cyber-physical systems and cloud-based manufacturing (Thames and Schaefer 2016). In particular, we recall some elements of the literature on digitalization and ICT technologies that can also apply to I4.0, but that have not yet been explicitly investigated by the I4.0 literature. The existing literature on ICT has mainly highlighted the difficulties in estimating the value generated by digital technologies (Grover and Kohli 2012; Yoo et al. 2012) and, consequently, in assessing the impact of the ongoing transformation. Due to the ever-increasing technological integration, the 'digital' side is difficult to evaluate separately from the 'non-digital' side.

Secondly, another problem is represented by the lack of shared criteria to identify what makes a business 'digital' or part of the I4.0 paradigm. Thus, the implementation and adoption of digital technologies by firms surely depend on the IT infrastructure. Although these are essential for further development, it may be misleading to consider this digital upgrading only as a part of an evolved ICT system (OECD 2014). Previous studies have also emphasized that digitalization and IT promote access to innovative ideas (Pisano and Verganti 2008), mainly sustaining the knowledge flow (Katz and Rice 2002) and changing how individuals interact (Hinds and Kiesler 2002). Therefore, openness and the creation of networks are essential in order for firms to compete. Firms will improve the relationship between individuals and business practices with internet-based technologies (Vaccaro and Madsen 2009), thus enabling digital technologies to create new types of innovation processes (Henfridsson et al. 2014).

Thirdly, firms need to design and implement an appropriate joint IT and business strategy depending on their competitive context, creating a digital organization and IT capabilities in order ultimately to be able to create value from digital innovation (Fichman 2012). Mere investments in IT infrastructure and related technologies are not enough, even though a well-designed IT architecture is essential to develop new products and processes (Fink 2007). Evidence shows that social and organizational capital both have a positive relationship with the adoption of innovations (Dost et al. 2016).

Fourthly, the ability to collect and manage multiple types of information is crucial for the innovation and exploitation of digital technologies (OECD 2015). Managing big data (Lycett 2013) is the key to creating value, employing information that is usually already available and whose potential only needs recognition in order to be released (Fosso Wamba et al. 2015). No evidence of a widespread awareness of the importance of data is available, as academics have in fact put forward very few models to evaluate the maturity level of data management (Comuzzi and Patel 2016). Thus, the main barriers to create value from data management and analytics are mainly managerial and cultural at the firm level rather than related to the technology itself (La Valle et al. 2011). Overcoming such barriers could lead to an improvement in firms' intellectual and human capital (Secundo et al. 2017), which might benefit both businesses and individuals. Furthermore, the impact of data management is not limited to already existing business models; it can also enable the creation of brand new data-driven business models (Hartmann et al. 2016).

Further, evidence shows that investments that do not involve human capital are less likely to lead to productivity gains, especially in small firms (Díaz-Chao et al. 2015). In fact, a positive relationship between product, service and process innovations and 'innovative human capital' has also been observed (McGuirk et al. 2015). Although there is no consensus that improving human and intellectual capital will enhance innovation in the broader sense (Buenechea-Elberdin 2017), it seems essential to accomplish digital transformation. For instance, Cirillo (2016) shows that hi-tech industries, influenced by international contexts, usually show greater productivity, accompanied by employment growth associated with high-skilled talent. Conversely, low-tech industries require lower-skilled workers, command lower wages and rely on more flexible labour. At present, learning by doing and intra-firm training are both essential. Evidence from Evangelista et al. (2014) indicates that in order to leverage the adoption of digital technologies, life-long learning seems to be more important than formal education.

Finally, openness to international markets has a positive impact on innovation activities in both large and small enterprises (Boermans and Roelfsema 2016). Access to international markets allows firms to benefit from economies of scale to pay back the fixed costs of innovation, and enables entrepreneurs, technicians and managers to be part of wider knowledge networks. A positive link exists not only between internationalization and innovation, but also between these two factors and productivity (Altomonte et al. 2013). Moreover, several empirical studies confirm a positive correlation between the use of digital technologies and export activities (Morgan-Thomas and Jones 2009; Higón and Driffield 2011; Bianchi et al. 2016; Cassetta et al. 2016). However, almost all of them consider the front-end applications of digitalization, using variables such as the use of ICT, social media and e-commerce. Conversely, the digitalization of productive processes has so far been under-studied.

7.3 Industry 4.0 in Italy

I4.0 has become a highly debated topic in Italy only in the last couple of years. For a long time, the discussion concerned a superficial interpretation of the German model, often focusing on a few single technologies. Recently, the attention has been shifting towards a more holistic and realistic vision.

From recent studies (Federmeccanica 2016; Fondazione Nord-Est 2015), it has emerged that the adoption processes of some technologies seem to be already in place. Indeed, views collected from entrepreneurs and managers seem to suggest that some technologies – such as additive printing, 3D scanning and advanced cutting systems – are basically an evolution of technologies already in use, greatly reducing the costs involved in the adoption of their later generations. On the other hand, the adoption of the IoT and virtual reality is, for instance, still limited and distant from many businesses' daily activities. This can be explained by the radical change of technological paradigm under way and thus of the consequent new business models that many of these technological solutions involve (e.g. in relation to the most extreme forms of servitization). In such a delicate transition, Italian firms tend to rely too little on the knowledge and expertise they could access from universities and research centres.

It is clear that the debate on the Fourth Industrial Revolution has so far been strongly linked to technological aspects, mostly driven by the narrow German model that has led the way. This technological primacy has contributed to creating a climate of mistrust and concern amongst businesses, especially amongst small and medium-sized firms which cannot fully understand the potentials that such technologies present to them. These doubts also arose from the way in which I4.0 was presented to companies with a strong emphasis placed on the adoption of, for instance, robotics, sensoring and relatively high-cost technologies, which small businesses have struggled to recognize as relevant for them, given the business model that has characterized their competitive advantage for years. Therefore, it is crucial to shift the debate on I4.0 from the mere technological aspects to a more systemic vision that has been captured in this volume using the term Industry 4.0+.

The Italian government launched a national plan to support the upgrading of firms' machinery stocks in 2016: the 'Piano Industria 4.0'. This provided financial support to firms of any size and industry to buy new machinery and equipment. Superficially, this seems to be endorsing an understanding of I4.0 as purely associated with the technological content of firms' capital stocks; however, the small size of the majority of Italian firms had prevented them in the recent past from undertaking the necessary investments to keep up with advances in technology. Besides, Italy has a very competitive and export-oriented mechanical engineering sector that nevertheless benefited from a boost in domestic demand. Therefore, the government plan must be understood as acting on two levels: firstly, to raise awareness of what I4.0 might mean and imply; and, secondly, to encourage firms to inject some technological upgrading in their production. The initial plan expected a private commitment of over €56 billion for the period 2017–2020, in view of a public commitment of around €24 billion.

7.4 Case study of I4.0 in Veneto

To analyse the diffusion of digital technologies in Veneto, a survey was administered to manufacturing, construction and services companies during the autumn of 2015. The aim of the survey was to investigate the awareness and diffusion among firms of the following technologies: automation and robotics, the industrial IoT, smart products, additive manufacturing, mixed reality, big data and the virtualization of IT systems. The survey also included in-depth questions on additive manufacturing. Firm case studies with structured interviews followed the collection of data.

7.4.1 Data and methodology

Primary data collection was carried out through an online survey administered in the autumn of 2015 to a stratified sample of firms in the Veneto region; the survey was facilitated by the Chamber of Commerce of Treviso and Belluno. The targeted sample of firms for the survey was selected according to the following criteria: manufacturing firms must have had at least six employees and a minimum of €1 million production value; construction firms must have had more than 20 employees; and service firms must have had at least three employees and a minimum production value of €250,000.

Table 7.1 shows the number of respondents, divided by sector. Sectors were identified according to the NACE rev. 2 classification. The sub-division was

Table 7.1 Respondents by sector: absolute numbers and percentages

Sector	*Respondents*	*Percentage of total*
Manufacturing	633	71.04
Construction	56	6.27
Services	202	22.69
Total	891	100

Source: Authors' elaboration.

operated as follows: manufacturing NACE section C; construction NACE section F; and services NACE sections J and M. The total number of respondents was respectively 633, 51 and 207; the sample is representative in terms of company size and industry.[1]

Firms were asked if they were familiar with and if they used any of the following digital technologies: robotics and automation, the industrial IoT, smart products, 3D printing, big data, mixed reality (virtual and augmented reality) and virtualization of IT systems. The questionnaire included an accurate definition of each technology in order to clarify and facilitate the comprehension of the task. In the construction and service sectors, 'digital users' were defined as firms adopting at least *one* of the digital technologies, and in the manufacturing sector, 'digital users' were firms that adopted at least *two* different technologies. This distinction was necessary in order to shed light on the effects of a combination of different technologies; this appears to be very important for the manufacturing sector.

For all surveyed firms, we were also able to collect administrative data on employment, trade and financial structure from secondary sources for the years 2007–2014. Data on human capital were sourced from 'Veneto Lavoro', the Regional Agency that records all the hiring and cessation movements occurring in the labour market. Data on import and export activities were extracted from the Infocamere and ISTAT databases. Finally, financial data were accessed from the AIDA database (the Italian database available from BvD). These three databases were aligned with the survey database, allowing us to build a unique firm-based dataset with information on the composition of the workforce, the import and export activities, and the financial structure. We analysed this rich database with robust descriptive statistics (Sections 7.5 and 7.6 below).

7.5 Main findings

7.5.1 Awareness and adoption of new digital technologies

The diffusion of digital technologies in the Veneto region varies across industries. The shares of digital users (as defined above) in the manufacturing and construction sectors are respectively 37% and 33%, while it is 64% for services. Therefore, awareness of digital technologies seems to be higher in services and lower in construction. We find the existence of different technological frontiers among sectors. Intensity of use and types of technologies are significantly different depending on firms' activity.

There is also an important gap between levels of awareness and adoption of technologies. Both seem to be the highest in relation to additive manufacturing: 60% of firms declare that they know of the technology, but less than 10% use it. The difference in this case – as well as for other technologies – is possibly due to the fact that firms do not use a specific technology in their specific business, but part of the adoption gap can also be explained by a superficial knowledge by firms of the possibilities and impact of such digital technologies on their business.

Analysing additive manufacturing in particular, what emerges is that it is only used in less than 10% of firms and it is weakly integrated in business processes. We find that smaller firms have been able to better integrate 3D printing technology in their business and there is no significant impact of the technology on the labour market. Very few jobs were created and in most cases its introduction did not require particular adjustments in terms of labour organization. Furthermore, 3D printing technology is still linked to prototyping, with more than 90% of firms using it for that purpose. Less than 30% of respondents declared that they use additive manufacturing for the fabrication of finished or usable products.

Given its sectoral specialization, Italy could greatly benefit from the large number of applications related to the adoption of the latest generations of additive manufacturing technology (Bai et al. 2017). However, the level of adoption in Veneto is still too limited: we find that 51% of firms are additive-detached, 37% are additive-integrated and only 12% can be considered as additive-oriented. Table 7.2 shows our findings in terms of firms' awareness and adoption of digital technologies. It is also worth noting the size of the gap between the firms that declare that they are familiar with some digital technologies and those that actually use them. As expected, we find considerable differences in the diffusion of digital technologies among sectors, with the virtualization of IT systems being the most widely adopted technology, whereas others are more sector-specific.

No relationship between the size of firms and the number of technologies adopted was found. This evidence is consistent with the idea of firms having their own technology frontiers, meaning that each firm selects a specific set of technologies and combines them according to their own specific needs and activities. For example, among the manufacturers of plastic products, it can be noted that 89% of them use robotics or automation, while none of them declare that they have introduced sensors in 'smart' products.

7.5.2 Clusters of technologies

We would argue that the multiple use of technologies can be more significant than the adoption of a single technology for firms. Having found that the size of firms does not play any role in relation to technological adoption, we began to explore whether firms' adoption could depend more on firms' specific technological frontiers or families of technologies they related to because of the sector or activities in which they were specialized. Within this logic, individual technologies were grouped together on the basis of complementarity. Figure 7.1 maps what we found from our survey in terms of technological combinations that firms disclosed. In this network of technologies, the size of the nodes denotes how many times a single technology is used together with another, while the thickness of the links represents how much two technologies

Table 7.2 Awareness and adoption of digital technologies (% of total)

Technology	*Manufacturing*		*Construction*		*Services*		*Total*	
	Knowledge	*Use*	*Knowledge*	*Use*	*Knowledge*	*Use*	*Knowledge*	*Use*
Robotics	52.66	26.59	32.08	4.04	29.81	7.68	48.82	24.13
Industrial IoT	37.04	13.84	21.49	9.37	33.06	9.25	38.16	15.71
Smart products	27.35	5.23	23.05	9.37	28.86	7.78	30.98	7.63
3D printing	58.57	8.34	44.06	1.56	52.27	6.68	58.47	13.13
Big data	25.60	9.49	28.18	12.94	36.49	20.96	34.34	17.06
Mixed reality	32.45	6.36	30.66	4.04	37.60	16.96	38.61	11.90
Virtualization of IT systems	39.93	16.87	40.32	30.22	55.56	45.21	53.65	33.67

Source: Authors' elaboration.

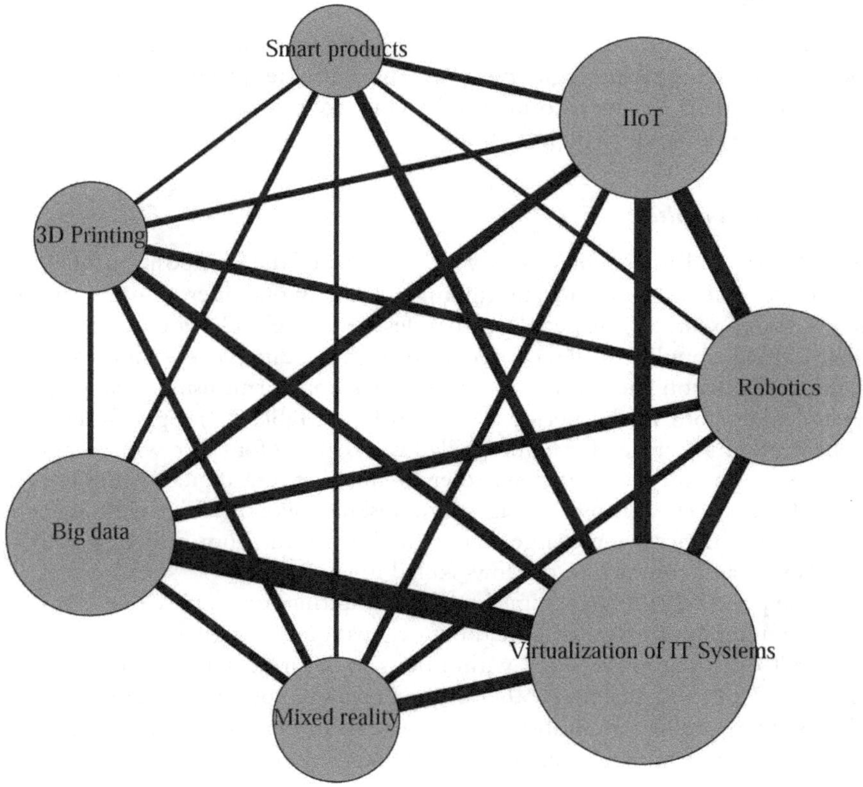

Figure 7.1 Combination of different technologies.

Source: Authors' elaboration.

Notes: The dimension of vertices expresses the number of times a single technology is used together with another. The width of the lines represents the number of times the two technologies are used together.

are used together. Some technologies show a higher level of complementarity than others. Potential clusters of technologies seem to emerge around robotics, the industrial IoT, big data and the virtualization of IT systems. This makes sense since all these technologies are often used together in advanced automation processes. Our evidence is coherent with the theoretical framework of I4.0, where value is created by combining different technologies (Schimtd et al. 2015). Furthermore, the creation of cyber-physical systems, which are the result of the application of I4.0 technologies, necessarily requires the combined adoption of multiple technologies such as robotics, the IoT and big data (Broy 2013; Evangelista et al. 2014).

7.6 Enabling factors

We move on to investigate three other enabling factors impacting on the adoption of digital technologies by firms. These are the quality of human capital in firms, their openness to international markets and their financial structure. We consider each of them in turn.

7.6.1 Human capital

Digital users and non-digital users vary in terms of the composition of their workforce. The most significant finding is that digital users employ more highly skilled workers, i.e. people with a degree or high school education (see Table 7.3). This applies to all sectors, even though the difference is more evident in the construction and service sectors. Furthermore, firms using technologies created more jobs in the period 2012–2014 (see Table 7.4). Specifically, the highest growth occurred for highly skilled workers and for those with a degree. Another important fact is that whether or not they use digital technologies, most of the surveyed firms no longer hire unskilled workers. This will result in firms having an increasingly large share of highly and medium-skilled people in their labour and contracting out low-skilled functions.

In the period 2012–2014, digital users (accounting for roughly one-third of the total number of firms) exhibited net occupational growth, recruiting more than 75% of all the jobs created within the sample firms. This is only partially consistent with evidence from other major European countries, where job creation is led by product innovation and an increase in value added (Cirillo 2016). Investments in technology can be interpreted as process innovation and should

Table 7.3 Composition of the workforce in 2014 (% of total employment)

	Manufacturing		*Construction*		*Services*		*Total*	
	Digital users	*Digital non-users*	*Digital users*	*Digital non-users*	*Digital users*	*Digital non-users*	*Digital users*	*Digital non-users*
No skills	12.31	10.91	10.64	16.65	0.49	3.88	10.90	10.80
Low skills	46.18	50.81	36.17	55.81	2.55	10.60	40.75	48.25
Medium skills	16.65	16.93	21.28	13.53	34.71	54.96	18.93	19.44
High skills	24.85	21.35	31.91	14.01	62.26	30.56	29.42	21.51
No academic qualifications	1.87	2.79	2.98	5.24	0.45	1.61	1.77	2.87
Compulsory schooling	38.41	46.54	36.14	59.81	4.57	14.13	34.33	45.03
High school	45.02	42.61	45.47	30.78	56.92	49.69	46.43	42.33
Degree	14.70	8.05	15.41	4.17	38.06	34.57	17.47	9.77

Source: Authors' elaboration.

Table 7.4 Employment growth 2012–2014 (% of total employment growth)

	Manufacturing		*Construction*		*Services*		*Total*	
	Digital users	*Digital non-users*	*Digital users*	*Digital non-users*	*Digital users*	*Digital non-users*	*Digital users*	*Digital non-users*
No skills	-1.24	-5.16	-9.52	21.93	-20.00	9.68	-1.88	-2.52
Low skills	6.67	1.43	0.31	6.15	13.51	10.71	6.35	1.93
Medium skills	6.76	3.75	-2.56	1.80	2.88	4.10	5.27	3.73
High skills	12.48	5.73	11.76	1.74	2.81	-2.19	10.01	4.68
Without academic qualifications	-5.53	5.31	-14.81	160.00	40.00	-7.14	-5.62	13.14
Compulsory schooling	-0.40	-4.15	-0.71	4.95	-5.33	-6.56	-0.50	-3.44
High school	12.18	8.14	1.15	0.88	3.76	5.53	10.22	7.51
Degree	23.28	12.58	19.00	29.17	1.72	4.49	16.78	10.73

Source: Authors' elaboration.

thereby have a negative impact on employment; however, our findings suggest that process innovation can be associated with employment growth, driven by productivity growth and new skills requirements. The data in Table 7.4 have to be interpreted in the light of the severe economic crisis that plagued the Veneto production base. Our findings suggest that access to high-skill labour was able to compensate for the negative business environment of the manufacturing and construction sectors in the mid-2010s; however, this was not the case for services, probably because the latter focused too narrowly on the local market (see Table 7.5).

7.6.2 Firms' internationalization

Firms' openness to international markets is one of the factors that enable and accelerate the adoption and diffusion of digital technologies. Our findings on the relationship between firms' import/export activities and firms' adoption of digital technologies are reported in Tables 7.5 and 7.6.

In the present analysis, we find that digital users are more open to international markets. The openness to international markets plays a significant role, but only if digital users are strictly defined (i.e. at least three technologies are used). Such a relationship can be seen from two different perspectives. Firstly, digital technologies can represent both a requirement for and a consequence of internationalization. Competing in international markets is likely to be more challenging than doing so in local markets, forcing firms to invest in digital technologies in order for them to reach productivity levels comparable to those of their international competitors. Thus, digital users have effectively higher

Table 7.5 Share of respondents that have export activities, divided by digital use (% of total)

	Digital users		*Digital non-users*	
	Export	*Do not export*	*Export*	*Do not export*
Construction	30.35	69.65	8.66	91.34
Manufacturing	73.69	26.31	58.27	41.73
Services	8.98	91.02	3.70	96.3

Source: Authors' elaboration.

Table 7.6 Share of respondents that have import activities, divided by digital use (% of total)

	Digital users		*Digital non-users*	
	Import	*Do not import*	*Import*	*Do not import*
Construction	48.51	51.49	10.59	89.41
Manufacturing	57.95	42.05	47.39	52.61
Services	5.83	94.17	8.30	91.70

Source: Authors' elaboration.

productivity performances than digital non-users. Secondly, engaging in import and export suggests that such internationally exposed firms operate in global value chains; for them, digital adoption might be necessary in order to collaborate with foreign partners in the supply chains.

7.6.3 Financial structure and economic performance

We finally looked at the financial position of firms in order to shed light on the relationship between the adoption of digital technologies and firms' economic performance, as well as looking at firms' access to capital. Specifically, the present investigation focused on the profitability (return on sales (ROS), return on equity (ROE) and return on investment (ROI)), productivity (value added per employee) and capital composition (Leverage, Net Financial Position and Debt/Equity) of firms (see Table 7.7 for details).

Digital users generally show a better financial composition (see Table 7.7). No great differences are evident on the leverage ratios, all being well below the limit of 3%. Additionally, the net financial position (NFP) is considerably higher for firms adopting digital technologies than for firms not adopting digital technologies.

Finally, considering profitability ratios, higher returns can be observed for firms that employ digital technologies in the construction and service sectors. Conversely, for manufacturing firms, the findings are less clear. In particular,

Table 7.7 Average financial ratios, separating the firms that adopt digital technologies from those that do not

	Manufacturing		*Construction*		*Services*	
	Digital users	*Digital non-users*	*Digital users*	*Digital non-users*	*Digital users*	*Digital non-users*
ROS	6.17	4.78	5.67	1.90	5.75	1.79
ROE	13.65	14.73	19.61	8.12	23.71	6.92
ROI	15.47	15.70	6.36	1.35	32.04	3.86
Value added per employee	65.27	56.45	73.89	49.98	60.62	65.08
Leverage (L)	1.28	1.52	2.34	1.29	1.17	2.07
Net financial position (NFP)	4.413	669	11.467	1.919	121	973
Debt/equity	1.03	0.82	0.70	1.80	0.47	1.37

Source: Authors' elaboration.

Note: The value added per employee and the net financial position are reported in thousands of €. ROS, ROE, ROI and Leverage are percentages.

digital users show a higher return on sales ratio, while ROE and ROI are higher for digital non-users. Nevertheless, the differences are not particularly significant. Additionally, the value added per employee ratio is higher for digital users in the manufacturing and construction sectors; however, in the service sector, digital users show a lower productivity ratio, suggesting that for them, the adoption of digital technologies does not translate into significant improvements in productivity.

However, we found the low profitability ratios for digital users in the manufacturing sector puzzling and we tried to understand the reasons for this. Our analysis finds that firms are adopting the first wave of I4.0 technologies, but have problems that are often related to learning processes. Moreover, innovative firms seems to have higher capital intensity and greater equity and risk capital in their financial position. This kind of capital allows firms to overcome asymmetric information constraining access to credit access and allows them to have more time to benefit from the initial investment.

Secondly, we find that human capital is most important in firms' value added; we looked at the ratio labour cost (wL) over value added (VA) and compared it with high capital intensity. We find that as firms employ more highly skilled employees, their wage bill increases and so does the wL/VA ratio. In other words, firms' lower business profitability in the short term is explained by investment in greater skills and to a lesser extent in fixed capital. Table 7.8 below shows human capital does not account for a greater share of value-added digital users across all sectors. Therefore, the explanation for the low profitability of manufacturing digital users might lie in the reinvestment of the created value and the longer-run ROI. The adoption of digital technologies requires a series of risk investments, such that the higher value created

Table 7.8 Distribution of the value added between human and risk capital

	Manufacturing		*Construction*		*Services*	
	Digital users	*Digital non-users*	*Digital users*	*Digital non-users*	*Digital users*	*Digital non-users*
wL/VA	0.63	0.76	0.71	0.86	0.71	0.84
EBITDA/VA	0.37	0.24	0.28	0.11	0.27	-0.02
EBIT/VA	0.26	0.12	0.19	0.03	0.17	-0.40

Source: Authors' elaboration

Note: Each indicator is calculated as an average over the last nine years, then considered in logarithmic value.

has to be reinvested in a company's activities instead of being distributed to shareholders. This would keep the ROI and ROE low. Although no data on the levels of investments are available, early indications point in this direction. For instance, the amount of the net fixed assets is four times higher for digital users than for digital non-users (€16 million against €4 million of digital non-users). This hypothesis needs further testing that is beyond the scope of this chapter (Aboal and Garda 2015).

The same conclusion can be drawn considering the Earnings Before Interest, Taxes, Depreciation and Amortization (EBITDA)/VA ratio (or EBIT/VA, thus mitigating the weight of capital-intense activities). In this case, though, a lower ratio would translate into a higher value added attributed to human capital.

7.7 Key findings from the empirical evidence

This chapter introduced the debate about I4.0 in Italy with the launch of the 'Piano Industria 4.0' by the government in 2016. We focused our attention on the diffusion of digital technologies in the Veneto region, as one of the country's most manufacturing-intensive regions. The main findings of the case studies are summarized below.

The first key finding is that firm size does not matter in terms of explaining the rate of adoption of I4.0, especially digital technologies. This confirms a similar result regarding Portuguese firms, also indicating a low correlation between size and the adoption of digital technologies (Faria et al. 2002).

The second key finding is that the adoption of digital technologies seems to cut across sectors. The present analysis shows the existence of different technological frontiers from one sector to another. However, we find that manufacturing firms are less likely to adopt technologies than those in the construction sector, and firms in the service sector show a more significant process of adoption. This finding can be explained by the nature of the manufacturing sector in Veneto, where small and medium-sized enterprises (SMEs) operate mainly in industries that have a competitive advantage in terms of design and innovation rather than in terms of price, the so-called 'made-in-Italy' industries such as eyewear, fashion, jewellery and furniture.

Thirdly, we find that firms' international exposure matters: firms' adoption of digital technologies is linked to their engagement in international markets, which is measured by the presence of import and/or export activities. This applies to the manufacturing and construction sectors, but not to services. We find a significant and positive relationship between firms' international exposure and the adoption of digital technologies. This relationship can be explained on two levels, since internationalization is simultaneously a consequence of and a requirement for the adoption of technologies. On the one hand, intense competition in international final markets requires flexibility and productivity levels which can only be achieved through digitalization; on the other hand, the growing need for firms to ingrate into the global supply chain can only be satisfied through ICT-related technologies, forcing them to keep up their technological readiness with global buyers.

Fourthly, another crucial finding is certainly that regarding human capital. The analysis shows that the quality of human capital is significant and positively related to the adoption of technology. We used two proxies for measuring the quality of human capital (the percentage of graduates among all employees and the percentage of highly skilled workers) and they both reinforce the argument that human capital is essential for the adoption of technologies. Analysis of the composition of skills suggests that digital users are characterized by more highly skilled and highly educated workers than digital non-users. Evidence from this study also shows that the digital users are mainly hiring skilled and educated workers. In the period 2012–2014, digital users from the present sample recorded net occupational growth: one-third of the firms accounted for 75% of all new jobs.

Finally, three different indicators were used to analyse the financial position of firms: the net financial position, the EBITDA and the debt/equity ratio. Of the three alternatives, the more significant indicator appears to be the EBITDA. Therefore, the ability of the firm to create significant and steady earnings seems to positively relate to the adoption of digital technologies. Lower ROI and ROE for digital users suggests that investments in new technologies will deliver over the longer term. Overall, digital users record a better productivity index than digital non-users. The empirical evidence suggests that internal resources represent a strong driver towards the adoption of technological innovation, as is the case in Guarascio and Pianta (2016).

7.8 Some policy considerations

Factors enabling an efficient use of digital technologies have to be identified to redirect companies and public investments. The present study and several others underline the value of intangible assets. Specifically, a specialized workforce, quality relations with suppliers, company know-how, wise management and accurate organization all allow the profitable exploitation of digital technologies. Hence, the adoption of a single technology might in itself be necessary, but far from sufficient. Therefore, our empirical analysis suggests the crucial role of human capital, which emerges as a key factor in the adoption of digital technologies. Consequently, public policies stimulating investments in the adoption of specific technologies (often embodied in machinery or equipment), like the Italian government's 'Piano Industria 4.0', should couple the technological aspect with the human capital aspect. In our view, the incentives in technology adoption should request a mandatory presence of adequate workers in the firm. Alternatively, the investments in new machinery should be combined with the hiring of new workers and/or with specific learning processes.

To capture all the potential value that digital transformation can add, it is necessary for a company to broaden its horizons and look beyond technological considerations. Hence, a supporting ecosystem that can promote and facilitate the adoption of technologies is essential to enable companies to keep up with their competitors. In doing so, any ideological position on technical revolutions and new industrial paradigms should be disregarded. Each company should choose its own model on the basis of its traditions and needs. Therefore, imposing the same business model on all companies is certainly not feasible and would surely deplete the efforts made and the potential benefits deriving from the implementation of the model. We have seen that digital technologies are not linked to a particular economic sector, but are used across all of them, although with different diffusion rates. This means that policies targeting firms as end-users of digital technologies should not be sector-specific, but should promote a diversity of firms and products, thus boosting territorial resources.

The complex 'job versus technology' issue should also be examined. Clearly, the labour market needs to adapt and adjust. However, concerns about robots replacing human workers are often likely to be speculative and not based on reality. Although the data presented in this work are limited and call for further analysis, our findings suggest that human capital is one of the most crucial elements for the digital transformation. Specifically, fieldwork conducted for this project clearly shows that a technological upgrade is generally accompanied by employment growth, especially in SMEs. This is very important in fragmented systems where no big players dominate the market, as is the case in Italy and most of Europe. Therefore, understanding the true situation is crucial for the realization of benefits and in order to avoid negative effects, whether we are observing a revolution or not.

7.9 Disclosure statement

No potential conflict of interest was reported by the authors.

Note

1 The composition of the sample was statistically tested. The chi-squared test (Pearson 1900; Plackett 1983) confirms that the composition of the universe and the sample correspond, both in terms of dimension and in terms of activities.

References

Aboal, D. and Garda, P. 2015. 'Technological and non-technological innovation and productivity in services vis-à-vis manufacturing sectors'. *Economics of Innovation and New Technology*, 25(5), 435–454. DOI: https://doi.org/10.1080/10438599.2015.1073478.

Altomonte, C., Aquilante, T., Békés, G. and Ottaviano, G.I. 2013. 'Internationalization and innovation of firms: evidence and policy'. *Economic Policy*, 28(76), 663–700.

Arthur, W.B. 2009. *The Nature of Technology: What it is and How it Evolves*. Simon & Schuster, New York.

Baur, C. and Wee, D. 2015. 'Manufacturing's next act'. *McKinsey Quarterly*, June.

Bai, X., Liu, Y., Wang, G. and Wen, C. (2017). 'The pattern of technological accumulation: the comparative advantage and relative impact of 3D printing technology', *Journal of Manufacturing Technology Management*, 28(1), 39–55.

Bianchi, C.C., Glavas, C. and Mathews, S.W. 2016. 'SME international performance in Latin America: the role of entrepreneurial and technological capabilities', *BALAS 2016 Annual Conference*, Guayaquil, Ecuador, available at: https://eprints.qut.edu.au/91536.

Bianchi, P. and Labory, S. 2018. *Industrial Policy for the Manufacturing Revolution: Perspectives on Digital Globalisation*. Edward Elgar, Cheltenham.

Boermans, M.A. and Roelfsema, H. 2016. 'Small firm internationalization, innovation, and growth'. *International Economics and Economic Policy*, 13(2), 283–296. DOI: https://doi.org/10.1007/s10368-014-0310-y.

Broy, M. 2013. 'Engineering cyber-physical systems: challenges and foundations'. In: Aiguier, M., Caseau, Y., Krob, D. and Rauzy, A. (eds), *Complex Systems Design & Management*. Springer, Berlin, Heidelberg, pp. 1–13.

Brynjolfsson, E. and McAfee, A. 2014. *The Second Machine Age: Work, Progress, and Prosperity in a Time of Brilliant Technologies*. WW Norton & Company, New York.

Buenechea-Elberdin, M. 2017. 'Structured literature review about intellectual capital and innovation'. *Journal of Intellectual Capital*, 18(2), 262–285. DOI: https://doi.org/10.1108/JIC-07-2016-0069.

Cassetta, E., Meleo, L. and Pini, M. 2016. 'The role of digitalization in the internationalization of Italian manufacturing firms'. *L'industria*, 37(2), 305–328.

Cirillo, V. 2016. 'Technology, employment and skills'. *Economics of Innovation and New Technology*, 26(8), 734–754. DOI: https://doi.org/10.1430/84077.

Comuzzi, M. and Patel, A. 2016. 'How organizations leverage big data: a maturity model'. *Industrial Management & Data Systems*, 116(8), 1468–1492. DOI: https://doi.org/10.1108/IMDS-12-2015-0495.

Cowen, T. 2013. *Average is over: Powering America beyond the Age of the Great Stagnation*. Penguin, New York.

Díaz-Chao, Á., Sainz-González, J. and Torrent-Sellens, J. 2015. 'ICT, innovation, and firm productivity: new evidence from small local firms'. *Journal of Business Research*, 68(7), 1439–1444. DOI: https://doi.org/10.1016/j.jbusres.2015.01.030.

Dost, M., Badir, Y.F., Ali, Z. and Tariq, A. 2016. 'The impact of intellectual capital on innovation generation and adoption'. *Journal of Intellectual Capital*, 17(4), 675–695. DOI: https://doi.org/10.1108/JIC-04-2016-0047.

EU Parliament. 2015a. 'Industry 4.0. Digitalisation for productivity and growth', available at: http://www.europarl.europa.eu/RegData/etudes/BRIE/2015/568337/EPRS_BRI(2015)568337_EN.pdf.

EU Parliament. 2015b. 'Industry 4.0', available at: http://www.europarl.europa.eu/RegData/etudes/STUD/2016/570007/IPOL_STU(2016)570007_EN.pdf.

Evangelista, R., Guerrieri, P. and Meliciani, V. 2014. 'The economic impact of digital technologies in Europe'. *Economics of Innovation and New Technology*, 23(8), 802–824. DOI: https://doi.org/10.1080/10438599.2014.918438.

Faria, A., Fenn, P. and Bruce, A. 2002. 'Determinants of adoption of flexible production technologies: evidence from Portuguese manufacturing industry'. *Economics of Innovation and New Technology*, 11(6), 569–580. doi: 10.1080/10438590214338.

Federmeccanica 2016. 'Industria 4.0 in Italia: l'indagine di Federmeccanica', Rome, available at: https://www.federmeccanica.it/archivio-eventi/dettaglievento/29/industria-4-0-in-italia-l-indagine-di-federmeccanica.html.

Fichman, R. 2012. 'Lecture note: digital innovation value maximization'. *Boston College*, available at: https://www2.bc.edu/~fichman/LN-Innovation-Value.Pdf.

Fink, L. 2007. 'Coordination, learning, and innovation: the organizational roles of e-collaboration and their impacts'. *International Journal of E-collaboration*, 3(3), 53–70.

Fondazione Nord-Est. 2015. Make in Italy. Il primo rapporto sull'impatto delle tecnologie digitali nel sistema manifatturiero italiano. Fondazione Make in Italy CDB.

Fosso Wamba, S., Akter, S., Edwards, A., Chopin, G. and Gnanzou, D. 2015. 'How "big data" can make big impact: findings from a systematic review and a longitudinal case study'. *International Journal of Production Economics*, 165, 234–246, DOI: https://doi.org/10.1016/j.ijpe.2014.12.031.

Frey, C.B. and Osborne, A.O. 2017. 'The future of employment: how susceptible are jobs to computerisation?' *Technological Forecasting & Social Change*, 114, 254–280, DOI: https://doi.org/10.1016/j.techfore.2016.08.019.

Gordon, R.J. 2016. *The Rise and Fall of American Growth: The US Standard of Living since the Civil War*. Princeton University Press, Princeton.

Grover, V. and Kohli, R. 2012. 'Cocreating IT value: new capabilities and metrics for multifirm environments'. *MIS Quarterly*, 36(1), 225–232.

Guarascio, D. and Pianta, M. 2016. 'The gains from technology: new products, exports and profits'. *Economics of Innovation and New Technology*, 26(8), 779–804. DOI: https://doi.org/10.1080/10438599.2016.1257446.

Hartmann, P.M., Zaki, M., Feldmann, N. and Neely, A. 2016. 'Capturing value from big data: a taxonomy of data-driven business models used by start-up firms'. *International Journal of Operations & Production Management*, 36(10), 1382–1406. doi: 10.1108/IJOPM-02-2014-0098.

Henfridsson, O., Mathiassen, L. and Svahn, F. 2014. 'Managing technological change in the digital age: the role of architectural frames'. *Journal of Information Technology*, 29(1), 27–43. DOI: https://doi.org/10.1057/jit.2013.30.

Heng, S. 2014. 'Industry 4.0: upgrading of Germany's industrial capabilities on the Horizon', available at: https://ssrn.com/abstract=2656608.

Hermann, M., Pentek, T. and Otto, B. 2015. 'Design principles for Industrie 4.0 scenarios'. DOI: https://doi.org/10.1109/HICSS.2016.488.

Higón, D.A. and Driffield, N. 2011. 'Exporting and innovation performance: analysis of the Annual Small Business Survey in the UK'. *International Small Business Journal*, 29(1), 4–24. DOI: https://doi.org/10.1177/0266242610369742.

Hinds, P.J. and Kiesler, S. 2002. *Distributed Work: New Research on Working across Distance Using Technology*. MIT Press, Cambridge, MA.

Hofmann, E. and Rüsch, M. 2017. 'Industry 4.0 and the current status as well as future prospects on logistics'. *Computers in Industry*, 89, 23–34. DOI: https://doi.org/10.1016/j.compind.2017.04.002.

Hsiao, C. 1996. 'Logit and probit models'. In *The Econometrics of Panel Data*, pp. 410–428. Springer, Dordrecht.

Kagermann, H., Helbig, J., Hellinger, A. and Wahlster, W. 2013. 'Umsetzungsempfehlungen für das Zukunftsprojekt Industrie 4.0: Deutschlands Zukunft als Produktionsstandort sichern; Abschlussbericht des Arbeitskreises Industrie 4.0. Forschungsunion'. *Abschlussbericht des Arbeitskreises Industrie.*

Kang, H.S., Lee, J.Y., Choi, S., Kim, H., Park, J.H., Son, J.Y., Kim, B.H. and Noh, S.D. 2016. 'Smart manufacturing: past research, present findings, and future directions', *International Journal of Precision Engineering and Manufacturing-Green Technology*, 3(1), 111–128. DOI: https://doi.org/10.1007/s40684-016-0015-5.

Katz, J.E. and Rice, R.E. 2002. *Social Consequences of Internet Use: Access, Involvement, and Interaction*. MIT Press, Cambridge, MA.

LaValle, S., Lesser E., Shockley, R., Hopkins, M.S. and Kruschwitz, N. 2011. 'Big data, analytics and the path from insights to value'. *MIT Sloan Management Review*, 52(2), 20–33.

Liao, Y., Deschamps, F., Loures, E.D.F.R. and Ramos, L.F.P. 2017. 'Past, present and future of Industry 4.0: a systematic literature review and research agenda proposal'. *International Journal of Production Research*, 55(12), 3609–3629. DOI: https://doi.org/10.1080/00207543.2017.1308576.

Lu, Y. 2017. 'Industry 4.0: a survey on technologies, applications and open research issues'. *Journal of Industrial Information Integration*, 6, 1–10. DOI: https://doi.org/10.1016/j.jii.2017.04.005.

Lycett, M. 2013. '"Datafication": making sense of (big) data in a complex world'. *European Journal of Information Systems*, 22(4), 381–386. doi: 10.1057/ejis.2013.10.

McGuirk, H., Lenihan, H. and Hart, M. 2015. 'Measuring the impact of innovative human capital on small firms' propensity to innovate'. *Research Policy*, 44(4), 965–976. DOI: https://doi.org/10.1016/j.respol.2014.11.008.

McQuivey, J. 2013. *Digital Disruption*. Forrester Research, Amazon Publishing, Las Vegas.

Morgan-Thomas, A. and Jones, M.V. 2009. 'Post-entry internationalization dynamics'. *International Small Business Journal*, 27(1), 71–97. DOI: https://doi.org/10.1177/0266242608098347.

OECD. 2014. *Measuring the Digital Economy: A New Perspective*. OECD Publishing, Paris.

OECD. 2015. *Data-Driven Innovation: Big Data for Growth and Well-Being*. OECD Publishing, Paris.

Pearson, K. 1900. 'On the criterion that a given system of deviations from the probable in the case of a correlated system of variables is such that it can be reasonably supposed to have arisen from random sampling'. *Philosophical Magazine Series 5*, 50(302), 157–175.

Pisano, G.P. and Verganti, R. 2008. 'Which kind of collaboration is right for you?' *Harvard Business Review*, 86(2), 78–86.

Plackett, R. 1983. 'Karl Pearson and the chi-squared test'. *International Statistical Review/Revue Internationale de Statistique*, 51(1), 59–72. DOI: https://doi.org/10.2307/1402731.

Platform I4.0. 2015. 'Von smarten Objekten und Maschinen', available at: http://www.plattform-i40.de.

Rullani, E. 1989. 'La teoria dell'impresa: soggetti, sistemi, evoluzione'. In Rispoli M. (ed.), *L'impresa industriale. Economia, tecnologia, management*. Il Mulino, Bologna, pp. 13–110.

Rüßmann, M., Lorenz, M., Gerbert, P., Waldner, M., Justus, J., Engel, P. and Harnisch, M. 2015. 'Industry 4.0: the future of productivity and growth in manufacturing industries'. *Boston Consulting Group*.

Schmidt, R., Möhring, M., Härting, R.C., Reichstein, C., Neumaier, P. and Jozinovic, P. 2015. 'Industry 4.0: potentials for creating smart products: empirical research results'. *Business Information Systems*, 16–27. DOI: https://doi.org/10.1007/978-3-319-19027-3_2.

Schröder, C. 2016. 'The challenges of Industry 4.0 for small and medium-sized enterprises'. Friedrich-Ebert-Stiftun, Division of Economic and Social Policy, Bonn.

Schwab, K. 2016. *The Fourth Industrial Revolution*. World Economic Forum, Geneva.

Secundo, G., Del Vecchio, P., Dumay, J. and Passiante, G. 2017. 'Intellectual capital in the age of big data: establishing a research agenda'. *Journal of Intellectual Capital*, 18(2), 242–261. DOI: https://doi.org/10.1108/JIC-10-2016-0097.

Shafiq, S.I., Sanin, C., Szczerbicki, E. and Toro, C. 2016. 'Virtual engineering factory: creating experience base for Industry 4.0'. *Cybernetics and Systems*, 47(1–2), 32–47. DOI: https://doi.org/10.1080/01969722.2016.1128762.

Shafiq, S.I., Sanin, C., Toro, C. and Szczerbicki, E. 2015. 'Virtual engineering object (VEO): toward experience-based design and manufacturing for Industry 4.0'. *Cybernetics and Systems*, 46(1–2), 35–50. DOI: https://doi.org/10.1080/01969722.2015. 1007734.

Sommer, L. 2015. 'Industrial revolution – Industry 4.0: are German manufacturing SMEs the first victims of this revolution?' *Journal of Industrial Engineering and Management*, 8(5), 1512–1532. DOI: https://doi.org/10.3926/jiem.1470.

Thames, L. and Schaefer, D. 2016. 'Software-defined cloud manufacturing for Industry 4.0'. *Procedia CIRP*, 52, 12–17. DOI: https://doi.org/10.1016/j.procir.2016.07.041.

Vaccaro, A. and Madsen, P. 2009. 'ICT and an NGO: difficulties in attempting to be extremely transparent'. *Ethics and Information Technology*, 11(3), 221–231. doi: 10.1007/s10676-009-9180-3.

Yoo, Y., Boland, R.J., Jr., Lyytinen, K. and Majchrzak, A. 2012. 'Organizing for innovation in the digitized world'. *Organization Science*, 23(5), 1398–1408. DOI: https://doi.org/10.1287/orsc.1120.0771.

8 Exploring Industry 4.0 production in Sweden

Claudio Fassio and Max Nathan

8.1 Introduction

Like many industries before it, manufacturing is being 'disrupted' by new technology. This 'Fourth Industrial Revolution' (Schwab, 2017) or 'Industry 4.0' (Brettel et al., 2014) promises substantive productivity and growth effects via the application of technologies such as sensors, nanotech, RFID chips, robotics, machine learning and AI to a vast range of industrial settings (Brynjolfsson and McAfee, 2014). The general purpose nature of many of these technologies (Bresnahan, 2010) is said to promote recombinant growth (Kremer, 1993) both through the reconfiguration of existing production lines, products and services, and the development of entirely new ones.

Much of the existing analysis on the Fourth Industrial Revolution and the implications for the so-called new manufacturing model called Industry 4.0 has focused on *users* and, more broadly, on industry awareness and levels of readiness in existing businesses (Brettel et al., 2014; Lee et al., 2014, 2015; Schwab, 2017). In contrast, we look at the evolution of Industry 4.0 *producers*, specifically science and technology companies in Sweden during the 2000s and early 2010s. We use rich microdata from the Swedish MONA dataset to do this, and provide results both at the national level and at the municipality level, identifying clusters in Stockholm and other Swedish cities.

Sweden is a particularly interesting country to study in relation to what Swedish policy makers call *smart manufacturing*. Its industrial heritage – in particular, its historic strengths in electrical engineering and mobile communications – means that hardware firms can potentially draw on a rich 'ecosystem' of high-value manufacturing knowledge, suppliers and collaborators, and a thick labour market of skilled and experienced workers (Brown and Mason, 2014; Spigel, 2017). Unlike Germany, which combines large conglomerates with the 'Mittelstand' of small and medium-size firms, Sweden's industrial economy remains dominated by large MNEs, plus a cadre of specialist ICT consulting companies (Gens et al., 2015; Giertz, 2015a). Furthermore, in the early 2000s, Ericsson shed around 50% of its workforce: many laid-off workers have either started their own businesses or have moved into consultancy roles, diffusing technical know-how further through the economy (Chaminade et al., 2010). Relatedly, Stockholm has become one of Europe's leading technology hubs, with both thousands of young tech companies and some global players such as Skype, Spotify, Mojang and Klarna (Semuels, 2017).

Furthermore, Sweden has a tradition of hands-on industrial policy: national and local policy makers are actively trying to encourage the adoption of new technology across a range of sectors and firm types and a shift towards smart manufacturing. Much of this has been in response to the so-called 'Swedish Paradox' – high levels of R&D spending but low productivity (Bitard et al., 2008; Ejermo and Kander, 2009), which, it was argued, may be partly explained in Schumpetarian terms by a lack of new entrants who bring new ideas to the market (Aghion et al., 2009).

The chapter is organised as follows. Section 8.2 sets out some key concepts and the country context. Section 8.3 describes our methodology. Section 8.4 discusses results. Section 8.5 gives brief conclusions.

8.2 Framework

8.2.1 Defining Industry 4.0

'Industry 4.0', the 'Industrial Internet' and the 'Fourth Industrial Revolution' (FIR) are fuzzy terms with no standardised definitions (Giertz, 2015a; Gens et al., 2015). Its components can usefully be seen as a 'technology-product-industry space'; that is, an evolving set of technologies, product/service applications and industry specifics.

Commonly cited FIR *technologies* include sensors and radio chips, AI, machine learning; 3D printing, nanotech and cloud computers. Many of these have general purpose characteristics (Bresnahan, 2010; Perez, 2010) and can be applied to a vast range of *products and services* (Brynjolfsson and McAfee, 2014). These include some wholly new or 'recombinant' use cases (Kremer, 1993), such as new 'smart objects' of varying complexity (such as wearables or drones), as well as existing activities (such as automated production lines), computerised/digitised products (such as medical devices) and components (such as airbags). These new products typically require associated *software*, in apps and or other control systems. In any given industry, a range of *services* also builds on these, especially data and analytics around a product (servitisation), consultancy and training.

Almost all manufacturers could be *users* of these new technologies. We focus on the (smaller) set of *producers* – firms whose sole or principal output are products in the FIR technology space, or services derived from such products. In practice, these firms cover a number of industries typically considered as science and technology, but also advanced manufacturing, medicine/pharma, consumer electronics and specialised software/support.

8.2.2 From technologies to ecosystems

More broadly, and following Freeman (1991) and Perez (2010), we can place these components in a larger, dynamic 'technology system', that is, a set of multiple technologies and its linked network of producers, suppliers, distributors and users. Technology systems benefit from (potentially substantial) internal spill-overs. Perez (2010: 187) argues that as 'technologies interconnect and tend to appear in the neighbourhood of other innovations', innovations in one part of the space tend to induce complementary (e.g. downstream) innovations in other parts. These spill-overs are likely to exist in both technology space (e.g. recombinant use cases) and physical space (clusters of firms that interact and learn from each other).

Industry 4.0 producers are knowledge-intensive businesses in which symbolic and physical product and service creation is a central activity. As Mudambi (2008) points out, value creation is mostly created at the upstream and downstream ends of a production function: ICTs, in theory, allow ever-finer levels of disaggregation and control. Nevertheless, while the costs of organising across long distances have fallen, the value of physical proximity for complex activity remains high, especially for building relationships, exchanging codified information and observing others (Glaeser, 2011). A number of studies have highlighted tools such as project-based organising (Grabher, 2002), virtual communities (Grabher and Ibert, 2014) and online tools (Bathelt, 2005) to mimic face-to-face interaction. In general, technology companies *both* make extensive use of these distance-based tools *and* tightly cluster into urban space (Nathan and Vandore, 2014; Martins, 2015).

How these local and non-local organising dynamics work in the Swedish case is an empirical question. In practice, we can observe co-location straightforwardly through structured data; firm–firm links and relationships are less easy to see.

8.2.3 The Swedish context

Sweden has a deep history of involvement in ICT production, especially electronic engineering, as well as closely related fields in advanced manufacturing (Giertz et al., 2015a, 2015b, from which this account draws heavily). Sweden industrialised late compared to its European rivals, but then developed very rapidly, particularly in telecoms: by 1855, for example, there were 5,000 telephone sets in Stockholm, the highest in the world at that time.

In the first half of the twentieth century, Sweden's ICT and manufacturing industries developed through a corporatist national policy framework, with private companies and the state co-creating key technologies and infrastructure, acting as developer and lead customer respectively. Some of these industrial policy bets worked out better than others: the Swedish personal computer industry faded away in the 1980s, for example, but the mobile communications industry did better. By 1969, a common Nordic mobile system had been developed; by 1985, Nordic Mobile Telephony (NMT) was the world's largest mobile network. The pan-European GSM standards group was formed in 1982, with Swedish companies heavily involved in developing the standard for its eventual launch in 1991; it subsequently became a global benchmark for telecoms, helping establish Ericsson as a global ICT player.

The corporatist policy framework, already under political attack in the 1970s and 1980s, was rolled back substantively during the 1990s after a fiscal crisis, when a number of pro-competition and pro-entrepreneurship policies were also introduced. In 1995 Sweden joined the European Community and deregulated energy, telecoms, postal services and the media, further altering its nationalised/corporatist economic development model.

The early 2000s saw Ericsson, the country's largest ICT firm, enter a period of crisis, driven by the dotcom crash and strategic miscalculations in 3G technology. By 2004, it had shed around half its workforce, with large job losses in Sweden. These company-level shifts had important knock-on effects in the country. Many laid-off engineers moved into hardware engineering, finance or banking, triggering a wave of entrepreneurship across ICT, especially software and the Internet.

In parallel, national level policy makers in Sweden introduced a number of measures to support new firm formation in the technology sector and other sectors. A policy consensus gradually grew on the need to raise levels of entrepreneurship in the country, especially in high-value activities. A number of subsequent reforms in the 1990s and 2000s – to tax and competition policy, for example – appear to have helped develop the country's entrepreneurship culture (Semuels, 2017). A national programme also provided subsidised PCs for households, with employers sharing costs; this widely diffused computers into society, including to households that otherwise would have been unable to afford them. Vinnova, the national innovation systems agency, was founded in 2001, as part of a major reorganisation of national economic development institutions. It takes a major interest in Industry 4.0, aiming to connect traditional industries to new digital processes and tools, especially in export industries.

8.3 Methodology

Our quantitative analysis uses microdata from the Statistics Sweden MONA database for the years 2007–2012 inclusive. We build industry and municipality-level panels from firm and worker-level microdata. The industry-level panel consists of 3,583 4-digit industry*year observations for 2007–2012. The municipality-level panel consists of 1,752 area*year observations for the same time period. Further details of the build are available on request.

To identify the set of tech firms that are Industry 4.0 producers, we start with a set of 'science and tech' industries drawn from an international benchmarking exercise conducted by the UK Office of National Statistics (Harris, 2015) and defined using 5-digit SICs. Drawing on the framework above, we refine this to proxy 'Industry 4.0' producer sectors, dropping a number of content activities (publishing, media, music, advertising) and science/health activities (life sciences, health), except where SIC descriptors directly pertain to R&D and/or manufacturing. We then crosswalk this to 4-digit SICs, which is identical to the NACE Rev 2 /SNI07 codes used in Sweden and other EU Member States.

We also select a set of STEM occupations from NESTA (Bakhshi et al., 2015), crosswalking these from UK SOC2010 occupation codes to SOC2008, then to the international ISCO08 and ISCO88 standards. The latter is identical to the SSYK-96 codes used in the Swedish data. Final lists of industries and occupations are given in the appendix, in Tables A1 and A2 respectively.

8.4 Results

Table 8.1 compares mean characteristics for the set of Industry 4.0 producing industries against the rest of the economy, pooled across the period 2007–2012. The right-hand column gives the result of a two-tailed T-test on means. We compare across a range of key characteristics in Panels 1 and 2. We can see that in almost all key characteristics, including workforce mix, these industries differ from the rest-of-industry average. Notably, while these industries produce substantively more patents than the rest of Sweden (covering over 75% of all Swedish patenting – see Table 8.2), and generate substantively higher exports, overall value added and turnover are not significantly different from other Swedish industries. This provides some support to the notion of the Swedish

Table 8.1 Industry 4.0 producers in Sweden: distinctiveness

Variable	*I4.0*	*Rest*	*Different?*
Total firms 5 years old or less	273,221	420,884	Y
Total large firms	2,161	1,628	Y
Total SMEs	882,073	1,582,661	Y
Total value added (mSEK)	3,579,333	3,211,102	N
Total net turnover (mSEK)	13,017,630	11,681,930	N
Total exports value (mSEK)	4,181,818	1,694,266	Y
Total patents weighted by applicants	13,830	3,012	Y
Total employment	4,395,439	4,209,906	N
Number of tertiary educated employees ≤ 3 yrs	826,717	636,933	Y
Number of tertiary educated employees > 3 yrs	1,396,159	783,519	Y
Total STEM workers	954,285	250,847	Y
Average science workforce intensity	0.013	0.010	Y
Average engineering workforce intensity	0.015	0.006	Y
Average tech workforce intensity	0.037	0.013	Y
Average stem workforce intensity	0.065	0.029	Y

Source: Statistics Sweden.

Notes: Graduates are those with 3 years or less tertiary education; + postgrads adds in those with more than 3 years tertiary education; STEM occupations defined from NESTA (2015); intensity = share of workers in science/engineering/tech/stem occupations, compared to all workers in these industries; tech industries defined using Harris (2015); turnover, value, added, exports value given in mSEK; patents weighted by applicants. Difference = two-tailed t-test, 5% significance or better.

Paradox. We can also see that compared to non tech-industries, 'sci-tech' and Industry 4.0 production have significantly more large firms, fewer start-ups and fewer small and medium-sized enterprises (SMEs).

Importantly, in Panel 3 we compare on the basis of STEM workforce 'intensity' and its component parts. The concept of workforce intensity draws on the idea of 'creative intensity' widely used in creative economy analysis (Bakshi et al., 2015). This defines a set of 'creative occupations' and then looks at how 'intensively' these are used across different industries. For a given industry *i*, creative intensity is defined as the share of workers in creative occupations in industry *i* out of all workers in *i*. Here, we substitute creative occupations for scientists, engineers, tech workers and the aggregate set of STEM workers. Again, we can see that Swedish Industry 4.0 producers are distinctive from the rest of Swedish firms in their use of scientists, engineers and technical staff.

Table 8.2 shows the main characteristics of the Industry 4.0 production sectors and covers the period 2007–2012 inclusive.

The top panel looks at workforce characteristics, while the middle and bottom panels cover firm characteristics. For each panel, we show totals by year, percentage change over the period, and these sectors' share of activity across all workers/all firms accordingly. We can see that in 2012, these sectors employed around 18% of all workers (top panel). Skilled workers make up a disproportionate share of this (these industries employ 21.6% of all graduates and just under 30% of all workers with postgraduate qualifications). Not surprisingly, over two-thirds of the country's workers in STEM jobs are employed in these sectors. While these industries' overall workforce share has fallen slightly between 2007 and 2012, shares of skilled and STEM workers have risen, often substantially.

Industry 4.0 production comprises just under 10% of all firms in Sweden (middle panel). This set of industries has grown by 17% since 2007 and its composition has changed, with a big rise in SMEs and start-ups, but a fall in large firms (those with over 250 staff). Nevertheless, the sector still contributes over a fifth of all large firms in Sweden. In terms of broader economic performance (bottom panel), turnover, value added and exports are all on an upward trend – yet, strikingly, patenting, a key innovation measure, has fallen since 2007.

Our analysis resonates with that of Giertz et al. (2015a), who classify Swedish ICT firms into eight cross-sector verticals. However, they focus on a much narrower range of established ICT firms (2,700 companies that have over five employees) compared with our sample. Within this smaller set, the 'hardware components' and 'complete systems' 'verticals' (closely related industry sets organised around common technologies, products or services) comprise around 14% of firms and over 20% of all ICT sector staff (over 26,000 of 132,000 FTE in 2011, compared with 459,000 in our data).

As in our ICT-wide data, hardware activity is a mix of a few large incumbents, plus a long tail of SMEs. The complete systems' vertical is dominated by a few large incumbents, with under 200 firms in total, of which Ericsson accounts for over 70% of all employees. By contrast, the hardware components' vertical is

Table 8.2 Industry 4.0 producers in Sweden: time trends

	Workers	*Graduates*	*+ Postgrads*	*STEM workers*
2007	464,683	85,516	135,288	90,503
2008	476,401	86,365	141,980	97,519
2009	455,653	84,132	143,814	99,395
2010	445,812	85,646	147,129	100,925
2011	459,503	88,853	153,370	104,161
2012	462,679	89,493	156,603	107,742
% change 2007–12	*−0.43%*	*4.65%*	*15.76%*	*19.05%*
% all, 2012	*17.73%*	*21.62%*	*29.97%*	*67.02%*
	Firms	*Start-ups*	*SMEs*	*Large firms*
2007	87,425	27,923	86,726	238
2008	90,552	28,274	89,483	237
2009	92,683	28,439	91,395	225
2010	87,493	27,415	85,912	221
2011	101,718	30,102	100,265	218
2012	102,606	29,703	101,043	220
% change 2007–12	*17.36%*	*6.37%*	*16.51%*	*−7.56%*
% all, 2012	*9.68%*	*11.40%*	*9.67%*	*22.00%*
	Turnover	*Value added*	*Exports*	*Patents*
2007	390,990	1,394,861	443,986	1,767
2008	376,374	1,427,239	459,208	1,690
2009	319,548	1,191,571	356,198	1,504
2010	381,274	1,260,775	410,137	1,677
2011	400,075	1,465,458	495,151	1,518
2012	383,141	1,448,182	465,684	
% change 2007–12	*−2.01%*	*3.82%*	*4.89%*	*−14.04%**
% all, 2012	*19.57%*	*18.67%*	*45.57%*	*76.93%**

Source: Statistics Sweden.

Notes: Tech industries defined using Harris (2015); graduates are those with 3 years or less tertiary education; + postgrads adds in those with more than 3 years tertiary education; STEM occupations defined from NESTA (2015); start-ups defined as firms 5 years old or less; turnover, value, added, exports value given in mSEK; patents weighted by applicants.

* Change and national shares given for 2011.

dominated by SMEs, with around ten employees on average; the few large firms have only a few hundred staff. Many of these firms are 'contracting manufacturing'. Many of the newer firms are start-ups producing 'fibre optics, nanotech, power electronics, printed electronics, control equipment, measuring and calibration, antennas, power transistors, alarms, lasers, sensors and actuators', and many are connected to universities.

The other hardware-relevant component of the Swedish ICT industry is R&D-focused consulting, which in Giertz et al. (2015a) comprised over 360 established firms and almost 12,400 staff in 2011. These firms work with other tech businesses on 'pure technical applications', including an important sub-set dealing with embedded systems and the Internet of Things. The roots of this consulting sector lie largely in corporate shake-ups, as discussed above.

8.4.1 Municipality analysis

Swedish Industry 4.0 producers are highly clustered, with Stockholm City and County the largest agglomeration of activity. Tables 8.3 and 8.4 give counts, shares and location quotients at municipality level for the years 2007–2012.

Table 8.3 looks at the 20 municipalities with the largest counts of Industry 4.0 firms. Over a quarter of these are in Stockholm County, with Stockholm Municipality having over twice as many firms as the next municipality (Gothenberg), over three times as many Industry 4.0 producer SMEs and around twice as many employees in these industries. Notably, tech SMEs make up almost all of the population of ICT firms and 9–18% of all SMEs in these municipalities. Stockholm County comprises around 47% of all Industry 4.0 employment in the 20 most ICT firm-dense municipalities.

Counts and shares do not fully control for the underlying economic structure of areas. Table 8.4 uses location quotients (LQs) to do this for the 20 municipalities with the highest LQs in 2007–2012. Lund has the highest LQ in Sweden in this period; Stockholm city has a rather lower LQ, reflecting its greater economic diversity. However, Stockholm County dominates the table: just under two-thirds of the Sweden's largest tech clusters are in Stockholm municipalities.

Other studies confirm this spatial picture. Chaminade et al. (2010) point to the Kista cluster of large tech MNEs (including Infosys, Huawei and Lenovo) just outside Stockholm city, as nationally important, alongside Skåne County (for computer games) and Linköping (for web servers). Over half the ICT employment identified by Giertz et al. (2015a) is located in Stockholm County[1] – over 60,000 FTE staff, far fewer than in Table 8.3 given the very restrictive sampling frame of those authors. Six of the eight verticals identified have over half their employees in the area. In hardware systems, Giertz et al. (2015a) highlight the fact that Ericsson has always been critically important to the Stockholm cluster – both through its location in Kista and elsewhere in the metropolitan area, and through its system-wide effects across the county and the country as a whole. Notably, the two *least*-concentrated sectors identified by Giertz et al. (ibid) are the focus of interest in this study. Around 77% of hardware components staff work outside Stockholm County, as do 65% of R&D-related consultancy staff. However, Stockholm remains the single largest location for these activities.

8.5 Conclusions

This chapter uses rich microdata to explore Industry 4.0 production in Sweden, a country with both a rich heritage in advanced manufacturing and an activist public policy tradition. Hardware products and services in Sweden can

Table 8.3 Firms and workers, top 20 Swedish municipalities by firm counts, 2007–2012

Code	*Municipality*	*County*	*Sci-tech firms*		*Sci-tech SMEs*			*Sci-tech workers*	
			Total	*% all firms*	*Total*	*% all SMEs*	*% all tech*	*Total*	*% all workers*
0180	Stockholm	Stockholm	17,176	13.84	17,114	14.04	99.64	121,529	17.32
1480	Gothenberg	Västra Götaland	6,881	14.32	6,853	14.51	99.59	64,989	32.93
1280	Malmö	Skåne	3,096	12.22	3,091	12.46	99.84	12,496	14.21
0380	Uppsala	Uppsala	2,353	13.43	2,351	13.64	99.92	6,932	21.19
1281	Lund	Skåne	1,854	17.90	1,850	18.12	99.78	11,685	41.25
0580	Linköping	Östergötland	1,531	13.83	1,529	14.09	99.87	13,039	42.65
1980	Västerås	Västmanland	1,337	14.11	1,332	14.31	99.63	15,099	41.55
0182	Nacka	Stockholm	1,281	13.82	1,279	14.03	99.84	2,544	19.59
1283	Helsingborg	Skåne	1,231	10.84	1,230	11.05	99.92	4,202	12.77
0160	Täby	Stockholm	1,214	16.95	1,214	17.23	100.00	1,978	14.70
2480	Umeå	Västerbotten	1,030	9.60	1,029	9.70	99.90	2,042	10.83
0184	Solna	Stockholm	1,026	15.74	1,022	16.02	99.61	4,946	6.19
0163	Sollentuna	Stockholm	1,014	17.35	1,014	17.63	100.00	1,855	11.13
0680	Jönköping	Jönköping	984	9.28	979	9.40	99.49	6,291	22.05
0581	Norrköping	Östergötland	948	10.52	946	10.70	99.79	2,908	10.33
1880	Örebro	Örebro	889	8.50	888	8.64	99.89	3,557	10.67
1384	Kungsbacka	Halland	888	11.43	887	11.59	99.89	1,146	12.19
0126	Huddinge	Stockholm	878	12.14	878	12.33	100.00	874	7.42
1490	Borås	Västra Götaland	797	9.01	795	9.12	99.75	4,040	17.25
1780	Karlstad	Värmland	783	9.92	782	10.07	99.87	2,384	13.57

Source: Statistics Sweden.

Notes: Tech industries defined using Harris (2015); start-ups defined as firms 5 years old or less.

Table 8.4 Location quotients, top 20 Swedish municipalities by firm counts, 2007–2012

Code	*Municipality*	*County*	*Firms*	*SMEs*	*Startups*	*Employees*
1281	Lund	Skåne	1.856	10.370	10.187	2.256
0163	Sollentuna	Stockholm	1.802	10.385	10.954	0.608
0160	Täby	Stockholm	1.758	10.386	10.395	0.802
0184	Solna	Stockholm	1.632	10.349	10.447	0.346
1262	Lomma	Skåne	1.603	10.392	9.925	0.984
1481	Mölndal	Västra Götaland	1.601	10.378	9.214	1.054
0183	Sundbyberg	Stockholm	1.571	10.377	11.006	0.688
0123	Järfälla	Stockholm	1.561	10.384	10.796	0.854
1402	Partille	Västra Götaland	1.507	10.392	9.647	0.693
0186	Lidingö	Stockholm	1.485	10.366	10.224	1.588
1480	Göteborg	Västra Götaland	1.484	10.349	10.554	1.793
0162	Danderyd	Stockholm	1.467	10.366	10.025	0.949
1980	Västerås	Västmanland	1.462	10.356	11.426	2.264
0180	Stockholm	Stockholm	1.435	10.354	10.836	0.944
0580	Linköping	Östergötland	1.433	10.375	10.489	2.324
0187	Vaxholm	Stockholm	1.432	10.392	10.923	0.532
0182	Nacka	Stockholm	1.432	10.382	10.687	1.067
0199			1.415	10.392	16.330	0.934
0117	Österåker	Stockholm	1.410	10.392	10.343	0.578
0128	Salem	Stockholm	1.403	10.392	10.122	0.382

Source: Statistics Sweden.

Notes: Tech industries defined using ONS/Harris (2015); start-ups defined as firms 5 years old or less.

draw on existing ecosystems, especially in electrical engineering and mobile communications. Swedish Industry 4.0 producers comprised around 10% of the country's firms in 2012, but around 20% of all large firms. They employed around 18% of all workers, but two-thirds of the country's STEM workers. These industries are nationally distinctive in their intensive use of skilled and STEM staff, high levels of patenting, turnover and exports. This setting presents both opportunities and challenges for Sweden as it develops readiness for Industry 4.0 (Nathan, 2018). Industry 4.0 producers can draw on a rich, perhaps unique, ecosystem of high-value knowledge, a web of potential suppliers and large numbers of skilled, experienced workers, much of which is already co-located in a few urban hubs. Unlike competitors such as Germany, in Sweden these industries are also dominated by a few large firms: there are relatively few start-ups and SMEs, although, as we have shown, their numbers are growing rapidly. Large incumbents are a striking feature of the Swedish ecosystem. They can act as key buyers of new products and services, and potentially partners in product/firm development. Historically, corporate shocks to large players – notably Ericsson – have helped feed subsequent growth in new entrants. Conversely, large firms in Sweden have tended towards incremental innovation conducted internally, which may present coordination problems for joint ventures. On top of policies to promote entrepreneurship and the growth of Stockholm as a leading European tech cluster, this suggests that future Swedish industrial policy will also need to look for tools to promote better links between emerging and existing industry actors in the national ecosystem.

Appendix

Table A1 List of sci-tech industries 'Science and tech' industries are drawn from an international benchmarking exercise conducted by the UK Office of National Statistics (Harris, 2015)

NACE	*NACE_descriptor*	*ONS_category*
1920	Mineral oil refining	other science_tech manufacture
2000	Manufacture of chemicals and chemical products	other science_tech manufacture
2010	Manufacture of basic chemicals, fertilisers and nitrogen compounds, plastics and synthetic rubber in primary forms	other science_tech manufacture
2011	Manufacture of industrial gases	other science_tech manufacture
2012	Manufacture of dyes and pigments	other science_tech manufacture
2013	Manufacture of other inorganic basic chemicals	other science_tech manufacture
2014	Manufacture of other organic basic chemicals	other science_tech manufacture
2015	Manufacture of fertilisers and nitrogen compounds	other science_tech manufacture
2016	Manufacture of plastics in primary forms	other science_tech manufacture
2017	Manufacture of synthetic rubber in primary forms	other science_tech manufacture
2020	Manufacture of pesticides and other agrochemical products	other science_tech manufacture
2030	Manufacture of paints, varnishes and similar coatings, mastics and sealants	other science_tech manufacture
2040	Manufacture of soap and detergents, cleaning and polishing preparations, perfumes and toilet preparations	other science_tech manufacture
2041	Manufacture of cleaning and polishing preparations	other science_tech manufacture
2042	Manufacture of perfumes and toilet preparations	other science_tech manufacture
2050	Manufacture of other chemical products	other science_tech manufacture
2051	Manufacture of explosives	other science_tech manufacture

(*continued*)

Table A1 Cont.

NACE	*NACE_descriptor*	*ONS_category*
2052	Manufacture of glues	other science_tech manufacture
2053	Manufacture of essential oils	other science_tech manufacture
2059	Manufacture of other chemical products n.e.c.	other science_tech manufacture
2060	Manufacture of man-made fibres	other science_tech manufacture
2521	Manufacture of central heating radiators and boilers	other science_tech manufacture
2530	Manufacture of steam generators, except central heating hot water boilers	other science_tech manufacture
2540	Manufacture of weapons and ammunition	other science_tech manufacture
2610	Manufacture of electronic components and boards	digital technologies
2611	Manufacture of electronic components	digital technologies
2612	Manufacture of loaded electronic boards	digital technologies
2620	Manufacture of computers and peripheral equipment	digital technologies
2630	Manufacture of communication equipment (other than telegraph and telephone apparatus and equipment)	publishing and broadcasting
2640	Manufacture of consumer electronics	digital technologies
2651	Manufacture of non-electronic instruments and appliances for measuring, testing and navigation, except industrial process control equipment	other science_tech manufacture
2652	Manufacture of watches and clocks	other science_tech manufacture
2660	Manufacture of irradiation, electromedical and electrotherapeutic equipment	life science and healthcare
2670	Manufacture of photographic and cinematographic equipment	publishing and broadcasting
2680	Manufacture of magnetic and optical media	digital technologies
2700	Manufacture of electrical equipment	other science_tech manufacture
2710	Manufacture of electric motors, generators, transformers and electricity distribution and control apparatus	other science_tech manufacture
2711	Manufacture of electric motors, generators and transformers	other science_tech manufacture
2712	Manufacture of electricity distribution and control apparatus	other science_tech manufacture
2720	Manufacture of batteries and accumulators	other science_tech manufacture
2730	Manufacture of wiring and wiring devices	other science_tech manufacture

Table A1 Cont.

NACE	*NACE_descriptor*	*ONS_category*
2731	Manufacture of fibre optic cables	other science_tech manufacture
2732	Manufacture of other electronic and electric wires and cables	other science_tech manufacture
2733	Manufacture of wiring devices	other science_tech manufacture
2740	Manufacture of electric lighting equipment	other science_tech manufacture
2750	Manufacture of domestic appliances	other science_tech manufacture
2751	Manufacture of electric domestic appliances	other science_tech manufacture
2752	Manufacture of non-electric domestic appliances	other science_tech manufacture
2790	Manufacture of other electrical equipment	other science_tech manufacture
2810	Manufacture of general purpose machinery	other science_tech manufacture
2811	Manufacture of engines and turbines, except aircraft, vehicle and cycle engines	other science_tech manufacture
2812	Manufacture of fluid power equipment	other science_tech manufacture
2813	Manufacture of compressors	other science_tech manufacture
2814	Manufacture of other taps and valves	other science_tech manufacture
2815	Manufacture of bearings, gears, gearing and driving elements	other science_tech manufacture
2821	Manufacture of ovens, furnaces and furnace burners	other science_tech manufacture
2822	Manufacture of lifting and handling equipment	other science_tech manufacture
2823	Manufacture of office machinery and equipment (except computers and peripheral equipment)	other science_tech manufacture
2824	Manufacture of power-driven hand tools	other science_tech manufacture
2825	Manufacture of non-domestic cooling and ventilation equipment	other science_tech manufacture
2829	Manufacture of other general-purpose machinery n.e.c.	other science_tech manufacture
2830	Manufacture of agricultural and forestry machinery	other science_tech manufacture
2840	Manufacture of metal forming machinery and machine tools	other science_tech manufacture
2841	Manufacture of metal forming machinery	other science_tech manufacture
2849	Manufacture of other machine tools	other science_tech manufacture

(*continued*)

Table A1 Cont.

NACE	*NACE_descriptor*	*ONS_category*
2890	Manufacture of other special-purpose machinery	other science_tech manufacture
2891	Manufacture of machinery for metallurgy	other science_tech manufacture
2892	Manufacture of machinery for mining, quarrying and construction	other science_tech manufacture
2893	Manufacture of machinery for food, beverage and tobacco processing	other science_tech manufacture
2894	Manufacture of machinery for textile, apparel and leather production	other science_tech manufacture
2895	Manufacture of machinery for paper and paperboard production	other science_tech manufacture
2896	Manufacture of plastics and rubber machinery	other science_tech manufacture
2899	Manufacture of other special-purpose machinery n.e.c.	other science_tech manufacture
2900	Manufacture of motor vehicles, trailers and semi-trailers	other science_tech manufacture
2910	Manufacture of motor vehicles	other science_tech manufacture
2920	Manufacture of bodies (coachwork) for motor vehicles (except caravans)	other science_tech manufacture
2930	Manufacture of parts and accessories for motor vehicles	other science_tech manufacture
2931	Manufacture of electrical and electronic equipment for motor vehicles	other science_tech manufacture
2932	Manufacture of other parts and accessories for motor vehicles	other science_tech manufacture
3000	Manufacture of other transport equipment	other science_tech manufacture
3010	Building of ships and boats	other science_tech manufacture
3011	Building of ships and floating structures	other science_tech manufacture
3012	Building of pleasure and sporting boats	other science_tech manufacture
3020	Manufacture of railway locomotives and rolling stock	other science_tech manufacture
3030	Manufacture of air and spacecraft and related machinery	other science_tech manufacture
3040	Manufacture of military fighting vehicles	other science_tech manufacture
3090	Manufacture of transport equipment n.e.c.	other science_tech manufacture
3091	Manufacture of motorcycles	other science_tech manufacture
3092	Manufacture of bicycles and invalid carriages	other science_tech manufacture

Table A1 Cont.

NACE	*NACE_descriptor*	*ONS_category*
3099	Manufacture of other transport equipment n.e.c.	other science_tech manufacture
3212	Manufacture of jewellery and related articles	other science_tech manufacture
3240	Manufacture of professional and arcade games and toys	other science_tech manufacture
3250	Manufacture of medical and dental instruments and supplies	life science and healthcare
3312	Repair of machinery	other science_tech manufacture
3313	Repair of electronic and optical equipment	digital technologies
3314	Repair of electrical equipment	other science_tech manufacture
3315	Repair and maintenance of ships and boats	other science_tech manufacture
3316	Repair and maintenance of aircraft and spacecraft	other science_tech manufacture
3317	Repair and maintenance of other transport equipment	other science_tech manufacture
5100	Air transport	other science_tech services
5110	Scheduled passenger air transport	other science_tech services
5120	Freight air transport and space transport	other science_tech services
5121	Freight air transport	other science_tech services
5122	Space transport	other science_tech services
5820	Software publishing	digital technologies
5821	Publishing of computer games	digital technologies
5829	Other software publishing	digital technologies
6200	Computer programming, consultancy and related activities	digital technologies
6201	Computer programming activities	digital technologies
6202	Computer consultancy activities	digital technologies
6203	Computer facilities management activities	digital technologies
6209	Other information technology and computed service activities	digital technologies
6310	Data processing, hosting and related activities; web portals	digital technologies

(*continued*)

Table A1 Cont.

NACE	*NACE_descriptor*	*ONS_category*
6311	Data processing, hosting and related activities	digital technologies
6312	Web portals	digital technologies
7100	Architectural and engineering activities; technical testing and analysis	other science_tech services
7110	Architectural and engineering activities and related technical consultancy	other science_tech services
7111	Architectural activities	other science_tech services
7112	Engineering activities and related technical consultancy	other science_tech services
7120	Technical testing and analysis	other science_tech services
7219	Other research and experimental development on natural sciences and engineering	other science_tech services
7220	Research and experimental development on social sciences and humanities	other science_tech services
7490	Quantity surveying activities	other science_tech services
8540	Higher education	other science_tech services
8541	Post-secondary non-tertiary education	other science_tech services
8542	Tertiary education	other science_tech services
9511	Repair of computers and peripheral equipment	digital technologies
9521	Repair of consumer electronics	other science_tech manufacture
9522	Repair of household appliances and home and garden equipment	other science_tech manufacture
9525	Repair of watches, clocks and jewellery	other science_tech manufacture

Note: The ONS set of industries is defined at 5- digit SIC2007 level. I refine this to focus on Industry 4.0, dropping a number of content activities (publishing, media, music, advertising) and science / health activities (life sciences, health), except where SIC descriptors directly pertain to R&D and/ or manufacturing. We then crosswalk this to 4- digit SIC, which is identical to the NACE Rev 2 / SNI07 codes used in Sweden and other EU states.

Table A2 List of STEM occupations STEM occupations are taken from NESTA (Bakhshi et al., 2015)

Category	*ISCO88*	*ISCO88_descriptor*
IT	1226	Production and Operations Department Managers in Transport, Storage and Communications
IT	1236	Computing Services Department Managers
IT	1316	General Managers in Transport, Storage and Communications
IT	1317	General Managers of Business Services
Science	2113	Chemists
Science	2211	Biologists, Botanists, Zoologists and Related Professionals
Science	2212	Pharmacologists, Pathologists and Related Professionals
Science	2111	Physicists and Astronomers
Science	2114	Geologists and Geophysicists
Science	2211	Biologists, Botanists, Zoologists and Related Professionals
Science	2212	Pharmacologists, Pathologists and Related Professionals
Engineering	2142	Civil Engineers
Engineering	2144	Mechanical Engineers
Engineering	2143	Electrical Engineers
Engineering	2144	Electronics and Telecommunications Engineers
Engineering	2149	Architects, Engineers and Related Professionals Not Elsewhere Classified
Engineering	2149	Architects, Engineers and Related Professionals NEC
Engineering	2150	Architects, Engineers and Related Professionals NEC
IT	2131	Computer Systems Designers and Analysts
IT	2132	Computer Programmers
IT	2139	Computing Professionals NEC
IT	2131	Computer Systems Designers and Analysts
IT	2132	Computer Systems Designers and Analysts
IT	2131	Computer Systems Designers and Analysts
IT	2132	Computer Programmers
IT	2139	Computing Professionals NEC
IT	2131	Computer Systems Designers and Analysts
IT	2132	Computer Programmers
IT	2139	Computing Professionals NEC
Science	2211	Biologists, Botanists, Zoologists and Related Professionals
Science	2212	Biologists, Botanists, Zoologists and Related Professionals
Science	1237	Research and Development Department Managers
Science	1319	General Managers NEC
Engineering	2148	Cartographers and Surveyors

Note: I crosswalk these from UK SOC2010 occupation codes to SOC2008, then to the international ISCO08 and ISCO88 standards. The latter is identical to the SSYK-96 codes used in the Swedish data.

Note

1 Stockholm County consists of 26 municipalities, out of 290 municipalities, and there are 20 counties in the whole of Sweden.

References

Aghion, P., Blundell, R., Griffith, R. et al. (2009) The effects of entry on incumbent innovation and productivity. *Review of Economics and Statistics* 91: 20–32.

Bakhshi, H., Davies, J., Freeman, A., et al. (2015) *The Geography of the UK's Creative and High-Tech Economies*. London: NESTA.

Bathelt, H. (2005) Geographies of production: growth regimes in spatial perspective (II) – knowledge creation and growth in clusters. *Progress in Human Geography* 29: 204–216.

Bitard, P., Edquist, C., Hommen, L. et al. (2008) Reconsidering the paradox of high R&D input and low innovation: Sweden. In: Edquist C. and Hommen L. (eds), *Small Country Innovation Systems: Globalization, Change and Policy in Asia and Europe*. Cheltenham: Edward Elgar, 237–280.

Bresnahan, T. (2010) General purpose technologies. In: Hall B.H. and Rosenberg N. (eds), *Handbook of the Economics of Innovation*. Amsterdam: North-Holland, 761–791.

Brettel, M., Friederichsen, N., Keller, M. et al. (2014) How virtualization, decentralization and network building change the manufacturing landscape: an Industry 4.0 oerspective. *International Journal of Mechanical, Industrial Science and Engineering* 8: 37–44.

Brown, R. and Mason, C. (2014) Inside the high-tech black box: a critique of technology entrepreneurship policy. *Technovation* 34: 773–784.

Brynjolfsson, E. and McAfee (2014) *The Second Machine Age: Work, Progress, and Prosperity in a Time of Brilliant Technologies*. New York: W.W. Norton & Company.

Chaminade, C., Zabala, J.M. and Treccani, A. (2010) *The Swedish national innovation system and its relevance for the emergence of global innovation networks*. CIRCLE Working Paper 2010/09. Lund: CIRCLE.

Ejermo, O. and Kander, A. (2009) The Swedish paradox revisited. In: Karlsson C., Johansson B. and Stough R. (eds), *Entrepreneurship and Innovation in Functional Regions*. Cheltenham: Edward Elgar, pp. 49–76.

Freeman, C. (1991) Networks of innovators: a synthesis of research issues. *Research Policy* 20: 499–514.

Gens, M., Giertz, E. and Rickne, A. (2015) ICT related technology shifts in the engineering sector. In: Giertz E., Rickne A. and Rouvinen P. (eds), *Small and Beautiful: The ICT Success of Finland & Sweden*. Stockholm: Vinnova, pp. 183–199.

Giertz, E. (2015a) The Swedish ICT sector today. In: Giertz E., Rickne A. and Rouvinen P. (eds), *Small and Beautiful: The ICT Success of Finland & Sweden*. Stockholm: Vinnova, pp. 106–121.

Giertz, E. (2015b) Understanding the Swedish saga through an historical exposé. In: Giertz E., Rickne A. and Rouvinen P. (eds), *Small and Beautiful: The ICT Success of Finland & Sweden*. Stockholm: Vinnova, pp. 62–95.

Glaeser, E. (2011) *The Triumph of the City*. London: Pan Macmillan.

Grabher, G. (2002) Cool projects, boring institutions: temporary collaboration in social context. *Regional Studies* 36: 205–214.

Grabher, G. and Ibert, O. (2014) Distance as asset? Knowledge collaboration in hybrid virtual communities. *Journal of Economic Geography* 14: 97–123.

Harris, J. (2015) *Identifying Science and Technology Businesses in Official Statistics*. London: ONS.

Kremer, M. (1993) The O-ring theory of economic development. *Quarterly Journal of Economics* 108: 551–575.

Lee, J., Bagheri, B. and Kao, H.-A. (2015) A cyber-physical systems architecture for Industry 4.0-based manufacturing systems. *Manufacturing Letters* 3: 18–23.

Lee, J., Kao, H.-A. and Yang, S. (2014) Service innovation and smart analytics for Industry 4.0 and big data environment. *Procedia CIRP* 16: 3–8.

Martins, J. (2015) The extended workplace in a creative cluster: exploring space(s) of digital work in silicon roundabout. *Journal of Urban Design* 20: 25–145.

Mudambi, R. (2008) Location, control and innovation in knowledge-intensive industries. *Journal of Economic Geography* 8: 699–725.

Nathan, M. (2018) 'Hardware is hard': manufacturing startups in an urban technology clusters. MAKERS working paper.

Nathan, M. and Vandore, E. (2014) Here be startups: exploring London's 'Tech City' digital cluster. *Environment and Planning A* 46: 2283–2299.

Perez, C. (2010) Technological revolutions and techno-economic paradigms. *Cambridge Journal of Economics* 34: 185–202.

Schwab, K. (2017) *The Fourth Industrial Revolution*. London: Crown Business.

Semuels, A. (2017) Why does Sweden have so many start-ups? *The Atlantic*, 28 September.

Spigel, B. (2017) The relational organization of entrepreneurial ecosystems. *Entrepreneurship Theory and Practice* 41: 49–72.

9 De-globalisation, value chains and reshoring

Diletta Pegoraro, Lisa De Propris and Agnieska Chidlow

9.1 Introduction

This chapter aims to review the recent debate on de-globalisation and to present some preliminary evidence that reconsiders the value of a manufacturing activity in light of the current geopolitical turmoil and new technological availabilities (*The Economist*, 2009). This is somehow important as changes in the nature of markets and technology can significantly impact on firms' location decisions in relation to manufacturing activities (Chidlow et al., 2009; Chidlow et al., 2015; Li and Bathelt, 2018; Mudambi et al., 2018). More specifically, such location decisions can relate to the adaptation of a reshoring strategy, which involves bringing manufacturing production (or part of it) back from abroad.

Since the 1970s, the intensification of exchanges in trade, capital and knowledge has fostered the inter-connectedness of economies on a global scale. Pushed by a neoliberal rationale, Western companies started expanding part of their business functions, *in primis* production and manufacturing, beyond their national borders. This was operationalised in two ways: either by relocating production facilities to a foreign location (in-house offshoring); or by outsourcing some functions to foreign suppliers (outsourcing offshoring). These strategies required production and manufacturing processes to be sliced up into smaller segments and to be coordinated by the lead firm (Jabbour, 2012; Timmer et al., 2014). In the 1990s, the global value chains (GVCs) framework was used to describe the increasing adoption of this fragmented production model by MNEs (Benito et al., 2019; Gereffi and Korzeniewicz, 1994). Since then, the GVC framework has been widely adopted by international organisations such as the Organisation for Economic Co-operation and Development (OECD), the World Trade Organization (WTO) and the United Nations Conference on Trade and Development (UNCTAD) to monitor the impact of this global organisation of production on host (and less so on home) economies, as well as on trends in globalisation and international trade. Many studies have looked at how countries were involved in GVCs through backward and forward linkages[1] and the impact of this involvement on their socio-economic development (Baldwin, 2016; Los et al., 2015; Timmer et al., 2014; Wang et al., 2017). In hindsight, the end of the 1990s and the beginning of the 2000s marked a time when globalisation and pro-globalisation forces peaked.

The global organisation of production in GVCs started to be challenged by the Global Financial Crisis (GFC) in 2008/2009 and following the collapse of the so-called Washington Consensus (Gereffi, 2014). The GFC brought to the fore not only the cost of having economies inter-linked and therefore at risk of shocks initiated elsewhere, but more crucially, it also highlighted the socio-economic cost of offshoring on home economies. The outcome has been a more critical approach to globalisation as businesses have also started to weigh the costs and benefits of coordinating worldwide production processes with changing markets and emerging new technologies. The current reconfiguration of GVCs is also led by geopolitical and trade forces, which this chapter only tangentially touches upon.

9.2 The world got smaller

The concept of modern globalisation is very recent. It was first introduced by the seminal work of Levitt (1983) for describing the novel phenomenon on the globalisation of markets. Since then, a large literature has flourished to try to define the concept and to identify key actors, drivers and operations, as well as discussing its benefits and costs and for whom.[2] The globalisation of markets was only the tip of the iceberg; however, the comfort of operating in a mature technological paradigm meant more aggressive price competition in domestic and international markets, forcing firms to seek cost reduction in production. At the same time, faster transport and easier communications really made the world a smaller place. In this context, multi-national enterprises (hereafter MNEs) saw the opportunity to extend their reach to markets that were global but fundamentally homogeneous, giving them scope to benefit from significant economies of scale (Baldwin, 2016).

Technology and the nature of competition constantly change the way in which the economy organises production and especially in the manufacturing sectors. The organisation of production had already moved away from the vertically integrated Fordist model (Chandler, 1962) to a stage-specialised and vertically dis-integrated flexible specialisation model from the 1960s onwards (Piore and Sabel, 1986). Networks of buyers and sellers replaced the factory model, as large firms became core buyers coordinating such networks (Saxenian, 1990). More generally, smaller and more specialised firms became parts of flexible and ever adjustable networks of buyers and suppliers located geographically closer to each other, thereby fostering agglomeration and external economies (Becattini, 1990 and Becattini et al., 2014; Porter, 1996), as well as flexibility, specialisation and innovativeness. These local production systems responded to a volatile and sophisticated demand eager for differentiated, innovative and fast-changing products. The introduction of new technologies such as electronics and mechatronics (with the transistor and microprocessor), as well as easily accessible telecommunications and computers since the 1960s allowed this reorganisation of production. The technological changes described above are often referred to as being part of the Third Industrial Revolution (see Chapter 1 in this volume).

Production processes that were already disintegrated and parcelled underwent another radical reorganisation from the 1980s onwards. Globalisation kicked in and firms, especially large buyers seeking cost efficiency to compete in global markets, started to move labour-intensive functions to lower labour-cost countries in Asia and China in particular. Indeed, this could not have taken place without the concomitant opening of China and Asia to the global economy as an attractive location to produce to export. The location decision choice of MNEs in relation to different portions of the supply chain created worldwide and complex global value chains (, Dicken, 2015; Feenstra, 1998; Gereffi, 1999; Krugman et al., 1995). Indeed, each stage of the production process was associated with varying degrees of value creation to which different costs were apportioned. Low and high-value added functions were geographically separated and for the first time the production process was unbundled (Baldwin, 2016), i.e. geographically dispersed contributing to an international fragmentation of production. Indeed, low-value-added functions were located in developing and emerging economies to benefit from raw materials or lower labour costs. In contrast, high-value-added functions (high-end design, R&D and product development) largely remained anchored in high-cost and high knowledge-intensive locations (Mudambi, 2007).

For decades, the operations of global value chains through 'offshoring' and foreign direct investment have redesigned the architecture of manufacturing activities worldwide. This created a thick web of exchanges between the East and West and transformed the economic and social profile of places, reshaping their identities (Mudambi, 2008; Mudambi and Venzin, 2010; Storper and Scott, 1995). There has always been a strand in the international business literature suspicious of the uneven distribution of the benefits of globalisation (Bailey et al., 2010; Chomsky, 2016), but their arguments were sidelined by an overwhelming enthusiasm for and obsession with globalisation (by hyper-globalists). This zeal for globalisation came to an end in 2008 with the GFC.

9.3 The de-globalisation debate

Economies and societies face unprecedented changes every time a worldwide economic and political shock occurs. Recently, the 2008 GFC profoundly disturbed the status quo of advanced economies and their societies: firstly, it was followed by a deep and somewhat long economic recession across Europe and the US which left firms uncertain about accessing finance and therefore investments (Gereffi and Luo, 2014); secondly, austerity and unemployment led to the emergence of populist movements in Western countries, and, in the EU, to a resentment towards European tight fiscal policies (Rodrik, 2018a); finally, protectionist policies and a reduction of outward investment from advanced countries – especially to developing countries – has stalled globalisation as it was perceived before.

In addition to these three aspects, there is one more whose importance has increased recently: technological change. There is a wave of new technologies that is emerging and the expectation is that they will change production models, the nature of sectors, markets and the terms of trade (Galvin et al., 2018). Some large firms and MNEs have been first-movers and actually driving the whole narrative on digitalisation and automation, together with innovative micro-firms in these frontier technologies at the other end of the spectrum. The more substantial impact on the form of supply chains is still to come. There is evidence that MNEs are reorienting their internationalisation strategies by changing the parameters of their production location choices.

The fallout from the GFC and the emergence of new technologies has had the unexpected consequence of stalling globalisation as firms have reassessed the true benefits of internationalisation. As GVCs appear to be shrinking and international investments fall, the world seems to be becoming a smaller place (Baldwin, 2016). Indeed, in the last decade the aggressive pro-globalisation narrative has been replaced by a more pragmatic and balanced view which has exposed the weaknesses and the risks inherent in globalisation and global value chains (Bailey and De Propris, 2014a), leading to a long-overdue and more open debate on the heterogeneous effects of globalisation across places, industries, communities and people.

Policy makers and leading scholars have started to shift their attention from the benefits that globalisation delivered to MNEs in the form of offshoring large parts of their value chains, to the costs entire communities were left to pay economically and socially in hollowed-out home regions (Bailey and Turok, 2016). Indeed, a first consequence of globalisation was the relocation of labour-intensive manufacturing operations away from historical industrial regions in the US and Europe (and especially the UK), causing deep unemployment and contributing to increasing levels of inequality in advanced societies (Davis, 2013; Davis and Cobb, 2010). A second and more systemic concern with manufacturing hollowing-out was that it weakened the ability in the European and US economies to promptly respond to external shocks, such as the 2008 GFC. The demise of manufacturing activities resulted in a loss of skills, competences and tacit knowledge across a sufficiently diversified suite of sectors, reducing economic diversity and eroding systemic economic resilience. Such *malaise* led to a revived interest around manufacturing and what forms of manufacturing could be relocated in countries such as the US or the UK to 'rebalance' their economies (Ancarani et al., 2015; Bayley and De Propris, 2014b; Gray et al., 2013; Kinkel, 2014; Tate et al., 2014) Opportunities for repopulating manufacturing industries were explored by the EU Commission (EU Commission, 2014) and by the Obama administration (White House Administration, 2012).

This renewed interest in manufacturing initiated a reflection on what manufacturing really meant in the 2010s. The outcome of the relationship between technological changes and sustainability concerns flourished in a new competitive context. A fast-moving debate on an emerging new manufacturing model shaped by a range of new technologies (considered as part of the Fourth Industrial Revolution) triggered a process of profound production reorganisation which could also result in a reconfiguration of global value chains. The OECD suggests that the Fourth Industrial Revolution has the potential to restore the competitiveness of advanced economies (OECD, 2017). The ambition and vision by policy makers to strengthen the presence of manufacturing across EU regions or US states was received positively by businesses, which were themselves sensing a change in the wind. The running 'offshoring train' that lots of firms had jumped on now started to slow down.

This offshoring slowdown spurred a rethink of businesses' strategies towards more regional and arm's-length controlled operations (Bailey and De Propris, 2014b). This trend was also recorded by macro-economic indicators such as foreign direct investment (FDI) (see Section 9.3 for more details). Firms are not the only actors playing a role in reducing the intensity of globalisation; society as a whole is involved. Protests on climate change, air pollution, gas emissions, but also movements for better labour conditions in developing countries, are leading the phenomenon of de-globalisation. Society as a whole is becoming more interested in issues relating to the Sustainable Development Goals (SDGs) and following a path that diverges from the neoliberalism position which was dominant for more than three decades (Lawrence and Almas, 2018).

9.4 The reorganisation of global production

As social dynamics are changing, so too is the global production system. The role of technology is of primary importance in this transformation. At the 2019 World Economic Forum, economists and policy makers discussed issues relating to the theme of 'Globalisation 4.0: Shaping a New Architecture in the Age of the Fourth Industrial Revolution' (Schwab, 2018). Industry 4.0 and its technological development profoundly shape sectors such as health, mobility, services, finance and manufacturing. Especially in manufacturing, Industry 4.0 triggers changes in shortening the process of product development, and the identification of new markets, flexibility, organisational hierarchy and efficiency (Lasi et al., 2014). Heavy investments in technological development by advanced economies paid off in terms of offering new solutions in the realm of robotics and AI together with other digital technologies such as cloud computing, big data and the sharing economy. This wave of technological change is often referred to as the Fourth Industrial Revolution (Lasi et al., 2014).

This revolution started in the early 2010s and its exponential growth is influencing actors across society. The production process paradigm in particular is shifting from mass-production to mass-customised production as new production technologies open up the opportunity to reduce the impact of labour cost on the overall production costs (Brettel et al., 2014; Rodrik, 2018). In so doing, the decision to locate low-value and high-labour content tasks in low labour cost countries might no longer be a mainstream value chain strategy.

New technologies to engage in the production process are not the only factors which influence the boundaries of a global production process (Schotter et al., 2017; Strange and Zucchella, 2017); other factors can play a role as well. Firstly, developing countries are still competitive in term of labour wages, but the gap with advanced countries is narrowing and eroding the short-term cost benefit of locating a business function there (Tate et al., 2014). Secondly, China – once the factory of the world – is heavily investing in the high-technology (AI and robots) and infrastructure sectors (the One Belt One Road Initiative) to support and foster its internal economic and demographic growth (Swaine, 2015). In the 2000s, its goal was hosting different types of manufacturing sectors by offering investment incentives and tax reduction. In the 2020s, its focus is to become a leader in green and sustainable technology (Ju and Yu, 2018). Thirdly, rising South-South trade and consumption in the Global South will prompt a reorganisation of GVCs (Horner and Nadvi, 2018). Finally, there are political uncertainties pervading Western economies, such as a weak EU and the the US-China trade war (Inglhart and Norris, 2016). These exogenous factors of a macro-political scale have an important effect on the organisation of manufacturing processes in MNEs and small and medium-sized enterprises (SMEs).

Some of the tangible examples of this fragile and kaleidoscopic scenario are Brexit, steel tariffs in the US and the reorganisation of the automotive supply chain in Germany and the wider European automotive industry. The first effect could lead towards an increase in supply chain complexity, and transportation and logistics costs in the near future in the UK (*Financial Times*, 2018a, 2018b). The second effect is the possibility of bringing back production from abroad inside US borders or establishing a closer relationship with domestic or Mexican suppliers (*The Economist*, 2018). The third example concerns losing ground in the automotive industry, as electric cars start to gain momentum and the German (and European) automotive business model is highly oriented towards petrol and diesel cars (Bormann et al., 2018).

From this brief list of tangible examples, new opportunities are arising, and among these, there is a chance that advanced economies might host again manufacturing activities, which are becoming increasingly higher value added, albeit less labour intensive. (Vanchan et al., 2018). Manufacturing functions are becoming higher in value than before, as they are no longer the mere assembly part of the value chain, but part of an integrated process that feed from innovation and meet consumers' need with reduced lead-time. This requires access to a highly skilled labour force and technological capabilities which advanced economies have. This is what in part is driving the current de-globalisation wave.

Having recognised that de-globalisation is a broader social movement created by a discontent with globalisation, this chapter continues to explore de-globalisation with some data at the macro-level before introducing the concept of manufacturing reshoring.

9.5 Some evidence of de-globalisation

In this section we piece together evidence on de-globalisation by looking at three trends: 1) recent trends in FDI[3] in terms of volume, geography, sector and operations; 2) the current reorganisation of GVC into shorter and more compact value chains; and 3) current firms' strategies to reshore production functions back to the home economy. We will discuss each of these in turn.

9.5.1 FDI trends

In the last few years, outward and inward global FDI has stagnated partly due to a contraction in the *volume of outward FDI* from advanced economies and inward FDI to developing economies. Figures 9.1a and 9.1b below show that inward and outward global FDI peaked in 2007, before dropping dramatically afterwards in 2008–2009, especially from advanced economies, and has not recovered to pre-crisis levels (for more evidence, see UNCTAD, 2018, Figure 9.5, p. 10). The lack of growth in FDI return on investment (ROI) in developing and transition economies in the period 2016–2017 and the rise of investments in asset-light forms of production suggest that an international production reorganisation is under way, especially in terms of a regionalisation of FDI (UNCTAD, 2017, 2018).

There is also evidence of a *changing geography of FDI*. Looking at regional levels of FDI in the period 2016–2017, inward FDI fell by 69% in Europe and 65% in North America, contributing to a total drop in inward FDI of 59% in 2017 with respect to the previous year in advanced economies. In the same period, there was no variation in inward FDIs into developing economies, as East and South Asia recorded a slight increase of 2%, while a negative figure was registered for West Asia and Africa of 21% and 27% respectively. Latin America and the Caribbean performed well by attracting 8% more FDI in 2017 than in the previous year (Figure 9.2). Equally, outward FDI fell by \$800 billion, reaching \$1 trillion in 2017 (\$1.8 trillion in 2007). Outward FDI from advanced economies – despite a recovery in 2015 – in 2017 was still well below the pre-crisis level in 2007, especially in terms of European and US FDI. Overall these two trends negatively impacted on the global picture, as FDI from other parts of the world is not compensating in value (see Figure 9.3).

The changing geography of FDIs seems to occur at the same time as a shift in the sectors and modes of entry. By distinguishing FDI according to sector destination, Table 9.1 shows that overall, there has been an increase in Announced Greenfield FDIs in the manufacturing sector in 2017. Sector data show that advanced countries invested much less abroad in particular in the primary (raw materials), energy and services sectors. However, it is noticeable that advanced countries were the favourite destination for more FDI in manufacturing sectors (with a 34% increase); chemicals and chemical products, electrical and electronic equipment, and motor vehicles sectors are leading the trend in this regard. The bottom part of Table 9.1 shows data on the destinations

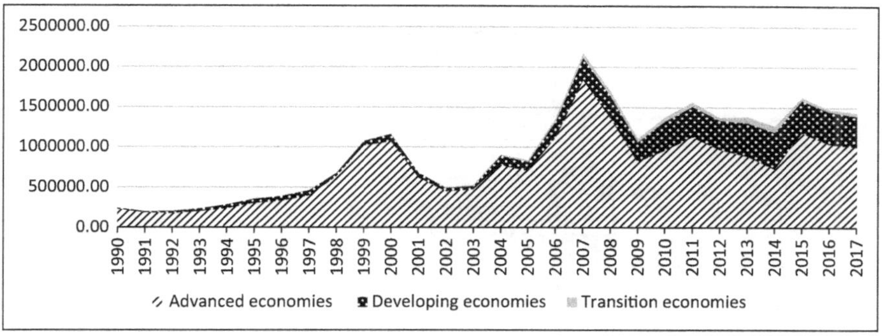

Figure 9.1a FDI outflows, 1990–2017.
Source: Authors' elaboration, based on UNCTAD (2018).

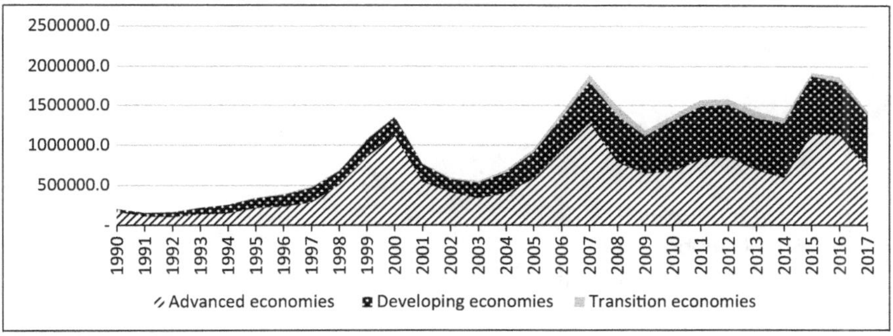

Figure 9.1b FDI inflows, 1990–2017.
Source: Authors' elaboration, based on UNCTAD (2018).

of greenfield FDI by macro-regions. Here we see more clearly that advanced countries have invested less in East and South Asia, South Asia and West Asia. Closer to home for the EU, FDI in transition economies in Eastern Europe has also dropped substantially. According to the data, advanced countries invested more in other advanced countries (i.e. US and Europe), with an increase of up to 32%. In other words, advanced countries are intensifying investments in other advanced countries and are reducing those in developing countries; this conforms with the view that de-globalisation is ongoing.

If we take a longer time horizon and look at the percentage of greenfield announcements between 2007 and 2017, both in value and number, we again find evidence of the changing patterns of FDI in support of a de-globalisation trend. By taking 2007 as a base year, Figure 9.4 shows that both the value and number of FDI projects to advanced economies increased, whilst those to

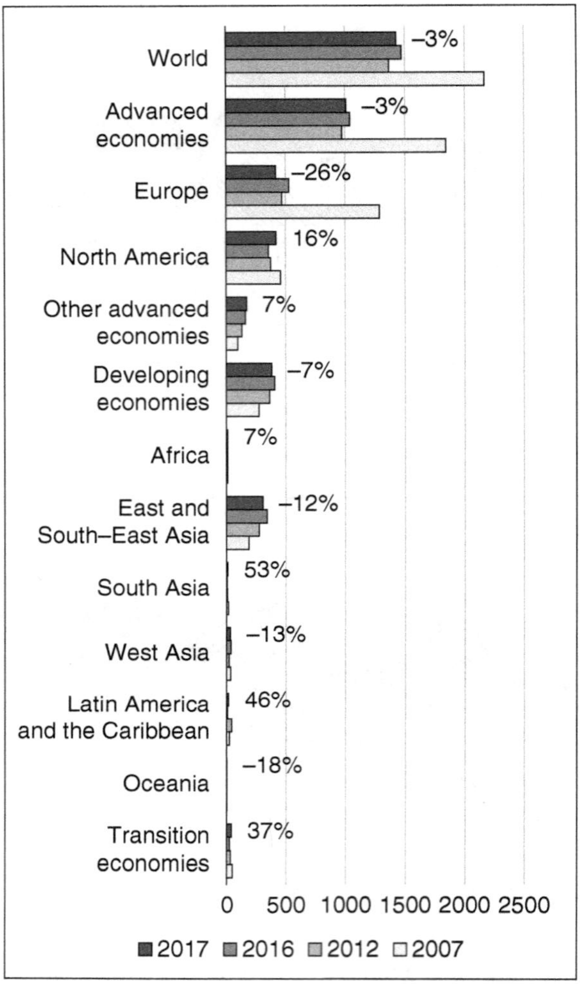

Figure 9.2 FDI outflows, by region and selected years (% variation 2016–2017).
Source: Authors' elaboration based on UNCTAD data (2018).

developing economies fell. In particular, the value of investments to advanced economies rose from 37% to 44%, while it fell from 55% to 51% to developing economies. However, it should be noted that in 2017, still half of the value of FDI was destined to developing economies. In terms of numbers, we observe similar patterns, but in 2017 a growing number of FDI projects were actually destined to advanced economies (58% of the total).

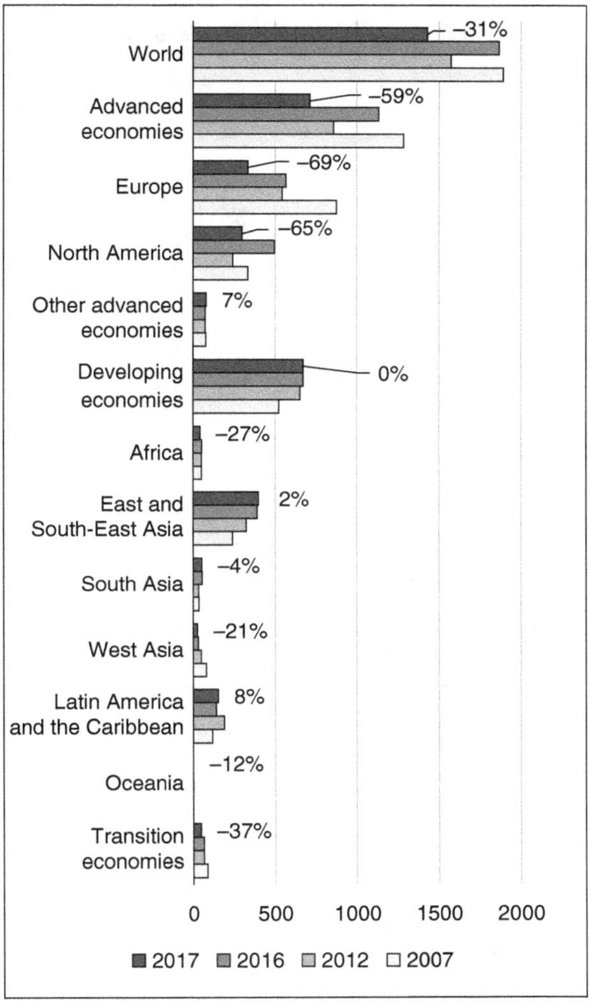

Figure 9.3 FDI inflows, by region and selected years, (% variation 2016–2017).
Source: Authors' elaboration with 2018 UNCTAD data.

Overall, the FDI data show that investment by advanced economies in Asia has contracted, whilst FDI flows within advanced economies have increased. The latter has involved in particular manufacturing sectors and some service sectors such as business services. This trend seems to suggest a change in the motives and destinations of foreign investments by MNEs from advanced economies.

Table 9.1 Announced greenfield FDI, 2016–2017

	Advanced countries as destination			*Advanced countries as investor*		
	2016	*2017*	*Var%*	*2016*	*2017*	*Var%*
Part I						
Total	254,187	318,406	20%	501,218	478,359	-5%
Primary	2,446	3,996	39%	47,371	18,415	-157%
Manufacturing	99,300	151,314	34%	197,404	212,357	7%
Textiles, clothing and leather	18,162	16,127	-13%	22,617	20,643	-10%
Chemicals and chemical products	12,813	32,060	60%	30,361	34,738	13%
Electrical and electronic equipment	8,161	21,669	62%	18,574	21,746	15%
Motor vehicles and other transport equipment	21,586	31,817	32%	44,561	47,555	6%
Services	152,441	163,096	7%	256,443	247,587	-4%
Electricity, gas and water	32,287	23,404	-38%	67,613	42,330	-60%
Construction	30,314	26,292	-15%	35,371	35,475	0%
Trade	15,823	20,967	25%	21,622	27,860	22%
Transport, storage and communication	15,498	12,954	-20%	31,220	32,356	4%
Business services	44,096	54650	19%	65,390	68,721	5%
Part II						
Announced greenfield FDI projects by macro-region, 2016–2017 (millions of dollars)						
	2016	*2017*	*Var%*	*2016*	*2017*	*Var%*
World	254,187	318406	20%	501,218	478,359	-5%
Advanced economies	204,031	255,003	20%	204,031	255,003	20%
Europe	127,061	150,934	16%	131,859	160,778	18%
North America	55,627	72,810	24%	54,370	70,537	23%
Other advanced countries	21,343	31,259	32%	17,802	23,687	25%
Developing economies	49,460	61,985	20%	242,827	204,501	-19%
Africa	1,411	1,961	28%	19,945	32,398	38%
East and South Asia	36,604	35,810	-2%	94,060	76,881	-22%
South Asia	6,759	5,986	-13%	46,873	23,479	-100%
West Asia	2,887	15,655	82%	23,159	13,579	-71%
Latin America and the Caribbean	1,799	2,572	30%	58,653	57,781	-2%
Transition economies	696	1,418	51%	54,360	18,855	-188%

Source: Authors' elaboration, based on UNCTAD (2018).

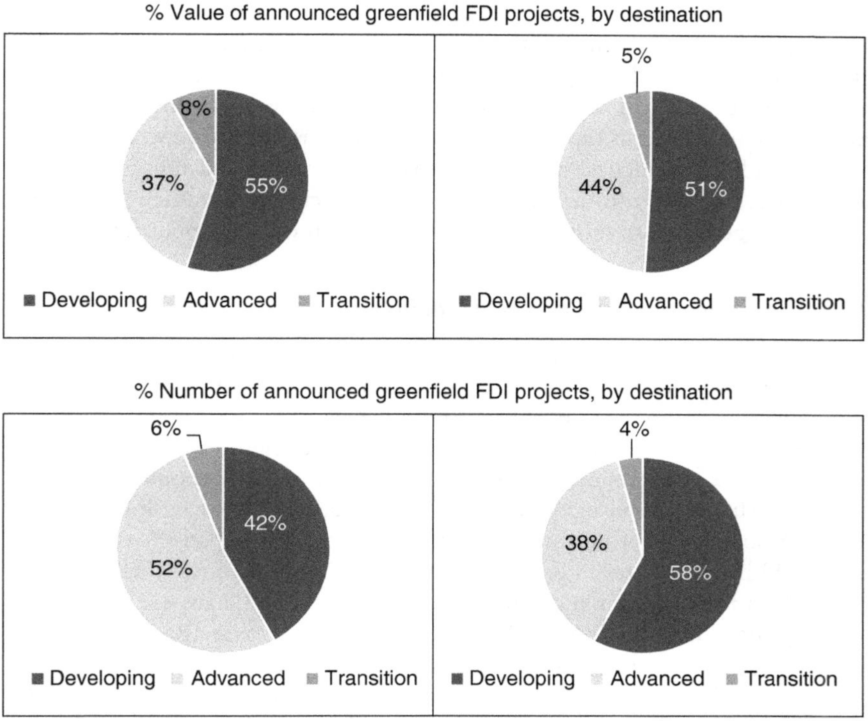

Figure 9.4 Number and value of greenfield FDIs, 2007 and 2017.
Source: Authors' elaboration, UNCTAD data (2018).

In parallel to the slowdown of worldwide FDIs flows, *geopolitical turmoil* also seems to weave a narrative around protectionism, trade wars and national interest. For long loud advocates of the free market, the US has recently embarked on a journey to curtail its trade in an effort to protect domestic jobs (White House, 2017).

According to UNTACD (2018), political factors and the emergence of strategic technologies will shape future FDI flows. Indeed, early moves by some political leaders in advanced economies to scrutinise FDI more closely can be seen as emerging signs of policy makers aiming to screen or block inward investment on public order and national security grounds. For example, the US Department of the Treasury introduced 'temporary regulations to protect critical American technology and intellectual property from potentially harmful foreign acquisitions' (US Treasury, 2018). Equally, tax reforms in the US that reward the repatriation of accumulated profits by American MNEs are aimed at cutting FDI outflows. In the EU, the International Trade Committee (INTA) proposed a harmonisation of FDI screening between Member States in order to cooperate over security and public order issues against emerging FDI inflows (EU Parliament, 2018).

Geopolitics and governments' concern with controlling emerging technologies are influencing the degree of openness to foreign investment and therefore countries' links in the GVC. Geopolitics is diffusing a sense of mistrust and uncertainty towards the motives of FDI, whereas protecting strategic technology explains countries' wariness to share knowledge and innovation. This seems to be less the case for exchanges within macro-regions such as Asia and Europe, suggesting a trend towards a regionalisation of investment activities.

9.5.2 Shorter and more compact value chains

FDI is not the only economic measure we can consider. Trade data gives us further insights on global economic trends and on the state of global production fragmentation, and hence on GVCs (Frederick, 2014).

The latest data (UNCTAD, 2017, 2018) provides significant evidence that EU GVCs are strongly integrated intra-EU; in particular, European GVCs in manufacturing are less integrated globally than expected: they have lower foreign sourcing percentage of intermediates (i.e. backward participation) and limited use of EU intermediates in exporting to non-EU countries (UNCTAD, 2018, p. 23). This is the culmination of trends that, since 2012, have seen EU firms sourcing more from within the EU, at the expense of extra-EU sourcing (see Figure 9.5). By extension, intra-regional exports of intermediate goods have risen within the EU and have dropped from outside the EU (see Figure 9.6).

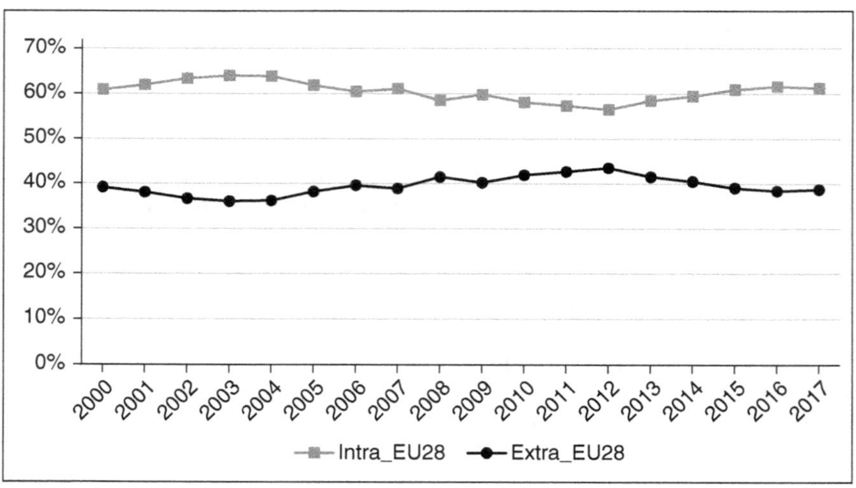

Figure 9.5 EU-28 intra-regional trade import in intermediate goods, 2000–2017 (% in regional total).

Source: Authors' elaboration with EUROSTAT data.

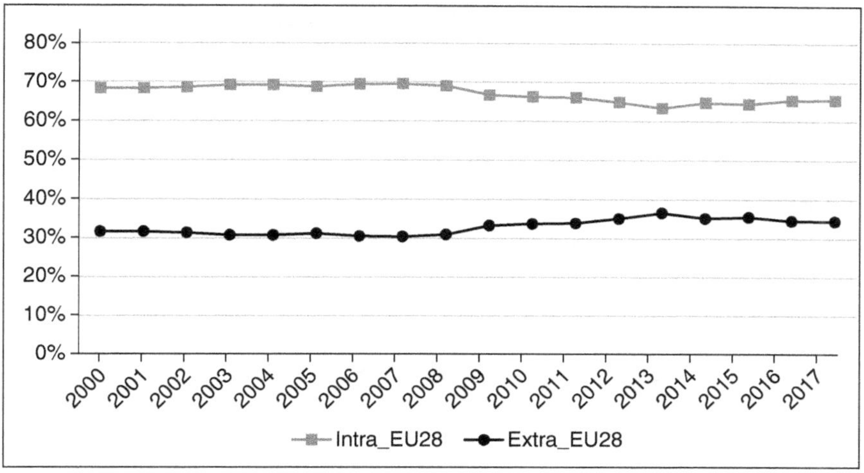

Figure 9.6 EU-28 intra-regional trade export in intermediate goods, 2000–2017 (% regional total).

Source: Authors' elaboration with EUROSTAT data.

Overall, the EU-28 presents a lower GVC participation rate (at 30%) than other economies (Backer and Miroudot, 2013).

This is consistent with UNCTAD (2018), which records a stagnation in the activities of post-2008 GVCs; in particular, the report found a change in the organisation of production of G7 economies (including the UK, Germany, France and Italy) between 2011 and 2015, with an increase in 'traditional trade production' (production to export) and a drop in 'simple GVCs' and 'complex GVCs'. The latter was particularly the case for manufacturing GVCs. Academic debate has started to observe such trends, suggesting that international production might be undergoing a structural reorganisation. Gereffi et al. (2014), for example, suggested that as assets became more intangible, firms required different skills and competencies, as well as adopted different internationalisation strategies by redrawing their value chain.

Another way of exposing changes in current patterns of production is to measure how much Foreign Value Added (FVA) is embodied in imports and exports. According to UNCTAD (2018), FVA measures how much of the value added produced originates from GVCs. It found that FVA peaked in 2010–2012 and that what appeared to be an adjustment post-crisis has now become structural. Indeed, UNCTAD (2018) reports FVA in imports falling year on year from 2015 to 2017, although the EU has a high FVA value, with 38% of its export value added being foreign compared to 13% for the US (ibid). This is not surprising given the dense nature of intra-EU trade fostered by the Single Market and underpinning EU-wide value chains.

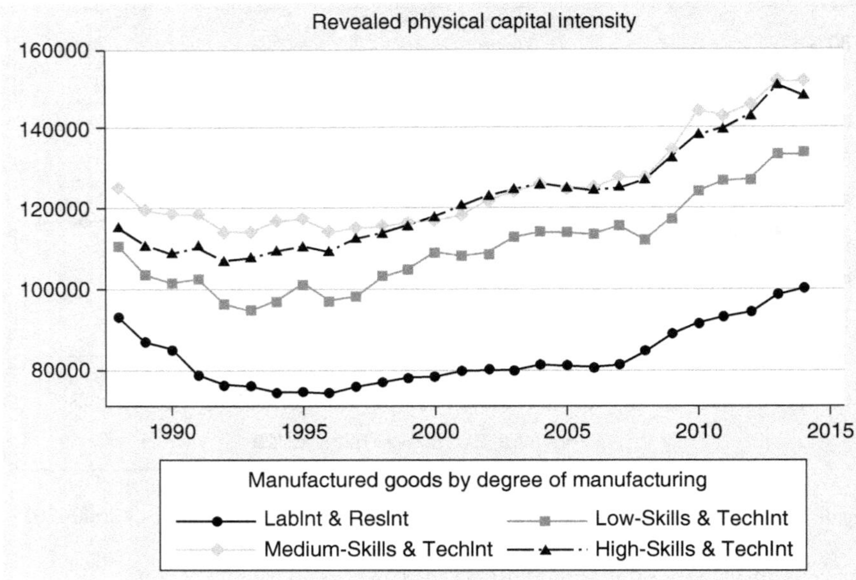

Figure 9.7 Revealed physical capital intensity in the US, 1988–2014.

Source: Authors' elaboration, based on UNCTAD (2018).

Note: UNCTAD distinguished four categories of capital intensity: (i) labour-intensive and resource-intensive; (ii) low-skill and technological-intensive; (iii) medium-skills and technological-intensive; and (iv) high-skills and technological-intensive.

At the same time, *technological change* is transforming the organisation of firms' internal production. As discussed in Chapter 1, firms are expected to become more efficient, agile, flexible and responsive thanks to the adoption of an array of new technologies. We have found an increase in firms' capital intensity as investment in robotisation gathers momentum. Data from UNCTAD shows that across manufacturing sectors with varying degrees of capital intensity, Revealed Physical Capital Intensity rose after the GFC (see Figure 9.7). This suggests that firms have started investing in new technologies by either upgrading existing machinery and equipment or replacing them. Of interest here is the fact that Revealed Physical Capital Intensity investment in medium-skills technological-intensive sectors has been greater than in high-skills sectors. Also, low-skills sectors seem to be those where capital intensity is even smaller, suggesting that new technologies are not replacing low-skill routine occupations. Indeed, we would argue that the penetration of robots at the middle-skill level confirms the rise of a completely different model of manufacturing whereby technology is integrated into production processes at high levels of sophistication (Goos et al., 2009).

In summary, the recent downward trend of FDI to and from advanced economies, and especially from advanced economies to developing ones, could be interpreted as a symptom of a progressive reduction in the length of GVCs. Indeed, the combined effect of a fragile macro-economic scenario and technological change seems to redefine firms' motives and location in terms of production organisation. This suggests in part a renewed attention to invest closer to home, which means either domestically or for European firms within the Single Market. A growing literature has looked at the opportunities and benefits of firms adopting a reshoring strategy, which will be discussed in the next section.

9.5.3 Firms' reshoring strategies

The empirical results in the previous section showed a trend of de-globalisation, which translated as a simultaneously shift of FDIs from developing countries to advanced countries and an increase and consolidation of EU-28 intra-trade. The macro-economic data combined with the revealed capital intensity data can give us a more detailed picture of de-globalisation. As technology is the key point for a reconfiguration of the production system, we can argue that the time is ripe for addressing this reconfiguration of the production system towards advanced countries by adopting the strategy of reshoring.

Reshoring has become something of a buzzword over the last few years. The American media flagged up that some large American MNEs, such as General Electrics and Caterpillar, as well as the largest US retailer Walmart, were bringing manufacturing operations or stocking back home to be able to seal production as being 'Made in USA'. Examples of reshoring have multiplied both in the US and in Europe, and in parallel a large academic and policy debate has expanded (e.g. EY, 2015; PwC, 2014; BCG, 2013). A discussion of the trends in the US and the EU will be discussed in later chapters in this volume.

9.5.4 What is reshoring?

Broadly speaking, in the literature the terms 'reshoring' and 'backshoring' have often been defined as the choice of a MNE to locate back to the home economy a production operation previously offshored: such relocations can include foreign investment or domestic outsourcing (Bailey and De Propris, 2014b). As such, reshoring and backshoring have been used interchangeably. However, we would argue that such a lack of clarity needs to be addressed. In order to conceptually clarify the phenomenon, we decide to consider two dimensions: geography and function. The *geography of firms' production organisation* matters. There is a vast debate on firms' location decision choices in the International Business literature (FDI theories and MNE theories). Yet, most of it has utilised cognitive categories to explain the internationalisation strategies of firms. In the context of reshoring, the 'where to' and 'where from' of movements in firms' production locations are important to the extent that they might be linked to the motives and drivers of such changes. Consider a home economy A and changes in the location choices of firms from and to A as captured by Figure 9.8 below. Starting from a similar point where a function has been previously offshored by a MNE, we suggest distinguishing four forms of reshoring. Although some terms have so far been used interchangeably, we suggest they should be meaningfully differentiated. These are: backshoring, near-shoring, home-shoring and hop-shoring (see Figure 9.9).

A second important aspect to consider is *what functions are actually reshored*. Offshoring strategies were explained by the well-known 'smile curve' (Mudambi, 2008) and tended to involve low-value-added functions; however, firms' current

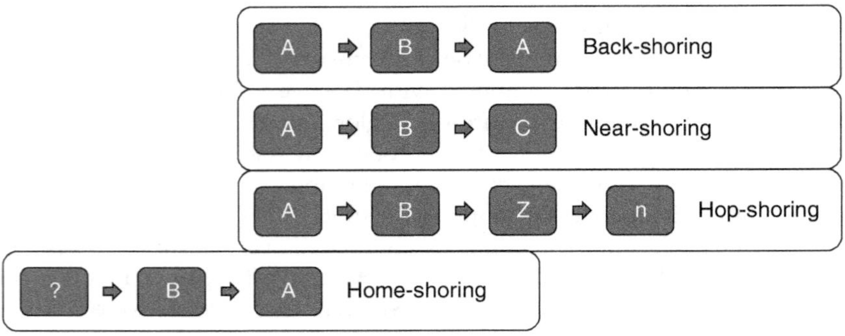

Figure 9.8 Taxonomy of reshoring.
Source: Authors' elaboration, 2018.

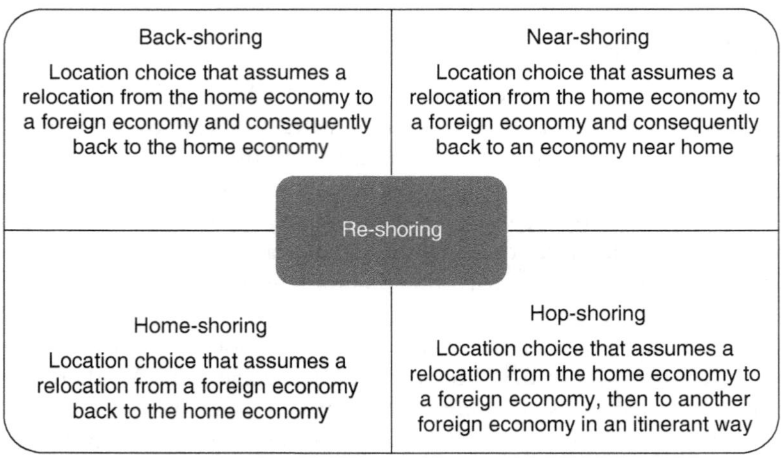

Figure 9.9 Forms of reshoring.
Source: Authors' elaboration, 2018.

location choices are driven by more complex decisions, not least because value chains are no longer linear, but can create multiple-value associated with similar functions in different competitive environments. Therefore, elements of the production function to monitor should be the labour to capital ratio, customisation, production flexibility, value creation, quality, reliability and technology intensity. The last point will be further developed in a later chapter in this volume.

9.5.5 Reshoring and the hidden costs of globalisation

Push and pull factors have been unpacked to understand and explain reshoring as a short-term adjustment to respond to, for instance, the hidden cost of offshoring (Gray et al., 2017; Espana, 2015; Kinkel and Meloca, 2009) or the increasing complexity of value chain governance (Lieb and Lieb, 2016; Lavissière et al., 2016). However, others have suggested that reshoring should be observed as part of firms' longer-term strategy to better face international competition (Moradlou et al., 2017; Młody, 2016a, 2016b; Navarro, 2013).

Some of the *push factors* driving reshoring are related to hidden long-term costs in offshoring strategies (Espana, 2015). Firms faced unexpected operational frictions such as monetary and time-related costs, as well as intangible costs derived from macro-political strategies and country-risk factors (Navarro, 2013). Gray et al. (2017) analysed the reshoring decisions of 19 American SMEs and found that reshoring was chosen to correct a previous decision as more intangible costs had emerged as compared to location advantages at home.

Flexibility, responsiveness and short lead time have been argued to have been key *pull factors*. The concept of 'responsiveness' is linked to the presence of intangible assets that can reduce supply chain frictions. Moradlou et al. (2017) took India as the host country of the UK's offshoring in the automotive, industrial goods, textiles and marine sectors. According to the study, responsiveness was linked to long production lead times and logistics and transportation features such as electricity storage, excessive paperwork and cultural differences in working attitudes. Moradlou et al. (2017) emphasise supply chain constrains rather than a location's limit. It also highlights the importance of cultural distance as a driver for pushing manufacturing production from India back to the UK. Another example is, for instance, the 'Amazon Effect' (Lieb and Lieb, 2016), that is the fast rise of e-commerce. Online shopping requires firms to control regional logistics that integrates with a shopping platform like Amazon. Closeness to consumers, tight control over the supply chain (fewer production tiers) and quicker exchanges (geographically closer suppliers) have been argued to have convinced firms to reshore either internally or externally previously offshored operations. B2C firms in particular have responded to shorter delivery time, small batches of product requests and frictionless supply chains by reshoring their production closer to the end market by leveraging the territorial infrastructure system (Martinez-Mora and Merino, 2014) and a shared coordinated quality management system (Uluskan et al., 2016).

Another crucial pull factor is geographical proximity and access to emerging new technologies. Tate et al. (2014) suggest that firms adopting advanced manufacturing technologies required skilled labour and access to innovation infrastructure, both of which were absent or underdeveloped in developing or emerging economies. This lured manufacturing firms to locate production back in their home economy. Stentoft et al. (2016) also argue that reshoring is not a simple U-turn, but a strategic choice driven by production innovation. They find empirical evidence that automation and innovation are linked to firms seeking a shorter value chain and adopting a reshoring strategy. Indeed, the emergence of a new manufacturing model (see Chapter 1 for more on this) create an urgency for firms to access relevant skills and technological capabilities that are most likely to be located in advanced economies. The empirical evidence of the nexus reshoring and Industry 4.0 is also provided in Chapter 11 of this volume.

As already discussed, FDI has stagnated over the past few years, possibly having peaked in 2007–2008; reshoring trends are in effect the mirror image of how MNEs are restructuring their international production system, which is the fundamental pillar of GVCs. Reshoring cannot be studied as a standalone strategy pursued by a single lead firm, but it has to take into account the territorial features underpinning the firm's choice. In other words, a multidisciplinary approach is required that combines approaches from international business, supply chain management with economic geography.

This means that in order to understand the dynamics of reshoring, we need to move away from the place-neutral approach implicit in firms' internationalisation strategy as conceptualised within the international business subject ('space neutral' is different here from 'space blind'), whereby offshoring location strategies were warranted by any place being relevant as long as they could provide cost savings or access to a specific resource. On the other hand, we would advocate for a different approach to be adopted in order to understand reshoring strategies: they are very much driven by a *place-based rationale*, whereby one place matters – that is, home. In this respect, reshoring can be considered as an expression of a de-globalising trend.

9.6 Conclusion

The aim of this chapter has been to offer insights into an emerging debate on de-globalisation and to provide some supporting evidence. We found that FDI was shrinking and MNEs' value chains were being regionalised within macro-regions. Indeed, trade intensity has increased at the macro-region level, with firms switching to more localised supply chains, even to the extent of shifting production or sourcing from abroad to locations closer to home. The reorganisation of their production process was also driven by the need to leverage the new technologies associated with Industry 4.0.

All this seems to suggest that MNEs are changing their internalisation strategies and are shifting away from polarised GVCs, whereby business functions are geographically dispersed to address a functional polarisation between high and low value-added functions. They are instead preferring to locate production nearer to the final market to accommodate and exploit an emerging business model that sees a continuum along the innovation-production-consumption spectrum. This imposes new priorities and a new urgency to firms' globalisation strategies, and in the aggregate it is reshaping global production around *macro-regional production platforms* where shortened and closer value chains can enable better monitoring, more flexibility, quicker turnaround, better quality control and better responsiveness. Understanding how these are structured and function is the next main challenge for research.

Notes

1 Backward linkages are measured as the share of value added in foreign input used for the production of exporting goods. Forward linkages are measured as the share of value added of a good exported to a trade partner and further processed and exported.
2 For a review of the recent debate on globalisation, see Stiglitz (2006, 2015) and Rodrick (1997, 2010); see Friedman (2005) for the globalisation and inequality growth nexus; and see Baldwin (2016, 2019) for the globalisation and technology nexus.
3 Data is computed from the Annex Table of the World Investment Report, available at: https://unctad.org/en/Pages/DIAE/World%20Investment%20Report/Annex-Tables.aspx.

References

Ancarani, A., Di Mauro, C., Fratocchi, L., Orzes, G. and Sartor, M. (2015) Prior to reshoring: a duration analysis of foreign manufacturing ventures. *International Journal of Production Economics*, 169, 141–155.

Bailey, D. and De Propris, L. (2014a) Recession, recovery and resilience? *Regional Studies*, 48(11), 1757–1760.

Bailey, D. and De Propris, L. (2014b) Manufacturing reshoring and its limits: the UK automotive case. *Cambridge Journal of Regions, Economy and Society*, 7(3), 379–395.

Bailey, D. and Turok, I. (2016) Resilience revisited. *Regional Studies*, 50(4), 557–560.

Bailey, D. de Ruyter, A., Michie, J., and Tyler, P. (2010) Global restructuring and the auto industry, *Cambridge Journal of Regions, Economy and Society*, 3(3), 311–318.

Baldwin, R. (2016) *The Great Convergence*. Harvard University Press.

Baldwin, R. (2019) *The Globotics Upheaval: Globalization, Robotics, and the Future of Work*. New York, Oxford University Press.

Becattini, G. (1990) The Marshallian industrial district as a socio-economic notion. In F. Pyke, G. Becattini and W. Sengenberger (eds), *Industrial Districts and Inter-firm Co-operation in Italy*. International Institute for Labour Studies, pp. 37–51.

Becattini, G., Bellandi, M. and De Propris, L. (eds) (2014) *A Handbook of Industrial Districts*. Edward Elgar.

Bormann, R., Fink, P., Holzapfel, H., Rammler, S., Sauter-Servaes, T., Tiemann, H., Waschke, T. and Weirauch, B. (2018) The future of the German automotive industry: transformation by disaster or by design? Available at: https://library.fes.de/pdf-files/wiso/14450.pdf.

Brettel, M., Friederichsen, N., Keller, M. and Rosenberg, M. (2014) How virtualization, decentralization and network building change the manufacturing landscape: an Industry 4.0 perspective. *International Journal of Mechanical, Industrial Science and Engineering*, 8(1), 37–44.

Boston Consulting Group (BCG) (2013) *The U.S. as One of the Developed World's Lowest-Cost Manufacturers behind the American Export Surge*. Boston: BCG.

Chandler, A.D. (1962) *Strategy and Structure: Chapters in the History of American Industrial Enterprises*. MIT Press.

Chidlow, A., Holmström-Lind, C., Holm., U. and Tallman, S. (2015) Do I stay or do I go? Sub-national drivers for post-entry subsidiary development. *International Business Review*, 24(2): 266–274.

Chidlow, A., Salciuviene, L. and Young, S. (2009) Regional determinants of inward FDI distribution in Poland. *International Business Review*, 18(2): 119–133.

Chomsky, N. (2016) *Who Rules the World*. Penguin.

Davis, G.F. (2013) After the corporation. *Politics & Society*, 41(2), 283–308.

Davis, G.F. and Adam Cobb, J. (2010) Resource dependence theory: past and future. In *Stanford's Organization Theory Renaissance, 1970–2000*. Emerald Group Publishing, pp. 21–42.

De Backer, K. and S. Miroudot (2013) *Mapping Global Value Chains*. OECD Publishing,

Dicken, P. (2015) *Global Shift: Transforming the World Economy*, 7th edn. Guilford Press.

The Economist (2009) Turning their backs on the world. Available at: https://www.economist.com/international/2009/02/19/turning-their-backs-on-the-world.

The Economist (2018) Tariffs on steel and aluminium are creating some winners. Available at: https://www.economist.com/finance-and-economics/2018/08/09/tariffs-on-steel-and-aluminium-are-creating-some-winners.

Ellram, L.M., Tate, W.L. and Petersen, K.J. (2013) Offshoring and reshoring: an update on the manufacturing location decision. *Journal of Supply Chain Management*, 49(2), 14–22.

España, J., 2015. Offshoring costs: a comprehensive model. *Journal of Business and Behavioral Sciences*, 27(2), 81–92.

EU Parliament (2018) EU framework for FDI screening. Available at: http://www.europarl.europa.eu/EPRS/EPRS-Briefing-614667-EU-framework-FDI-screening-FINAL.pdf.

European Commission (2014) For a European industrial renaissance. Available at: https://eur-lex.europa.eu/legal-content/EN/TXT/HTML/?uri=CELEX:52014DC0014&from=EN.

EY (2015). *Reshoring Manufacturing: Time to Seize the Opportunity*. EY.

Feenstra, R.C. (1998) Integration of trade and disintegration of production in the global economy. *Journal of Economic Perspectives*, 12(4), 31–50.

Financial Times (2018a) Logistics industry says 'too late' to avoid Brexit disruption. Available at: https://www.ft.com/content/5631e0f2-68bb-11e8-b6eb-4acfcfb08c11.

Financial Times (2018b) Sterling's long-term decline. Available at: https://www.ft.com/content/30dd70be-a9cb-11e7-ab66-21cc87a2edde.

Frederick, S. (2014) September: combining the global value chain and global IO approaches. In *Center on Globalization, Governance & International Conference on the*

Measurement of International Trade and Economic Globalization Aguascalientes, Mexico, vol. 29.

Friedman, T. (2005) *The World is Flat*. Penguin.

Galvin, J., Han, F., Hynes, S., Qu, J., Rajgopal, K. and Shek, A. (2018) Synergy and disruption: ten trends shaping Fintech. McKinsey Global Banking Report.

Gereffi, G. (1999) International trade and industrial upgrading in the apparel commodity chain. *Journal of International Economics*, 48(1), 37–70.

Gereffi, G. (2014) Global value chains in a post-Washington Consensus world. *Review of International Political Economy*, 21(1), 9–37.

Gereffi, G. and Korzeniewicz, M. (eds) (1994) *Commodity Chains and Global Capitalism*. ABC-CLIO.

Gereffi, G. and Luo, X., 2014. *Risks and Opportunities of Participation in Global Value Chains*. World Bank.

Gozman, D. and Willcocks, L. (2019) The emerging cloud dilemma: balancing innovation with cross-border privacy and outsourcing regulations. *Journal of Business Research*, 97, 235–256.

Gray, J.V., Esenduran, G., Rungtusanatham, M.J. and Skowronski, K. (2017) Why in the world did they reshore? Examining small to medium-sized manufacturer decisions. *Journal of Operations Management*, 49, 37–51

Gray, J.V., Skowronsky, K., Esenduran, G. and Rungtudanatham, M.J. (2013) Reshoring phenomenon: what supply chain academics ought to know and should do. *J. Supply Chain Manag.*, 49(2), 27–33.

Goos, M., Manning, A. and Salomons, A. (2009) Job polarization in Europe. *American Economic Review*, 99, 58–63.

Horner, R. and Nadvi, K. (2018) Global value chains and the rise of the Global South: unpacking twenty-first century polycentric trade. *Global Networks*, 18(2), 207–237.

Inglehart, R. and Norris, P. (2016) *Trump, Brexit, and the Rise of Populism: Economic Have-Nots and Cultural Backlash*. Harvard Kennedy School Working Paper, RWP16-026.

Jabbour, L. (2012) Slicing the value chain internationally: empirical evidence on the offshoring strategy by French firms. *The World Economy*, 35(11), 1417–1447.

Ju, J. and Yu, X. (2018) China's opening up after 40 tears: standing at a historic turning point. *China & World Economy*, 26(2), 23–49.

Kinkel, S. (2014) Future and impact of backshorin: some conclusions from 15 years of research on German practices. *Journal of Purchasing and Supply Management*, 20(1), 63–65.

Kinkel, S. and Maloca, S. (2009) Drivers and antecedents of manufacturing offshoring and backshoring: a German perspective. *Journal of Purchasing and Supply Management*, 15(3), 154–165.

Krugman, P. and Venables, A.J. (1995) Globalization and the inequality of nations. *Quarterly Journal of Economics*, 110(4), 857–880.

Lasi, H., Fettke, P., Kemper, H.G., Feld, T. and Hoffmann, M. (2014) Industry 4.0. *Business & Information Systems Engineering*, 6(4), 239–242.

Lavissière, A., Mandják, T. and Fedi, L. (2016) The key role of infrastructure in backshoring operations: the case of free zones. *Supply Chain Forum: An International Journal*, 17(3), 143–155.

Lawrence, G. and Almas, R. (2018) *Globalisation, Localisation and Sustainable Livelihoods*. Routledge.

Levitt, T. (1983) The globalisation of markets. *Harvard Business Review*, May–June.

Li, P. and Bathelt, H. (2018) Location strategy in cluster networks. *Journal of International Business Studies*, 49(8), 967–989.

Lieb, R.C. and Lieb, K.J. (2016) 3PL CEO perspectives on the current status and future prospects of the third-party logistics industry in North America: the 2014 survey. *Transportation Journal*, 55(1), 78–92.

Los, B., Timmer, M.P. and de Vries, G.J. (2015) How global are global value chains? A new approach to measure international fragmentation. *Journal of Regional Science*, 55(1), 66–92.

Martínez-Mora, C. and Merino, F. (2014) Offshoring in the Spanish footwear industry: a return journey? *Journal of Purchasing & Supply Management*, 20(4), 225–237.

May, C. (2015) *The Global Political Economy of Intellectual Property Rights: The New Enclosures*. Routledge.

Młody, M. (2016a) Backshoring in light of the concepts of divestment and de-internationalization: similarities and differences. *Entrepreneurial Business & Economics Review*, 4(3), 167–180.

Młody, M. (2016b) Reindustrialisation of the European Union Member States in the context of reshoring. *Reindustrializacja krajów Unii Europejskiej w kontekście reshoringu*, 35(1), 455–467.

Moradlou, H., Backhouse, C. and Ranganathan, R. (2017) Responsiveness, the primary reason behind re-shoring manufacturing activities to the UK. *International Journal of Physical Distribution & Logistics Management*, 47(2/3), 222–236.

Mudambi, R. (2007) Offshoring: economic geography and the multi-national firm. *Journal of International Business Studies*, 38(1), 206–210.

Mudambi, R. (2008) Location, control and innovation in knowledge-intensive industries. *Journal of Economic Geography*, 8(5), 699–725.

Mudambi, R., Li, L., Ma, X., Makino, S., Qian, G. and Boschma, R. (2018) Zoom in, zoom out: geographic scale and multinational activity. *Journal of International Business*, 49(8), 929–941.

Mudambi, R. and Venzin, M. (2010) The strategic nexus of offshoring and outsourcing decisions. *Journal of Management Studies*, 47(8), 1510–1533.

Navarro, P. (2013) China 2013: the year of reshoring to America? *Financial Executive*, 29(1), 33–35.

OECD (2017) *The Next Production Revolution: Implications for Governments and Business*. OECD Publishing, https://doi.org/10.1787/9789264271036-en.

Piore, M.J. and Sabel, C.F. (1986) *The Second Industrial Divide: Possibilities for Prosperity*. Basic Books.

Porter, M.E. (1996) Competitive advantage, agglomeration economies, and regional policy. *International Regional Science Review*, 19(1–2), 85–90.

PwC (2014) *Reshoring: A New Direction for the UK Economy*. PwC.

Rodrik, D. (1997) *Has Globalization Gone Too Far?* Institute for International Economics.

Rodrik, D. (2011) *The Globalization Paradox: Democracy and the Future of the World Economy*. W.W. Norton.

Rodrik, D. (2018) Populism and the economics of globalization. *Journal of International Business Policy*, 1–22.

Saxenian, A. (1990) Regional networks and the resurgence of Silicon Valley. *California Management Review*, 33(1), 89–112, https://doi.org/10.2307/41166640.

Schotter, A.P., Mudambi, R., Doz, Y.L. and Gaur, A. (2017) Boundary spanning in global organizations. *Journal of Management Studies*, 54(4), 403–421.

Schwab, K. (2018) Globalization 4.0: what it means and how it could benefit us all. Available at: https://www.weforum.org/agenda/2018/11/globalization-4-what-does-it-mean-how-it-will-benefit-everyone.

Stentoft, J., Mikkelsen, O.S. and Jensen, J.K. (2016) Flexicurity and relocation of manufacturing. *Operations Management Research*, 9(3–4), 133–144.

Stiglitz, J. (2006) *Making Globalization Work*. W.W. Norton.

Stiglitz J. (2015) *The Great Divide: Unequal Societies and What We Can Do about Them*. W.W. Norton.

Storper, M. and Scott, A.J. (1995) The wealth of regions: market forces and policy imperatives in local and global context. *Futures*, 27(5), 505–526.

Strange, R. and Zucchella, A. (2017) Industry 4.0, global value chains and international business. *Multinational Business Review*, 25(3), 174–184.

Swaine, M.D. (2015) Chinese views and commentary on the 'One Belt, One Road' initiative. *China Leadership Monitor*, 47(2), 3–27.

Tate, W.L., Ellram, L.M., Schoenherr, T. and Petersen, K.J. (2014) Global competitive conditions driving the manufacturing location decision. *Business Horizons*, 57(3), 381–390.

Timmer, M.P., Erumban, A.A., Los, B., Stehrer, R. and De Vries, G.J. (2014) Slicing up global value chains. *Journal of Economic Perspectives*, 28(2), 99–118.

Uluskan, M., Joines, J.A. and Godfrey, A.B. (2016) Comprehensive insight into supplier quality and the impact of quality strategies of suppliers on outsourcing decisions. *Supply Chain Management*, 21(1), 92–102.

UNCTAD (2017) World Investment Report. Available at: https://unctad.org/en/PublicationsLibrary/wir2017_en.pdf.

UNCTAD (2018) World Investment Report. Available at: https://unctad.org/en/PublicationsLibrary/wir2018_en.pdf.

US Treasury (2018) Summary of the Foreign Investment Risk Review Modernization Act of 2018. Available at: https://www.treasury.gov/resource-center/international/Documents/Summary-of-FIRRMA.pdf.

Vanchan, V., Mulhall, R. and Bryson, J. (2018) Repatriation or reshoring of manufacturing to the US and UK: dynamics and global production networks or from here to there and back again. *Growth and Change*, 49(1), 97–121.

Wang, Z., Wei, S.J., Yu, X. and Zhu, K. (2017) *Measures of Participation in Global Value Chains and Global Business Cycles*. National Bureau of Economic Research.

White House (2017) Remarks of President Donald J. Trump. Executive Office of the President. Available at: https://www.whitehouse.gov/briefings-statements/remarks-president-trump-joint-address-congress.

White House Report (2012) Investing in America: building an economy that lasts. Available at: https://obamawhitehouse.archives.gov/sites/default/files/investing_in_america_report_final.pdf.

10 Reshoring in the US and Europe

Steffen Kinkel, Diletta Pegoraro and Rosemary Coates

10.1 Introduction

The reshoring phenomenon in both the European Union (EU) and the United States (US) is a 'hot' topic as Industry 4.0 is shortening global value chains (GVCs) and new players from emerging markets are aggressively entering the global arena. Securing a strong and competitive industrial base is a focal requisite for advanced economies to remain competitive in today's business environment. This chapter provides evidence of the reshoring phenomenon in the EU and the US. Motives and challenges will be highlighted as well as the role of policy makers in supporting a possible reshoring strategy.

At first glance, we can say that reshoring in the EU is not so relevant, but it is an interesting phenomenon to take into account for revitalizing or for maintaining competitiveness in important industrial zones. In contrast, reshoring in the US is a predominant topic for policy makers, with arguments focused on bringing back jobs to the US.

After an overview section which compares the EU and US contexts, three selected European regions, namely Veneto in Italy, Baden-Württemberg in Germany and the West Midlands in the United Kingdom UK), are presented by way of exploring whether a reshoring strategy is a viable solution for sustainable competitiveness or not. Section 10.7 presents evidence on reshoring in the US, with three criteria highlighted to be considered in adopting a reshoring strategy. Finally, the conclusion presents an overarching list of motives that are driving reshoring decisions in both the EU and the US.

10.2 Reshoring trends from data in the EU and the US

Based on a rich literature review, we have analysed and compared empirical evidence that quantitatively measures reshoring activities in the EU, in selected single European countries and in the US (Kinkel et al., 2017). The following studies have been included:

- The 2012 Eurostat international sourcing survey (Rikama et al., 2013).
- The Uni-CLUB MoRe reshoring dataset (complied by the Italian Universities of Catania, L'Aquila, Udine and Bologna; e.g. Ancarani et al.,

2015; Fratocchi et al., 2014, 2016; Wan et al., 2017) and the subsequent *European Monitor of Reshoring* (*EMR*) (e.g. Ancarani et al., 2017), a collaboration between the EU Eurofound and the Italian CLUB Universities, based on a keyword search in secondary data of the major business-related newspapers, magazines and reports, white papers of major consulting companies and an internet search.

- Studies on European companies' backshoring activities, based on data from the *European Manufacturing Survey* (*EMS*) (e.g. Dachs and Kinkel, 2013; Dachs and Zanker, 2014).
- Longitudinal evidence on offshoring and backshoring activities in the German manufacturing industry (e.g. Kinkel et al., 2017; Kinkel, 2014; Kinkel 2012; Kinkel and Maloca, 2009).
- An online survey of buyers and purchasing managers from companies located in France and Western Europe (Fel and Griette, 2016).
- Results of surveys of UK-based manufacturers (Li et al., 2017; Bailey and De Propris, 2014).
- A comprehensive study on the 'Relocation of Nordic Manufacturing' in the Nordic countries of Denmark, Finland and Sweden (Heikkilä, 2017).
- The 2011 Boston Consulting Group report 'Made in America again' and related follow-up work (Boston Consulting Group, 2011, 2012).

Based on these sources, we have drawn conclusions on evidence of reshoring in the EU and the US, and on the potential and limitations of existing approaches to measure the reshoring phenomenon. The main results and conclusions of this secondary study on similar and differentiating patterns of EU and US companies' reshoring activities can be briefly summarized as follows.

Reshoring seems to be a more common phenomenon in the US than in most European countries. In 2013, more than 20% of the surveyed executives of US companies were actively engaged in reshoring manufacturing, with more than half of executives planning or considering reshoring activities (Boston Consulting Group, 2012). In Europe, the average share of companies active in reshoring at all manufacturing companies, 'adjusted' to a comparable timeframe of two years of activity, is around 4% (Table 10.1). It varies significantly from around 1% in Eastern European countries like Romania and Bulgaria to over 3% in large industrial countries like Germany and the UK, 4% in Nordic countries like Denmark and Finland, around 6% in Belgium and France, and up to 9% in Sweden and Ireland. However, it is very difficult to compare these figures, as they originate from different timeframes (from two to eight years) and, in the case of US surveys, even include companies that are only considering reshoring activities or investing in (new) manufacturing capacities in the US instead of in an offshore country. Thus, comparisons of reshoring levels between different countries need to be interpreted with great care.

Table 10.1 'Adjusted' shares of companies active in reshoring for selected European countries

Country	*Share of companies active in reshoring*	*Timeframe (years covered)*	*'Adjusted' share of companies active in reshoring over a two-year period*
Sweden	27.0%	6	9.0%
Ireland	13.0%	3	8.7%
Belgium	9.5%	3	6.3%
Slovakia	9.0%	3	6.0%
France	14.0%	5	5.6%
Denmark	13.0%	6	4.3%
Finland	13.0%	6	4.3%
DACH	4.0%	2	4.0%
Portugal	6.0%	3	4.0%
The Netherlands	6.0%	3	4.0%
Selected European countries (*EMS* survey)	**4.0%**	**2**	**4.0%**
The UK	13.0%	8	3.3%
Germany	3.0%	2	3.0%
Estonia	3.5%	3	2.3%
Lithuania	2.0%	3	1.3%
Bulgaria	2.0%	3	1.3%
Romania	1.0%	3	0.7%

Note: Source countries for reshoring by US companies are mostly China and other Asian countries, while for European companies, Western and in particular Eastern European countries are most important. However, China and India have also become more important as source countries for European companies' reshoring activities over time.

10.3 The region of Veneto in Italy

10.3.1 Veneto and its manufacturing industry

The Veneto region is located in the north-east of Italy and has for decades been the heartland of Italian manufacturing, hosting a variety of industries that emerged in the post-Second World War period; it has been part of the so-called *Third Italy* (Bagnasco, 1977). Much has been written on the Third Italy, especially in relation to it being characterized by the presence of a large number of industrial districts (Becattini et al., 2014), which flourished in the 1970s and 1980s and some of which are still present today. In Veneto, three main factors favoured the growth of industrial districts: (i) the export-oriented attitude of local firms; (ii) richness in local social capital; and (iii) a long period of domestic economic growth driven by the availability of a large labour pool thanks to internal migration from the southern regions in conjunction with a favourable monetary policy (Tattara and Anastasia, 2003; Bentivogli and Gallo, 2011). In the 1990s, the fast growth of the manufacturing sector and its export success took a new turn, with profound modifications in firms' division of labour (Giunta et al., 2012). Firms in labour-intensive sectors such as textiles and apparel and leather and footwear (TALF) started to delocalize the manufacturing functions to low labour-cost economies (Corò et al., 2013; Crestanello and Tattara, 2011; Dunford, 2006). Since small and medium-sized enterprises (SMEs) in industrial districts tended to be family-owned, their internationalization strategy tended to proceed mostly via offshored outsourcing and joint ventures rather than pure outward foreign direct investment (FDI) (Furlan et al., 2007). However, this offshoring pressure to seek cost-efficiency brought the region to a profound sense of 'crisis',[1] and what was left of traditional manufacturing sectors presented a high degree of heterogeneity both within and across industrial districts (De Marchi et al., 2014). The 2008 Global Financial Crisis added an additional layer of problems mostly due to the long national recession that followed. By the end of 2017, after ten years of profound reorganization, manufacturing in the region still accounted for 97% of micro- and small firms and 55% of the active labour force. The fabricated metal products and TALF sectors are the largest in terms of the number of firms, accounting for 20% and 15% of the total number of firms in the region, respectively.[2]

10.3.2 Evidence on reshoring in the region of Veneto

There is evidence that previously offshored activities are being reshored back to Veneto. A few studies have started to look at the reshoring phenomenon in Italy at the national level (Kinkel et al., 2017), within industrial districts (Bettiol et al., 2017) and as a marketing strategy (Grappi et al., 2015). These studies agree the Veneto region has the highest percentage of firms that have adopted a reshoring strategy.

This section aims to shed further light on the specifics of the reshoring phenomenon in the Veneto region. By combining several sources such as local newspapers, microdata from the Union Chamber of Veneto and analysis of financial reports, we have compiled a list of 311 companies that have adopted reshoring strategies. From this data set we have extracted key information about firms' reshoring strategies. Firstly, we found that of these, one-third are small, one-third are medium-sized and one-third are large companies. Looking closer at sectorial composition, we found that TALF firms have been the most active, especially small-sized firms. On the other hand, in the Machinery and Equipment sector, medium-sized firms have more visibly adopted reshoring strategies. With a 6.4% growth rate in the first quarter of 2018, the industrial variation index for the Machinery & Equipment sector was double the total for the regional economy (3.2%) and the sector also saw investments finally overtake the 2010 level[3] (Callegari and Trevisanato, 2018). Secondly, in relation to the Machinery & Equipment sector, analysing firms' financial statements, we found that reshoring strategies were adopted largely due to internal reorganization or through mergers and acquisition (M&A) activities. Only a few companies in the TALF sectors adopted reshoring strategies to leverage 'Made in Italy' marketing brand value or to reduce lead time. From a careful analysis of financial statements, we found that very few firms reshored via plant closure, and the majority of firms decided to reshore a single product line or to invest in new facilities in Veneto to produce small volumes of high-value products. A third observation is that reshoring seems to co-exist with some offshoring, in that firms have 'brought back' only high-value and niche productions which can command the highest margins.

These observations were subsequently tested with a questionnaire. The survey was administered by the Union Chamber of Veneto in the last quarter of 2017 by adding one specific question on reshoring in the quarterly survey 'VenetoCongiuntura'. Firms were asked if they had in the period 2012–2017 done any of the following activities:

1. Closed a production site abroad and opened a new one in Veneto.
2. Reduced production in a foreign plant and increased production in a domestic plant.
3. Reduced the use of foreign suppliers and increased the use of domestic suppliers.
4. None of the above.

We defined a reshoring strategy as options 1–3 above. We had a sample of 1,200 firms, of which 26 declared as having adopted reshoring strategies. A first result confirms that reshoring in a strict sense (option 1 or 2) is small, with only five firms having selected option 1. It should be noted that these firms have more than 50 employees and operate in the intermediary goods sector. Firms' characteristics endorse the first and second observation, regarding dimension and sector. Of particular note is the finding that 21 firms selected option 3: of these, one is a large company, 16 are of medium size and the rest are micro-firms. In terms of sector composition, 42% of respondents were firms in heavy industries such as mechanics equipment and metal production, while 33% of respondents were in light industries (e.g. textile, leather and eyewear). Finally, of the 26 firms that adopted a reshoring strategy, all of them engaged both in reshoring and offshoring strategies at the same time, which confirms that reshoring was adopted to bring back only high-value, top-end and niche productions.

10.4 The region of Baden-Württemberg in Germany

10.4.1 Baden-Württemberg and its manufacturing industry

Baden-Württemberg is one of the leading economic regions in Germany, with well-known global companies located there, such as Daimler, Bosch and SAP and with many SMEs which are competing successfully in international markets and creating the basis for industrial efficiency and excellence. Two-thirds of all jobs, 80% of trainee positions and more than half of the revenues in Baden-Württemberg are provided by medium-sized companies.

In Baden-Württemberg, the manufacturing industry records a higher share of value added than in any other German state. In 2017, more than 34% of gross value added was attributed to the manufacturing industry. Its macro-economic impact is even larger, as it is strongly inter-connected to industry-related services. In 2017, Baden-Württemberg's manufacturing industry counted 8,200 companies, whose 1.284 million employees generated sales of around €360 billion euros. The federal state's industrial sector has an international focus: the export ratio, measured as foreign sales at total sales, exceeded 55% (2017).

Baden-Württemberg's manufacturing industry features three leading industries: mechanical engineering (25% of employees and 22% of sales in the region, and a 64% export ratio), car manufacturing (18% of employees, 29% of sales and a 72% export ratio), and electrical engineering and electronics (13% of employees, 11% of sales and a 55% export ratio). Together they generate around two-thirds of total manufacturing industry revenues. Alongside these lead industries, the metal-processing industry is also a major element of Baden-Württemberg's industrial profile.

Of all federal states in Germany, Baden-Württemberg invests by far the most in research and development (R&D), with a 4.9% share of R&D expenditures of GDP in 2016. Baden-Württemberg is also the number one region in Germany in terms of patents per capita, with 132 patent applications per 100,000 inhabitants in 2017. Universities, external research institutes (e.g. Max Planck and Fraunhofer) and transfer centres (e.g. Fraunhofer and Steinbeis) between the scientific and business communities are key components of its research infrastructure and successful technology transfer, particularly to SMEs.

10.4.2 Reshoring and Industry 4.0 adoption in Baden-Württemberg

In Germany, only 9% of manufacturing companies offshored parts of their production abroad from 2013 to mid-2015. As will be shown in more detail in Chapter 11, this value is barely higher than the lowest level ever measured since the 1990s. Over the past 12 years, fewer and fewer German companies have reduced their domestic production capacities in favour of foreign locations. In the same timeframe from 2013 to mid-2015, about 3% of German manufacturing companies engaged in the reshoring of foreign production capacities to Germany (Kinkel and Jäger, 2017). Hence, there is currently one reshoring company for every three offshoring companies. While this does not seem to be a major trend, it is nevertheless a relevant phenomenon.

We use data from the same data source, the *EMS* 2015 edition, to illustrate and describe the respective reshoring patterns in Baden-Württemberg. The EMS is a firm-level survey that investigates products, processes, services and organizational innovation in European manufacturing. *EMS* is organized by a consortium coordinated by the Fraunhofer Institute for Systems and Innovation Research (ISI). The survey addressed all manufacturing sectors (NACE Rev. 2 classes 10–33) with at least 20 employees.

The Baden-Württemberg subset of the *EMS* 2015 edition comprises data from a total of 244 randomly selected companies and provides a representative picture of the manufacturing sector in terms of size classes and sector structure.

Of the surveyed companies, 38% have less than 50 employees, 44% have 50–249 employees and 18% have 250 or more employees. Around 24% of the companies belong to the metal processing industry (20% in the parent population), 21% to mechanical engineering (18% in the parent population) and 6% to car manufacturing (4% in the parent population). To further improve the representativeness of the results on offshoring and reshoring behaviour, data was weighted in terms of size classes and sectors.

From 2013 to mid-2015, 2% of manufacturing companies in Baden-Württemberg have performed a reshoring of production capacities from abroad. This is a noticeable but not significantly lower level than the 3% share in Germany as a whole. This lower level might be partly due to the high share of metal processing and mechanical engineering companies in Baden-Württemberg, which overall reported below-average reshoring ratios of 1.9% and 1.4%, respectively. Another reason might be the very high international orientation of the manufacturing industry in Baden-Württemberg, which led to many early, market-driven and sustaining offshoring activities, as local customers could be served directly from foreign locations. This customer-driven approach might have provided a stronger 'glue' and stamina to stay at the foreign location than might have been the case for activities in low-wage locations with respective customers elsewhere.

At the same time, manufacturing companies in Baden-Württemberg show a superior level of adoption of digitization technologies in manufacturing (Industry 4.0). More companies use technologies from all three digital technology fields (digital management systems, wireless human-machine communication and cyber-physical-systems), qualifying them as advanced users (level 3) using the I4.0 readiness index described in Chapter 11. In Baden-Württemberg, 35% of manufacturing companies belong to this advanced group, compared to only 27% of all German manufacturing companies. Conversely, only 16% of the manufacturing companies in Baden-Württemberg belong to the non-users (level 0) of digital technologies in manufacturing, compared to 23% of all German manufacturing companies. Overall, manufacturing companies in Baden-Württemberg on average seem to be more advanced in Industry 4.0 technology use and readiness. This is not surprising, given the innovation strength of the Baden-Württemberg industry and the high importance of Industry 4.0-related industries like car manufacturing or mechanical engineering.

However, this excellent I4.0 readiness index in Baden-Württemberg does not seem to translate into a superior reshoring ratio, as other factors seem to keep most foreign manufacturing activities at their locations. One reason might be that the argument of flexible production of individual products in local value chains might in this case work at least partly in favour of staying at the foreign location, as early on many companies from Baden-Württemberg successfully built up foreign factories close to local customers. Another factor might be that many Baden-Württemberg companies are acting as suppliers or equipment providers for large multi-national lead firms, mainly from the automotive sector.

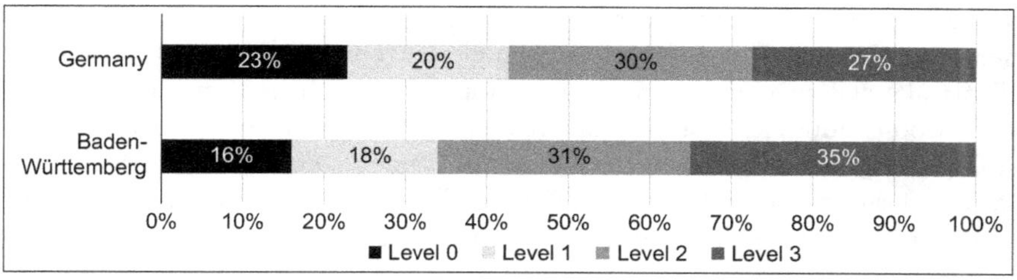

Figure 10.1 Industry 4.0 readiness index in the German and Baden-Württemberg manufacturing industry.

They have built up offshore locations to be close to their lead customers, and these close customer relations seem to provide an effective incentive to keep manufacturing activities of supplier companies at the foreign location, leading to a reduced likelihood of reshoring (Dachs et al., 2017).

10.5 The region of the West Midlands in the UK

10.5.1 The West Midlands and its manufacturing industry

The West Midlands is a UK region with a long tradition in the manufacturing sector. It comprises the Birmingham/Solihull area, the 'Black Country', Coventry, Stoke-on-Trent plus other shires (e.g. Staffordshire, Warwickshire and Worcestershire). The Midlands were the cradle of the First Industrial Revolution with the first large concentration of manufacturing firms in the metal, leather, glass and ceramics industries (MacNeill and Bailey, 2010). Thanks to the availability of labour and embedded know-how in metal materials, a cluster of automotive and aerospace industries flourished. However, since the 1960s, the manufacturing sector has gone through a severe industrial reorganization in the form of functional offshoring and increased foreign ownership (Donnelly et al., 2017), resulting in a significant loss of manufacturing jobs and firms. What was left, however, had to be high technology and positioned at the very top end producing high-value outputs (Bryson et al., 2013).

In recent years, the restructuring of manufacturing in the West Midlands saw a specialization in basic metals and metal products, and transportation and equipment. The specialization in those sectors fostered industries such as advanced manufacturing and engineering, and the aerospace and automotive industries (Eurostat, 2018). According to the West Midlands Industrial Strategy (2018), the automotive sector in the region counts 20 vehicle-manufacturing sites and 35 automotive original equipment manufacturers (OEMs), employs 46,000 people and generates £3.2 billion in gross value added (GVA). The major players in the cluster are Jaguar Land Rover, Aston Martin Lagonda and BMW. However, small and niche innovative companies such as the London Electric Vehicle Company (owned by the Chinese firm Geely) are flourishing. The region also hosts 10% of the British aerospace industry, with companies such as Rolls-Royce, UTC Aerospace System and Moog leading the cluster. The rail sector is linked to its historical metals production and remains important for the region, together with low carbon industries that are attracting innovative companies addressing the broader national sustainable agenda. The high-value medical technology and life science cluster is also crucial for the West Midlands economy through the application of AI, digital technologies and data analytics trials.

10.5.2 Reshoring in the West Midlands

In the last four years, the UK manufacturing sector steadily increased the number of employees up to 145,000 units in March 2018. However, the productivity index is reversing, suggesting that companies are hiring more people but not investing in new technologies. Some analysis confirms this, as one-third of the employment recorded in March 2018 was in low-tech activity (e.g. cutlery, radiators and screws). However, the transportation sector revealed signs of an opposite trend, employing highly skilled labour. In the automotive sector, there was an employment increase of 42,000 plus another 13,000 in other mobility-related sectors (e.g. aerospace, ship and train) up to 2018. Some commentators believe that this positive trend in manufacturing employment could be driven by a reshoring trend (*Financial Times*, 2018).[4]

Reshoring in the UK, especially in the West Midlands, has not been investigated in detail as yet. There have been no surveys on reshoring in West Midlands and official data do not capture the motives for bringing back manufacturing activity. However, De Propris and Bailey (2014) highlight the opportunities and challenges of reshoring in the automotive sector. Currently, the automotive sector is undergoing a disruptive technological transformation with the introduction of electric and driverless vehicles (Bailey, 2018). To unlock these challenges, Jaguar Land Rover for example invested £3.7 million in a R&D project called CORTEX in partnership with the University of Birmingham to further develop autonomous and connected cars (Jaguar Land Rover, 2018). The firm is also investing £500 million at its Whitley site in Coventry (Mullen, 2018), and in 2019 announced – despite job losses – investment in electric drivetrain assembly at its i54 engine plant and battery assembly at a new plant at Hams Hall, near Birmingham, as well as electric vehicle manufacturing at Castle Bromwich. While Jaguar Land Rover has expanded its manufacturing sites in China and Slovakia, it is keen to stress that it is also investing in British manufacturing sites for those activities related to high-value manufacturing, demonstrating its goal to pursue a truly international strategy.

In the West Midlands, another case of home-shoring was Mondelez-owned Cadbury. Mondelez has invested £75 million over the last few years in upgrading its manufacturing plant in Bourneville, Birmingham and 'brought home' the production of some Dairy Milk bars from Poland and Dairy Milk Tiffin and Dairy Milk Oreo from Germany (*Daily Telegraph*, 2017). The limited production run of Dairy Milk Tiffin in the summer of 2016 became permanent in the summer of 2017, leveraging a consumer trend for nostalgic products (Mintel, 2018).

In the broader Midlands region (including the East Midlands), the textile and fashion industries are also historically significant. Lead firms in these sectors highlighted speed and flexibility as key drivers for offering 'fast-fashion' products, as well as the value of premium British-based brands able to leverage the authenticity of a 'Made in the UK' label. In Leicester, the fashion and textile industries in 2017 employed 9,500 people in 1,480 businesses. Further exogenous factors such as currency fluctuation and/or Brexit could further trigger a reshoring of production in the area. Business opportunities suggest that businesses in this sector should invest in technical textiles, composite and intermediate textile goods in order to satisfy valuable niche markets (Focus, 2017). The city of Leicester is the second-largest hub of fashion and textiles in the UK; some concerns have been raised about some instances of 'modern slavery' in some of its firms (*Just-Style*, 2018) and this could be a problem as sourcing is increasingly scrutinized by ethically conscious consumers; major retailers such as Asos and New Look expect the highest standards in order to decide to locate in the UK and in particular to reshore production to Leicester.

10.6 Challenges in adopting a reshoring strategy in the EU

Adopting a reshoring strategy is an intense and costly effort, whether a company decides to bring home production home either by opening a plant or by home-sourcing. The first implies heavy investment, while the second requires establishing trust with domestic suppliers, and a vibrant local supply chain (Bailey and De Propris, 2014). In particular, a common challenge faced by firms in adopting a reshoring strategy is the availability of skills and a competent workforce. In particular, high-skilled manufacturing roles are predominant in driving a reshoring strategy both in Veneto (Italy) and in the West Midlands (UK). For example, it took an Italian firm four years to upgrade its workforce internally with competent engineers and to reorganize its supply chain for more flexible production.[5] In the West Midlands case, Jaguar Land Rover is investing £100 million a year into its JLR Academy, which has already upskilled 7,000 master-educated employees since 2010.[6] In contrast to these two European regions, the Baden-Württemberg region does not suffer from a lack of technological skills of its workforce, due to its superior commitment to I4.0. However, specialists with corresponding digital skills (e.g. software development, data analysis and IT design) have become very scarce in the meantime. This shortage of skilled workers is a central challenge, especially for SMEs. Thus, as highlighted previously, the adoption of I4.0 technology in Baden-Württemberg companies is rarely translated into a reshoring strategy, but it is fundamental for the prosperity of the region as an important value-adding node embedded in GVCs. This last point is key for German firms, as their competitiveness is also driven by their participation in GVCs and therefore highly dependent on the lead firm's strategy. Many Baden-Württemberg companies are suppliers or equipment providers for large multi-national lead firms, mainly in the automotive sector, as shown above. They have to adopt advanced manufacturing and I4.0 technologies to be able to participate in these highly competitive value chains. They also need to build up offshore locations to be close to their lead customers' foreign factories. As noted, these close customer relations of supplier companies seem to provide an effective incentive to keep their manufacturing activities at the foreign location and to reduce the likelihood of reshoring (Dachs et al., 2017).

10.7 Reshoring in the US

10.7.1 Offshoring and the momentum for bringing manufacturing back to the US

Offshoring to China and other low-cost countries has caused the loss of about five million US manufacturing jobs over 20 years, has helped contribute to worker wage erosion and has had a negative effect on workers and the economy across America. Local communities have lost approximately 27% of their manufacturing workforce since 2000. About 63% of the job losses are due to the offshoring of jobs.[7] During the 2012 US presidential election, both Barack Obama (Democrat) and Mitt Romney (Republican) were blaming the sluggish economy on the outsourcing of US manufacturing to China. This rhetoric gave rise to serious executive conversations about the possibility of bringing manufacturing back to the US, if economically feasible, and for patriotic reasons, termed 'Economic Patriotism' by the Reshoring Institute.[8] Beginning in 2012, reshoring and manufacturing expansion (those companies that decide to expand domestically instead of moving overseas) have enjoyed steady growth. This growth can be attributed to several factors:

- intellectual property theft concerns in China;
- rising Chinese wages for high-labour-content manufacturing;
- low energy costs in the US;
- introduction of automation such as 3D printing, robotics and advanced machine tools;
- reduction of latency in deliveries to US consumers;
- lower corporate tax rates (2017 reduction to 21%);
- lower tax rates for repatriation of overseas funds (2017 reduction to 15%);
- relaxation of environmental regulations;
- consumer preference for goods made in the US.

During this same period, individual states offered significant local tax and other incentives such as training credits and infrastructure development to attract and keep manufacturers in their state. In some cases, state and local governments offered free property, data services and cash incentives to attract manufacturers. This is because manufacturing has an economic magnifier effect on local economies, promising new jobs and a greater tax base. For every $1.00 spent in manufacturing, another $1.89 is added to the US economy. That is the highest multiplier effect of any economic sector. In addition, for every one worker in manufacturing, there are another four employees hired elsewhere (National Association of Manufacturers).[9]

In 2017, the average manufacturing worker in the US earned $84,832 annually, including pay and benefits. The average worker in all non-farm industries earned $66,847. Looking specifically at wages, the average manufacturing worker earned more than $27 per hour, according to the latest figures, not including benefits.[10] These numbers put manufacturing workers squarely in the American middle class.

Taking a more informed and analytical approach to global manufacturing strategies and the cost of overseas production, American executives started to evaluate the possibility of bringing manufacturing home. In addition, American politicians began campaigning heavily on a 'jobs platform'. The momentum for this kind of informed analysis has grown over the past ten years, especially since the election of a Republican government – the party most favoured by American manufacturers for its policies on reducing taxes and eliminating environmental regulations.

For the first time in decades, more manufacturing jobs are returning to the US than are going offshore. Reshoring, plus foreign direct investment (FDI) surged in 2017. Manufacturing job announcements reached 171,000, up 50% from 2016 and a remarkable 2,800% from 2010. This brings the total number of manufacturing jobs brought to the US from offshore to over 576,000 since the manufacturing employment low of 2010. The 171,000 reshoring and FDI job announcements equal 90% of the 189,000 total manufacturing jobs added in 2017.[11]

The resurgence of US manufacturing and other jobs has been on a steady incline since the Great Recession of 2008–2010. Job growth rates climbed under the Obama Administration and the Trump Administration. However, enthusiasm for manufacturing is typically greater under Republican administrations. Coupled with tax rate restructuring, manufacturing is experiencing a positive rebirth and outlook in America.

10.7.2 Selected case studies

GE Appliances

GE Appliances provides an interesting reshoring example. In the 1990s, the CEO of GE, Jack Welsh, shut down much of GE's domestic appliance manufacturing, moving operations mostly to China. Even Asian appliance manufacturers and OEMs such as Samsung established primary manufacturing in China. This was done to leverage very low labour costs, low operating costs and the resulting increased profit margins. For GE, the manufacture of traditional water heaters was well suited to low-cost Chinese manufacturing to supply the US market and the burgeoning Chinese consumer market. But when Jeff Immelt became CEO in 2002, he challenged GE engineers to develop new products and technologies. One of the newest products was a heat-on-demand water heater called Geo-spring. The primary market for the Geo-spring was the US, due to its expensive price tag.

GE manufacturing engineers worked with design engineers to automate a very efficient production line that minimized labour and was cost-efficient. Lean manufacturing was added to Six Sigma programmes to keep quality high and costs low. GE then reopened manufacturing in Louisville, Kentucky at GE Appliance Park. In addition, GE worked with local labour unions for wage concessions and eventually rehired 4,000 workers for several new production lines. The GE Appliance division was later sold to Haier Appliances, a Chinese company, for $5.4 billion in 2016. Haier now operates the Appliance Park facility.[12]

iRT Wheels: technology for elite cyclists

The use of advanced technology in manufacturing can reduce labour requirements and cost, improve quality and reduce supply chain latency. One example is iRT Wheels in Pasadena, California. CEO Ray Asante is an engineer by training and a former competitive cyclist. He began manufacturing and selling wheel hubs for elite cyclists in the early 2000s. Initially iRT Wheels designed the hubs in California, then ordered wheel hub prototypes from Taiwan at a cost of $7,000–$10,000, plus $5,000–$10,000 in duty, taxes and shipping fees to be delivered within 60–90 days. If the prototype was not correct, the process would have to be repeated, making new moulds, with more costs and time delay. Prototypes were sent back to California for adjustments, then sent back to Taiwan for manufacture.

In 2013, iRT Wheels purchased a 3D printer and started printing the prototypes and hubs in California. This process reduced per-unit costs, improved quality and allowed for the delivery of new hubs to elite cyclists within 48 hours. Rush orders can be delivered in 24 hours. In the competitive cycling world, this is a remarkable competitive advantage. This move to 3D printing saved the iRT Wheels $100,000 over two years and significantly improved customer service.

Use of Foreign Trade Zones: Lam Research, Silicon Valley

The introduction of technology is important to the overall cost factors in making reshoring decisions, but it is not the only factor. Process and strategy can also be important decision factors. For example, the use of a Foreign Trade Zone allows for in-zone manufacturing, assembly, manipulation or storage. No customs duty is changed on the goods in a Zone until they are removed from the Zone and formally imported into the US. If the goods are subsequently exported form the Zone, they are not imported or taxed in the US.

Lam Research, a $14 billion manufacturer of semiconductor equipment in Silicon Valley, uses Foreign Trade Zones extensively as part of its product and global logistics strategy. Parts from worldwide suppliers are brought into multiple Silicon Valley Foreign Trade Zones, to be incorporated into finished products, combined with domestic parts and products, or warehoused as spares. This carefully controlled physical environment is considered 'outside US Customs Territory' and goods kept there are considered foreign and restricted.

Once an order from a Lam Research customer is received, the products ordered are assembled inside the designated Zone and are then either shipped to a foreign customer or imported to be sold domestically. Each customer order is highly configured and unique.

Use of the Lam Research FTZs keeps manufacturing jobs in the US, delays or avoids the payment of Customs duties, and creates hundreds of new jobs managing the Foreign Trade Zone warehouses and operations.

Buy American

According to a study by *Consumer Reports* magazine, eight out of ten American consumers say they would prefer to buy an American-made product than an imported one. In several studies conducted by Walmart, the world's largest retailer, and other consumer groups, over 60% of shoppers say they are willing to pay 10–15% more for items made in the US.[13] These statistics are used to drive reshoring decisions based on economic factors. If a manufacturer can produce products that are no more than 15% more expensive than similar foreign-made products, Americans will choose the US product.

In determining the economics of competitive manufacturing in the US, the Reshoring Institute uses the 15% margin target to guide total cost of ownership (TCO) modelling. The TCO can help guide the executive decision to bring manufacturing home.

The decision to manufacture in America is therefore guided by three decision criteria:

1. *Economic analysis* including the total cost of ownership modelling and cost reduction through automation and process efficiencies.
2. *Government support* through state and local incentives and federal corporate tax cuts, and reduction of regulations regarding manufacturing.
3. *Consumer Buying Preference* for products made and labelled 'Made in the USA'.

10.8 Conclusion

The magnitude of reshoring depends on the sectoral and value chain composition of the firms in a territory, as a reshoring strategy is more likely to be implemented by companies pursuing an individual customer-oriented strategy in the domestic market. The main motivations for reshoring are different between the territories of the EU and the US, and to some degree also between different regions in the EU. Table 10.2 below shows the push and pull factors

Table 10.2 Push and pull factors for reshoring in the EU and the US

	EU	*US*
Push Factors	Quality issues Loss of flexibility Delivery time Transportation costs Reduction of labour cost gaps Total costs of sourcing	Loss of know-how, intellectual property theft Reduction of labour cost gaps Total costs of sourcing Transportation costs Costs of control Delivery time Quality issues
Pull Factors	'Made in' preference Proximity to lead firms Investment in technology for advanced manufacturing Incentives for investment in I4.0 technologies	Low energy costs (in the US) Investment in automation technology Vicinity of production to R&D Relaxation of environmental regulations Lower corporate tax rates and tax rates for repatriation of overseas funds 'Made in' preference Feeling of patriotism

that trigger a reshoring strategy, differentiated by the EU and the US as home regions. Some factors are shared between the two territories, while others are related only to a single territory.

The most important push factors for reshoring activities of European manufacturing companies are quality issues, loss of flexibility and delivery time, transportation costs, the reduction of labour cost gaps and the total costs of sourcing. The most important pull factors are the 'Made in' reputation effect, the proximity to lead firms in the home country, and investments and incentives to implement advanced manufacturing and I4.0 technologies to make production at the home base more competitive. Innovation-related factors like the loss of know-how or the vicinity of production to R&D are less important for reshoring of European companies in the regions studied here,[14] as are some other manufacturing costs such as energy costs.

In the US, different cost factors, like rising labour costs at the offshore country, the total costs of sourcing, transportation costs or the costs of control, represent some of the most important push factors for reshoring. Also, intellectual property theft concerns in the offshore country and the consequent loss of know-how are seen as a very important boost for reshoring activities. The most important pull factors for reshoring to the US are: low energy costs in the US; the introduction of automation technologies such as additive manufacturing, robotics or advanced machine tools; the vicinity of production to R&D; lower corporate tax rates; and lower tax rates for the repatriation of overseas funds.

Overall, the narrowing cost levels between emerging and developed countries seem to be more important for US companies' than for European companies' reshoring activities. Conversely, quality issues and losses of flexibility and delivery time seem to be relatively more important for European companies. Also, the exploitation of the 'Made in' buying preference effect is a reshoring driver that seems to be more important for European than for US manufacturers.

In addition, policy plays a different role for supporting reshoring activities in the EU and the US. Reshoring in the US is more directly supported by policy makers, e.g. by lower corporate tax rates, state and local incentives or by direct pressure on US companies to produce and buy in their home country. The US federal government also enforces the Buy American Act of 1933, requiring US government agencies to always purchase products made in the US unless they are not made or available in the US (US Code 41 U.S.C. §§ 8301–8305).

The US 232 and 301 import penalty tariffs have negative effects on the manufacturing performance of US companies, as they damage export strategies and make foreign imports of raw materials, parts and products simply more expensive. In the EU, reshoring activities are more indirectly supported by the focus of European industrial policies on more inclusive growth. Promising measures to potentially support reshoring activities indirectly without having to subsidise them directly could include, among others:

- supporting regional clusters and local value chains;
- supporting local demand for innovative and more sustainable solutions (e.g. public procurement and 'Made in' local value chains);
- supporting the development and adoption of smart production systems (e.g. I4.0, agile and individualized manufacturing, additive manufacturing);
- supporting the development of smart, data-driven services and business models for B2B;
- supporting the education, qualification and competence development of skilled personnel, and limiting bottlenecks in digital key competences.

Despite these differences in motivations and supporting policies, manufacturing reshoring is considered to be an important strategy to increase the value of the territory, both in the EU and in the US.

Notes

1 Between 2007 and 2012, Italy faced both the Global Financial Crisis and the European debt crisis.

2 Data on firms dimensions, employee numbers and sectors compositions have been provided by the Union of Chamber of Commerce ofVeneto, December 2017.

3 Data from the Eurostat series 'Annual detailed enterprise statistic for industry' (NACE Rev, 2, B-E), 'Code sbs_na_ind_r2'.

4 However, a combination of a fall in sales in China, the decline in diesel sales and Brexit uncertainty led to around 1400 job losses at Jaguar Land Rover in 2018, with another 4000+ job losses announced by the firm in early 2019.

5 2016 anonymous firm's Financial Statement.
6 2018 JLR Financial Statement.
7 US Department of Labor, Bureau of Labor Statistics, www.bls.gov/.
8 www.reshoringinstitute.org.
9 www.nam.org.
10 Bureau of Economic Analysis and Bureau of Labor Statistics, 2017 www.bls.gov.
11 Reshoring Initiative,www.reshorenow.org.
12 Reshoring Institute Case Studies, www.ReshoringInstitute.org.
13 See www.reshoringinstitute.org.
14 For a counter view on production and R&D in Spanish manufacturing 'home sourcing' see Bailey et al. (2018).

References

Ancarani, A., Di Mauro, C., Fratocchi, L., Orzes, G. and Sartor, M. 2015. Prior to reshoring: a duration analysis of foreign manufacturing ventures. *International Journal of Production Economics*, 169, 141–155.

Bagnasco, A. 1977. *Tre Italia. La Problematica Territoriale dello Sviluppo Economico Italiano.* Bologna: il Mulino.

Bentivogli, C. and Gallo, M. 2011. Nord Est: metamorfosi di un modello. *L'economia del Nord Est. Report of the Bank of Italy*, pp. 16–67.

Bailey, D. 2018. Comment: we need more backing for West Mids manufacturers. *Birmingham Post*, 19 June, Available at: www.birminghampost.co.uk/business/business-opinion/comment-need-more-backing-west-14802440.

Bailey, D. and De Propris, L. 2014. Manufacturing reshoring and its limits: the UK automotive case. *Cambridge Journal of Regions, Economy and Society*, 7(3), 379–395.

Bailey, D, Corradini, C, and De Propris, L. 2018. 'Home-sourcing' and closer value chains in mature economies: the case of Spanish manufacturing. *Cambridge Journal of Economics*, 42(6), 1567–1584, Available at: https://academic.oup.com/cje/advance-article/doi/10.1093/cje/bey020/5067309.

Becattini, G., Bellandi, M. and De Propris, L. (eds). 2014. *A Handbook of Industrial Districts*. Cheltenham: Edward Elgar.

Bettiol, M., Burlina, C., Chiarvesio, M. and Di Maria, E. 2017. From delocalisation to backshoring? Evidence from Italian industrial districts. *Investigaciones Regionales – Journal of Regional Research*, 39, 137–154.

Boston Consulting Group. 2011. Made in America, again. Why manufacturing will return to the US. Available at: www.bcg.com/documents/file84471.pdf.

Boston Consulting Group. 2012. *Made in America, Again: U.S. Manufacturing Nears the Tipping Point*. Boston: Boston Consulting Group.

Bryson, J.R., Clark, J. and Mulhall, R. 2013. The competitiveness and evolving geography of British manufacturing: where is manufacturing tied locally and how might this change. *Future of Manufacturing Project: Evidence Paper*, 3.

Callegari, F. and Trevisanato, A. 2018. VenetoCongiuntura I trimestre 2018. Slides Conference Press, 25 May. Available at: www.ven.camcom.it/userfiles/ID251__VER2018_slide_UCV_defver02.pdf.

Corò, G., Schenkel, M. and Volpe, M. 2013. International offshoring, local effects: an inquiry on Italian firms. *Symphonya. Emerging Issues in Management*, 2, 88–99.

Crestanello, P. and Tattara, G. 2011. A global network and its local ties, in N. De Liso and R. Leoncini (eds), *Internationalization, Technological Change and the Theory of the Firm*. London, Routledge, pp. 239–258.

Dachs, B., Kinkel, S. and Jäger, A. 2017. Bringing it all back home? Backshoring of manufacturing activities and the diffusion of Industry 4.0. *Proceedings of the 6th European Conference on Corporate R&D and Innovation, Seville, Spain, 27–29 September.*

Daily Telegraph. 2017. Cadbury comes home as Dairy Milk production set to return to UK. 7 April. Available at: www.telegraph.co.uk/news/2017/04/06/cadburys-comes-home-dairy-milk-production-set-return-uk.

De Marchi, V., Lee, J. and Gereffi, G. 2014. Globalization, recession and the internationalization of industrial districts: experiences from the Italian gold jewellery industry. *European Planning Studies*, 22(4), 866–884.

Donnelly, T., Begley, J. and Collis, C. 2017. The West Midlands automotive industry: the road downhill. *Business History*, 59(1), 56–74.

Dunford, M. 2006. Industrial districts, magic circles, and the restructuring of the Italian textiles and clothing chain. *Economic Geography*, 82(1), 27–59.

Eurostat. 2018. Regional Innovation Monitor Plus, West Midlands. Available at: https://ec.europa.eu/growth/tools-databases/regional-innovation-monitor/base-profile/west-midlands.

Fel, F. and Griette, E. 2016. Determinants for French firms' reshoring decisions: a proposed typology. *Proceedings of the 23rd International Annual EurOMA Conference, Trondheim, Norway, 19–21 June.*

Financial Times. 2018. Manufacturing enjoys longest period of jobs growth for 40 years. 13 September. Available at: www.ft.com/content/6e60e386-ab9a-11e8-89a1-e5de165fa619.

Focus. 2017. Leicester and Leicestershire Enterprise Partnership Leicester Textiles/Leicester Fashion Hub Study Composite Report. Available at: www.llep.org.uk/wp-content/uploads/2017/05/Leicester-Fashion-Hub-Report-May-2017.pdf.

Fratocchi, L., Ancarani, A., Barbieri, P., Di Mauro, C., Nassimbeni, G., Sartor, M., Vignoli, M. and Zanoni, A. 2016. Motivations of manufacturing reshoring: an interpretative framework. *International Journal of Physical Distribution & Logistics Management*, 46(2), 98–127.

Fratocchi, L., Di Mauro, C., Barbieri, P., Nassimbeni, G. and Zanoni, A. 2014. When manufacturing moves back: concepts and questions. *Journal of Purchasing & Supply Management*, 20(1), 54–59.

Furlan, A., Grandinetti, R. and Camuffo, A. 2007. How do subcontractors evolve? *International Journal of Operations & Production Management*, 27(1), 69–89.

Giunta, A., Nifo, A. and Scalera, D. 2012. Subcontracting in Italian industry: labour division, firm growth and the north–south divide. *Regional Studies*, 46(8), 1067–1083.

Grappi, S., Romani, S. and Bagozzi, R.P. 2015. Consumer stakeholder responses to reshoring strategies. *Journal of the Academy of Marketing Science*, 43(4), 453–471.

Heikkilä, J. (ed.). 2017. *Relocation of Nordic Manufacturing*. Tampere: Tampere University of Technology.

Jaguar Land Rover. 2018. Land Rover is making all-terrain autonomy a reality. 30 March. Available at: https://media.jaguarlandrover.com/news/2018/05/land-rover-making-all-terrain-autonomy-reality.

Just-Style. 2018. UK manufacturing: a ticking time bomb or sourcing gold? Available at: www.just-style.com/analysis/uk-manufacturing-a-ticking-time-bomb-or-sourcing-gold_id134105.aspx.

Kinkel, S. 2012. Trends in production relocation and back-shoring activities: changing patterns in the course of the global economic crisis. *International Journal of Operations & Production Management*, 32(6), 696–720.

Kinkel, S. 2014. Future and impact of backshoring – some conclusions from 15 years of research on German practices. *Journal of Purchasing & Supply Management*, 20(1), 63–65.

Kinkel, S., Dewanti R.T., Zimmermann P. and Coates, R. 2017. MAKERS Deliverable 4.1. Measuring reshoring trends in EU and the US. Available at: www.makers-rise.org/wp-content/uploads/2018/02/D4.1-Measuring-reshoring-trends-in-the-EU-protected.pdf.

Kinkel, S. and Jäger, A. 2017. *Auslandsverlagerungen, Rückverlagerungen und Digitalisierungsverhalten in der deutschen Industrie. Trends und Auswirkungen für den Produktionsstandort Deutschland*. Hochschule Karlsruhe: Technik und Wirtschaft.

Kinkel, S. and Maloca, S. 2009. Drivers and antecedents of manufacturing offshoring and backshoring: a German perspective. *Journal of Purchasing & Supply Management*, 15(3), 154–165.

Li, D., Godsell, J. and Karatzas, A. 2017. The current state of manufacturing reshoring in the UK. *Proceedings of the 24th International Annual EurOMA Conference, Edinburgh, 3–5 July*.

MacNeill, S. and Bailey, D. 2010. Changing policies for the automotive industry in an 'old' industrial region: an open innovation model for the UK West Midlands? *International Journal of Automotive Technology and Management*, 10(2–3), 128–144.

Mintel, 2018. Report – chocolate confectionery – UK, May.

Mullen, E. 2018. Jaguar Land Rover gets approval for huge Coventry expansion. 19 June. Available at: www.coventrytelegraph.net/news/coventry-news/jaguar-land-rover-coventry-whitley-14923641.

Rikama, S., Nielsen, M.E., Bøegh Nielsen, P. Alajääskö, P. and Roodhuijzen, A. 2013. International sourcing of business functions, Eurostat.

Tattara, G. and Anastasia, B. 2003. How was that the Veneto region became so rich? Time and causes of a recent success. MPRA Paper No. 18458.

Wan, L., Orzes, G., Sartor, M., Di Mauro, C. and Nassimbeni, G. 2017. Entry modes in reshoring strategies: an empirical analysis. *Proceedings of the 24th International Annual EurOMA Conference, Edinburgh, 3–5 July*.

West Midlands Industrial Strategy, Consultation Document. 2018. West Midlands Combined Authority. Available at: www.wmca.org.uk/media/2627/west-midlands-industrial-strategy.pdf.

11 Industry 4.0 and reshoring

Steffen Kinkel

11.1 Introduction

The rise of global value chains (GVCs) has transformed the global manufacturing landscape dramatically in recent decades (Timmer et al., 2016; Brennan et al., 2015). Globally fragmented production processes often result in products consisting of components from a variety of countries, which can be best described as 'made in the world' (WTO, 2011).

However, highly fragmented supply chains come at a price. Disadvantages include higher coordination efforts, a longer time-to-market, quality issues, a loss of flexibility and a loss of the ability to react quickly to changes in market demand (e.g. Fratocchi et al., 2014, 2016; PricewaterhouseCoopers, 2014; Kinkel, 2012; BCG, 2011; Kinkel and Maloca, 2009). Moreover, the rise of GVCs and the offshoring of production activities have been blamed for job losses in manufacturing sectors of the US and European countries.

As a result, the so-called reshoring or backshoring of once-offshored manufacturing capacities back to the home country has recently received broad attention in the academic literature (e.g. De Backer et al., 2016; Di Mauro et al., 2018; Kinkel, 2014; Stentoft et al., 2016; Wiesmann et al., 2017), and even more by policy makers and in public debates. The debate on re-industrialization (Pisano and Shih, 2009, 2012) in the US and Europe is to some extent based on expectations that reshoring activities of manufacturing companies might help to restore industrial competitiveness in high-wage countries. It is fuelled by the assumption that cost advantages of important low-wage countries, in particular China, may be gradually eroded by higher wage increases in the next five to ten years (BCG, 2011).

This chapter investigates the relationship between investments in new digital production technologies, which are currently discussed under headings such as 'Industry 4.0' (I4.0) or 'Industrial Internet of Things (IIoT)', and reshoring or backshoring decisions of manufacturing companies.

It is assumed that the use of I4.0 technologies may affect GVCs in two ways: first, because increased productivity provided by I4.0 production technologies may neutralize the factor cost advantages of offshoring locations and make labour arbitrage less appealing; and, second, because increased flexibility provided by I4.0 technologies may provide an incentive for firms to locate production close to their European customers and regain some of the responsiveness lost by having finely sliced their global supply chains.

The empirical test is based on a large dataset of almost 1,300 German manufacturing companies from the *European Manufacturing Survey* (*EMS*). This dataset has the advantage of including variables on both reshoring and investments in modern production technologies, and a number of additional control variables.

11.2 Definitions and some theory on reshoring and I4.0

11.2.1 Reshoring/backshoring

Reshoring or backshoring is the decision to relocate manufacturing activities back to the home country of the parent company (Kinkel and Maloca, 2009; Arlbjørn and Mikkelsen, 2014; Fratocchi et al., 2014; Foerstl et al., 2016). Reshoring or backshoring can origin from and be relocated to wholly owned production sites of the company (captive mode) as well as from foreign suppliers or to home-based suppliers (outsourced mode), thus covering different ownership modes of manufacturing in the host and home countries. In this context, Gray et al. (2013) distinguish four different reshoring options (see Figure 11.1): (a) in-house reshoring, when a company is relocating manufacturing activities being performed in wholly owned offshore facilities back to wholly owned facilities in the home country; (b) reshoring for outsourcing, when a company is relocating manufacturing activities being performed in wholly owned offshore facilities back to home-based suppliers; (c) reshoring for insourcing, when a company is relocating manufacturing activities being performed by offshore suppliers back to wholly owned facilities in the home country; and (d) outsourced reshoring, when a company is relocating

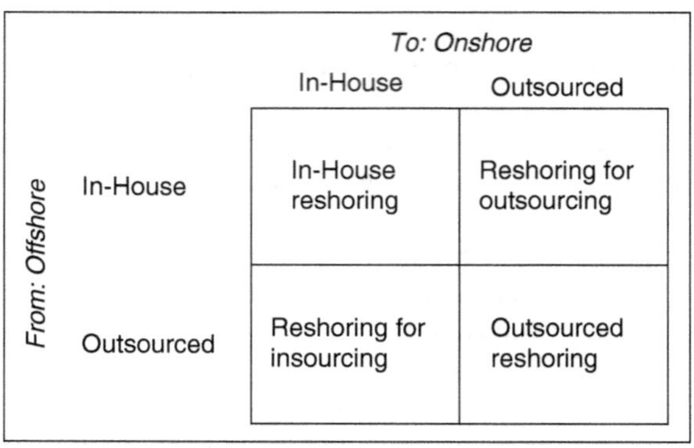

Figure 11.1 Reshoring options.
Source: Gray et al. (2013).

manufacturing activities being performed by offshore suppliers back to home-based suppliers. The authors characterize all these different options basically as location decisions.

There is no explicit theory of reshoring or backshoring. The literature explains reshoring in the framework of existing theories of the multi-national firm, as a reverse or subsequent decision of a previous offshoring decision (Bals, et al., 2013; Ellram et al., 2013; Gray et al., 2013; Tate, 2014; Foerstl et al., 2016). To put it simply, reshoring takes place when the trade-offs between cost advantages, market and knowledge seeking, transaction costs and maintaining control are no longer advantageous for the firm.

Through the lens of *internalization theory* (Buckley and Casson, 1976; Casson, 2013; Rugman, 2010) and Dunning's 'eclectic paradigm' (Dunning, 1980, 1988), reshoring is the result of changes in the ownership, location and/or internalization advantages from international production, or a consequence of a wrong assessment of these advantages (Ellram et al., 2013; Fratocchi et al., 2016). The international expansion of multi-national firms was fuelled by labour arbitrage, a substantial lowering of import barriers for intermediate goods, lower cost of cargo transport and the rapid development of ICTs which supported trans-border communication and coordination (Dicken, 2014). Factors that contributed to a wrong assessment of location, internalization or ownership advantages include rising labour costs in foreign locations and narrowing wage differentials, transport costs and long lead-times in transport, currency fluctuations, the cost for obsolete materials ordered according to a long-term and incorrect forecast, unforeseen coordination costs such as additional travelling expenses, or a loss of intellectual property to foreign competitors or suppliers (Handfield, 1994; Kinkel and Maloca, 2009; Holweg at al., 2011; Nassimbeni, 2006). Case studies have shown that some managers have offshored manufacturing activities based on simple comparisons of easily measurable costs, in particular labour costs (Kinkel and Maloca, 2009).

The *resource-based view* (RBV) of the firm (Wernerfelt, 1984; Prahalad and Hamel, 1990) can also be applied to explain reshoring strategies. Firms can develop organizational processes and routines that cannot be acquired over markets, enabling them to use resources and develop capabilities more efficiently and effectively (Barney, 1991; Teece et al., 1997, 2002). Reshoring decisions may thus result from the limited abilities of companies to sufficiently develop and maintain such critical capabilities in foreign locations, or to exploit the host country's resources in order to create competitive advantage for the multi-national company as a whole (Canham and Hamilton, 2013). Here, advanced production technologies also come into play. Some organizations are able to adopt manufacturing processes to develop unique and barely imitable competences at specific locations and to exploit these resources in a specific and more effective way (Broedner et al., 2009; Grant, 1991).

Transaction cost theory (TCT) can also help us understand reshoring. High and growing transaction and coordination costs can be strong arguments for reconcentrating manufacturing activities via reshoring. TCT points to various reasons for a wrong assessment of the 'hidden' costs of offshoring. *Bounded rationality* and possible contingencies in transactions across companies and countries may lead to inaccuracy of the projected cost and performance of manufacturing offshoring decisions (Pisano, 1990; Pisano and Shih, 2009; Lewin et al., 2009; Cabral et al., 2013), higher than expected costs, poorer than expected quality and higher than expected efforts for the management of trans-border activities (Fredriksson and Jonsson, 2009; Tate et al., 2009). Biases in decision making such as the 'bandwagon effect' (Abrahamson and Rosenkopf, 1993), aiming at imitating competitor behaviour and 'following the herd', can also be explained by bounded rationality (Barthélemy, 2001).

The *level of uncertainty* is also influencing companies' offshoring and reshoring decisions. Foerstl et al. (2016) differentiate between environmental uncertainty, supply chain complexity and task uncertainty as possible drivers for reshoring decisions. *Environmental uncertainty* encompasses the perceived degree of volatility and unpredictability of a foreign market, including unforeseen cost increases, quality and flexibility issues, raw material shortages and currency fluctuations (Ellram et al., 2013; Gray et al., 2013; Tate, 2014). *Supply chain complexity* includes vertical complexity, horizontal complexity, geographical dispersion and the length of the supply chain (Choi and Hong, 2002). It can lead to excessive coordination and monitoring efforts, rising transportation cost or high amounts of working capital in safety stock (Lewin et al., 2009; Tate et al., 2011; Ritter and Sternfels, 2004). *Task uncertainty* is another factor influencing offshoring and reshoring decisions. Here, to some extent, the uncertain potential of technological innovations in manufacturing processes, e.g. by an intensified use of I4.0, come also into play. A greater adoption of I4.0 might enable more flexible, autonomous and less labour-intensive production modes, giving advantages to reshoring decisions over low-wage manufacturing activities (Handley and Benton Jr., 2013; Lasi et al., 2014). *Asset specificity* is also closely linked to the implementation of new product or production technologies, e.g. I4.0 technologies. It involves specific durable investments such as technology or knowledge and skills that are required to realize efficient processes and transactions. A high degree of asset specificity appears to be most critical for the integration of manufacturing activities and their control under unified governance (Williamson, 1985), in particular in cases of high product or process complexity (McIvor, 2009). The higher and more specific investments in advanced production technology are, the higher the possibility to integrate the specific manufacturing operations at one focal plant, favouring reshoring rather than additional offshoring activities.

11.2.2 Industry 4.0

Many observers today agree that we are witnessing a technological revolution in manufacturing (Brynjolfsson and McAfee, 2014; Ford, 2015; OECD, 2016, 2017). This revolution is based on a variety of digital production technologies (e.g. sensors and actors, networked production, advanced robotics and 3D printing), new materials and IT-enabled management processes (e.g. enterprise resource planning and production control, data analytics and artificial intelligence). In the manufacturing context, this group of technologies is often labelled as the Fourth Industrial Revolution – after mechanization, electrification and automation (Figure 11.2) – or I4.0 (Kagermann et al., 2013; Spath et al., 2013; Bauernhansl, 2014). The German term 'Industry 4.0' is widely used in the European context and sums up a group of production technologies where components and machines communicate and coordinate their operations in factories and (global) value chains (Brennan et al., 2015; Bauernhansl, 2014; Kagermann et al., 2013; Spath et al., 2013; OECD, 2017; UNCTAD, 2017). Observers expect that I4.0 will allow a highly flexible and at the same time highly efficient production which makes it possible to produce individualized products under the economic conditions of a mass producer (Lichtblau et al., 2015).

A main component of I4.0 are cyber-physical systems (CPSs), which comprise 'smart machines, warehousing systems and production facilities that have been developed digitally and feature end-to-end ICT-based integration, from inbound logistics to production, marketing, outbound logistics and service' (Kagermann et al., 2013, p. 14). This is done by embedding technology that can take on tasks like sensing or automation into physical objects and connecting them via the Internet. In other words, CPSs integrate all stages of the physical production process over the Internet in order to create a seamless exchange of information between these two worlds.

11.2.3 Research question

This chapter tests the assumption that firms' adoption of I4.0 technologies – via productivity and flexibility effects – affects location decisions of manufacturing activities. If I4.0 really leads to higher productivity, a higher degree of customization and more flexibility to manufacturing firms, this may offset the labour cost advantages firms enjoy in offshoring locations. As a consequence, Western Europe may become again a more attractive location for manufacturing because firms benefit from geographical proximity to their customers – 'in the market and for the market' (Brennan et al., 2015) – without suffering from higher production costs. Proximity to the customer is increasingly competing with the long-dominant GVCs, incorporating a variety of operations from different low-wage countries, resulting in high complexity and increasing flexibility disadvantages, especially in the case of short-term and individual customer requests (Kinkel et al., 2016).

Against this background, the *research question* is posed as follows:

> *Is there a positive relationship between the propensity for reshoring/backshoring and the use of I4.0 technologies in manufacturing companies, once we correct for other firm characteristics?*

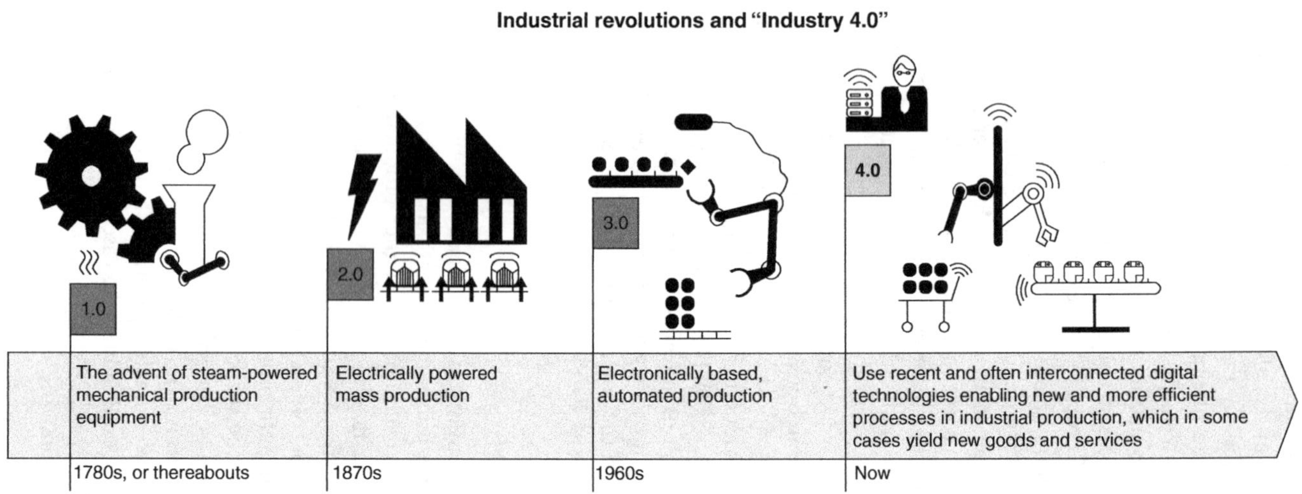

Figure 11.2 Industrial revolutions of the past and I4.0.
Source: OECD (2017).

11.3 Data

The relationship between reshoring/backshoring activities and the use of I4.0 technologies is tested with German data from the 2015 edition of the *EMS*. The *EMS* is a firm-level survey that investigates product, process, service and organizational innovation in European manufacturing. It is organized by a consortium coordinated by the Fraunhofer Institute for Systems and Innovation Research (ISI).

The *EMS* includes detailed information on the degree of utilization of a number of production technologies, on innovation input such as research and development (R&D) expenditure, innovation output such as the introduction of new products to the market, the qualification structure of the employees, and a number of control variables such as firm size, exports, the position of the firm in the value chain and the characteristics of the main product and of the production process. This makes it possible to study the effects of reshoring/backshoring and investment in production technologies in detail.

The German subset of the *EMS* 2015 comprises data from a total of 1,282 randomly selected companies (Kinkel and Maloca, 2009). It provides a representative picture of the manufacturing sector in Germany in terms of size classes, sector structure and regional distribution. The survey addressed all manufacturing sectors in Germany (NACE Rev. 2 classes 10–33 with at least 20 employees). In order to ensure the representativeness of the results and comparability with earlier analyses, the descriptive data on offshoring and backshoring behaviour were weighted in terms of size classes, sectors and regional structure analogously to the population of all manufacturing enterprises with 20 or more employees.

The *EMS* measures reshoring/backshoring asking firms whether they had relocated production activities from their own affiliates or from suppliers back to the home country during the past two years. As a consequence, backshoring is not just divestment of assets abroad; it also includes activities which have been contracted out to third parties. In other words, backshoring firms do not necessarily possess affiliates and production activities abroad.

I4.0 technologies are counted with an array of questions on the use of eight different digitization technologies that can be understood as enabling technologies for digital networked production according to the I4.0 model.

11.4 Descriptive results on reshoring

As the descriptive results of the survey round of 2015 show, the backshoring of production capacities has risen slightly compared to the 2012 survey results. From 2013 to mid-2015, about 3% of German manufacturing companies have shored parts of their foreign production capacities back to Germany (Kinkel and Jäger, 2017). This does not necessarily mean that a foreign site had to be closed, as partial capacities may also have been transferred back. At the same time, production offshoring activities abroad continued to stay at a low level.

Only 9% of German manufacturing companies offshored parts of their production abroad from 2013 to mid-2015. This value is only barely higher than the 8% at the last survey in 2012, which represented the lowest level measured since the start of the survey in the mid-1990s (Figure 11.3). Thereby the declining trend of the past 12 years has not yet reversed. Fewer and fewer German companies reduce domestic production capacities in favour of foreign locations.

Hence, there is currently one backshoring company for every three offshoring companies. A share of about 3 per cent of firms choosing to backshore suggests that backshoring is not a big trend. However, it is a relevant phenomenon. When extrapolated to the entire German manufacturing sector, absolute numbers account actually for around 500–550 German companies performing backshoring activities per year. Further time-series analysis of panel data shows that every fourth to sixth offshoring activity is countered by a backshoring activity within two to five years (Kinkel, 2014). Approximately 20% of German companies' backshoring decisions can be characterized as mid- to long-term reactions to changing local environments, whereas 80% can still be characterized as short- to mid-term corrections of prior location misjudgements (Kinkel, 2014; Kinkel and Maloca, 2009).

The main source countries of German companies' backshoring activities were the Western European EU 15 countries (32%), followed by other (than China) Asian countries (23%), North America (16%), China (13%), and the Middle and Eastern European EU 13 countries (10%). In the previous surveys of 2012, 2009 and 2006, the EU 13/12/10 have been much more important for German companies' backshoring activities, accounting for around 50% of the backshoring cases in each round.

The most important reasons for the backshoring activities of German manufacturing companies are the lack of flexibility (56%) at the offshored location or in the resulting supply chain and a low quality (52%) of the goods produced. Both reasons are relevant for more than half of all backshoring decisions and remained virtually unchanged since the last survey. The reduced flexibility and delivery capability may be due to problems and distances in their own supply chain between the sites, as well as limited access to local supplier networks abroad. Quality issues stem from underestimated efforts to ensure the desired product and process quality in countries with a different mentality and culture, as well as internal quality assurance efforts. On the other hand, innovation-relevant factors such as the risk of loss of know-how at the foreign location (6%), the proximity to domestic R&D (5%) or the availability or fluctuation of skilled workers at the foreign site (0%) play a minor or no role for the reshoring decisions of German manufacturing companies.

11.5 Descriptive results on the use of digitization technologies/Industry 4.0-enabling technologies

The *EMS* includes questions on the use of eight different digitization technologies that can be understood as enabling technologies for I4.0. These were assigned to the following three technology fields:

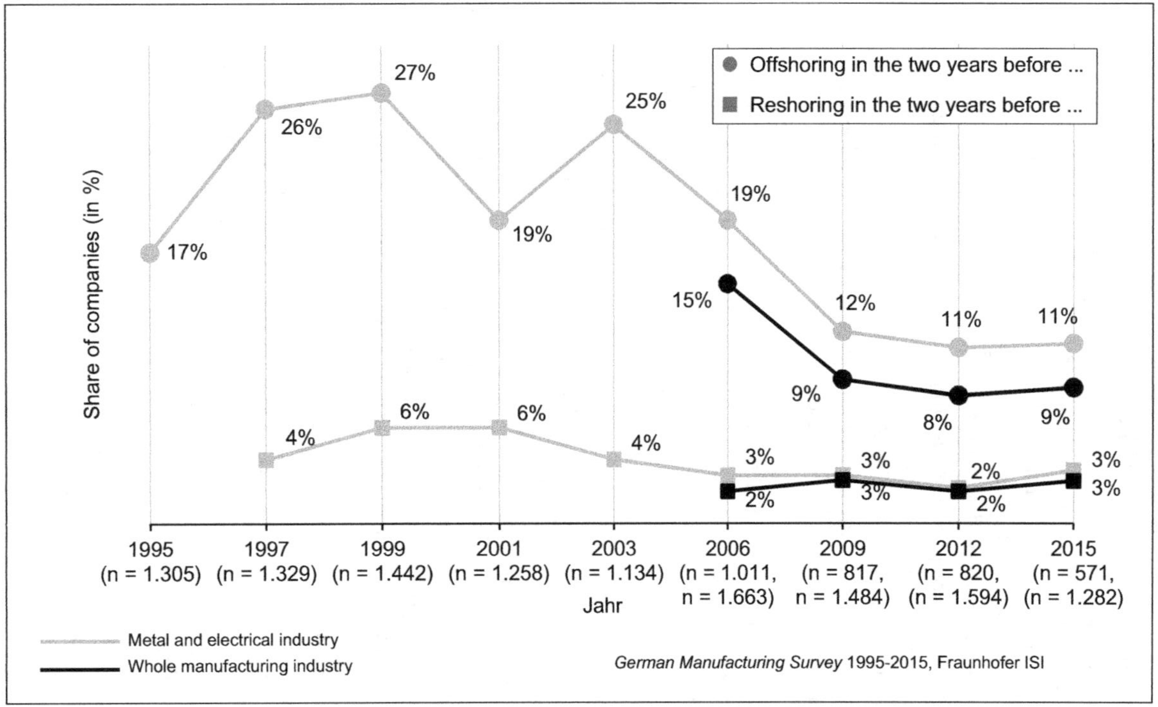

Figure 11.3 German manufacturing companies' offshoring and backshoring activities over time.

- *Digital management systems* comprise two basic technologies for the management of IT-related processes of production and product development:
  - software systems for production planning and control (enterprise resource planning (ERP));
  - product lifecycle management (PLM) systems.
- *Wireless human-machine communication* encompasses two workplace-supporting IT implementations:
  - digital visualization in the workplace;
  - mobile/wireless devices for the programming and operation of systems.
- *CPSs* encompass production-integrated enabler technologies for I4.0:
  - digital exchange of disposition data with suppliers or customers (supply chain management (SCM));
  - techniques for automation and control of internal logistics;
  - a real-time manufacturing execution system (MES).

The share of German manufacturing companies already using these digitization technologies in their manufacturing processes is displayed in Figure 11.4.

As expected, enterprise resource planning (ERP) systems are the most widespread; two out of three manufacturing companies are using this technology. They are already an established standard in production systems. PLM systems, the second technology from the field of digital management systems, are used by only 11% of the companies and thus much less frequently. The systematic and customer-specific retention and management of product data therefore still seems to place high demands on the management and production processes of companies. Diffusion is quite low, with 6% of the companies planning to introduce such systems in the next three years. In the case of production and planning systems, this is due to the already high level of penetration; in the case of PLM, however, this is rather sobering and raises questions about the usage barriers.

One-third of the companies use technologies for the digital visualization of the most important information at the workplace in their own production processes. The second technology from the field of wireless human-machine communication, mobile devices for programming and operating systems and machines, is being used by almost one-fifth of the companies. Both technologies in this field also show a comparatively high dynamic of 8–10% of the companies planning to introduce these technologies in the next three years.

A good quarter to almost a third of the surveyed manufacturing companies use the three digitization technologies in the field of CPS-related operations, Digital Data Exchange with customers and/or suppliers to enable SCM, technologies for the Automated Logistics and Real-time Production Control System. This means that the technologies in this field are used on a comparably broad basis. However, the dynamics of the launches planned for the next three years vary. In the case of Digital Data Exchange with customers and/or suppliers, only a further 5% of companies plan to introduce this technology, which indicates a certain degree of maturity of this technology to support

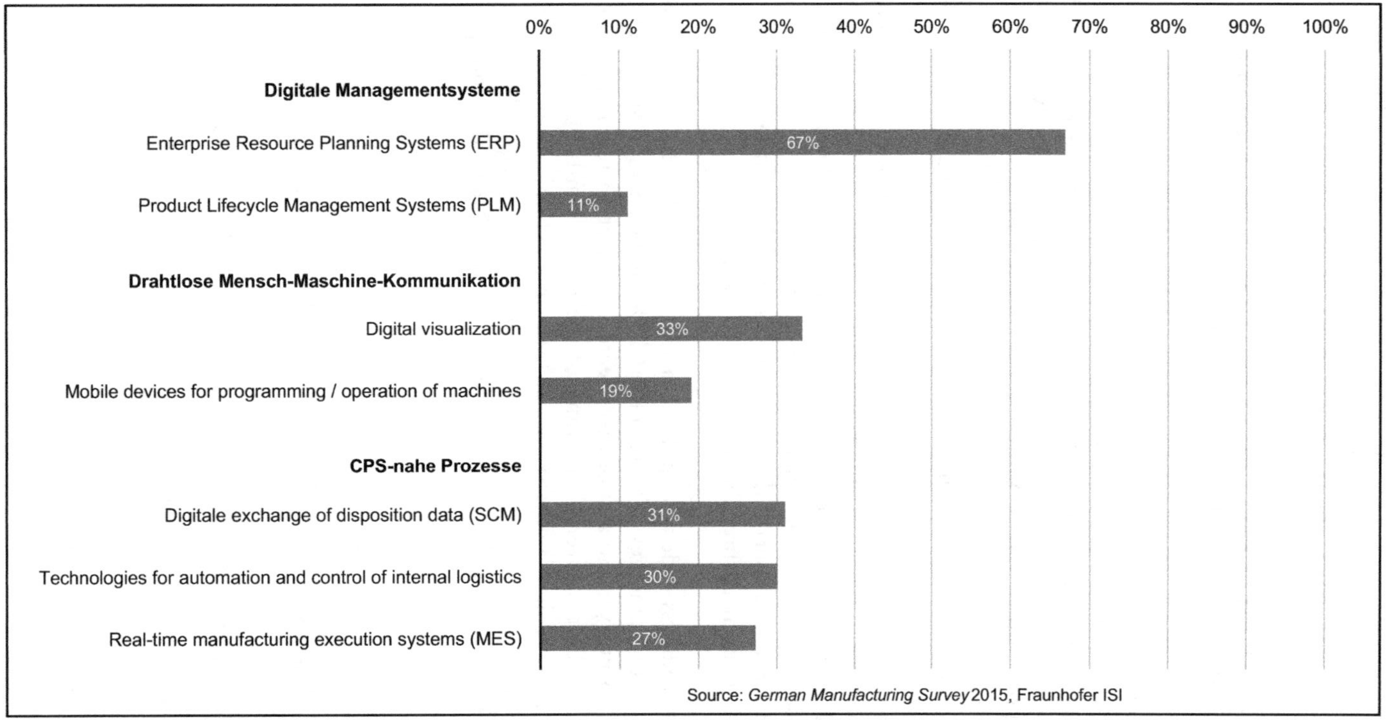

Figure 11.4 Use of I4.0-enabling technologies in the German manufacturing industry

Source: Kinkel and Jäger (2017).

SCM. With the Automated Logistics and the Real-time Production Control System, the dynamics are much higher, with 10% of the companies planning to introduce these technologies in the next three years.

11.6 The relationship between the backshoring of production activities and the use of digitization technologies in manufacturing

A recent study by Kinkel and Jäger (2017) investigates the relationship between reshoring/backshoring of production activities and the use of digitization technologies in manufacturing (I4.0). In order to measure this relationship, the information on the usage of single I4.0-enabling technologies was used to create an I4.0 readiness index. This index can take four values:

Level 0 (non-user) if the company has not yet introduced any technology from the three technology fields.
Level 1 (beginner) if the company has introduced at least one technology from one of the three different technology fields.
Level 2 (active user) if the company has introduced technologies from at least two of the three different technology fields.
Level 3 (advanced user) if the company has introduced at least one technology from all three different technology fields.

If this I4.0 readiness index is applied to the data of the 2015 survey, the following picture emerges (Figure 11.5): 23% of German manufacturing enterprises do not yet use any of the selected digitization technologies and are therefore still at the very beginning of the path towards I4.0 (level 0 – non-users); 20% of the enterprises use at least one technology in one of the technology fields (level 1 – beginners); 30% use at least one technology in two of the technology fields (level 2 – active users); and 27% of the enterprises

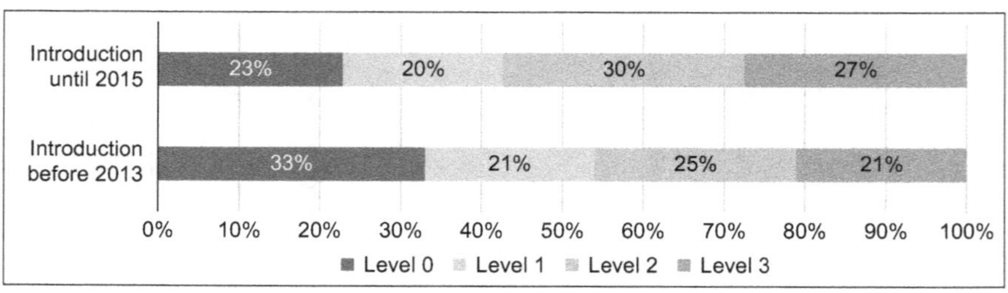

Figure 11.5 Distribution of I4.0 readiness index values.

Source: Kinkel and Jäger (2017), translated from German language.

use at least one technology from each of the three technology fields (level 3 – advanced users). The 'advanced' companies are already positioned in such a way that they have already gained experience with today's enabling technologies in all three of the technology fields relevant for I4.0. However, this group is remarkably small, with just over a quarter of German industrial companies in this category.

As the reshoring activities are surveyed for the years from 2013 to 2014 and the impact of previous technology usage was to be examined, only the introduction of digitization technologies before 2013 is considered in the following regression model (Figure 11.5). The descriptive analysis shows that 33% of the German manufacturing companies did not use any of the selected digitization technologies before 2013 (level 0). The group which introduced at least one technology in one of the technology fields before 2013 (level 1) includes 21% of the companies. About 25% of the companies belong to level 2 and a relatively small group of 21% to level 3.

Based on this I4.0 readiness index before 2013, we ran a logistic regression model to explain the likelihood of a German manufacturing company to have been active in backshoring manufacturing operations during 2013–2014. The model is significant and shows satisfactory model quality (Table 11.1).

Table 11.1 Logit model for the backshoring propensity of German manufacturing companies

Cox & Snell: 0.055	*Nagelkerkes: 0.230*	*Regression coefficient B*	*Sig.*
Step 1	Ln#employees	.072	.673
	sec24_metal & metal components	–.093	.938
	sec26_Data processing equipment, electronic and optical products	.691	.561
	sec27_electrical equipment	.439	.724
	sec28_machinery &equipment	–1.023	.415
	medium batch size	.329	.593
	large batch size	-.152	.850
	medium complex products	-.383	.532
	complex products	–.248	.730
	supplier company	–1.485	.004
	maincompetition factor: price/cost	.574	.310
	Lnimport quota of inputs-	.143	.468
	Lnexport quota of inputs1	.101	.004
	Ln share ofunskilled workers	.137	.439
	I40-enabling-use-til-2013_level11	.884	.095
	I40-enabling-use-til-2013_level21	.932	.076
	I40-enabling-use-til-2013_level32	.618	.016
	Constant	–8.946	.000

Source: Kinkel and Jäger (2017).

The results show that supplier companies show a significant lower backshoring propensity than manufacturers of end products (original equipment manufacturers (OEMs)). This can be explained by close ties with customer companies at the foreign location, which often have to be supplied flexibly from a short distance, so that proximity to the customer is advantageous. In addition, the backshoring propensity increases with the export rate of the companies. For German companies that rely on an export model, the quality and flexibility of their production are decisive factors, which are also the most important motives for backshoring activities. In addition, the label 'Made in Germany' is often helpful for these companies in order to successfully sell their premium products abroad.

The results also display a *significant positive correlation between the use of digitization technologies in manufacturing and the backshoring propensity of German manufacturing companies*.

Advanced users (level 3), which introduced at least one technology from each of the three technology fields before 2013, have significantly more often shifted foreign production activities back to the German location than non-users (level 0) of digitization technologies. According to the estimation model, advanced users of digitization technologies display on average a ten times higher backshoring propensity (approx. 5%) than non-users of digitalization technologies (approx. 0.5%). Also, beginners (level 1) and active users (level 2) are showing a higher backshoring propensity than non-users (level 0), albeit at a lower 10% level of significance.

Two arguments can be used to explain this correlation:

- First, the use of digitization technologies can lead to increased automation and productivity at the German production site, so that the labour cost ratio becomes lower, labour arbitrage in low-wage countries is less appealing and economies of scale at the remaining factory sites in developed countries become more important.
- Second, the use of digitization technologies can be used to increase the flexibility and ability for customized production in small batches with very low marginal cost, which allows the efficient and timely serving of individual customer requirements, and offers incentives to companies to bring back or hold production close to their European customers (leading to local value chains).

According to both arguments, the intensive use of digitalization technologies can significantly contribute to more attractive production conditions with increased added value at the German location.

11.7 Conclusions

Overall, the pressure for greater flexibility and responsiveness is likely to grow in the future, thus suggesting increasing consideration of backshoring options. Our results suggest that companies are continuing to internationalize their activities, but with greater sensitivity to critical factors than in the past. The advantages of cost-based offshoring activities to low-wage countries seem to diminish more and more as time passes, while market-related expansion investments in emerging markets, in order to get closer to the local customers and serve their needs in time, might gain further significance.

However, it is not easy to restore product and process competences outsourced some years ago and restore their 'industrial commons' (Pisano and Shih, 2009). In many cases it might be easier to build up capabilities for the next generation of products or technology, e.g. in the new and vibrant area of I4.0 technologies, as relearning of once-outsourced competences can be a difficult process and only results in catching up rather than becoming a market leader (Kinkel, 2014).

In light of the new potential of I4.0 and smart digitized manufacturing technologies, companies are increasing their focus on utilizing the strengths and potentials of their home base in high-wage countries in Europe. Therefore, we might envisage the beginning of a new strategic imperative of *relocalized manufacturing* (Brennan et al., 2015; Kinkel, 2014) in important markets, with a strong focus on regional concentration and specialization of the necessary engineering and manufacturing competences. Complete solution providing capabilities will be installed in all relevant markets, bidding farewell to further slicing value chains over locations with least-cost advantages, which has led to very complex, multi-stage global supply chains that often comprise many different players and locations. Such global chains are also vulnerable to damage in one of their links, endangering the reliability and responsiveness of the whole chain, which is a crucial condition for the success of companies in today's global economy.

Other factors supporting localized manufacturing (Brennan et al., 2015; Foresight, 2013) are as follows:

- Providing customized products and services, making it necessary to develop and produce customized solutions in smart and agile (responsive) modes close to local clients (Forfas, 2013; Foresight, 2013; McKinsey Global Institute, 2012).
- Rising labour costs in emerging countries as a result of their economic catching-up processes, rendering their comparative cost advantages more and more marginal compared to developed countries with a highly skilled workforce and lower wage volatility (Forfas, 2013; Foresight, 2013).
- Reduced weight of labour costs in total production costs, due to continuing automation and efficiency improvements in many manufacturing firms. For example, currently in the German manufacture industry, direct labour costs account for only around 10% or less of production output value. These progresses are paced by innovations in information and communication technologies and manufacturing technologies towards smart and digital factories, and I4.0 technologies play a vital role here.

References

Abrahamson, E. and Rosenkopf, L. (1993) Institutional and competitive bandwagons: using mathematical modeling as a tool to explore innovation diffusion. *Academy of Management Review*, 18: 487–517.

Arlbjørn, J. and Mikkelsen, O. (2014) Backshoring manufacturing: notes on an important but under-researched theme. *Journal of Purchasing & Supply Management*, 20(1): 60–62.

Bals, L., Jensen, P. D. Ø., Larsen, M. M. and Pedersen, T. (2013) Exploring layers of complexity in offshoring research and practice. In T. Pedersen, L. Bals, P. D. Ørberg Jensen and M. Møller Larsen (eds), *The Offshoring Challenge: Strategic Design and Innovation for Tomorrow's Organization*. London: Springer, pp. 1–18.

Barney, J. (1991) Firm resources and sustained competitive advantage. *Journal of Management*, 17(1): 99–120.

Barthélemy, J. (2001) The hidden costs of IT outsourcing. *Sloan Management Review*, 42(3): 60–69.

Bauernhansl, T. (2014) Die vierte industrielle revolution – der weg in ein wertschaffendes produktionsparadigma. In T. Bauernhansl, M. ten Hompel and B. Vogel-Heuser (eds), *Industrie 4.0 in Produktion, Automatisierung und Logistik*. Wiesbaden: Springer, pp. 5–35.

BCG (2011) Made in America, again. Why manufacturing will return to the U.S. Boston Consulting Group. Available at: www.bcg.com/documents/file84471.pdf.

Brennan, L., Ferdows, K., Godsell, J., Golini, R., Keegan, R., Kinkel, S., Srai, J. S. and Taylor M. (2015) Manufacturing in the world: where next? *International Journal of Operations & Production Management*, 35(9): 1253–1274.

Broedner, P., Kinkel, S. and Lay, G. (2009) Productivity effects of outsourcing: new evidence on the strategic importance of vertical integration decisions. *International Journal of Operations & Production Management*, 29(2): 127–150.

Brynjolfsson, E., and McAfee, A. (2014) *The Second Machine Age: Work, Progress, and Prosperity in a Time of Brilliant Technologies*. New York: Norton Publishers.

Buckley, P. J. and Casson, M. (1976) *The Future of Multinational Enterprise*. London: Macmillan.

Cabral, S., Quelin, B. and Maia, W. (2013) Outsourcing failure and reintegration: the influence of contractual and external factors. *Long Range Planning*, 47(6): 1–14.

Canham, S. and Hamilton, R. T. (2013) SME internationalisation: offshoring, 'backshoring', or staying at home in New Zealand. *Strategic Outsourcing: An International Journal*, 6(3): 277–291.

Casson, M. (2013) Economic analysis of international supply chains: an internalization perspective. *Journal of Supply Chain Management*, 49(2): 8–13.

Choi, T. Y. and Hong, Y. (2002) Unveiling the structure of supply networks: case studies in Honda, Acura, and DaimlerChrysler. *Journal of Operations Management*, 20(5): 469–493.

De Backer, K., Menon, C., Desnoyers-James, I. and Moussiegt, L. (2016) Reshoring: myth or reality? *OECD Science, Technology and Industry Policy Papers* No. 27.

Di Mauro, C., Fratocchi, L., Orzes, G. and Sartor, M. (2018) Offshoring and backshoring: a multiple case study analysis. *Journal of Purchasing and Supply Management*, 24(2): 108–134.

Dicken, P. (2014) *Global Shift: Mapping the Changing Contours of the World Economy*. London: Sage Publications.

Dunning, J. H. (1980) Towards an eclectic theory of international production: some empirical tests. *Journal of International Business Studies*, 11(1): 9–31.

Dunning, J. H. (1988) The eclectic paradigm of international production: a restatement and some possible extensions. *Journal of International Business Studies*, 19(1): 1–31.

Ellram, L. M., Tate, W. L. and Petersen, K. J. (2013) Offshoring and reshoring: an update on the manufacturing location decision. *Journal of Supply Chain Management*, 49(2): 14–22.

Foerstl, K., Kirchoff, J. F. and Bals, L. (2016) Reshoring and insourcing: drivers and future research directions. *International Journal of Physical Distribution and Logistics Management*, 46(5): 492–515.

Ford, M. (2015) *Rise of the Robots: Technology and the Threat of Mass Unemployment*. New York: Basic Books.

Foresight (2013) The Future of Manufacturing: A new era of opportunity and challenge for the UK, Summary Report, Government Office for Science, London.

Forfas (2013) Making it in Ireland: Manufacturing 2020, Dublin.

Fratocchi, L., Ancarani, A. Barbieri, P., Di Mauro, C., Nassimbeni, G., Sartor, M., Vignoli, M. and Zanoni, A. (2016) Motivations of manufacturing reshoring: an interpretative framework. *International Journal of Physical Distribution & Logistics Management*, 46(2): 98–127.

Fratocchi, L., Di Mauro, C., Barbieri, P., Nassimbeni, G. and Zanoni, A. (2014) When manufacturing moves back: concepts and questions. *Journal of Purchasing and Supply Management*, 20(1): 54–59.

Fredriksson, A. and Jonsson, P. (2009) Assessing consequences of low-cost sourcing in China. *International Journal of Physical Distribution & Logistics Management*, 39(3): 227–249.

Grant, R. M. (1991) The resource-based theory of competitive advantage: implications for strategy formulation, *California Management Review*, 33: 114–135.

Gray, J.V., Skowronski, K., Esenduran, G. and Rungtusanatham, M. (2013) The reshoring phenomenon: what supply chain academics ought to know and should do. *Journal of Supply Chain Management*, 49(2): 27–33.

Handfield, R. B. (1994) US global sourcing: patterns of development. *International Journal of Operations & Production Management*, 14(6): 40–51.

Handley, S. M. and Benton Jr., W. C. (2013) The influence of task- and location-specific complexity on the control and coordination costs in global outsourcing relationships. *Journal of Operations Management*, 31(3): 109–128.

Holweg, M., Reichhart, A. and Hong, E. (2011) On risk and cost in global sourcing. *International Journal of Production Economics*, 131: 333–341.

Kagermann, H., Wahlster, W. and Helbig, J. (eds) (2013) *Recommendations for Implementing the Strategic Initiative INDUSTRIE 4.0: Securing the Future of German Manufacturing Industry*. Final report of the Industrie 4.0 Working Group. acatech – Deutsche Akademie der Technikwissenschaften e.V., Berlin.

Kinkel, S. (2012) Trends in production relocation and back-shoring activities: changing patterns in the course of the global economic crisis. *International Journal of Operations & Production Management*, 32(6): 696–720.

Kinkel, S. (2014) Future and impact of backshoring: some conclusions from 15 years of research on German practices. *Journal of Purchasing & Supply Management*, 20(1): 63–65.

Kinkel, S. and Jäger, A. (2017) Auslandsverlagerungen, Rückverlagerungen und Digitalisierungsverhalten in der deutschen Industrie. Trends und Auswirkungen für den Produktionsstandort Deutschland. Hochschule Karlsruhe – Technik und Wirtschaft.

Kinkel, S. and Maloca, S. (2009) Drivers and antecedents of manufacturing offshoring and backshoring: a German perspective. *Journal of Purchasing and Supply Management*, 15(3): 154–165.

Kinkel, S., Rieder, B., Horvath, A. and Jäger, A. (2016) Productivity and flexibility advantages of in-house manufacturing and local sourcing – The limits of global value chains? Proceedings of the 42nd Annual Conference of the European International Business Academy (EIBA).

Lasi H., Fettke, P., Kemper H. G., Feld T. and Hoffmann, M. (2014) Industry 4.0. *Business and Information Systems Engineering*, 6(4): 239–242.

Lewin, A.Y., Massini, S. and Peeters, C. (2009) Why are companies offshoring innovation? The emerging global race for talent. *Journal of International Business Studies*, 40(6): 901–925.

Lichtblau, K., Stich, V., Bertenrath, R., Blum, M., Bleider, M., Millack, A., Schmitt K., Schmitz E. and Schröter, M. (2015) *Industrie 4.0-Readiness*. Aachen: IMPULS-Stiftung.

McIvor, R. (2009) How the transaction cost and resource-based theories of the firm inform outsourcing evaluation. *Journal of Operations Management*, 27(1): 45–63.

McKinsey Global Institute (2012) *Manufacturing the Future. The Next Era of Global Growth and Innovation*. Seoul: McKinsey Global Institute.

Nassimbeni, G. (2006) International sourcing: empirical evidence from a sample of Italian firms. *International Journal of Production Economics*, 103(2): 694–706.

OECD (2016) *OECD Science, Technology and Industry Outlook 2016*. Paris: Organisation for Economic Co-operation and Development.

OECD (2017) *Enabling the Next Production Revolution: The Future of Manufacturing and Services*. Paris: Organisation for Economic Co-operation and Development.

Pisano, G. P. (1990) The R&D boundaries of the firm: an empirical analysis. *Administrative Science Quarterly*, 35(1): 153–176.

Pisano, G. P. and Shih, W. C. (2009) Restoring American competitiveness. *Harvard Business Review*, 87(7/8): 2–14.

Pisano, G. P. and Shih, W. C. (2012) *Producing Prosperity: Why America Needs a Manufacturing Renaissance*. Boston, MA: Harvard Business Review Press.

Prahalad, C. K. and Hamel, G. (1990) The core competence of the corporation. *Harvard Business Review*, May/June: 79–91.

PricewaterhouseCoopers (2014) Reshoring: a new direction for the UK economy? UK Economic Outlook, March, pp. 25–33.

Ritter, R. and Sternfels, R. (2004) When offshore manufacturing doesn't make sense. *McKinsey Quarterly*, 4: 124–127.

Rugman, A. M. (2010) Reconciling internalization theory and the eclectic paradigm. *Multinational Business Review*, 18(2): 1–12.

Spath, D., Ganschar, O., Gerlach, S., Hämmerle, M., Krause, T. and Schlund, S. (2013) *Produktionsarbeit der Zukunft – Industrie 4.0*. Stuttgart: Fraunhofer Verlag. Available at: www.produktionsarbeit.de/content/dam/produktionsarbeit/de/documents/Fraunhofer-IAO-Studie_Produktionsarbeit_der_Zukunft-Industrie_4_0.pdf.

Stentoft, J., Olhager, J., Heikkilä, J. and Thoms, L. (2016) Manufacturing backshoring: a systematic literature review. *Operations Management Research*, 9(3): 53–61.

Tate, W. L. (2014) Offshoring and reshoring: U.S. insights and research challenges. *Journal of Purchasing and Supply Management*, 20(1): 66–68.

Tate, W. L., Dooley, K. J. and Ellram, L. M. (2011) Transaction cost and institutional drivers of supplier adoption of environmental practices. *Journal of Business Logistics*, 32(1): 6–16.

Tate, W. L., Ellram, L., Bals, L. and Hartmann, E. (2009) Offshore outsourcing of services: an evolutionary perspective. *International Journal of Production Economics*, 120(2): 512–524.

Teece, D. J., Pisano, G. and Shuen, A. (1997) Dynamic capabilities and strategic management. *Strategic Management Journal*, 18(7): 509–533.

Teece, D. J., Pisano, G. and Shuen, A. (2002) Dynamic capabilities and strategic management. In G. Dosi, R. R. Nelson and S. G. Winter (eds), *The Nature and Dynamics of Organizational Capabilities*. New York: Oxford University Press, pp. 334–362.

Timmer, M. P., Los, B., Stehrer, R. and De Vries, G. J. (2016) An anatomy of the global trade slowdown based on the WIOD 2016 release. *GGDC Research Memorandum 162*, Groningen.

UNCTAD (2017) *World Investment Report 2017: Investment and the Digital Economy*. New York: United Nations.

Wernerfelt, B. (1984) A resource-based view of the firm. *Strategic Management Journal*, 5(2): 171–180.

Wiesmann, B., Snoei, J. R., Hilletofth, P. and Eriksson, D. (2017) Drivers and barriers to reshoring: a literature review on offshoring in reverse. *European Business Review*, 29(1): 15–42.

Williamson, O. E. (1985) *The Economic Institutions of Capitalism*. New York: Free Press.

World Trade Organization (WTO) (2011) Made in the World Initiative (MiWi). Available at: www.wto.org/english/res_e/statis_e/miwi_e/miwi_e.htm.

12 Technological readiness in Europe

EU policy perspectives on Industry 4.0[1]

Mafini Dosso

12.1 Introduction

The new technological and innovative developments promised by the next industrial revolution come with their corollaries of optimistic and pessimistic scenarios for our societies. Today, public policy is still tackling digital transition issues; meanwhile, it is already acting on and anticipating the challenges and opportunities, and the risks and uncertainties, of the emerging Industry 4.0 (I4.0) paradigm. This chapter acknowledges these trends and provides an insider view on the background of the policy support given by the European Union (EU)[2] to the transition towards the new industrial age.

While the third production revolution brought its waves of innovations through a wider penetration of information and communications technology (ICT) and automation, I4.0 is expected to extend, accelerate, connect and scale up these disruptions and transformations, and to trigger a wider integration across domains and discoveries. It will enable this through the multiplication of interactions across the physical, digital and biological spheres (Schwab, 2016)[3] allowed by the convergence of new and emerging technologies and materials and the related technology-enhanced processes and systems, including 3D printing, the Internet of Things (IoT), big data and cloud computing, artificial intelligence (AI), advanced robotics, smart factories, precision farming and agriculture, fintech, neurotechnology, micro-engineering, predictive medicine, synthetic biology and predictive gene-based healthcare. The transformational and disruptive nature of the ongoing and upcoming technology-enabled or -pushed changes are already altering our learning, education, consumption, distribution, productive, financial, legal and governance systems (see e.g. Smit et al., 2016; Ulmann 2017; Craglia et al., 2018). They modify our established conceptions of privacy and ownership, work organisation, industries and competitive markets, and prompt the adoption of new business and governance models, as well as new collaborative and sharing practices.

From a policy perspective, these developments call for, amongst other things, adequate public anticipations and responses in terms of societal awareness raising and acceptance, learning and training, technology adoption and diffusion, support to production systems upgrading and value creation, data security, and standards and regulatory frameworks across various industries and socio-economic domains. While they also entail a variety of opportunities to rethink public policy and its (participatory) processes, the (un)expected and unprecedented transformations of I4.0 are indeed already requiring more agile and anticipatory governance. At the EU level, I4.0 can be considered as a central component of innovation, industry and digital policies, even if in practice the responsibilities are distributed across EU-level institutions and the Member States with their governments and administrative bodies, institutions and agencies.

Setting up the foundations of the Europe 2020 Strategy[4] for smart, sustainable and inclusive growth, the EU has designed dedicated flagship initiatives – 'Innovation Union', 'An industrial policy for the globalisation era' and 'A digital agenda for Europe' flagships (European Commission, 2010a) – to strengthen the framework conditions and environment in the EU economy. Through these early broad and thematic policy initiatives, the Commission has put the development and adoption of emerging and digital technologies at the centre of its growth and modernisation agendas (European Commission, 2010b, 2010c, 2010d). Already, around a decade ago, the game-changing potential of key enabling technologies was underlined for the development of entirely new industries and as a response to societal challenges in areas relating, for instance, to energy, environment and resource scarcity (European Commission, 2009, 2010d). This study departs from these early initial policy steps and examines the main evolutions in the background and policy rationales for the support for the transition towards I.4.0 in Europe. The qualitative analysis mainly relies upon official European Commission communications[5] and EU reports as well as thematic national and regional strategies. It brings together an updated and structured picture of some of the rationales and directions of I4.0-enabling policies in the EU.

The remainder of the chapter is organised as follows. Section 12.2 describes the EU policy background and underlines the main related rationales for the support for the transition towards I4.0. Section 12.3 presents and compares the recently formulated I4.0 policy strategies at the national levels. Then selected regional strategies are discussed, focusing on the policy objectives and formulation as underlined in their innovation strategies for smart specialisation.

12.2 Industry 4.0: EU policy background and main rationales

12.2.1 EU policy background: an overview

The initial efforts to develop key enabling technologies (KETs)[6] and advanced manufacturing as engines of the EU's growth trajectory led to the identification of priority action lines for the EU's industrial policy and investments into new technologies. Building upon the 2010 communication (European Commission, 2010d), the policy proposals for *A Stronger European Industry for Growth and Economic Recovery* (European Commission, 2012) put forward six fast-growing initial priority areas, including: markets for advanced manufacturing technologies for clean production; markets for key enabling technologies (micro- and nano-electronics, advanced materials, industrial biotechnology, photonics, nanotechnology and advanced manufacturing systems); bio-based product markets; sustainable industrial policy, construction and raw materials; clean vehicles and vessels; and smart grids (European Commission, 2012). These priority markets and technological areas constitute essential components of the industrial policy responses to the economic crisis and formed the basis for the development and modernisation of'the industrial infrastructure needed for what has been identified as a new "Industrial Revolution"[7]' (ibid, p. 7). High in the concerns was thus the need to speed up investment in breakthrough technologies in fast-growing areas and to capitalize upon and exploit their transformative potential in order to reverse the manufacturing decline. Based on the works of dedicated tasks forces, further policy priorities along the initial areas were proposed for a *European Industrial Renaissance* (European Commission, 2014). These included, for instance, the implementation of knowledge and innovation communities, public–private partnerships (PPPs), the identification of projects of European interests, thematic initiatives, inter-regional cooperative efforts to realise joint investment projects, and dedicated funding schemes for enabling and industrial technologies and breakthrough advances, for instance, under the EU Horizon 2020 programme[8] (see also European Commission, 2015a for an early assessment of the European strategy for KETs).

In addition to the more supply-oriented initiatives, the Commission has gradually integrated a lead user market approach also enshrined in the strategy for the Digital Single Market (DSM)[9] (European Commission, 2015b, 2016a; Burh and Stehnken, 2018; Smit et al., 2016). Lead market strategies intend to stimulate the demand for adoption and diffusion of novel innovation designs (Beise and Cleff, 2004). The DSM communications recognise the multiple opportunities of digital technologies and the major challenges for *Digitising European Industry* deriving, for instance, from the large disparities across firms and European territories, the need for digitally skilled workers, an improved supply of digital consumer products and Web services, a critical mass of investments in digital innovation and infrastructure, and the importance of designing targeted policy actions in the field of data regulation and standardisation. On this latter point, five priority areas for standardisation have been selected focusing on 5G, cloud computing, the IoT, (big) data technologies and cyber-security (European Commission, 2016b) as the technology building blocks of the DSM.

Beyond the technological issues, the digital transition has wider social and economic implications and is changing the labour market conditions and the nature of work and skill mixes (e.g. digital and complementary entrepreneurial, engineering and power or soft skills – see Smit et al., 2016; Ulmann 2017). Acknowledging these structural changes, *A New Skills Agenda for Europe* underlined the main proposals to address the digital skills gaps in Europe and to encourage the development of digital skills strategies across Member States

(European Commission, 2016c). The many important challenges and opportunities of digital and key enabling technologies are again underlined in the successive and more recent communications on industry and innovation policies (see, for instance, European Commission, 2017a, 2018). These different proposals have paved the way and have contributed to the recent establishment of dedicated platforms (e.g. the European Platform of National Initiatives on Digitisation and digital industrial platforms). In parallel, key funding sources have been identified, for instance, from the European Fund for Strategic Investments,[10] Horizon 2020 as well as the European Structural and Investments Funds (ibid).[11]

The priority areas underlined in the previous communications also constituted important building blocks of the EU Regional and Cohesion Policy for the period 2014–2020. Within this policy framework, regions were required to design their Smart Specialisation Strategies[12] as an 'ex-ante conditionality' to access the European Regional Development Fund.[13] Smart specialisation strategies (S3) are socio-economic transformation agendas that aim at identifying priority research and innovation (R&I) investment domains in order to build up sustainable competitive advantages in the regional economies. As part of their smart specialisation strategies, regions were encouraged to collaborate through the Smart Specialisation Platform for Industrial Modernisation (S3P-Industry). Launched in 2016, S3P-Industry intended to facilitate the establishment of inter-regional partnerships and joint investment projects in areas relating to digital technologies and I4.0, and to reinforce the links among industrial value chains across Europe (Hegyi and Rakhmatullin, 2017).

The aim of this section has been to underline some of the fundamental orientations of the EU policy for industrial innovation and technological development. Taken together, EU official communications provide important conceptual pillars of the EU policy background for the digital era and for the transition towards I4.0. Besides, they make it possible to highlight common and consensual motivations across the different thematic policy intervention areas. The next section examines in further detail these key communications in order to put forward the broad policy rationales advanced to support the European digitalisation and industrial transition towards I4.0.

12.2.2 Broad policy rationales

Strengthening the manufacturing sector in the EU through the adoption of new technologies constitutes one of the fundamental rationales for I4.0-enabling policies. The role of the manufacturing sector in terms of direct and indirect jobs, export and private research, and innovation efforts in the EU economy has been acknowledged in successive communications from the European Commission. These latter policy documents have also made explicit the need to reverse manufacturing decline and to bring back to 20% the weight of industry in the EU's gross domestic product (GDP) by 2020. The 20% target has also been underlined in the political guidelines for the current European Commission as a necessity in order to strengthen the EU's industrial base (Juncker, 2014). This objective raises major scale and policy challenges beyond the sole realm of innovation and industrial policies. One structural issue, as underlined by Berger (2014), resides in the current structure and de-industrialisation trends in EU, which do not leave much room for manoeuvre, also considering the decline of manufacturing (and the parallel rising value-added share of services) observed in other advanced and even emerging economies (Berger, 2014; European Parliamentary Research Service, 2015). Moreover, achieving the target requires coordination across a broader scope of policy areas such as energy, raw materials, capital, trade, education and training, business services, advanced technologies, standards, intellectual property (IP) and the single market in order to improve the overall framework conditions for industrial development (European Commission, 2012, 2014a; Veugelers, 2013; European Parliamentary Research Service, 2015). This means that continued enhanced coordination across the Commission's Directorates and Member States may well contribute to improving the general industrial environment in Europe with an industrial policy that can enhance the impact of targeted investment in new technologies for the advancement of manufacturing systems and the modernisation of industry.

In addition to its importance for economic growth, the manufacturing sector, and its role in research and development (R&D) and innovation, can provide both resources and potential solutions to tackle and address the societal challenges faced by the EU, such as health, climate change, food security and the development of a safe and secure society. A main rationale is that the adoption of I4.0 technologies can enable completely new kinds of better-quality and customised products and services across all economic sectors, while also allowing production to be more efficient from economic, social and environmental perspectives. Also, new and smart technologies are perceived as enablers for environmentally and socially sustainable manufacturing and for the set-up of economically and ecologically sustainable value chains across the EU. From the perspective of more integrated value chains in the EU, the single market is thus seen as pivotal, even vital, for a successful adoption and diffusion of new technological developments, and thus as a driver of the EU's industrial competitiveness (see, for instance, the industrial policy communication: European Commission, 2017a).[14] Yet, much is still to be done to advance or reinforce the lead in the global competition in green and clean technologies and smart manufacturing. Some of the answers will certainly lie in the EU strategic value chains that will be selected and supported and, eventually, in our ability to integrate and connect innovation systems and clusters across Europe, as well as to attenuate the (effects of) disparities that exist between regions, industries and firms (see European Commission, 2016a; Innobarometer,[15] Business Innovation Observatories, Digital Economy and Society Index (DESI)[16] in European Commission, 2017c; Digital Innovation Monitor[17] 2018 in European Commission, 2018a; and Vezzani et al., 2018 for comparisons of innovation performances in the EU).

By encouraging inter-regional collaborations and bottom-up initiatives for industrial modernisation, the Cohesion Policy's smart specialisation framework might actually hold some keys to unlock I4.0-enabled and sustainable cross-regional value chains in the EU. This also means that partnerships should be based on evidence-based matchings and assessments of related-industrial capabilities, skills and potential for critical mass, and that capacities for adequate monitoring and benchmarking need to be built up or reinforced. For the great diversity of European micro-firms and SMEs, important constraints on their transition towards I4.0 come from their awareness and understanding of the new model, of the benefits of absorption, the technology uncertainty, the costs of investment, economic impact assessments, issues around security, and the availability of I4.0 competences and skilled workers. At the same time, pressures to reinvent the ways in which firms deliver value to customers and markets and inter-connect through current and future value chains are no less important (Smit et al., 2016; Ulmann 2017). Nevertheless, hopes that I4.0 can allow the EU's industry to become attractive again for production and manufacturing activities are rising. In other words, advanced manufacturing technologies can be instrumental to aid reshoring in the EU (see Chapter 11 in this volume).

I4.0-oriented skills are required for the modernisation and digitalisation of EU industry. The skills shortage and mismatches in fields such as ICTs, green technologies, advanced industrial processes, fast-growing industries, science, technology, engineering and mathematics (STEM) subjects, research, creativity and entrepreneurship, and the importance of anticipating digital and I4.0-enabling skills needs are widely recognised in the EU policy background. In the ICT field in particular, it is estimated that Europe could have a major shortfall of ICT professionals in the short to medium term. Modernising the EU industrial skills bases and filling (digital) vacancies pose many imperatives for our traditional education systems, vocational education and training, as well as our lifelong learning frameworks and mechanisms. Especially in the transition towards I4.0, such investments should rely upon the development of dedicated tools to monitor and anticipate needs and mismatches at the EU, country, regional, local and industrial levels. Recent multi-stakeholder initiatives such as the 'Blueprint for Sectoral Cooperation on Skills'[18] and the 'Digital Skills and Jobs Coalition' are expected to contribute to address digital and sectoral skills mismatches in the EU (European Commission, 2016c). In addition to skills shortages, growing tensions are emerging within the exiting workforce due to the ongoing and pressing changes at both the organisational and factory-floor levels, leading, for instance, to complex imbalances between control, liability, flexibility, autonomy and empowerment, and to the greater human–machine interactions enabled by the adoption and diffusion of smarter technologies (see e.g. Craglia et al., 2018; Cirillo et al., 2018; UN DESA/DPAD, 2017). The scale and depth of these imbalances may differ greatly across industries and types of occupations (see e.g. Brynjolfsson et al., 2018; Frey and Osborne, 2017). These changes have come with the phenomena of polarisation, jobs creation, destruction and transformation, and a series of labour market shocks, which call for enhanced skills planning capabilities and forward-looking governance mechanisms to anticipate, for instance, potential worker displacements due to the introduction of new production technologies and new labour rights in the digital economy. I4.0 technologies and processes also bring to the fore many legal and accountability concerns and would certainly require the setting-up of completely new forms of working and social contracts, which could account better for the socio-political aspects of digitalisation (European Parliamentary Research Service, 2014; Burh and Stehnken, 2018).

Timely regulation and standards for I4.0 technologies are critical for realising I4.0. 'A standard is a document, established by a consensus of subject matter experts and approved by a recognised body that provides guidance on the design, use or performance of materials, products, processes, services, systems or persons' (International Organization for Standardization [ISO]).[19] Standards are essential for the development and dissemination of new products and services, and enable comparability and inter-operability across firms, industries, regions and countries. Since the beginning of the decade, many EU-led initiatives[20] have been implemented jointly to foster the European Standardisation System (ESS) and the single market, as essential framework conditions for industrial innovation and enhanced competitiveness. In the I4.0 era, industry-wide adoption of standards is an even more critical requirement to facilitate the global networking of production and global functioning applications, and, above all, to allow for the realisation of economies of scale and productivity gains, as expected from the adoption of new advanced technologies (Smit et al., 2016). Moreover, anticipation in the area of standards can secure the digitalisation and modernisation of EU industries. According to a recent Joint Research Centre (JRC) study, broad thematic areas for standardisation include standards for integration, environmental sustainability, quality and performance, service standards and de-risking standards (Scapolo et al., 2015).

Regulation and anticipatory regulation help cope with the pace of change induced by the transition to I4.0. 'Anticipatory regulation is an emerging method of regulation that is proactive, iterative and responds to evolving markets' (NESTA, 2017). With faster technological change, the anticipation of regulation or de-regulation is necessary to limit technical (e.g. regarding open internet) and legal barriers (e.g. on the use and sharing of data; see also OECD, 2017) and also to address obsolete regulation, IP issues and their scope, the identification of final ownership and security of data, the liability for autonomous systems, cyber-security, and labour rights and workplace conditions. As already achieved in terms of data privacy regulation (the General Data Protection Regulation (GDPR); European Commission, 2016d), the EU is expected to become even more proactive considering the uncertainties related to smart technologies, their interactions with and effects on human beings, and the current and coming data-related concerns (see, for instance, Craglia et al., 2018 on AI-related challenges; and European Commission, 2018b for recent proposals on data and public information regulations by the Commission).

The EU has taken many initiatives to foster the DSM and to facilitate the uptake of new technologies and the generation of technology-enabled products, services and processes. Nevertheless, more action and greater investment will be required to enhance the coordination and the continuity of different national strategies and to better account for industry-region-specific contexts in order to enable an inclusive and sustainable transition towards I4.0. The next section touches upon such strategies at the national and regional levels and compares the different uptake of strategies focusing on the formulation of policy objectives in the transition towards I4.0.

12.3 Stimulating, accelerating and monitoring I4.0 in the EU

12.3.1 I4.0-enabling national initiatives in the EU

A number of EU Member States have designed a strategy to address the challenges of digitalisation and the transition towards I4.0. At the EU level, these strategies are monitored by the Digital Transformation Monitor (DTM), as part of the European Platform of National Initiatives. Launched at the beginning of 2017, the European Platform aims at facilitating more inclusive coordination and best practice exchanges for the achievement of the *Digitising European Industry* (see European Commission, 2016a). It also intends to stimulate collaborations and joint investments in order to reach the critical mass required to meet the goals set in terms of digitalisation of industry across Europe. As of October 2017, 15 Member States had already launched national initiatives for the digitisation of industry.[21] Seven more initiatives were under preparation. The DTM enables an EU-level monitoring of digital transformation in order to support a coordinated EU-wide effort. The Web platform provides statistics and information about initiatives for and the challenges related to digital transformation at the EU, national, sectoral and technological levels. As an integral element of the European Platform of National Initiatives on Digitising Industry, the DTM allows us to compare the framework conditions of national digital policies, for instance, through the Digital Transformation Scoreboard (2018) (DTS). The most recent DTM report covers a total of 19 strategies and programmes for digitalisation and relies mainly on desk research and interviews. The DTS provides Country Profile Reports (CPRs) for each Member State and offers a comparative overview in terms of framework conditions, main strengths and areas for improvement, as well as interesting policy practices.

In addition, the DTM makes available on the platform the documents of individual Member State, which present the main features of national initiatives, such as the policy levers, pillars and objectives, the budget and funding models, the strengths and weaknesses, the implementation strategy, the results achieved so far and uniqueness factors. Table 12.1 uses information from these documents in order to suggest a comparative overview of some of the national initiatives.[22] While these initiatives are collected under the thematic digital transformation,[23] many Member States actually refer more or less explicitly to I4.0.

As also underlined in the DTM analyses, the initiatives present many similarities in terms of policy objectives, but differ greatly, for instance, in terms of strategy design, focus, budget and related funding mechanisms, implementation approaches, coordination mechanisms and timing in terms of implementation and results achieved so far (Digital Transformation Scoreboard [2018] and national initiatives documents). Whilst such differences limit strict comparisons across national initiatives, they provide a relevant basis for benchmarking and experience exchanges.

Often initiated by the government or PPPs, many initiatives are now led or coordinated through multi-stakeholder partnerships with the close involvement of industry, academia and research. Indeed, a majority of national I4.0-enabling policies follow a bottom-up approach for the implementation of the initiatives. Moreover, the component 'awareness raising about I4.0, I4.0-related or digital technologies' is considered by many as critical to address the uncertainties associated with the emerging paradigm and to exploit the relevant opportunities offered by new technologies. As part of their strategies for digitalisation, many Member States and regions support the implementation of Digital Innovation Hubs (DIHs).[24] DIHs are one-stop-shops for SMEs, mid-caps and more mature or established companies, which provide a range of supporting services, including technology testing, financing advice, market intelligence, training, promotion and marketing, and networking opportunities. Two hundred hubs are already fully operational and about the same number are expected to be implemented. The WATIFY campaign[25] also complements the national and regional efforts, through awareness events, success storytelling and matchmaking events, in order to stimulate the modernisation of the EU industry, the technological transformation through digitisation and the uptake of advanced technologies. Working on different timescales, such national initiatives vary in terms of what they have achieved; indeed, whilst some Member States were actually still preparing implementation plans, others were already implementing their actions (e.g. the Czech Republic, Hungary, Slovakia and Slovenia; see Table 12.1). As initiatives differ in relation to the specific targets, their achievements also take different forms, such as network development, the number of supported, funded or awarded companies, identification of experts, R&I support (funding, programmes established), research cooperation and workers' training, depending, amongst other things, on the objectives and national specific contexts and industrial structures.

Furthermore, it is becoming apparent that Member States' initiatives and programmes also differ in terms of the weaknesses and threats of the initiatives adopted. Some initiatives show some weaknesses in relation to: the lack of a clear funding model or the lack or low level of public and or private funding; the definition of implementation plans and target setting; the low business culture and inadequate or costly internet and ICT infrastructure; bottlenecks in the deployment at the shop-floor level; the balance between small and large firms; or the definition of adequate company-level monitoring indicators. Threats also vary in terms of: regional inequalities; imbalances or divergence between

Table 12.1 Overview of selected national initiatives*

Countries	*Names of the initiatives (launch, adoption or official year of announcement)*	*Broad policy objectives (examples)*	*Main targets*	*Dedicated budgets (approximate)*
Austria	Plattform Industrie 4.0 (2015)	- Leverage multi-stakeholder interests - Accompany digitisation and provide knowledge and services on I4.0 - Define fields of action and advise policy makers - Develop joint strategies with high leverage on I4.0 - Steer regional, national and international activities - Enable exchanges of experience, best practices, data and studies	Companies, research, academia, policy makers, trade unions, employees' associations	€300,000 a year from founding members and €200,000 from fees (est. 2017)
Belgium	Made Different (launched in Flanders, 2013) Made Different-Digital Wallonia (launched in 2017)	- Foster move towards I4.0 - Support digital transformation of production and operational processes - Transform manufacturing into Factories of the Future	Manufacturing companies, esp. SMEs	No dedicated funding scheme, but availability of public grants
Czech Republic	Průmysl 4.0 (2016)	- Enhance competitiveness in the wake of I4.0 - Foster ability of companies to participate in GVCs - Improve manufacturing efficiency - Improve multi-stakeholder cooperation for the development of software solutions, patents, production lines and export know-how	Policy makers, private sector, R&D organisations, industry associations, academia	No additional budget earmarked

(continued)

Table 12.1 Cont.

Countries	*Names of the initiatives (launch, adoption or official year of announcement)*	*Broad policy objectives (examples)*	*Main targets*	*Dedicated budgets (approximate)*
Denmark	Manufacturing Academy of Denmark, MADE (2015)	- Increase competitiveness through industrial-based research in manufacturing - Strengthen Danish technical research community - Create an enabling ecosystem for research, innovation and knowledge sharing - Optimise education for manufacturing	Manufacturing SMEs, research and academia stakeholders	€50 million for 2014–2019 from participating companies, universities, associations, private foundations and public funds
France	Industries du Futur (2015)	- Developing cutting-edge technology - Business transformation - Upskilling the workforce - International cooperation on standards and alliances - Promotion of Industries du Futur	Industry and production SMEs, mid-tier companies and technology providers, academia and public bodies	Approx. €10 billion from public sources, including IftF funding from 2017 onwards, supported by private funding
Germany	Industrie 4.0 (2011)	- Technology deployment - Integration of cyber physical systems & IoT in industry processes - Enhance productivity, efficiency and flexibility of production processes	Manufacturing and production SMEs, entrepreneurs, large corporation, Policy makers	€200 million from public and contribution from industry
Hungary	IPAR 4.0 National Technology Platform (2016)	- Enhance information exchange and cooperation - Accelerate innovation in key areas of digitalisation and production - Innovative adaptation - Fasten responses to challenges and foster bold steps towards innovation	Policy makers, private sector, R&D organisations, industry associations, universities, social circles, businesses	In progress (incl. planned state support)

Italy	Industria 4.0 (2017)	- Innovative investment - Uptake of innovative technologies related to I4.0 - Development of skills with I4.0 education programmes	SMEs, micro-enterprises and large companies	>€18 billion for the period 2017–2020
Latvia	National Industrial Policy Guidelines 2014–2020	- Align workforce supply and education to the economy's needs - Foster manufacturing in industrialised areas and reduce energy costs - Improve financing availability - Promote an innovative environment and stimulate exports	National industry, managers, employees, students, clusters, etc.	Public funds (EU and national) amount to more than €6 billion for 2014–2020, complemented by private sector financing
Lithuania	Pramonė 4.0 (2017)	- Reinforce the competitiveness and productivity of the industry - Advance the integration of digital solutions and new technologies in the national industry	Industrial companies, enterprises and universities	€79.8 million foreseen for industry digitalisation in 2017–2020
Luxembourg	The Third Industrial Revolution Strategy Powered by Transformational Investments (initiated in 2015)	- Prepare the economy and society for megatrends and disruptions and for new economic models - Foster digital capabilities and competencies - Support firms and employees in the digital transition process	Public and private stakeholders, and specific industries	Project-based
Poland	Initiative for Polish Industry 4.0 – the Future Industry Platform (announced in 2016)	- Improve competitiveness of industry and establish conditions for I4.0 - Improve competitiveness of domestic machines, devices and software - Consolidate supply chains - Improve labour market attractiveness	Public and private stakeholders, esp. SMEs and domestic 4.0 solution suppliers, academia, research	In progress

(*continued*)

Table 12.1 Cont.

Countries	*Names of the initiatives (launch, adoption or official year of announcement)*	*Broad policy objectives (examples)*	*Main targets*	*Dedicated budgets (approximate)*
Portugal	Indústria 4.0 (2017)	- Provide industry with knowledge, information and tools for transformation and empower the national workforce - Enable conditions for the development of i4.0 start-ups and national technological solutions in an international context - Make Portugal an international hub	SMEs	€4.5 billion over four years
Slovakia	Smart Industry (2016)	- Bring company closer to I4.0 principles and thinking - Strengthen the economy and support the digital transformations of businesses	Industry, SMEs, R&D organisations, education providers and civil society	No additional budget earmarked
Slovenia	Slovenian Digital Coalition (2016)	- Foster development of the digital economy - Stimulate the creation of digital jobs - Support the exploitation of opportunities of ICT and internet	Civil society, public and private sector, industry	No dedicated budget
Spain	Industria Conectada 4.0 (2014)	- Increase the industrial added value and employment - Support the Spanish model for the industry of the future - Develop the local digital solutions - Develop differential competitive levers to promote industry and exports	Industrial enterprises, esp. SMEs and micro-enterprises	€97.5 million for project calls and related programmes, €68 million for ICT firms; €10 million for innovative clusters
Sweden	Produktion 2030 (2013)	- Modernise the industry base - Support sustainable production and customised, high-end industrial services - Upskill the workforce - Facilitate investments in production R&D	Research institutes, universities and companies/SMEs from industry and services	€25 million from VINNOVA 2013–2018 and €25 million from industry

The Netherlands	Smart Industry (2016)	- Catch up with I4.0 frontrunners - Support industry use of ICT and related opportunities - Strengthen knowledge, skills and ICT conditions - Enhance industry and manufacturing competitiveness	Business community with sectoral focus	€25 million for 2014–2017 complemented by industry co-financing
UK	High Value Manufacturing Catapult (HVMC) (2011)	- Accelerate new concepts to commercial reality and create sustainable high-value manufacturing - Innovation support improving manufacturing competitiveness - Innovation support for new sectors and markets - Target innovation support to SMEs - Support the development of the next-generation technologies to transform UK manufacturing	Business, industry and research organisations	€164 million from UK government on 2012–18 For 2015/16: €79.7 million commercial income vs. €61.3 million public funding and €62 million for collaborative R&D

Source: Elaborations from the 19 country documents available at https://ec.europa.eu/growth/tools-databases/dem/monitor/category/national-initiatives.

Note: Dates of the latest versions of websites range between January 2017 and May 2018.

* This table does not intend to cover the detailed and thematic programmes under one or several policy objectives; neither does it reflect the diversity of I4.0 policy perspectives (e.g. at the regional level).

relevant stakeholders' interests and involvement; the insufficient reach of micro-enterprises and small companies; decreasing mobilisation; mismatches between industry needs and qualifications; the discouraging effects of I4.0 complexity; instability of funding; social rejection; cyber-security-related threats; and political and economic instability.

12.3.2 The I4.0 in Research & Innovation Strategies for Smart Specialisation (RIS3)

Under the reformed cohesion policy for 2014–2020, several regions and Member States have designed their smart specialisation strategies as the basis for the identification of priority domains for R&I investments. S3 processes unfold into six fundamental steps, including an analysis of regional strengths, weaknesses and potential; a dedicated and inclusive governance; the adoption of a shared vision for local development; the identification and selection of priority R&I areas; the design of policy mixes; and the establishment of monitoring and evaluation frameworks (Foray et al., 2012). The priority or strategic domains can be reviewed and revised, and should help regions and countries to build up or reinforce competitive advantages through the development of unique innovation niches. Ideally, priorities should foster the development of new businesses and, eventually, block easy replication or imitation outside the region (European Parliamentary Research Service, 2018). The selection of strategic domains is based on bottom-up approaches and wide stakeholder involvement – the so-called Entrepreneurial Discovery Process (EDP). EDPs intend to be inclusive and participatory processes for decision making, which bring together business enterprises, government, research and academic institutions, and civil society/consumer groups in order to identify new domains for innovation and market opportunities (see, for instance Foray, 2015). The EDP features and the implementation strategies and approaches reflect the diversity of regional and national contexts, challenges and cultures, and the selected strategic domains (see Gianelle et al., 2016; OECD, 2013).

RIS3 strategies are monitored through the Smart Specialisation Platform, which aims at providing evidence-based advice and assistance for the design and implementation of the strategies. It offers, among other things, online inventory and benchmarking tools, technical reports and experts reviews. Since 2014, more than 100 S3 strategies have been developed and more than €40 billion (and more than €65 billion including national co-financing) have been allocated to regions for priority funding through the European Regional Development Fund (European Commission, 2017b). In practice, S3 strategies are implemented by the Operational Programmes (OPs).[26] Such OPs are plans in which Member States and/or regions detail how funding from the European Structural and Investment Funds will be spent during the programming period. The European Structural and Investment Funds include the European Regional Development Fund, the European Social Fund, the Cohesion Fund, the European Agricultural Fund for Rural Development, and the European Maritime and Fisheries Fund.

In order to stimulate and enhance the coordination for joint projects and investments for socio-economic transformation and modernisation, the Commission has set up the Thematic Smart Specialisation Platforms (or S3 Thematic Platforms)[27] in areas relating to energy (launched in 2015), agri-food and industrial modernisation (launched in 2016). Overall, the platforms involve over 120 regions and 28 inter-regional partnerships working together with the objective of realising joint investment projects (European Commission, 2017b). The platforms are meant to be developed and led by regions relying on wide stakeholder involvement, and new partnerships can be set up through expressions of interests on the thematic platforms. In particular, I4.0 technologies are expected to play a key role in industrial transitions and modernisation across EU regions. In terms of regional scope, the S3 Thematic Platform of Industrial Modernization is expected to be crucial for further I4.0-oriented transnational and inter-regional collaborations at different stages of the R&D and innovation value chains. From this perspective, the Vanguard Initiative is seen as inspirational to develop inter-territorial spaces and organisations to reinforce industrial modernisation across EU regions in priority areas or techno-industrial domains.[28]

Originally developed as a strategic development support tool, Eye@RIS3 provides information on the priorities, including their description, economic domains and scientific domains, and EU policy objectives.[29] Data and information come from national and regional public managers and from the European Commission staff, and are updated according to the outcomes of the (continuous) EDPs. Overall, KETs and Digital Agenda feature in at least one priority for more than half of the regions. Under the broad KETs category, sub-domains include, for instance, advanced manufacturing systems and materials and industrial biotechnology (see Hegyi and Rakhmatullin, 2017 for the main evolutions of the S3P-Industry). The S3P-Industry initiative, a multi-regional partnership on I4.0, explicitly aims at showing the benefit of I4.0 solutions and technologies to SMEs.[30] As a key component of the Digitising European Industry initiative, the DIHs are also actively involved in the S3 processes, either by leading a S3 priority area or by carrying more horizontal missions.[31] Additional support to the thematic platform is provided by the EU-funded ReConfirm project through evidence-based analyses for partnerships, collaboration labs and strategic workshops (matchmaking, roadmaps making assistance, etc.).

Table 12.2 presents selected information about RIS3 for some regions with different encoded policy objectives associated with the priorities or strategic domains selected by the Member States or regions. The search terms for the selection of regions included 'industry 4.0', 'industry 40, KETs', 'key enabling technologies' and '4.0 and digital technologies' in order to flag up examples of how 4.0-related technologies have been integrated into RIS3 designs.

More detailed information about each strategy is made available by the search and selection of the Member States or regions. The scope of this chapter unfortunately does not allow us to provide a comprehensive study of the variety of I4.0-related priorities and their different implementation stages at the

Table 12.2 Examples of I4.0-related policy objectives for selected RIS3 (Eye@RIS3)

NUTS ID	*Region/country name*	*Policy objectives related to priorities*	*Date source*
BE3	Walloon Region	D – Digital transformation, D.22 – Cleaner environment & efficient energy networks and low energy computing, D.25 – E-Commerce & SMEs online, D.26 – e-Government (e.g. e-Procurement, open data & sharing of public sector information), D.27 – e-Health (e.g. healthy ageing), D.28 – e-Inclusion (e.g. e-Skills, e-Learning), D.29 – ICT trust, cyber security & network security, D.30 – Intelligent inter-modal & sustainable urban areas (e.g. smart cities), D.33 – New media & easier access to cultural contents (e.g. heritage), D.35 – Robotics, autonomous and cyber physical systems (e.g. vehicles, embedded systems) J – Sustainable innovation, J.63 – Eco-innovations, J.66 – Smart green & integrated transport systems	Dec-14
DE3	Berlin	D – Digital transformation, D.19 – Artificial intelligence, cognitive systems, augmented and virtual reality, visualisation, simulation, gamification & interaction technologies, D.24 – Digitising Industry (Industry 4.0, smart and additive manufacturing) E – KETs, E.37 – Advanced manufacturing systems	Nov-13
DK04	Midtjylland	D – Digital transformation, D.24 – Digitising Industry (Industry 4.0, smart & additive manufacturing)	Jan-16
EL11	Anatoliki Makedonia, Thraki	D – Digital transformation, D.24 – Digitising Industry (Industry 4.0, smart and additive manufacturing) E – KETs, E.37 – Advanced manufacturing systems, E.38 – Advanced materials, E.39 – Industrial biotechnology, E.40 – Micro/Nano-electronics, E.41 – Nanotechnology, E.42 – Photonics	July-14
ES21	País Vasco	B – Blue growth, B.13 – Offshore mining, oil & gas E – KETs, E.37 – Advanced manufacturing systems, E.38 – Advanced materials	Dec-14
ES61	Andalucía*	A – Aeronautics & space, A.01 – Aeronautics, A.02 – Aeronautics & environment, A.03 – Bio fuels & energy efficiency, A.04 – Remotely piloted aircrafts, A.05 – Safety & security, A.06 – Space, A.07 – Transport & logistics	Jan-14
ITC4	Lombardia	E – KETs, E.37 – Advanced manufacturing systems	Oct-14

LU	Luxembourg	A – Aeronautics & space, A.06 – Space, A.07 – Transport & logistics D – Digital transformation, D.18 – Advanced or High performance computing, D.19 – AI, cognitive systems, augmented and virtual reality, visualisation, simulation, gamification & interaction technologies, D.20 – Big data, data mining, database management … D.25 – E-Commerce & SMEs online … D.35 – Robotics, autonomous & cyber physical systems (e.g. vehicles, embedded systems), D.36 – Smart system integration E – KETs, E.37 – Advanced manufacturing systems H – Service innovation, H.51 – New or improved organisational models, H.52 – New or improved service processes, H.53 – New or improved service products (commodities or public services)	Dec-17
PL22	Slaskie	E – KETs, E.37 – Advanced manufacturing systems, E.38 – Advanced materials	Dec-12
SI	Slovenia	D – Digital transformation, D.18 – Advanced or High performance computing, D.19 – Artificial intelligence, cognitive systems, augmented and virtual reality, visualisation, simulation, gamification & interaction technologies, D.20 – Big data, data mining, database management, ..., D.25 – E-Commerce & SMEs online, D.31 – Internet of Things (e.g. connected devices, sensors and actuators networks), D.35 – Robotics, autonomous and cyber-physical systems (e.g. vehicles, embedded systems), D.36 – Smart system integration E – KETs, E.37 – Advanced manufacturing systems	Sept-15

Source: Eye@RIS3 database, December 2018.

Notes:

* Information from Draft RIS3 Document or other (otherwise from final document)

Eye@RIS3 was fully upgraded in September 2018. Data are regularly updated based on inputs from European regional and national authorities and their stakeholders.

regional level.[32] Nevertheless, as for the national initiatives, it might still be too early a stage to assess the impact of dedicated efforts to support the transition towards I.4.0. But it may not be too late to provide evidence-based and multi-dimensional considerations of the I4.0 readiness of EU regions in order to anticipate, for instance, a territory-specific lack of adequate resources and cost-efficient infrastructure, or obstacles to partnership, or even cases of workforce and social rejections.

12.4 Conclusions

The EU has taken several important steps and has advanced on many fronts to stimulate, coordinate, monitor and strengthen framework conditions for the uptake of digital and enabling technologies in order to accompany the modernisation of its industrial bases and systems. Nevertheless, much remains to be done to ensure consistent and sustainable I4.0-driven or I4.0-enabled socio-economic and industrial transformations. Importantly, on the one hand, the imperatives of developing a critical mass do not relate solely to target funding or infrastructure, but also, and maybe more fundamentally, to the levels of awareness and readiness of our society and citizens in relation to I4.0 technologies and their transformational potential. On the other hand, the adoption and diffusion of new technologies and models should be fast-tracked in the majority of our regions in order to considerably reduce the territorial imbalances that can seriously undermine the inclusiveness and sustainability of such modernisation and transition paths.

From a governance and policy practitioner perspective, the level of horizontal and multi-level coordination required and the limited scope for experimentation and learning pose even more complex challenges in this transition period, especially when combined with the management of increasingly open and inter-connected territories. In this context, approaches such as smart specialisation can help to address these new challenges by offering renewed possibilities for evidence-informed collaborative innovation and industrial policy making. As underlined during the European Week of Regions and Cities,[33] critical to the success of these bottom-up initiatives are the territorial competences and assets needed to generate and sustain new dynamics for value creation and capture (Bailey et al., 2018), and the ability to match policy actions with territory-specific needs.

Notes

1 Disclaimer: the analyses presented in this chapter do not necessarily represent the views of the European Commission. Neither the European Commission nor anyone acting on its behalf can be held responsible for any use made thereof. The author would like to thank her colleagues Hegyi F., Rissola G. from the Smart Specialisation Platform, Tuebke A., Hervas F. from JRC-Unit B3 and Batalla Masana M. and Engelmann U. from DG GROW for their constructive comments and feedback on the chapter.

2 The EU is a union of 28 Member States and their citizens. Many institutions are involved in decision-making processes at the EU level, including the European Parliament (elected by EU's citizens), the European Council (heads of state or governments; see European Commission, 2018b), the Council or the Council of the European Union (representatives of governments) and the European Commission, which generally proposes new laws to be adopted by the Parliament and the Council. In this chapter, the focus is on the policy directions and proposals as reflected in the European Commission's communication and documents (see Publication Office of the European Union: https://publications.europa.eu/en/home).

3 See also at https://ec.europa.eu/digital-single-market/en/fourth-industrial-revolution.

4 The Europe 2020 Strategy is the EU's agenda for growth and jobs for the decade 2010–2020. It puts forward three priority dimensions, five headline targets and seven flagship initiatives.

5 The communications of the Commission refer here to the official documents, which provide the main rationales, levers and action lines, as well as the Commission's proposals regarding a given thematic and policy area or issue.

6 The European strategy for KETs combined the efforts of different Directorate-Generals (DGs) of the European Commission, including DG Research and Innovation, DG Communications Networks, Content and Technology, DG Regional Policy, DG Trade and DG Competition, under the political leadership of DG Internal Market, Industry, Entrepreneurship and SMEs. A high-level group on KETs is advising the European Commission on the implementation of KETs. For more about the European strategy for KETs, see https://ec.europa.eu/growth/industry/policy/key-enabling-technologies/european-strategy_en.

7 In reference to Rifkin (2011).

8 Horizon 2020 is the financial instrument of the Innovation Union flagship and constitutes the largest EU Research & Innovation programme ever, with about €80 billion of funding available between 2014 and 2020. The work programme for 2014–2015 included KETs pilot lines in areas identified by the High-Level Expert Group.

9 Digital Single Market – Policies: The Fourth Industrial Revolution, https://ec.europa.eu/digital-single-market/en/fourth-industrial-revolution.

10 The European Fund for Strategic Investment (EFSI) is one of the three pillars of the Investment Plan for Europe, which finances strategic investments in key areas such as infrastructure, R&I, education, renewable energy and energy efficiency, as well as risk finance for small and medium-sized enterprises (SMEs). For more details on this, see https://ec.europa.eu/commission/priorities/jobs-growth-and-investment/investment-plan-europe-juncker-plan/what-investment-plan-europe_en.

11 European Structural and Investment Funds: https://ec.europa.eu/info/funding-tenders/funding-opportunities/funding-programmes/overview-funding-programmes/european-structural-and-investment-funds_en. See also the early guidelines for enabling synergies between the funds at https://ec.europa.eu/regional_policy/sources/docgener/guides/synergy/synergies_en.pdf.

12 Smart Specialisation Platform: http://s3platform.jrc.ec.europa.eu.

13 Regulation EU 1301/2013. See also Foray et al (2012) for an official guide on smart specialisation strategies; and European Commission (2017b) for a recent communication on the regional policy.

14 Single Market Act I and Single Market Act II: http://ec.europa.eu/growth/single-market/smact_en.
15 Innobarometer and Business Innovation Observatory (DG GROW): http://ec.europa.eu/growth/industry/innovation/facts-figures_en.
16 Digital Economy and Society Index (DESI): https://ec.europa.eu/digital-single-market/en/desi.
17 Digital Transformation Monitor: https://ec.europa.eu/growth/tools-databases/dem/monitor.
18 Blueprint for Sectoral Cooperation on Skills: https://ec.europa.eu/social/main.jsp?catId=1415&langId=en.
19 https://www.iso.org/sites/ConsumersStandards/1_standards.html.
20 See European Commission (2016b) for ICT priority standards and the different EU initiatives in the area of standards at http://ec.europa.eu/growth/single-market/european-standards_en. See also the Vademecum at https://ec.europa.eu/growth/single-market/european-standards/vademecum_en, which compiles key documents from the European Commission on European standardisation policy and related practice. It provides guidance without having legal status.
21 See also a more detailed List of Active National Policy Initiatives for Digitisation of Industry at https://ec.europa.eu/futurium/en/system/files/ged/list_of_policy_initiatives_on_digitising_industry_across_eu_211117.pdf (last updated November 2017).
22 See https://ec.europa.eu/futurium/en/implementing-digitising-european-industry-actions/national-initiatives-digitising-industry.
23 In this chapter, policies for digital transformation are considered as I4.0-enabling policies. See Rifkin (2011) for conceptual discussions about the complementarity between I4.0 and Third Industrial Revolution paradigms in driving industrial transformation.
24 See https://ec.europa.eu/digital-single-market/en/news/digital-innovation-hubs-annual-event-2018. See also additional background information at https://ec.europa.eu/futurium/en/system/files/ged/digital_innovation_hubs_in_digital_europe_programme_final2_december.pdf.
25 https://ec.europa.eu/growth/tools-databases/dem/watify.
26 Operational Programmes adopted by the European Commission at the beginning of a programming period can be found at: https://ec.europa.eu/regional_policy/index.cfm/en/atlas/programmes.
27 Thematic Smart Specialisation Platforms: http://s3platform.jrc.ec.europa.eu/s3-thematic-platforms.
28 See https://www.s3vanguardinitiative.eu/
29 Eye@RIS3 database: http://s3platform.jrc.ec.europa.eu/eye-ris3.
30 Partnership webpage: http://s3platform.jrc.ec.europa.eu/eu/sme-integration-to-industry.
31 In practice, they can also result from an S3 process; see Rissola and Sörvik (2018) for dedicated cases studies on DIHs and S3. A catalogue of DIHs monitored by the S3 platform is available at: http://s3platform.jrc.ec.europa.eu/digital-innovation-hubs-catalogue.
32 See, for instance, Gianelle et al. (2016); European Parliamentary Research Service (2018).
33 See the reports and presentations of the workshop session on 'Thirty Years of EU Cohesion Policy: What Works? Where? for Whom?', co-organised by DG REGIO during the European Week of Regions and Cities 2018, at: https://europa.eu/regions-and-cities/programme/sessions/154_en.

References

Bailey D., Pitelis C. and Tomlinson P. R. (2018). A Place-Based Developmental Regional Industrial Strategy for Sustainable Capture of Co-created Value. *Cambridge Journal of Economics*, 42(6): 1521–1542, https://doi.org/10.1093/cje/bey019.

Beise M. and Cleff T. (2004). Assessing the Lead Market Potential of Countries for Innovation Projects. *Journal of International Management*, 10(4): 453–477.

Berger R. (2014). *Industry 4.0: The New Industrial Revolution, How Europe Will Succeed*. Munich: Strategy Consultants, March.

Brynjolfsson E., Mitchell T. and Rock D. (2018). What Can Machines Learn, and What Does it Mean for Occupations and the Economy? *AEA Papers and Proceedings*, 108. Available at: www.aeaweb.org/articles?id=10.1257/pandp.20181019.

Buhr D. and Stehnken T. (2018). Industry 4.0 and European Innovation Policy – Big Plans, Small Steps. *WISO Diskurs* 12/2018, Friedrich-Ebert-Stiftung, Germany. Available at: https://library.fes.de/pdf-files/wiso/14455.pdf.

Cirillo V., Rinaldini M., Staccioli J. and Virgillito M. E. (2018). Workers' Awareness Context in Italian 4.0 Factories. *LEM Papers Series* 2018/13, Laboratory of Economics and Management (LEM), Sant'Anna School of Advanced Studies, Pisa, Italy.

Craglia M., Annoni A., Benczur P., Bertoldi P., Delipetrev P., De Prato G., Feijoo C., Fernandez Macias E., Gomez E., Iglesias M., Junklewitz H., López Cobo M., Martens B., Nascimento S., Nativi S., Polvora A., Sanchez I., Tolan S., Tuomi I. and Vesnic Alujevic L. (eds) (2018). *Artificial Intelligence – A European Perspective*. EUR 29425 EN. Luxembourg: Publications Office of the European Union.

Digital Transformation Scoreboard (2018). Available at: https://ec.europa.eu/growth/tools-databases/dem/monitor/sites/default/files/Digital%20Transformation%20Scoreboard%202018_0.pdf.

European Commission (2009). *Preparing for Our Future: Developing a Common Strategy for Key Enabling Technologies in the EU*. COM(2009) 512 final, {SEC(2009) 1257}.

European Commission (2010a). *Europe 2020: A Strategy for Smart, Sustainable and Inclusive Growth*. COM(2010) 2020 final.

European Commission (2010b). *A Digital Agenda for Europe*. COM(2010)245 final.

European Commission (2010c). *Europe 2020 Flagship Initiative Innovation Union*. COM(2010) 546 final / SEC(2010)/ 1161.

European Commission (2010d). *An Integrated Industrial Policy for the Globalisation Era – Putting Competitiveness and Sustainability at Centre Stage*. COM(2010) 614 final.

European Commission (2012). *A Stronger European Industry for Growth and Economic Recovery – Industrial Policy Communication Update*. COM(2012) 582 final.

European Commission (2014). *For a European Industrial Renaissance*. COM(2014) 14 final.

European Commission (2015a). *KETs: Time to Act*. Final report of the High-Level Expert Group on Key Enabling Technologies. Available at: www.kowi.de/Portaldata/2/Resources/horizon2020/coop/Report-KETs-HLG.pdf.

European Commission (2015b). *A Digital Single Market Strategy for Europe*. COM(2015) 192 final.

European Commission (2016a). *Digitising European Industry – Reaping the Full Benefits of a Digital Single Market*. COM(2016) 180 final.

European Commission (2016b). *ICT Standardisation Priorities for the Digital Single Market*. COM(2016) 176 final.

European Commission (2016c). *A New Skills Agenda for Europe – Working Together to Strengthen Human Capital, Employability and Competitiveness.* {SWD(2016) 195 final} COM(2016) 381 final.

European Commission (2016d). *Regulation (EU) 2016/679 of the European Parliament and of the Council of 27 April 2016 on the Protection of Natural Persons with Regard to the Processing of Personal Data and on the Free Movement of Such data, and Repealing Directive 95/46/EC* (General Data Protection Regulation), OJ L119.

European Commission (2017a). *Investing in a Smart, Innovative and Sustainable Industry – A Renewed EU Industrial Policy Strategy.* COM(2017) 479 final.

European Commission (2017b). *Strengthening Innovation in Europe's Regions – Strategies for Resilient, Inclusive and Sustainable Growth.* COM(2017) 376 final – {SWD(2017) 264 final}.

European Commission (2017c). *Regional Innovation Scoreboard 2017.* Brussels.

European Commission (2018a). *European Innovation Scoreboard 2018.* Brussels.

European Commission (2018b). *The European Union: What it is and What it Does.* Luxembourg: Publications Office of the European Union.

European Parliamentary Research Service (2014). *Reshoring of EU Manufacturing.* 21 March, BRI(2014)140791.

European Parliamentary Research Service (2015). *Industry 4.0 – Digitalisation for Productivity and Growth.* September.

European Parliamentary Research Service (2018). *New Technologies and Regional Policy – Towards the Next Cohesion Policy Framework.* Available at: www.europarl.europa.eu/RegData/etudes/STUD/2018/614546/EPRS_STU(2018)614546_EN.pdf.

Foray D. (2015). *Smart Specialisation, Opportunities and Challenges for Regional Innovation Policy.* Abingdon: Routledge.

Foray D. et al. (2012). *Guide to Research and Innovation Strategies for Smart Specialisation (RIS 3).* European Commission. Available at: http://s3platform.jrc.ec.europa.eu.

Frey C. B. and Osborne M. A. (2017). The Future of Employment: How Susceptible are Jobs to Computerisation? *Technological Forecasting and Social Change,* 114: 254–280.

Gianelle C., Kyriakou D., Cohen C. and Przeor M. (eds) (2016), *Implementing Smart Specialisation: A Handbook.* Luxembourg: Publication Office of the EU.

Hegyi F. B. and Rakhmatullin R. (2017). *Implementing Smart Specialisation – Thematic Platform on Industrial Modernisation.* EUR 28769 EN. Luxembourg: Publications Office of the European Union.

Juncker J.-C. (2014). *A New Start for Europe: My Agenda for Jobs, Growth, Fairness and Democratic Change.* Political Guidelines for the next European Commission – Opening Statement in the European Parliament, Strasbourg, 15 July. Available at: https://ec.europa.eu/commission/sites/beta-political/files/juncker-political-guidelines-speech_en.pdf.

NESTA (2017). Anticipatory Regulation. Available at: www.nesta.org.uk/feature/innovation-methods/anticipatory-regulation/

OECD (2013). *Innovation-Driven Growth in Regions: The Role of Smart Specialisation* (preliminary version). Paris: OECD.

OECD (2017). *Enabling the Next Production Revolution: A Summary of Main Messages and Policy Lessons.* Meeting of the OECD Council at Ministerial Level, Paris, 7–8 June. OECD: Paris.

Rifkin J. (2011). *The Third Industrial Revolution: How Lateral Power is Transforming Energy, the Economy, and the World*. New York: Palgrave Macmillan.

Rissola G. and Sörvik J. (2018). *Digital Innovation Hubs in Smart Specialisation Strategies*. EUR 29374 EN. Luxembourg: Publications Office of the European Union.

Scapolo F., Churchill P., Viaud V., Antal M., Córdova H. and de Smedt P. (2015). *How Will Standards Facilitate New Production Systems in the Context of EU Innovation and Competitiveness in 2025?* Final report. JRC Foresight Study.

Smit J., Kreutzer S., Moeller C. and Carlberg M. (2016). *Industry 4.0 – Study for the ITRE Committee*. European Commission's Directorate General for Internal Policies, Policy Department A: Economic and Scientific Policy.

Schwab K. (2016). *The Fourth Industrial Revolution*. Cologny: World Economic Forum.

Ulmann L. (ed.) (2017). Industry 4.0: The New Industrial Revolution for Europe. *The European Files*, January, n. 45.

UN DESA/DPAD (2017). The Impact of the Technological Revolution on Labour Markets and Income Distribution. Frontiers Issues, July. Available at: www.un.org/development/desa/dpad/wp-content/uploads/sites/45/publication/2017_Aug_Frontier-Issues-1.pdf.

Veugelers R. (ed.) (2013). *Manufacturing Europe's Future*. Bruegel: Blueprint 21. Available at: http://bruegel.org/2013/10/manufacturing-europes-future.

Vezzani A., Pugliese E. and Gkotsis P. (2018). *Socio-economic Regional Microscope Series – EU Regions and the Upgrading for the Digital Age*. Luxembourg: Publications Office of the European Union.

13 Industry 4.0 and transformative regional industrial policy[1]

David Bailey and Lisa De Propris

13.1 Introduction

It can be argued that modern EU regional policy was introduced in the 1990s with the reform of the Structural Funds and the introduction of a clear set of objectives aimed at reducing income disparities across the EU via multi-level governance. This marked a shift away from a pure redistributive mechanism whereby funding was re-allocated from the richer to the poorer Member States (Bailey and De Propris, 2002) towards a bottom-up process that introduced regions as key actors in the policy-making process. Indeed, the new process enabled regions to enter into dialogue directly with the EU and meant that regions could spend EU funds on interventions that they would design and implement within an operating framework with broad objectives set by the EU and national governments.

Between the 1990s and 2013, the allocation of EU funding still had an underlying compensative rationale to the extent that the share of the allocated funding privileged low-income regions. In fact, EU regional and cohesion policies were designed to compensate low-performing and lagging regions for the possible costs they would have had to incur to cope with asymmetric shocks, whether internal or external. The introduction of the Smart Specialisation Strategy in the 2014–2020 cycle marked a further step change as EU policy became very much a growth-driven policy or a regional-level innovation policy.

As a new post-2020 cycle is dawning, one can see via DG Regio announcements that 'EU regional policy is an investment policy. It supports job creation, competitiveness, economic growth, improved quality of life and sustainable development'.[2] A decade on from the Global Financial Crisis and with austerity increasingly questioned, attention should shift to identifying clear, well-funded and achievable growth targets; however, the EU finds itself firefighting on many fronts, including Brexit, trade wars and an anaemic level of enthusiasm towards the EU encouraged by populist parties from north to south.

Against this backdrop, the EU risks underestimating the fundamental role that policy and public interventions must play just as the economy and wider society are embarking on transformations that will shape work, industry, mobility, communications and more broadly our way of life for the next 50–60 years, as has been detailed in this volume. These are times of radical and disruptive change, and inevitably – we would argue – EU regional and industrial policies must move towards having truly transformative power; this could, for example, render smart specialisation strategies with a heightened level of attention paid towards the creation and adoption of Fourth Industrial Revolution (FIR) technologies in different regions.

The objective of this chapter is to reflect on the extent to which technological change will require adjustments to EU regional and cohesion policies in order to allow the latter to have a 'transformative' power. To do so, we start by considering the evolution of EU policies in terms of vision, objectives and instruments since the 1990s. Priorities have changed over time, but, we argue, have always been underpinned by a fundamental concern for inter-regional socio-economic cohesion. The ever-present trade-off between efficiency and equity in recent EU integration (Bailey and De Propris, 2002) has often been reconciled by having declarations of a grand aspiration for growth and jobs that are then complemented by much of the funding being allocated to lagging regions to reassure the latter of the equitable nature of EU membership.

The disruptions brought about by the technologies of the FIR have the potential to introduce new layers of socio-economic divides. We will discuss if and how new technologies will widen economic divergence between low- and high-performing regions and states or, alternatively, if and how they might allow some regions to 'leap-frog' with a consequent faster catching up.

The chapter proceeds as follows: Section 13.2 discusses the evolution of EU cohesion policy over time, highlighting the shift from compensation to smart upgrading; Section 13.3 notes the effort to upgrade regional development via smart specialisation approaches; Section 13.4 summarises the scale of change coming with the FIR; Section 13.5 reviews current levels of digital disparities and considers the impact of the FIR on spatial disparities going forward; Section 13.6 issues a 'call to arms' for a transformative industrial policy given the scale of change coming; and Section 13.7 concludes the chapter.

13.2 EU cohesion policy so far: from compensation to smart upgrading

While reforms to EU regional policy in the late 1970s and early 1980s brought about minor changes and budget increases, it was the 1988 reform which essentially redesigned the entire framework of regional support. The overhaul was wide-ranging as the Structural Funds were required to make an impact on the less developed regions and countries of the EU in order to compensate them for the imbalances brought about by the completion of the Single Market (Bliss and de Macedo, 1990) and to enable them to catch up with the wealthier regions (Bailey and De Propris, 2002).

The key concern was over a polarisation of wealth and diverging growth paths across different regions: 'to ward off the threat of a two-speed Europe, the EC has reformed the structural funds. The aim is to give the weakest regions the resources to catch up progressively by making more rapid progress than the others, in spite of their handicap' (European Commission, 1992, p. 10). Following on from this change, we would argue that the rationale of EU support for lagging Member States has since evolved over time, from being redistributive at the national level (pre-1990s) to being compensative at the regional level (1990s–2013) and currently to favouring regional upgrading (2014–2020). The link between regional development and innovation became more explicit with the Lisbon Strategy, where one can read the aspirational nature of policy:

> The Union has [today] set itself a new strategic goal for the next decade: to become the most competitive and dynamic knowledge-based economy in the world capable of sustainable economic growth with more and better jobs and greater social cohesion.[3]

After the launch of the Lisbon Strategy in 2000, the EU pursued a growth agenda that was then reinforced by the adoption of the 'Europe 2020 Strategy' in 2010 that aimed to drive the EU towards smart, sustainable and green growth. Ever since, innovation has underpinned EU policies and especially regional and cohesion policies (which had traditionally been associated with equity priorities by reducing income disparities). Indeed, the two rounds of Structural Funds over the periods 2007–2013 and 2014–2020 have seen an increased emphasis on funding destined for research and development (R&D) and related interventions.

Since the entry of Greece, Spain and Portugal in the early 1980s, which saw a significant widening of socio-economic disparities across Member States, social and economic cohesion has been a paramount concern for EU policy makers, given the fear that deep divisions between Member States might undermine the EU project. The +12 enlargement over the period 2004–2007 and in parallel the creation of the eurozone further heightened concerns over widening inter-regional disparities. The external shock of the 2008 Global Financial Crisis hit EU Member States severely, deeply and also asymmetrically. The simultaneous processes of internal deepening and enlarging together with austerity post-2008 left some EU Member States and regions on a path of virtual zero growth for almost a decade. The result is that now, after three decades of EU intervention through regional and cohesion policies, many regions still have gross domestic product (GDP) per capita levels below 75% of the EU average.

13.3 Upgrading regions with smart specialisation strategies

The concept of smart specialisation was introduced in the late 2000s (Foray, David and Hall, 2009) as a new way of tackling regional development. Foray (2015, p. 1) proposed that 'the notion of smart specialisation described the capacity of an economic system (a region for example) to generate new specialities through the discovery of resources and competences in these domains'. The approach has become the cornerstone of EU regional and cohesion policies and has been implemented thought the Research Innovation Strategies for Smart Specialisation (RIS3) in the 2013–2020 funding round.

A number of elements of this approach are worth noting as relevant specifically for this chapter. One is the aspiration to drive regional upgrading via 'structural changes' (Foray, 2017b, p. 39) that can open up new development paths. With the term 'smart', it is suggested that RIS3 must be designed to allow regions to build on their existing specialisations by creating innovation capabilities that are compatible with such sectors. Framed as sector-specific innovation policies, RIS3 arguably re-invests governments with the task of developing capabilities that are connected with their territory, without being accused of 'picking-winners'. This idea went against the previous tendency, whereby policy makers were seen as jumping on the bandwagon of pursuing sectors that were seen as fashionable or desirable, but completely disjointed from their existing specialisations (Foray, 2015).[4] However, it is crucial to highlight that in reality, RIS3 has encouraged regions to upgrade or create a 'competitive advantage' in sectors in which they were already active rather than pursuing a true structural change.

The second element is the idea of embeddedness (McCann and Ortega-Argiles, 2015). Indeed, some form of path dependency is acknowledged whereby 'for many regions, the point is not innovating at the frontier, but rather (to) generate innovations complementarities in existing sectors' (Foray, 2017, p. 47). Smart specialisation was conceptualised at a time when the technological paradigm was known and consolidated. The adoption and multiplication in countless incremental variants of the dominant technologies in different sectors and regions were perceived as crucial keys to unlock some form of *specialised diversification* (McCann and Ortega-Argiles, 2015) in regions that were lagging behind or underperforming. Smart specialisation also drew upon a well-established literature that understood the systemic nature of innovation with its spatial and connected prerogatives. In order to do this, it endorsed reliance on delivery infrastructures such as regional innovation systems with their triple helix approach.

The third element to note here is the process of entrepreneurial discovery that would motivate firms and institutions to explore and experiment with different interventions over what opportunities might arise (Foray, 2015). The novelty here is to envisage that policy makers have the ingenuity and risk-taking outlook – as well as the institutional capacity[5] – to explore and experiment with policy objectives and tools. In other words, policy design and implementation requires some entrepreneurial spirit not only from firms, but also from other key stakeholders in the regional system of innovation, underpinned by what Foray (2015) calls entrepreneurial knowledge that can reside not only within businesses but is also dispersed systemically.

So, in terms of regional policy, smart specialisation has been used to emphasise the need to exploit related variety, build regional embeddedness and enable strategic diversification. This relates to a final feature, notably the need for regional actors (government, firms, universities, research institutions, etc.) to collaborate, recognising the current starting point for the region in terms of skills, technologies and institutional governance, and then to build on these capabilities rather than trying to start 'from scratch'.

This approach sees the capacity of territories to root their economic activity in the local institutional fabric as being central to their economic success, through the generation, acquisition and exchange of knowledge. Yet such knowledge is uncertain and is embedded in localities; this needs to be uncovered through participatory and bottom-up processes to build consensus and trust (Barca et al., 2012). This place-based smart specialisation approach has strong parallels with Rodrik's (2004, 2008) perspective of industrial policy as a process of discovery requiring strategic collaboration between the private sector and state in unlocking growth opportunities, but set within a framework of multi-level governance so as to enable a process of local collaboration and discovery.

In this vein, industrial and regional policies which facilitate a process of discovery through strategic collaboration are seen as relevant under smart specialisation perspectives and require appropriate institutions to engender this. In fact, this is largely how modern, intelligent industrial policy design is conceived of in contemporary debates (see Rodrik, 2004, 2008), with industrial policy ideally having the quality of 'embedded autonomy', whereby it is not captured by firms and sectors, but where, as noted above, it focuses on the discovery process, where firms and the state learn about underlying costs and opportunities, and engage in strategic coordination. Given the uncertainty generated by the FIR and the need for a process of knowledge discovery, we will return to policy implications below.

13.4 Technological change and the FIR

As has been stressed throughout this volume, a wave of new technologies is arguably driving a shift in our techno-socio-economic paradigm (Perez, 2010). Indeed, these technologies are expected not only to change the organisation of production inside and between firms, as well as the balance between capital and labour, but to fundamentally change the workplace, the physical environment and the way we live our lives. There include artificial intelligence (AI) biotech, nanotech, neurotechnologies, green and renewables, information and communications technology (ICT) and mobile tech, cloud technology, big data, 3D printing, the Internet of Things, robotics, sensoring, space technology and drones.

The introduction of these technologies was first noticed through a debate in the late 1990s and early 2000s on the importance of general purpose technologies (GPTs) and key enabling technologies (KETs). As the name suggests, GPTs are those that can find a myriad of applications across different sectors and markets (Bresnahan and Trajtenberg, 1995). These have included nanotechnology and biotechnologies, ICT and the internet. On the other hand, KETs 'act as a platform for the diversification of firms' competencies into a broader set of technologies fields' (Corradini and De Propris, 2017, p. 198); in other words, KETs tend to be multi-disciplinary to the extent that their adoption can generate technologies that in turn can feed into diverse applications. These include micro-/nano-electronics, nanotechnology, photonics, advanced materials, industrial biotechnology and advanced manufacturing technologies.[6] Some of the current debate on the FIR (Rifkin, 2011) suggests that these new technologies are indeed KETs. Certainly, there is little doubt as to their pervasiveness and disruptive potentials.

13.5 Current levels of digital disparities

Much of the literature on the impact of technological change on socio-economic disparities has focused on IT first and more recently on internet and digital technologies. Serious concerns have been raised about the risk of so-called *digital divides* (OECD, 2001) which could emerge between regions in the same country, between countries and, more crucially, between the rich and poor in society (Hundley et al., 2003).

We focus in this chapter on cross-country divides that technological change can trigger. The EU has always been concerned with income disparities – as mentioned above – but there is evidence that these can in turn underpin broader variations in terms of access to and adoption of technology, which can subsequently result in wider socio-economic disparities.

There are many factors that can cause digital divides and these include differences in human capital and human capital development, infrastructural capabilities, institutional set-ups and policy, access to finance and culture (including attitudes to risk and failure) (Hundley et al., 2003). Going forward, knowledge will matter more than ever in relation to understanding and using new technologies. However, knowledge is embedded in people and for this it is uneven, cumulative and sticky. Human capital endowments will give some places advantages that others will not have; equally, knowledge will age quicker than before, so human capital development cannot stop with education, but must stretch into lifelong learning, training and retraining.

This takes us to the second discriminating factor, i.e. that infrastructural capability includes education and innovation systems. These again can vary greatly in terms of quality and content, although the EU has made huge progress in aligning qualifications to enable frictionless labour mobility across EU Member States. The EU has favoured the conservation of national and regional institutional set-ups and policy frameworks that reflect the peculiarity of Member States. This was very much endorsed by the subsidiarity principle adopted as a cornerstone of the reform of Structural Funds. This means that the mechanisms for change that are driven by policy and institutions also vary greatly. In terms of access to finance, for example, firms face a more similar landscape; indeed, according to Hundley et al. (2003), the EU overall lacks risk capital that enables the formation of new and innovative firms, especially at times of high risk, such as when technology is changing – this goes hand in hand with an overall more risk-averse attitude in the EU than the US for instance (ibid).

Some evidence presented below will show that EU Member States and regions present clear divides and that a major issue for EU policy makers is the extent to which technological change will lock regions into some path-dependency development that will ultimately exacerbate such cleavages. Indeed, recent evidence from the EU Regional Innovation Scoreboard confirms that when considering aggregate innovation inputs and outputs, certain innovation leaders and laggards across the EU can be identified. Here we take two indicators to sketch the complexity of the situation. If we look at the number of firms across EU Member States that employ ICT specialists as a proxy for *digital skills*, a clear divide emerges between northern European countries and southern and eastern ones (see Figure 13.1). Equally, considering the level of automation and digitalisation in the production process, the evidence shows that countries characterised by industries reliant on scale economies and that are therefore larger in size, such as Germany, tend to have a greater number of enterprises whose business processes are already automatically linked to suppliers/customers. This can of course deliver greater efficiency and labour productivity (see Figure 13.2). Finally, the degree of digital penetration can be measured by people's digital skills; however, data shows that the picture is quite different; core EU countries show much less digital dexterity than Italy, Spain, the UK and the Scandinavian economies (see Figure 13.3). The reasons for this might be manifold, including the extent of infrastructural investment and societal readiness.

13.6 Towards a new, transformative industrial policy?

The scale and speed of the challenge posed by the FIR brings into focus both the need and possibilities for a broader canvass on which to draw transformative industrial and regional policies approaches. Space constraints preclude exploring this in detail in this chapter, but this could include, for example, fostering regional industrial policy as a process of discovery so as to identify opportunities and challenges and ways to overcome such challenges (Rodrik, 2004, 2008), new forms of technology policy to ensure that the 'general purpose' nature of new technologies reaches different sectors and regions, skills and (re)training policy, access to finance and support for small and medium-sized enterprises (SMEs), policies to support 'reshoring' as global value chains change and so on.[7]

Firstly, on training, the FIR will see AI and automation both destroy jobs and also create new ones (see World Economic Forum, 2018). This raises a profound risk of further labour market polarisation, and there will be a need to not only develop the skills required for the FIR to be applied in different sectors and regions, but also, as noted above, a need to develop more of a lifelong approach to training and retraining throughout workers' careers. On this, European countries and regions might learn from successful experience elsewhere, such as in Singapore with its 'Skills Future' programme, as well as regional examples in the EU itself. An instructive example is industrial policy since 2015 in Emilia-Romagna, particularly through its 'Patto per il Lavoro' (Pact for Employment and Growth) (Bianchi and Labory, 2018). The Pact lays out a long-term vision

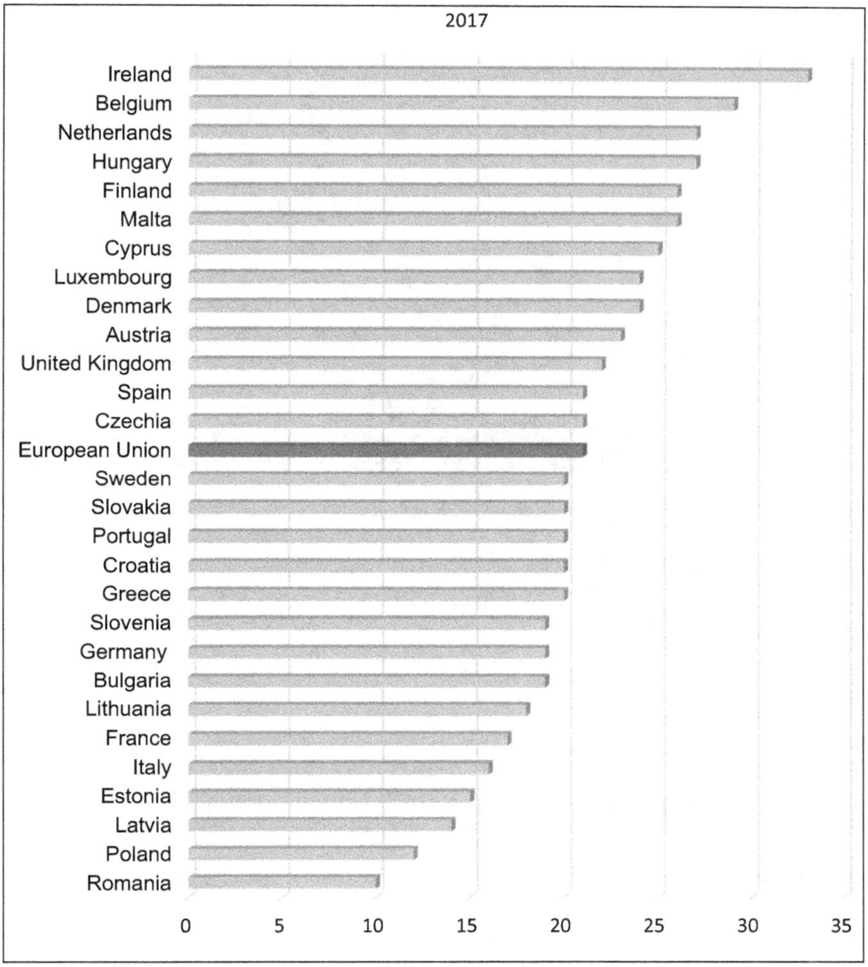

Figure 13.1 Enterprises that employ ICT specialists (% of enterprises).
Source: Authors' elaboration from EUROSTAT.

for regional development, comprising a shared understanding of challenges and a joint approach to foster investment, growth and better jobs, with interventions to leverage the region's strategic assets.[8]

Secondly, and picking up form earlier discussions, on technology policy, policy makers will have to nurture and engage with ecosystems of open, interconnected networks of stakeholders, cooperating to a much greater extent through strategic partnerships (Bachtler et al., 2017). Such ecosystems will be more dependent on their business environments to source knowledge regionally

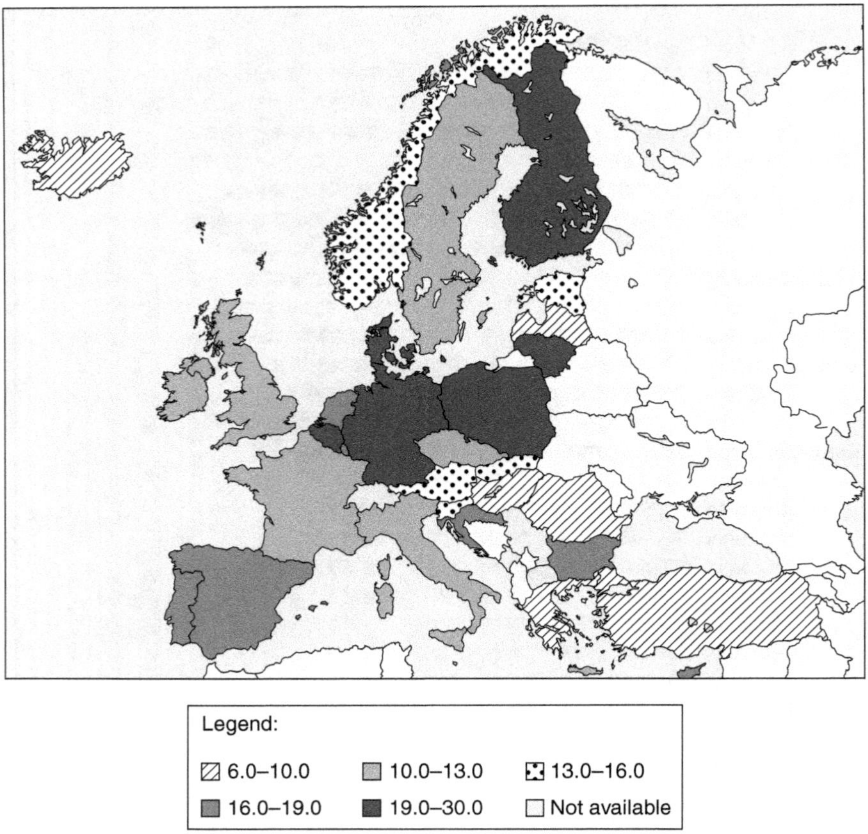

Figure 13.2 Enterprises whose business processes are automatically linked to suppliers/customers.

Source: Authors' elaboration from EUROSTAT.

Note: Enterprises with at least ten employees, NACE sectors, 2009–2017.

and internationally. A number of factors are relevant here for value creation and capture in ecosystems as Bailey et al. (2018) highlight.

Thirdly, the rapid pace of technological and other changes inherent in the FIR pose considerable uncertainty and risks for firms and governments alike (Andreoni and Chang, 2016). Managing this calls for the pooling of resources and risk-sharing, and requires the use of joint support services and infrastructures. On this, Bachtler et al. (2017) highlight, for example, 'living-labs' where multi-national companies and start-ups can interact and benefit from each other's competencies. Such ecosystem support needs to be regionally provided, but positioned within a multi-level governance framework, and to be able to integrate with innovation systems internationally. Moreover, as

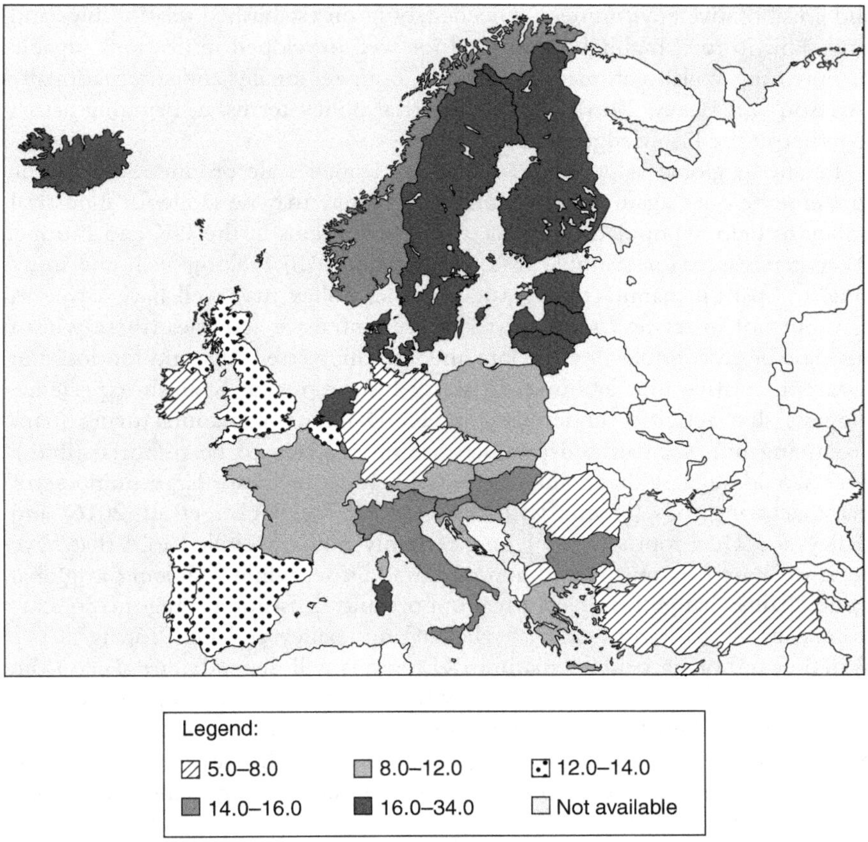

Figure 13.3 Internet skills (individuals who have carried out five out of six internet-related activities).

Source: Authors' elaboration from EUROSTAT.

Notes: Internet skills are measured using a self-assessment approach, depending on how many internet-related tasks have been carried out, without these skills being assessed, tested or actually observed. The internet-related tasks are as follows: used search engine, sent mail with attachment, posted messages to chatrooms/newsgroups or online discussion forum, made phone calls, done peer-to-peer file sharing or created a webpage. Individuals' ages 16–74. Year 2013.

Bailey et al. (2018) stress, these need regular reviewing to ensure consistency with regional needs.

Fourthly, disruptive innovation often requires inter-disciplinary approaches and 'open' models of collaboration (Chesbrough, 2003). As the OECD (2016) has noted, 'pieces of knowledge required come from various actors and activities are rarely available inside a single organisation … it is important therefore to support the generation, diffusion and use of many sorts of knowledge and types of collaboration' (OECD, 2016, p. 68). For this 'mixing' to occur, an open and collaborative environment is needed, built on established relationships and trust. This in turn highlights the need for well-developed institutions capable of nurturing collaboration and networks both regionally and internationally (Amison and Bailey, 2014) and, in industrial policy terms, in bringing actors together in the knowledge-discovery process.

Finally, as global value chains change and small-scale production possibilities emerge once again closer to innovation, there may be scope for industrial policy to help 'repopulate' manufacturing ecosystems in the UK and Europe. Recent research, for example by Bailey et al. (2018) looking at 'home sourcing' in Spanish manufacturing, suggests that policy may well have a role to play, but not in trying to bring back labour-intensive activities (these will in any case be susceptible to wage rate and exchange rate shifts, and footloose in nature as relative unit labour costs shift). Instead, recent Spanish experience suggests that activities undertaken by R&D-intensive manufacturing firms producing non-standardised products are more likely to be reshored (ibid.). This would suggest that reshoring is unlikely to re-create large numbers of manufacturing jobs (in line with the work of De Backer et al. (2016) and Bailey and De Propris (2014)), and certainly not low-skilled jobs that have been offshored or outsourced abroad. In addition, while reshoring as global value chains change is indeed a real opportunity, it is not a foregone conclusion, as its actual logistics can be challenging (Bailey and De Propris, 2014). Whether reshoring benefits mature EU regions will depend, *inter alia*, on the availability of skills, innovation capacity, the supply chain base, support services and the role of institutions. Maintaining an ecosystem of firms and agencies provides firms with a 'deal-breaking' anchor, making home-sourcing a viable option (this correlates to the US and British reshoring experience; see Bailey and De Propris, 2014).

13.7 Concluding comments and policy recommendations

To conclude, policy interventions should form part of a more holistic industrial strategy for stimulating business investment and new firm formation to rebuild value creation and capture, and safeguard manufacturing ecosystem competitiveness. Policy needs to take this on board, for example, in private–public-sector dialogue to identify opportunities to rejoin supply chain functions. This would be in line with modern conceptions of industrial policy as a collaborative process of discovery of information involving the public and private sectors.

As the FIR will play out differently across sectors and regions, this will have implications for the focus and innovation aspirations of EU cohesion policy. The integration of sectors with new technologies will be fundamental in allowing the former to be truly transformed in the light of the new technologies. A transformative industrial policy therefore needs to 'join up' technologies, sectors and places. The challenge for the new round of RIS3 will be to acknowledge the transformative necessity of policy intervention as against a more incremental upgrading.

A transformative industrial policy needs to think beyond sectors alone and instead identify, nurture and diffuse the key cross-cutting technologies (e.g. digitalisation, the Internet of Things, robotics and AI) that have an enabling role across manufacturing and services. Linked to this, industrial strategy needs to recognise and exploit such technologies by making them accessible to businesses in different regions. Furthermore, a transformative industrial strategy needs to be developed both nationally and regionally in a holistic sense (for example, on skills, access to finance, clusters, supply chains and innovation) so as to enable policy to be better suited to the distinctive characteristics and advantages of different scales. This could entail examining what a regional industrial strategy might look like, identifying sectoral trends, analysing emerging strengths and opportunities identified, and carrying out analysis of the export potential of key sectors in which the region already holds emergent strengths and which can be built on in a 'smart specialisation' sense.

Such an approach requires regionally based industrial development strategies promoting 'related diversification' capitalising on the FIR. Such strategies need to recognise: (i) the need to bring together different but related activities in a region via cross-cutting FIR technology platforms (such as via living-labs or digital demonstration hubs); and (ii) the differing potentials of regions to diversify, due to different industrial, knowledge and institutional structures linked to specific regional historical trajectories. Rather than 'starting from scratch' or applying 'one-size-fits-all policies', regional industrial strategies for the FIR instead require tailor-made policy actions embedded in and linked to the specific needs and available resources of regions, starting with the existing knowledge and institutional base in that region. These need to capitalise on region-specific assets rather than attempting to replicate and apply policies that may have worked in quite different places (Bailey et al., 2018).

However, to transform the region's potential based on 'unrelated variety' and to broaden and renew the region's industrial structure by helping it branch into new related activities, policy could encourage crossovers between manufacturing (and service) industries and between manufacturing and new technologies. This could come via knowledge transfer mechanisms that connect related *and* unrelated industries (see Grillitsch et al., 2018), such as by: (i) enhancing entrepreneurship from unrelated industries (targeting such entrepreneurs would not only increase the likelihood of successful policy, but could also contribute to regional diversification); (ii) encouraging labour mobility between related and unrelated industries, as it transfers knowledge between industries and may lead to new 'recombinations' of knowledge (such labour mobility could also increase the level of human capital, as firms and employees learn from experience in related sectors, and in turn could help regional resilience as workers can move between sectors); (iii) promoting exposure to new technologies via institutional intermediaries; and (iv) supporting collective research collaboration with partners from related and unrelated competences (ibid).

Other elements would involve, *inter alia*, the need for: new skills to be developed and constant reskilling and upskilling processes as the FIR progresses; enabling SMEs to have access to funding and finance to embrace digital technologies; recognising and exploiting possibilities to reposition firms, industries and regions on new parts of the global value chain as the value added of manufacturing changes over time; seizing reshoring opportunities as relocalisation opportunities open up, involving policies to rebuild supply chains in Europe; infrastructure investment to embrace new technologies (e.g. 5G) and so on as part of a holistic regional industrial policy.

Acknowledgements

The writing of this chapter has been supported by the EU Horizon 2020 project 'MAKERS – Smart Manufacturing for EU growth and prosperity', which is a project funded by the Horizon 2020 Research and Innovation Staff Exchange Programme, which is a Research and Innovation Staff Exchange under the Marie Sklodowska-Curie Actions, grant agreement number 691192. Ethical disclaimer: the secondary data used in the chapter was collected before the MAKERS project. David Bailey also acknowledges the support of the Economic and Social Research Council's UK in a Changing Europe programme, Grant Reference: ES/T000848/1.

Notes

1 This chapter builds on and develops the discussion in Bailey and De Propris (2019).
2 http://ec.europa.eu/regional_policy/en.
3 www.europarl.europa.eu/summits/lis1_en.htm.
4 The term 'specialisation' is in a sense misleading as 'smart diversification' better represents this line of thinking.
5 This can be challenging. Relating to the earlier reform of the structural funds, for example, Bailey and De Propris (2002) stressed that the 1988 reform of the EU Structural Funds gave EU regions an entitlement to participate in the design and implementation of regional policy, but that some of the weakest regions lacked the institutional capacity to actually access and implement the funds allocated to them. Regional inequalities subsequently increased and only later started to narrow. Only after a process of institutional capacity building and learning were some regions able to interact with the European Commission and national governments on regional policy issues, and only then where gatekeeping Member States allowed it.
6 http://ec.europa.eu/growth/industry/policy/key-enabling-technologies_en.
7 In the context of the FIR, this could involve more radical forms of change, including path diversification and path change (see Grillitsch et al., 2018).
8 On some lessons from Germany's training system being applied internationally, see Wiemann and Fuchs (2018).

References

Amison, P. and Bailey, D. (2014) Phoenix industries and open innovation? The Midlands advanced automotive manufacturing and engineering industry. *Cambridge Journal of Regions, Economy and Society*, 7(3): 397–412.

Andreoni, A. and Chang, H.-J. (2016) Industrial policy and the future of manufacturing. *Economia e Politica Industriale*, 43(4): 491–502.

Bachtler, J., Martins, J.O., Wostner, P. and Zuber, P. (2017) *Towards Cohesion Policy 4.0. Structural Transformation and Inclusive Growth*. Brussels: RSA Europe.

Bailey, D. and De Propris, L. (2002) EU Structural Funds, regional capabilities and enlargement: towards multi-level governance? *Journal of European Integration*, 24(4): 303–324.

Bailey, D. and De Propris, L. (2014) Manufacturing reshoring and its Limits: the UK automotive case. *Cambridge Journal of Regions, Economy and Society*, 7(3): 379–398.

Bailey, D. and De Propris, L. (2019) Industry 4.0, regional disparities and transformative industrial policy. In M. Barzotto, C. Corradini, F.M. Lai, S. Labory and P.R. Tomlinson (eds), *Revitalising Lagging Regions: Smart Specialisation and Industry 4.0*. London: Taylor & Francis, pp. 67–78.

Bailey, D., Corradini, C. and De Propris, L. (2018) 'Home-sourcing' and closer value chains in mature economies: the case of Spanish manufacturing. *Cambridge Journal of Economics*, 42(6): 1567–1584.

Barca, F., McCann, P. and Rodrigues-Pose, A. (2012) The case for regional development intervention: place-based versus place-neutral approaches. *Journal of Regional Science*, 52(1): 134–152.

Bailey, D., Pitelis, C. and Tomlinson, P. (2018) A place-based developmental regional industrial strategy for sustainable capture of co-created value. *Cambridge Journal of Economics*, 42(6): 1521–1542.

Bianchi, P. and Labory, S. (2018) *Industrial Policy for the Manufacturing Revolution. Perspectives on Digital Globalisation*. Cheltenham: Edward Elgar.

Bliss, C. and de Mecedo, J.B. (1990) *Unity with Diversity in the European Economy: The Community's Southern Frontier*. Cambridge: Cambridge University Press.

Bresnahan, T.F. and Trajtenberg, M. (1995) General purpose technologies: engines of growth? *Journal of Econometrics*, 65: 83–108.

Chesbrough, H.W. (2003) The era of open innovation. *MIT Sloan Management Review*, 44(3): 35–41.

Corradini, C. and De Propris, L. (2017) Beyond local search: bridging platforms and inter-sectoral technological integration. *Research Policy*, 46(1): 196–206.

Bailey, D. and L. De Propris (2002) The 1988 reform of the Structural Funds: entitlement or empowerment? *Journal of European Public Policy*, 9(3).

De Backer, K., Menon, C., Desnoyers-James, I. and Moussiegt, L. (2016) *Reshoring: Myth or Reality?, OECD Science, Technology and Industry Policy Papers, No. 27*. Paris: OECD Publishing.

European Commission (1992) *Reform of the Structural Funds: A Tool to Promote Economic and Social Cohesion*, Luxembourg: CEC.

Foray, D. (2015) *Smart Specialisation*. London: Routledge.

Foray, D. (2017) The economic fundamentals of smart specialization strategies. In S. Radosevic, A. Curaj, R. Gheorghiu, L. Andreescu and I. Wade (eds), *Advances in the Theory and Practice of Smart Specialization*. London: Elsevier, pp. 37–50.

Foray, D., David, P.D. and Hall, B.H. (2009) Smart specialization: from academic idea to political instrument, the surprising career of a concept and the difficulties involved in its implementation. Available at: https://pdfs.semanticscholar.org/29ad/6773ef30f362d7d3937c483003d974bc91c5.pdf.

Grillitsch, M., Asheim, B. and Trippl, M. (2018) Unrelated knowledge combinations: the unexplored potential for regional industrial path development. *Cambridge Journal of Regions, Economy and Society*, 11(2): 257–274.

Hildreth, P. and Bailey, D. (2013) The economics behind the move to 'localism' in England. *Cambridge Journal of Regions, Economy and Society*, 6(2): 233–249.

Hundley, R. O., Anderson, R.H., Bikson, T.K. and Neu, C.R. (2003) *The Global Course of the Information Revolution: Recurring Themes and Regional Variations*. Santa Monica, CA: RAND Corporation.

McCann, P. and Ortega-Argilés, R. (2015) Smart specialization, regional growth and applications to European Union cohesion policy. *Regional Studies*, 49(8): 1291–1302.

OECD (2001) Understanding the digital divide. *OECD Digital Economy Papers No. 49*, https://www.oecd-ilibrary.org/docserver/236405667766.pdf?expires=1541427281&id=id&accname=guest&checksum=2A1BC64F8ADA994938D8725D4CE12C54.

OECD (2016) The next production revolution – an interim project report. Document prepared by the Directorate for Science, Technology and Innovation, 25 February.

Perez, C. (2010). Technological revolutions and techno-economic paradigms. *Cambridge Journal of Economics*, 34(1), 185–202.

Rifkin, J. (2011) *The Third Industrial Revolution*. Basingstoke: Palgrave Macmillan.

Rodrik, D. (2004) *Industrial Policy for the 21st Century*. Cambridge, MA: John F. Kennedy School of Government.

Rodrik, D. (2008) *One Economics, Many Recipes: Globalization, Institutions, and Economic Growth*. Princeton: Princeton University Press.

Wiemann, J. and Fuchs, M. (2018) The export of Germany's 'secret of success' dual technical VET: MNCs and multiscalar stakeholders changing the skill formation system in Mexico. *Cambridge Journal of Regions, Economy and Society*, 11(2): 373–386.

World Economic Forum (2018) *The Future of Jobs Report 2018*. Available at: www3.weforum.org/docs/WEF_Future_of_Jobs_2018.pdf.

Index

Note: Page numbers in *italics* indicate figures and in **bold** indicate tables on the corresponding pages.

For Product Safety Concerns and Information please contact our EU representative GPSR@taylorandfrancis.com
Taylor & Francis Verlag GmbH, Kaufingerstraße 24, 80331 München, Germany

www.ingramcontent.com/pod-product-compliance
Lightning Source LLC
LaVergne TN
LVHW011119300926
849160LV00008B/449

* 9 7 8 1 0 3 2 2 3 6 6 2 9 *